Dr. John Chung's

SAT II

Mathematics

Level 2

Good Luck!

Dear Beloved Students,

With this SAT II Subject Test Math Level 2 Third Edition, I like to thank all students who sent me email to encourage me to revise my books. As I said, while creating this series of math tests has brought great pleasure to my career, my only wish is that these books will help the many students who are preparing for college entrance. I have had the honor and the pleasure of working with numerous students and realized the need for prep books that can simply explain the fundamentals of mathematics. Most importantly, the questions in these books focus on building a solid understanding of basic mathematical concepts. Without understanding these solid foundations, it will be difficult to score well on the exams. These book emphasize that any difficult math question can be completely solved with a solid understanding of basic concepts.

As the old proverb says, "Where there is a will, there is a way." I still remember vividly on fifth-grader who was last in his class who eventually ended up at Harvard University seven years later. I cannot stress enough how such perseverance of the endless quest to master mathematical concepts and problems will yield fruitful results.

You may sometimes find that the explanations in these books might not be sufficient. In such a case, you can email me at drjcmath@gmail.com and I will do my best to provide a more detailed explanation. Additionally, as you work on these books, please notify me if you encounter any grammatical or typographical errors so that I can provide an update version.

It is my great wish that all students who work on these books can reach their ultimate goals and enter the college of their dreams.

Thank you.

Sincerely,

Dr. John Chung

Contents
61 Tips

Practice Tests

Tips

TIP 01   Identical Equation

An **identical equation** is an equation which is true for all values of the variable.

$10x + 5x = 15x$ is **an identical equation** because it is always true for all real x.

$10x + 5 = 15$ is **an algebraic equation** because it is true for $x = 1$ only.

- Identical equation has infinitely many solutions.
- In an identical equation, the expressions of both sides are exactly same.

  Example 1: $5x + 5 = 5x + 5$

  Example 2: $ax + b = 0$ for all real values of x $\rightarrow$ $ax + b = 0x + 0$ $\rightarrow$ $a = 0$ and $b = 0$

PRACTICE

1. If $ax - b = 3x + 2$ is always true for all real x, what are the values of a and b?

2. If $a(x+1) + b(x-1) = x + 9$ is true for all real values of x, what are the values of a and b?

3. If $x^2 + 2x + 6 = a(x-1)^2 + b(x+1) + c$ is true for all real x, where a, b, and c are constants, what are the values of a, b, and c?

EXPLANATION

1. The coefficients must be equal.

2. $ax + a + bx - b = (a+b)x + a - b$, $(a+b)x + (a-b) = x + 9$
   Coefficients must be equal.
   $a + b = 1$ and $a - b = 9$
   Therefore, $a = 5$, $b = -4$.

3. Since $x^2 + 2x + 6 = ax^2 + (b-2a)x + a + b + c$, then $a = 1$, $b - 2a = 2$, and $a + b + c = 6$.
   Therefore, $a = 1$, $b = 4$, and $c = 1$.

   Answer: **1.** $a = 3, b = -2$ **2.** $a = 5, b = -4$ **3.** $a = 1, b = 4, c = 1$

Tips

Remainder Theorem

When polynomial $P(x)$ is divided by $(x-a)$, the remainder R is equal to $P(a)$.

Polynomial $P(x)$ can be expressed as follows.

$$P(x) = (x-a)Q(x) + R$$

The identical equation is true for any value of x, especially $x = a$. Therefore,

$$P(a) = R$$

Example: If $P(2) = 5$, then you can say that "When polynomial $P(x)$ is divided by $(x-2)$, the remainder is 5.

PRACTICE

1. If a polynomial $f(x) = 2x^2 - 3x + 5$ is divided by $(x-1)$, what is the remainder?

2. If a polynomial $g(x) = x^3 + 2x^2 + 2x + 3$ is divided by $(x-1)(x-2)$, then what is the remainder?

EXPLANATION

1. $R = f(1) = 2(1)^2 - 3(1) + 5 = 4$

2. $g(x) = (x-1)(x-2)Q(x) + ax + b$ When divided by degree 2 polynomial, the remainder is represented by $ax + b$

   At $x = 1$ $g(1) = 8 = a + b$

   At $x = 2$ $g(2) = 23 = 2a + b$ Therefore, $a = 15$ and $b = -7$.

   The remainder is $15x - 7$

   Also the remainder can be obtained using long-division or synthetic division.

Tips

TIP 03   Factor Theorem

If $p(a)=0$, then $p(x)$ has a factor of $(x-a)$.

Polynomial $p(x)$ can be expressed with a factor of $(x-a)$ as follows.

$p(x)=(x-a)Q(x)$, where $Q(x)$ is quotient.

If $(x-a)$ is a factor of $p(x)$, then the remainder after division should be 0.

Example: If $p(5)=0$, then $p(x)$ has a factor of $(x-5)$.

PRACTICE

1. If a polynomial $P(x)=x^2+kx-8$ has a factor of $(x-2)$, then what is the value of constant k?

2. If a polynomial $f(x)=x^3+ax^2+bx+1$ has a factor of (x^2-1), what are the values of a and b?

EXPLANATION

1. Using the factor theorem,

   $P(2)=0 \quad \rightarrow \quad 2^2+2k-8=0 \quad \rightarrow \quad k=2$

2. Since $x^3+ax^2+bx+1=(x+1)(x-1)Q(x)$,

   $f(1)=a+b+2=0$ and $f(-1)=a-b=0$

   Therefore, $a=-1$ and $b=-1$.

   Answer: **1.** $k=2$ **2.** $a=-1$ and $b=-1$

Tips

For a polynomial $P(x) = a_n x^n + a_{n-1} x^{n-1} + a_{n-2} x^{n-2} + \cdots + a_1 x + a_o = 0$

Sum of the roots $= -\dfrac{a_{n-1}}{a_n}$

Product of the roots $= \dfrac{a_o}{a_n}(-1)^n$, where n is the degree of the polynomial

Example 1: $P(x) = ax^2 + bx + c = 0$, r and s are the roots of the quadratic equation.

     Sum of the roots: $r + s = -\dfrac{b}{a}$

     Difference of the roots: $(r-s)^2 = (r+s)^2 - 4r \cdot s$

     If r and s are real and $r > s$, then

$$r - s = \sqrt{(r+s)^2 - 4rs} \;\rightarrow\; r - s = \sqrt{\frac{b^2}{a^2} - \frac{4c}{a}} = \frac{\sqrt{b^2 - 4ac}}{|a|}$$

     Product of the roots: $r + s = \dfrac{c}{a}(-1)^2 = \dfrac{c}{a}$

Example 2: $P(x) = Ax^3 + Bx^2 + Cx + D = 0$

     Sum of the three roots $= -\dfrac{B}{A}$

     Product of the three roots $= = \dfrac{D}{A}(-1)^3 = -\dfrac{D}{A}$

PRACTICE

1. If the roots of a quadratic equation $2x^2 + 5x - 4 = 0$ are α and β, what is the value of $\dfrac{1}{\alpha} + \dfrac{1}{\beta}$?

2. What is the sum of all zeros of a polynomial function $P(x) = 2x^7 + 3x^3 - 5x^2 + 4$?

3. What is the product of all zeros of $g(x) = 3x^7 - 5x^3 + 3x^2 + x - 2$?

4. If one of the roots of a quadratic equation is $2 - i$, what is the equation?

Tips

EXPLANATION

1. Since $\alpha + \beta = -\dfrac{5}{2}$ and $\alpha \times \beta = -\dfrac{4}{2} = -2$, therefore $\dfrac{1}{\alpha} + \dfrac{1}{\beta} = \dfrac{\alpha + \beta}{\alpha\beta} = \dfrac{5}{4}$.

2. Because the coefficient of x^6 is 0, the sum of the roots $= -\dfrac{a_{n-1}}{a_n} = -\dfrac{0}{2} = 0$

3. Because the product of all zeros is $\dfrac{a_o}{a_n}(-1)^n = \dfrac{-2}{3}(-1)^7 = \dfrac{2}{3}$

4. The quadratic equation can be defined by $x^2 + \dfrac{b}{a}x + \dfrac{c}{a} = 0$.

   The sum of the roots $= (2-i) + (2+i) = 4 = -\dfrac{b}{a}$ $\quad \rightarrow \quad \dfrac{b}{a} = -4$

   The product of the roots $= (2+i)(2-i) = 5 = \dfrac{c}{a}$ $\quad \rightarrow \quad \dfrac{c}{a} = 5$

   Therefore, the equation is $x^2 - 4x + 5 = 0$.

   Proof
   Sum of the two roots:

   $$\dfrac{-b + \sqrt{b^2 - 4ac}}{2a} + \dfrac{-b - \sqrt{b^2 - 4ac}}{2a} = \dfrac{-2b}{2a} = -\dfrac{b}{a}$$

   Product of the two roots:

   $$\left(\dfrac{-b + \sqrt{b^2 - 4ac}}{2a}\right)\left(\dfrac{-b - \sqrt{b^2 - 4ac}}{2a}\right) = \dfrac{(-b)^2 - \left(\sqrt{b^2 - 4ac}\right)^2}{4a^2}$$

   $$= \dfrac{4ac}{4a^2} = \dfrac{c}{a}$$

Answer: **1.** $\dfrac{5}{4}$ **2.** 0 **3.** $\dfrac{2}{3}$ **4.** $x^2 - 4x + 5 = 0$

Tips

Complex Number

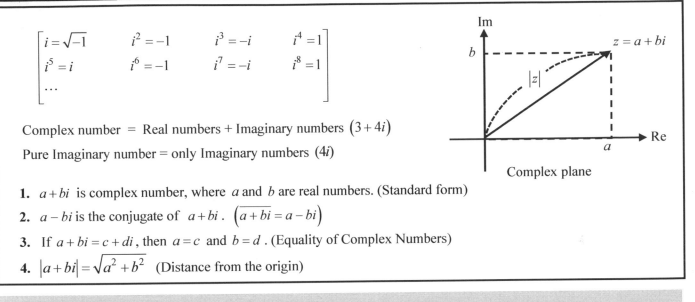

$$\begin{bmatrix} i = \sqrt{-1} & i^2 = -1 & i^3 = -i & i^4 = 1 \\ i^5 = i & i^6 = -1 & i^7 = -i & i^8 = 1 \\ \dots \end{bmatrix}$$

Complex number = Real numbers + Imaginary numbers $(3 + 4i)$

Pure Imaginary number = only Imaginary numbers $(4i)$

1. $a + bi$ is complex number, where a and b are real numbers. (Standard form)
2. $a - bi$ is the conjugate of $a + bi$. $\left(\overline{a + bi} = a - bi\right)$
3. If $a + bi = c + di$, then $a = c$ and $b = d$. (Equality of Complex Numbers)
4. $|a + bi| = \sqrt{a^2 + b^2}$ (Distance from the origin)

PRACTICE

1. What are the additive inverse and multiplicative inverse of the complex number $3 - i$?

2. What is the value of $|3 - 4i|$?

3. If $a + b + (a - b)i = 6 - 4i$, what are the values of a and b?

EXPLANATION

1. Additive inverse: $(3 - i) + (a + bi) = 0 \rightarrow -3 + i$.   Multiplicative inverse: $\dfrac{1}{(3 - i)} \dfrac{(3 + i)}{(3 + i)} = \dfrac{3 + i}{10}$

2. $|3 - 4i| = \sqrt{3^2 + (-4)^2} = \sqrt{25} = 5$

3. $a + b = 6$ and $a - b = -4$. Therefore, $a = 1$ and $b = 5$.

   Answer: **1.** $-3 + i$, $\dfrac{3}{10} + \dfrac{1}{10}i$ **2.** 5   **3.** $a = 1$, $b = 5$

Tips

TIP 06 | Conjugate Roots

If a polynomial function $P(x)$ has one variable with real coefficients, and $a+bi$ **is**

a root with a **and** b **real numbers, then its conjugate** $a-bi$ **is also a root of** $P(x)$.

1. If $x^2+x+1=0$, the roots are $\dfrac{-1}{2}+\dfrac{i\sqrt{3}}{2}$ and $\dfrac{-1}{2}-\dfrac{i\sqrt{3}}{2}$.

2. A polynomial $x^2+5=0$ has the roots of $i\sqrt{5}$ and $-i\sqrt{5}$.

PRACTICE

1. If one of the roots of a quadratic equation $f(x)=0$ is $-3+2i$, what is the quadratic equation?

2. If one of the roots of $mx^2+(4m-1)x+k=0$ is $-1-2i$, where m and k are real numbers, then what is the value of k?

EXPLANATION

1. **Using the roots**

   $\left(x-(-3+2i)\right)\left(x-(-3-2i)\right)=0 \;\rightarrow\; (x+3-2i)(x+3+2i)=0 \;\rightarrow\; (x+3)^2-(2i)^2=0$

   Therefore, $x^2+6x+13=0$.

   Using sum and product of the roots. $\quad x^2+\dfrac{b}{a}x+\dfrac{c}{a}=0$

   Sum: $-\dfrac{b}{a}=(-3+2i)+(-3-2i)=-6$ and Product: $\dfrac{c}{a}=(-3+2i)(-3-2i)=13$.

   The equation is $x^2+6x+13=0$

2. Sum: $-\dfrac{(4m-1)}{m}=-1-2i+(-1+2i)=-2,\;\rightarrow\; m=\dfrac{1}{2}$

   Product: $\dfrac{k}{m}=(-1-2i)(-1+2i)=5,\quad k=5m$. Therefore, $k-\dfrac{5}{2}$.

   Answer: **1.** $x^2+6x+13=0$ **2.** $k=\dfrac{5}{2}$

Tips

Linear Function

For two linear functions:

$$y = m_1 x + b_1 \quad \text{and} \quad y = m_2 x + b_2$$

1. If $m_1 = m_2$ and $b_1 \neq b_2$, then these two lines are parallel. (Inconsistent)

2. If $m_1 = m_2$ and $b_1 = b_2$, then these two lines coincide. (Dependent)

3. If $m_1 \cdot m_2 = -1$, then these two lines are perpendicular.

4. If $m_1 \neq m_2$, these two lines are intersecting. (Consistent)

PRACTICE

1. What is the equation of the line which is equidistant from two points $A(4, 0)$ and $B(0, 2)$?

2. If the two lines $2x - 3y + 2 = 0$ and $3x - ky - 1 = 0$ are perpendicular, then $k =$

3. If the two lines $2x + ay = 1$ and $ax + (a + 4)y = 2$ are parallel, then $a =$

EXPLANATION

1. The midpoint $= (2, 1)$ and the slope of $\overline{AB} = -\dfrac{1}{2}$. The perpendicular line has slope of 2 and passes through $(2, 1)$. Therefore, the equation is $y = 2x - 3$.

2. The product of the slopes is -1. $\quad \dfrac{2}{3} \cdot \dfrac{3}{k} = -1 \quad \rightarrow \quad k = -2$

3. The slopes are equal. $-\dfrac{2}{a} = -\dfrac{a}{a+4} \quad \rightarrow \quad (a-4)(a+2) = 0 \quad \rightarrow \quad a = 4$ or -2. But the y-intercepts are

   $\dfrac{1}{a}$ and $\dfrac{2}{a+4}$. At $a = 4$, the two y-intercepts are equal (coincide). Therefore, $a = -2$

   Answer: **1.** $y = 2x - 3$ **2.** $k = -2$ **3.** $a = -2$

Tips

Distance from a Point to a Line

Distance D from a point (x_1, y_1) to a line $ax + by + c = 0$:

$$D = \frac{|ax_1 + by_1 + c|}{\sqrt{a^2 + b^2}}$$

Distance between two points $D = \sqrt{(x_2 - x_1)^2 + (y_2 - y_1)^2}$

Distance between two straight lines is the minimum distance which is perpendicular to the lines.

PRACTICE

1. What is the distance from a point $(7, 9)$ to a line $12x - 5y = 0$?

2. What is the distance from the origin to a line $3x + 4y = 8$?

3. What is the distance between two parallel lines $3x + y = 12$ and $mx + 2y = 4$?

EXPLANATION

1. $D = \dfrac{|12(7) - 5(9)|}{\sqrt{12^2 + (-5)^2}} = \dfrac{39}{13} = 3$

2. Origin $(0, 0)$, and the equation of the line is $3x + 4y - 8 = 0$.

   Therefore, $D = \dfrac{|3(0) + 4(0) - 8|}{\sqrt{3^2 + 4^2}} = \dfrac{8}{5}$.

3. Since they are parallel, $m = 6$. Choose any point on $3x + y = 12$. $\rightarrow$ $(4, 0)$

   Distance between $(4, 0)$ and $6x + 2y - 4 = 0$ is

   $D = \dfrac{|6(4) + 2(0) - 4|}{\sqrt{6^2 + 2^2}} = \sqrt{10}$

   Answer: **1.** 3   **2.** $\dfrac{8}{5}$ **3.** $\sqrt{10}$

Tips

TIP 09   Distance from a Point to a Plane

Distance from point $A(x_2, y_2, z_2)$ to point $B(x_1, y_1, z_1)$ in space :

$$D = \sqrt{(x_2 - x_1)^2 + (y_2 - y_1)^2 + (z_2 - z_1)^2}$$

Distance from a point (x_1, y_1, z_1) to a plane $ax + by + cz + d = 0$:

$$D = \frac{|ax_1 + by_1 + cz_1 + d|}{\sqrt{a^2 + b^2 + c^2}}$$

Distance from the origin to a point (a, b, c) is $D = \sqrt{a^2 + b^2 + c^2}$.

PRACTICE

1. What is the distance from a point $(1, \ 2, -3)$ to a plane $3x - 4y + 12z = -2$?

2. What is the length of the diagonal of a rectangular solid with dimensions 3, 4, and 12?

3. What is the distance between point $A(1, -1, \ 2)$ and point $B(3, 4, 1)$?

EXPLANATION

1. $D = \dfrac{|3(1) - 4(2) + 12(-3) + 2|}{\sqrt{3^2 + 4^2 + 12^2}} = \dfrac{39}{13} = 3$

2. $D = \sqrt{3^2 + 4^2 + 12^2} = 13$

3. $D = \sqrt{(3-1)^2 + (4 - {}^-1)^2 + (1-2)^2} = \sqrt{30}$

     Answer: **1.** 3   **2.** 13   **3.** $\sqrt{30}$

Tips

Quadratic Function

Polynomial function of x with degree n is defined as follows.

$$P(x) = a_n x^n + a_{n-1} x^{n-1} + a_{n-2} x^{n-2} + \cdots + a_2 x^2 + a_1 x + a_o$$

1. If $f(x) = a_o$, then $f(x)$ is a constant function.

2. If $f(x) = ax^2 + bx + c$, then $f(x)$ is a quadratic function.

   If $a > 0$, f has a minimum at $x = -\dfrac{b}{2a}$.   If $a < 0$, f has a maximum at $x = -\dfrac{b}{2a}$.

3. $f(x) = ax^2 + bx + c$: standard form.

4. $f(x) = a(x - x_1)(x - x_2)$: factored form, where x_1 and x_2 are the roots of $f(x) = 0$

5. $f(x) = a(x - h)^2 + k$: vertex form

   Axis of symmetry: $x = h$,   Vertex: (h, k)

PRACTICE

1. If $f(x) = -x^2 + 6x - 8$, what are the coordinates of the vertex?

2. If a manufacturer of game computers has daily production costs of $C(n) = 1200 - 24n + 0.5n^2$, where C is the total cost, in dollars, and n is the number of units produced, how many game computers should be produced each day to minimize cost?

EXPLANATION

1. Axis of symmetry $x = -\dfrac{b}{2a} = -\dfrac{6}{2(-1)} = 3$, $y = f(3) = -3^2 + 6(3) - 8 = 1$

2. Axis of symmetry $n = -\dfrac{(-24)}{2(0.5)} = 24$, C has a minimum at $n = 24$.

   Therefore, the minimum cost $C(24) = 1200 - 24(24) - 0.5(24^2) = 912$

   Answer: **1.** $(3, 1)$ **2.** 24

Tips

TIP 11 | Discriminant

Discriminant determines the nature of the roots of a quadratic equation $ax^2 + bx + c = 0$.

$$\text{Roots} = \frac{-b \pm \sqrt{b^2 - 4ac}}{2a}, \quad \text{Discriminant } D = b^2 - 4ac$$

1. If $D > 0$, then the roots are real and unequal.

2. If $D = 0$, then the roots are real and equal.

3. If $D < 0$, then the roots are imaginary. (No real roots)

PRACTICE

1. If a quadratic equation $2x^2 - kx + 3 = 0$ have imaginary roots, what is the value of k ?

2. If the roots of $x^2 + (k+1)x + 4 = 0$ are real and equal, what is the value of k ?

3. If $y = 3x^2 - 2x + k$ is positive for all x, then what is the smallest integral value of k ?

Explanation

1. $D = k^2 - 24 < 0 \rightarrow \left(k - 2\sqrt{6}\right)\left(k + 2\sqrt{6}\right) < 0$. Therefore, $-2\sqrt{6} < x < 2\sqrt{6}$.

2. $D = (k+1)^2 - 16 = 0 \rightarrow (k+5)(k-3) = 0$. $k = -5$ or 3.

3. That means "no x-intersections," or "imaginary roots."

$D = 4 - 12k < 0 \rightarrow 12k > 4 \rightarrow k > \dfrac{1}{3}$, The smallest integer k is 1.

Answer: **1.** $-2\sqrt{6} < k < 2\sqrt{6}$ **2.** $k = 3$ or -5 **3.** $k = 1$

Tips

Circle

A circle is the locus of points equidistant from a given point, known as the center.

The standard equation of a circle whose center is at the point (h, k) is

$$(x - h)^2 + (y - k)^2 = r^2, \quad r = \text{radius}$$

PRACTICE

1. What is the area of a circle whose equation is $x^2 - 4x + y^2 + 2y = 11$?

2. The graph of the equation $x^2 + y^2 + 2ax - 4y + 2a^2 = 0$ represents a circle. What is the greatest possible integer value of a ?

3. What is the circumference of a circle whose equation is $x^2 + y^2 - 6y = 16$?

EXPLANATION

1. The standard equation is $(x - 2)^2 + (y + 1)^2 = 16$, $r^2 = 16$

   Therefore, the area is $\pi r^2 = 16\pi$.

2. The standard equation is $(x + a)^2 + (y - 2)^2 = -a^2 + 4$

   To form a circle, $r^2 = -a^2 + 4 > 0 \rightarrow a^2 - 4 < 0 \rightarrow (a + 2)(a - 2) < 0$

   Since $-2 < a < 2$, the greatest integer a is 1.

3. The standard equation is $x^2 + (y - 3)^2 = 25$. $r = 5$.

   Therefore, the circumference of the circle is $2\pi r = 10\pi$.

   Answer: **1.** 16π **2.** 1   **3.** 10π

Tips

An ellipse is the set of all points (x, y) in a plane, the sum of whose distances from two distinct fixed point (foci) is constant.

The standard equation of an ellipse with center (h, k) is

if $a > b$

$$\frac{(x-h)^2}{a^2} + \frac{(y-k)^2}{b^2} = 1 \quad : \text{Major axis is horizontal}$$

$$\frac{(x-h)^2}{b^2} + \frac{(y-k)^2}{a^2} = 1 \quad : \text{Major axis is vertical}$$

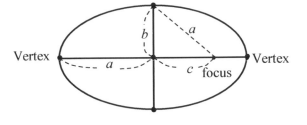

1. The center of the ellipse is at point (h, k)
2. Length of major axis is $2a$. Length of minor axis is $2b$.
3. If c is the length from the center to the focus, then $c^2 = a^2 - b^2$.

PRACTICE

1. What is the center of an ellipse whose equation is $x^2 + 4y^2 - 6x + 8y + 9 = 0$?

2. What is the length of the major axis of the ellipse whose equation is $\frac{x^2}{5} + \frac{y^2}{27} = 1$?

3. The ellipse is given by $4x^2 + y^2 = 36$. What are the coordinates of the foci?

4. If a line $y = x + k$ is tangent to an ellipse whose equation is $x^2 + \frac{y^2}{4} = 1$, what is the value of k ?

Tips

1. The standard equation is $(x-3)^2 + 4(y+1)^2 = 4$ $\rightarrow$ $\dfrac{(x-3)^2}{4} + \dfrac{(y+1)^2}{1} = 1$.

Center $(3, -1)$

2. $a^2 = 27$ $\rightarrow$ $a = 3\sqrt{3}$, Therefore major axis is $2a = 6\sqrt{3}$.

3. The standard equation is $\dfrac{x^2}{9} + \dfrac{y^2}{36} = 1$. (Major axis is vertical)

$a^2 = 36$ and $b^2 = 9$

$c = \pm\sqrt{a^2 - b^2} = \pm\sqrt{27}$

Therefore the coordinates of foci is $f\left(0, \pm3\sqrt{3}\right)$.

4. Substitute. $4x^2 + (x+k)^2 = 4$ $\rightarrow$ $5x^2 + 2kx + k^2 - 4 = 0$

Since the line is tangent to the ellipse, its **discriminant must be 0**.

$D = 4k^2 - 4(5)(k^2 - 4) = 0$ $\rightarrow$ $16k^2 = 80$ $\rightarrow$ $k^2 = 5$

Therefore, $k = \pm\sqrt{5}$.

Answer: **1.** $(3, -1)$ **2.** $6\sqrt{3}$ **3.** $\left(0, \pm3\sqrt{3}\right)$ **4.** $\pm\sqrt{5}$

Tips

A parabola is the set of all points in a plane that are equidistant from a fixed line, the directrix, and a fixed point, the focus.

1. The standard form of the equation with vertex at the origin (0, 0) is

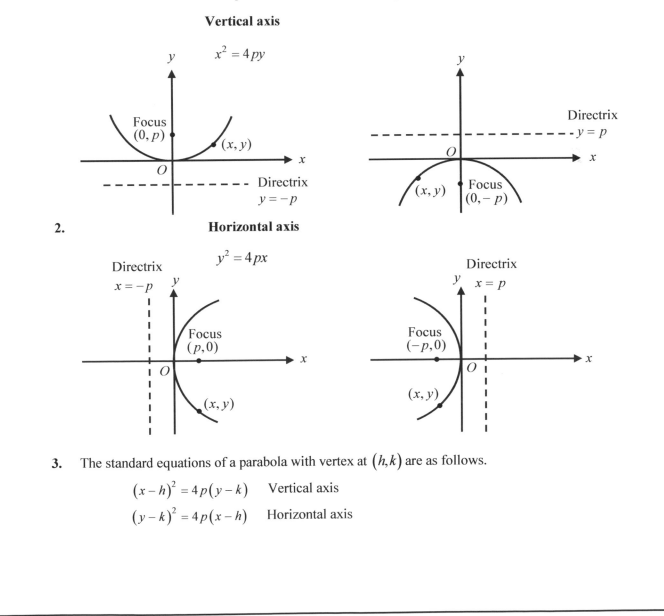

2.

3. The standard equations of a parabola with vertex at (h, k) are as follows.

$$(x-h)^2 = 4p(y-k) \quad \text{Vertical axis}$$
$$(y-k)^2 = 4p(x-h) \quad \text{Horizontal axis}$$

Tips

1. What are the focus and directrix of the parabola whose equation is given by $y = \dfrac{1}{16}x^2$?

2. Find the focus of the parabola given by $y = -\dfrac{1}{4}x^2 - x + \dfrac{1}{4}$.

3. Find the standard form of the equation of the parabola with the vertex at $(1, 0)$ and the **focus** at $(2, 0)$.

EXPLANATION

1. $\quad x^2 = 16y \;\rightarrow\; x^2 = 4(4)y \quad$ focus $(0, 4)$ and directrix $y = -4$

2. $\quad y - \dfrac{1}{4} = -\dfrac{1}{4}\left(x^2 + 4x\right) \quad$, Standard form is

$\quad y - \dfrac{5}{4} = -\dfrac{1}{4}(x + 2)^2 \;\rightarrow\; (x + 2)^2 = 4(-1)\left(y - \dfrac{5}{4}\right)$

Therefore, the focus $(h, k + p) = \left(-2, \dfrac{5}{4} - 1\right) = \left(-2, \dfrac{1}{4}\right)$

3. Because the axis of symmetry is horizontal, passing through $(1, 0)$ and $(2, 0)$,

The standard equation is

$(y - k)^2 = 4p(x - h)$, where $h = 1$, $k = 0$, and $p = 2 - 1 = 1$.

Therefore the equation is

$(y - 0)^2 = 4(1)(x - 1) \;\rightarrow\; y^2 = 4(x - 1)$

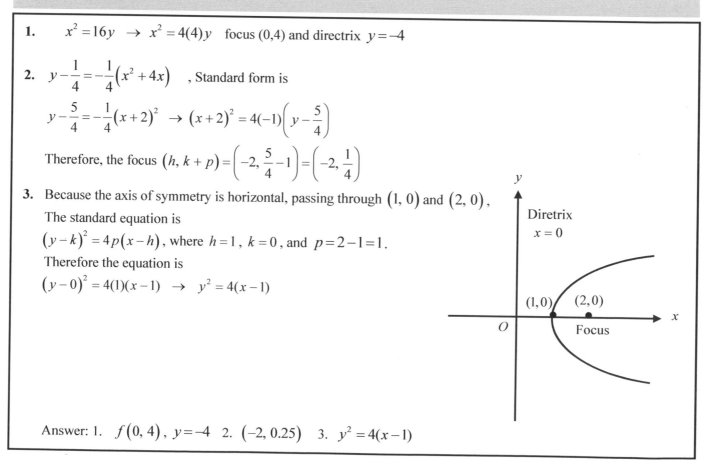

Answer: 1. $f(0, 4)$, $y = -4$ 2. $(-2, 0.25)$ 3. $y^2 = 4(x - 1)$

Tips

A hyperbola is the set of points in a plane, the difference of whose distances from two distinct foci is constant. The standard form of the equation with the center at $(0, 0)$ is

$$\frac{x^2}{a^2} - \frac{y^2}{b^2} = 1$$

Transverse axis is horizontal

$$\frac{y^2}{a^2} - \frac{x^2}{b^2} = 1$$

Transverse axis is vertical

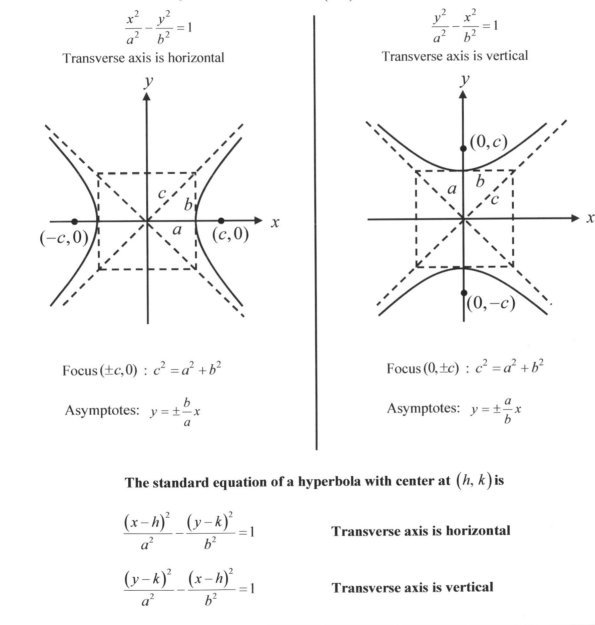

Focus $(\pm c, 0)$: $c^2 = a^2 + b^2$

Asymptotes: $y = \pm \dfrac{b}{a} x$

Focus $(0, \pm c)$: $c^2 = a^2 + b^2$

Asymptotes: $y = \pm \dfrac{a}{b} x$

The standard equation of a hyperbola with center at (h, k) is

$$\frac{(x-h)^2}{a^2} - \frac{(y-k)^2}{b^2} = 1$$ **Transverse axis is horizontal**

$$\frac{(y-k)^2}{a^2} - \frac{(x-h)^2}{b^2} = 1$$ **Transverse axis is vertical**

Tips

1. If the equation of a hyperbola is given by $\dfrac{x^2}{25} - \dfrac{y^2}{16} = 1$, what are the equations of its asymptotes?

2. Find the asymptotes and foci of the hyperbola whose equation is $\dfrac{y^2}{16} - \dfrac{x^2}{4} = 1$.

3. The equation of a hyperbola is defined by $9x^2 - y^2 - 36x - 6y + 18 = 0$.
Find the center.

EXPLANATION

1. Asymptotes: $y = \pm \dfrac{b}{a} x$. Since $a = 5$ and $b = 4$, the asymptotes is $y = \pm \dfrac{4}{5} x$.

2. Asymptotes: $y = \pm \dfrac{a}{b} x$. $a = 4$ and $b = 2$. Therefore, the asymptotes is $y = \pm \dfrac{4}{2} x \;\rightarrow\; y = \pm 2x$.

For the foci $(0, c)$:

$$c = \pm \sqrt{a^2 + b^2} = \pm \sqrt{16 + 4} = \pm 2\sqrt{5}$$

3. Perfect squared form: $9\left(x^2 - 4x + 4\right) - \left(y^2 + 6y + 9\right) = -18 + 36 - 9$

$$9(x-2)^2 - (y+3)^2 = 9 \;\rightarrow\; \dfrac{(x-2)^2}{1} - \dfrac{(y+3)^2}{9} = 1$$

Center at $(2, -3)$

Answer: **1.** $y = \pm \dfrac{4}{5} x$ **2.** $y = \pm 2x$, $f\left(0, \pm 2\sqrt{5}\right)$ **3.** $(x-2)^2 - \dfrac{(y+3)^2}{9} = 1$, Center $(2, -3)$

Tips

TIP 16   Function

A **function** f from a set X to a set Y is a relation that assigns to each element in set X **exactly one element** in the set Y.

    Domain is the set of X (input).   **Range** is the set of Y (output).

1. x is the independent variable and y is the dependent variable.

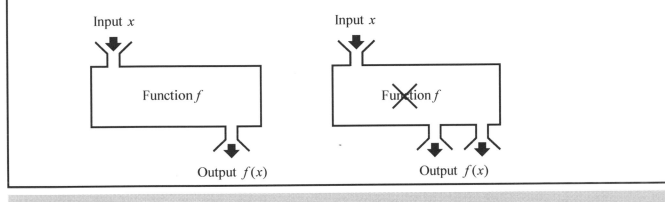

PRACTICE

1. What are the domain and range of the function $f(x) = \sqrt{16 - x^2}$?

2. What is the domain of the function $f(x) = \dfrac{\sqrt{x - 10}}{x - 15}$?

3. What is the range of the function $f(x) = 3|x - 5| - 4$?

EXPLANATION

1. $16 - x^2 \geq 0 \quad \rightarrow \quad (x + 4)(x - 4) \leq 0 \quad \rightarrow \quad -4 \leq x \leq 4$

2. $x - 10 \geq 0$ but $x \neq 15 \quad \rightarrow \{10 \leq x < 15\} \cup \{x > 15\}$ or   interval notation: $[10, 15) \cup (15, \infty)$

3. Minimum of f is -4. You can a graphing calculator

    Answer: **1.** Domain: $-4 \leq x \leq 4$, Range: $0 \leq y \leq 4$ **2.** $\{10 \leq x < 15\} \cup \{15 < x\}$

            3. $y \geq -4$

Tips

TIP 17   Domain and Range of a Composite Function

Domain of a composite function is the intersection of domains of the starting and final function.

Range of a composite function is the range of final function restricted by starting function.

Example:

$$f(x) = \frac{1}{x+2}, \quad g(x) = \frac{x}{x-3} \quad : \qquad \begin{array}{l} g(x) \rightarrow \text{starting function}, \quad f(x) \rightarrow \text{second function} \\ f(g(x)) \rightarrow \text{final function} \end{array}$$

Domain of starting function $g(x)$ is $x \neq 3$. (All real numbers except 3)

$$f(g(x)) = \frac{1}{\dfrac{x}{x-3}+2} = \frac{x-3}{3(x-2)} \quad \rightarrow \quad \text{Domain of final function is } x \neq 2.$$

Therefore, the domain of $f(g(x))$ is all real numbers x except 2 and 3.

Now let's find the range. First find the range of the final function.
From the function, we can find two asymptotes.

$$\begin{cases} x = 2 : \text{ Vertical asymptote} \\ y = \lim\limits_{x \to \infty} \dfrac{x-3}{3(x-2)} = \dfrac{1}{3} : \text{Horizontal asymptote} \end{cases}$$

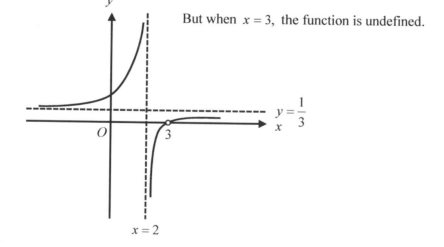

But when $x = 3$, the function is undefined.

$$y = \frac{1}{3}$$

$$x = 2$$

Therefore, the range of $f(g(x))$ is $(-\infty, 0) \vee \left(0, \dfrac{1}{3}\right) \vee \left(\dfrac{1}{3}, \infty\right). \rightarrow$ All real numbers y except 0 and $\dfrac{1}{3}$

Tips

PRACTICE

1. If $f(x) = \sqrt{x}$ and $g(x) = x - 1$, what is the domain and range of $(g \circ f)(x)$?

2. If $f(x) = \dfrac{1}{x}$ and $g(x) = \dfrac{1}{x - 1}$, what is the domain and range of $(g \circ f)(x)$?

EXPLANATION

1. Domain of $f(x)$ is $x \geq 0$.

$(g \circ f)(x) = \sqrt{x} - 1$: Domain of $(g \circ f)(x)$ is $x \geq 0$. There, the domain of the final function is $x \geq 0$.

The range of the final function is $y \geq -1$.

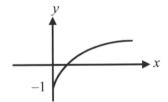

2. Domain of $f(x)$ is $x \neq 0$. (All real numbers except 0)

$$(g \circ f)(x) = \frac{1}{\dfrac{1}{x} - 1} = \frac{x}{1 - x}$$

Domain of $(g \circ f)(x)$ is $x \neq 1$. Therefore, actual domain is all real numbers except 0 and 1.

Range of $(g \circ f)(x)$:

$\begin{cases} \text{Vertical asymptote: } x = 1 \\ \text{Horizontal asynptote: } y = \lim\limits_{x \to \infty} \dfrac{x}{1 - x} = -1 \end{cases}$

From the first function $f(x)$,

$x \neq 0 \;\to\; (g \circ f)(0)$ is undefined.

Therefore, the range of $g(f(x))$ is all real numbers

except $y = -1$ and $y = 0$.

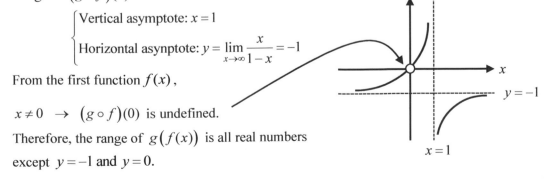

Tips

TIP 18 — Piecewise-Defined Function

A **piecewise-defined function** is a function that is defined by two or more equations over a specified domain.

$f(x) = |x|$ is a piecewise-defined function as follows.

$$f(x) = |x| = \begin{cases} x, & \text{when } x \geq 0 \\ -x, & \text{when } x < 0 \end{cases}$$

PRACTICE

1. What are the domain and range of the piecewise-defined function as follows?

$$f(x) = \begin{cases} x^2 + 1, & x < 0 \\ x - 1, & x \geq 0 \end{cases}$$

EXPLANATION

1. The graph shows that the domain is all real x and the range is $y \geq -1$.

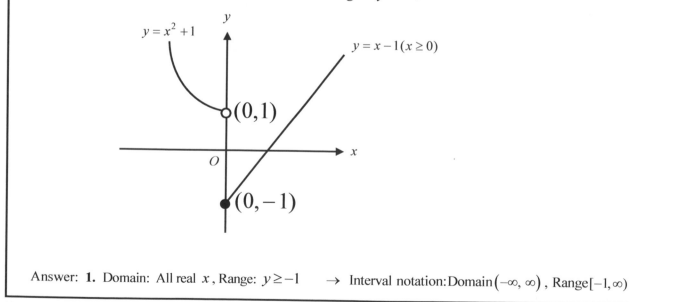

Answer: **1.** Domain: All real x, Range: $y \geq -1$ → Interval notation: Domain $(-\infty, \infty)$, Range $[-1, \infty)$

Tips

TIP 19 — Odd and Even Functions

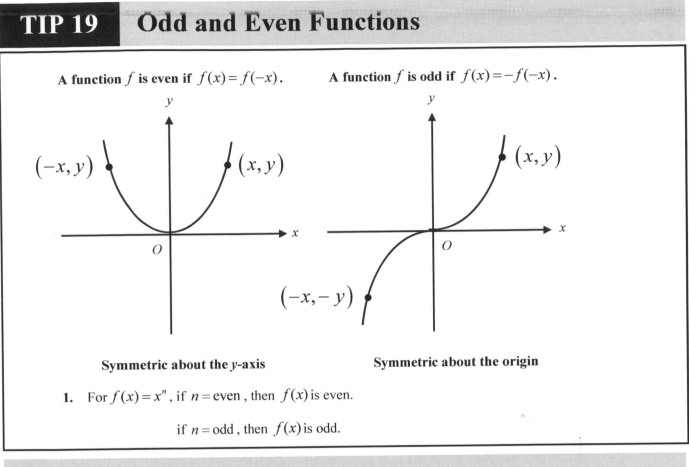

A function f is even if $f(x) = f(-x)$.

A function f is odd if $f(x) = -f(-x)$.

Symmetric about the y-axis

Symmetric about the origin

1. For $f(x) = x^n$, if $n = $ even , then $f(x)$ is even.

   if $n = $ odd , then $f(x)$ is odd.

PRACTICE

Determine whether each function is even, odd, or neither.

1. $f(x) = x^3 - 2x$
2. $g(x) = x^4 + 2x^2 + 5$
3. $h(x) = x^3 - 1$

EXPLANATION

1. Since $f(x) = -f(-x)$, $f(x)$ is odd.

2. Since $g(x) = g(-x)$, $g(x)$ is even.

3. $h(x)$ is neither , because $h(x) \neq h(-x)$ or $h(x) \neq -h(-x)$.

   Answer: 1. Odd   2. Even   3. Neither

Tips

TIP 20	Combinations of Functions

Sum:	$(f+g)(x) = f(x) + g(x)$
Difference:	$(f-g)(x) = f(x) - g(x)$
Product:	$(fg)(x) = f(x) \cdot g(x)$
Quotient:	$\left(\dfrac{f}{g}\right)(x) = \dfrac{f(x)}{g(x)}, \; g(x) \neq 0$
Compositions:	$(f \circ g)(x) = f\big(g(x)\big)$

PRACTICE

1. If $f(x) = 2x + 3$ and $g(x) = 2x - 3$, then $(fg)(4) =$

2. If $f(x) = \log_3(x-3)$ and $g(x) = \log_3(x+3)$, then $(f+g)(6) =$

3. If $f(x) = \log_2(x^2 - 3x + 2)$ and $g(x) = \log_2(x-2)$, then $(f-g)(9) =$

4. If $f(x) = e^x$ and $g(x) = 3\ln(x-3)$, then $f\big(g(5)\big) =$

EXPLANATION

1. Since $fg = (2x+3)(2x-3) = 4x^2 - 9$, $(fg)(4) = 55$. Or, $f(4) = 11$ and $g(4) = 5$. $f(4)g(4) = 55$.

2. Since $f + g = \log_3(x-3)(x+3) = \log_3(x^2 - 9)$,

   $(f+g)(6) = \log_3(36 - 9) = 3\log_3 3 = 3$.

3. $f - g = \log_2(x-2)(x-1) - \log_2(x-2) = \log_2\dfrac{(x-2)(x-1)}{(x-2)} = \log_2(x-1)$

   Therefore, $(f-g)(9) = \log_2(9-1) = 3\log_2 2 = 3$

4. Since $f\big(g(x)\big) = e^{3\ln(x-3)} = (x-3)^3$, $f\big(g(5)\big) = (5-3)^3 = 8$.

   Answer: **1.** 55   **2.** 3   **3.** 3   **4.** 8

Tips

Periodic Functions

If a function f is periodic if there exists a number p such that

$$f(x+p) = f(x) \text{ for all number } x.$$

1. The smallest period is called the fundamental period of the function.

2. If a periodic function f has period p , then

    1) $y = cf(x)$ still has period p.

    2) $y = f(cx)$ has period $\dfrac{p}{c}$.

3. **The smallest period is simply called the period.**

PRACTICE

1. If a function $f(x) = \sin x$ has period 2π, then what is the period of the function
    $f(x) = -3\sin 3x$?

2. What is the period of the function $y = -2\cos\left(\pi x - \dfrac{\pi}{12}\right) + 5$?

3. If a function is defined by $f(x) = f(x+2\pi)$, what is the period of the function?

EXPLANATION

1. $p = \dfrac{2\pi}{c} = \dfrac{2\pi}{3}$

2. $p = \dfrac{2\pi}{\pi} = 2$

3. $p = 2\pi$

Tips

TIP 22 | Inverse Functions

An inverse function is a function that reverses function f. If f is a function mapping x to y, then the inverse function of f maps y back to x.

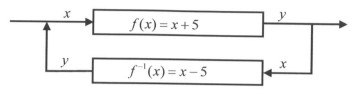

If $\quad f(x) = x + 5 \quad : \{(1, 6), (2, 7), (3, 8), (4, 9)\}$

then $\quad f^{-1}(x) = x - 5 \quad : \{(6, 1), (7, 2), (8, 3), (9, 4)\}$

In order to form inverse function of f just interchange x and y coordinates and express y in terms of x.

If the function g is the inverse function of f,

1. $f(g(x)) = x$ and $g(f(x)) = x$.

2. The domain of f is the range of g and the range of f is the domain of g.

3. $f^{-1}(x)$ is a reflection of the graph of f in the line $y = x$.

4. If point (a, b) lies on graph of f, then point (b, a) must lie on the graph of f^{-1}.

PRACTICE

1. What is the inverse function of $f(x) = \dfrac{3x - 5}{2}$?

2. If $f(4) = 35$, then $f^{-1}(35) =$

EXPLANATION

1. $x = \dfrac{3y - 5}{2}, \quad f^{-1} : y = \dfrac{2x + 5}{3}$

2. $f : (4, 35) \rightarrow f^{-1} : (35, 4)$

Answer: **1.** $y = \dfrac{2x + 5}{3}$ **2.** 4

Tips

TIP 23   The Existence of an Inverse Function

If a function f is one-to-one, then its inverse is a function.

1. If f is increasing on its entire domain, then f is one-to-one.
2. If f is decreasing on its entire domain, then f is one-to-one.
3. If f is increasing on its entire domain, then f^{-1} is a function.
4. If f is decreasing on its entire domain, then f^{-1} is a function.

To check one-to-one, the horizontal line test can be used.

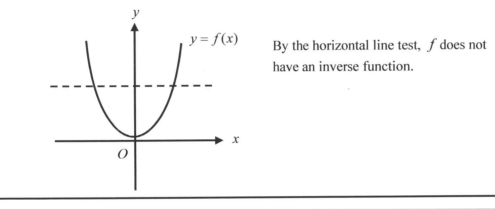

By the horizontal line test, f does not have an inverse function.

PRACTICE

1. Does the function $f(x) = \sqrt{x-2} + 3$ have an inverse function?

2. Does the function $g(x) = |x+3|$ have an inverse function?

EXPLANATION

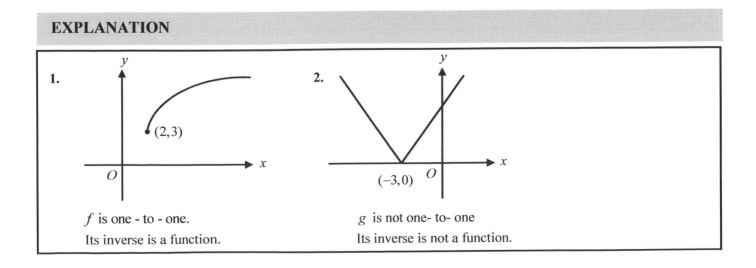

1. f is one - to - one.
Its inverse is a function.

2. g is not one- to- one
Its inverse is not a function.

Tips

TIP 24 Leading Coefficient Test (Behavior of Graph)

Whether the graph of a polynomial rises or falls can be determined by **the Leading Coefficient Test** as follows.

$$P(x) = a_n x^n + a_{n-1} x^{n-1} + \cdots + a_1 x + a_o \quad : \quad a_n \text{ is the leading coefficient.}$$

1. When n is odd and a_n is positive, the graph falls to the left and rises to the right.
2. When n is odd and a_n is negative, the graph rises to the left and falls to the right.

3. When n is even and a_n is positive, the graph rises to the left and right.
4. When n is even and a_n is negative, the graph falls to the left and right.

PRACTICE

1. What are the right-hand and left-hand behaviors of the graph of $f(x) = x^5 + 2x^3 - 3x + 5$?

EXPLANATION

1. Using the test, leading coefficient is positive and n is odd.

$$\lim_{x \to \infty} x^5 = +\infty \quad \text{and} \quad \lim_{x \to -\infty} x^5 = -\infty$$

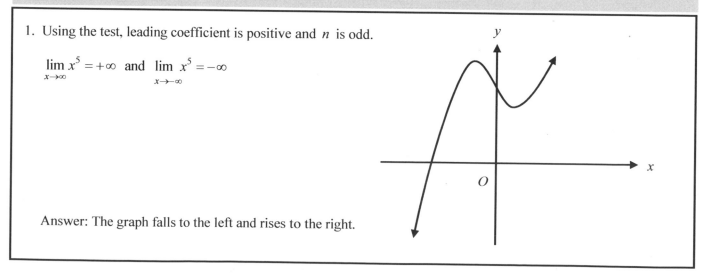

Answer: The graph falls to the left and rises to the right.

Tips

TIP 25   Arithmetic Sequences

A sequence is **arithmetic** if the differences between consecutive terms are the same.

If $a_1 = a$ and d is the **common difference**, then **the nth term** of an arithmetic sequence is
$$a_n = a + (n-1)d.$$

And **the sum** of a finite arithmetic sequence with n terms is
$$S_n = \frac{n(a_1 + a_n)}{2}$$

PRACTICE

1. If the first term of a sequence $\{a_n\}$ is $a_1 = 3$ and $a_{n+1} = a_n + 4$, what is a_{25}?

2. If three numbers m, a, and k form an arithmetic sequence in that order, the sum of the numbers is 21, and the product of the numbers is 315, what is the greatest number in the sequence?

3. If the first term of an arithmetic sequence is 5 and the common difference is 3, what is the sum of the first 100 terms?

EXPLANATION

1. Since $a_1 = 3$, $a_{n+1} - a_n = 4$, and $d = 4$, $a_{25} = a + (n-1)d = 3 + 24 \cdot 4 = 99$.

2. Let three numbers be $a-d$, a, $a+d$. Then $a-d+a+a+d = 3a = 21 \rightarrow a = 7$
   In an arithmetic sequence, the middle number (median) is equal to the average.
   $(7-d) \cdot 7 \cdot (7+d) = 315 \rightarrow 49 - d^2 = 45 \rightarrow d^2 = 4 \rightarrow d = \pm 2$
   Therefore, three numbers are 5, 7, 9

3. Since $a_1 = 5$ and $d = 3$, then $a_{100} = 5 + (100-1) \cdot 3 = 302$ and number of terms is 100.
   Therefore, $S_{100} = \dfrac{100(5+302)}{2} = 15,350$

   Answer: **1.**   99   **2.**   9   **3.**   15,350

Tips

A sequence is **geometric** if the ratios of consecutive terms are the same.

If $a_1 = a$ and the common ratio is r, then

     1) the nth term of the geometric sequence is $a_n = ar^{n-1}$ and

     2) the sum of the sequence is $S_n = \dfrac{a(1-r^n)}{1-r}$.

     3) **The sum of the infinite series** is given by $S_\infty = \lim\limits_{n \to \infty} S_n = \lim\limits_{n \to \infty} \dfrac{a(1-r^n)}{1-r}$.

         If $|r| < 1$, then the sum of the infinite series is as follows.

$$S_\infty = \frac{a}{1-r}$$

PRACTICE

1. The first term of a geometric sequence $\{a_n\}$ is 2 and $a_{n+1} = 2a_n$. What is the value of a_{10} ?

2. In a geometric sequence, the second term is 3 and fifth term is 24. What is the 8th term?

3. What is the sum of the infinite series $15 - 3 + \dfrac{3}{5} - \dfrac{3}{25} + \cdots$?

EXPLANATION

1. Since $a_1 = 2$ and $r = 2$, then $a_{10} = 2(2)^9 = 2^{10}$.

2. $a_2 = a_1 r = 3$ and $a_5 = a_1 r^4 = 24$, $\dfrac{a_5}{a_2} = \dfrac{a_1 r^4}{a_1 r} = \dfrac{24}{3}$ $\rightarrow r^3 = 8$.

     Therefore $r = 2$ and $a_1 = \dfrac{3}{2}$. The 8th term $a_8 = \left(\dfrac{3}{2}\right)(2)^7 = 192$

3. Since $r = -\dfrac{1}{5}$, $S_\infty = \dfrac{a}{1-r} = \dfrac{15}{1-(-1/5)} = 12.5$

     Answer: **1.**   1024   **2.**   192   **3.**   12.5

Tips

TIP 27 — Exponential Functions

A. Laws of Exponents:

If a, b, and c are positive integers.

1. $x^a \cdot x^b = x^{a+b}$: Multiplication Law

2. $x^a \div x^b = x^{a-b}$: Division Law

3. $\left(x^a\right)^b = x^{ab}$: Power Law

4. $(xy)^a = x^a \cdot y^a$: Power of a Product Law

5. $\left(\dfrac{x}{y}\right)^a = \dfrac{x^a}{y^a}$: Power of a Quotient Law

6. $x^o = 1 \ (x \neq 0)$: Zero Exponent

7. $x^{-a} = \dfrac{1}{x^a} = \left(\dfrac{1}{x}\right)^a \ (x \neq 0)$: Negative Exponent

8. $x^{\frac{a}{b}} = \sqrt[b]{x^a} = \left(\sqrt[b]{x}\right)^a$: Fractional Exponent

B. Exponential Function f with base a :

     $f(x) = a^x$, where $a > 0$, $a \neq 1$, and x is any real number.

C. Graphs of Exponential Functions

     1) $a > 1$ 2) $0 < a < 1$

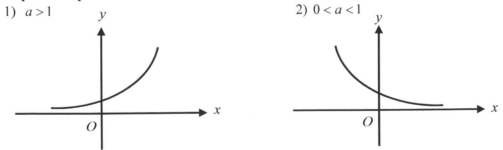

The graph of $y = 2^{-x}$ is the reflection in the y-axis of the graph of $y = 2^x$.

     Domain: $(-\infty, \infty)$, **Range:** $(0, \infty)$, **Horizontal asymptote:** $y = 0$

D. The natural base e $(e \approx 2.718281828)$

$$e = \lim_{x \to \infty}\left(1 + \frac{1}{x}\right)^x \quad \text{or} \quad e = \lim_{x \to 0}(1 + x)^{\frac{1}{x}}$$

Tips

1. If a total of $10,000 is invested at an annual interest rate of 5%, compounded annually, what is the balance in the account after 5 years?

2. If $5,000 is invested at an annual interest rate of 6%, compounded quarterly, what is the amount of the balance after 5 years?

3. If $3^{2x} - 3^x - 72 = 0$, what is the value of x?

4. If $\dfrac{2^{x^2+1}}{2^{x-1}} = 16$, then $x =$

EXPLANATION

1. $A = 10,000(1+0.05)^5 \approx 12762.82$

2. $A = 5,000\left(1 + \dfrac{0.06}{4}\right)^{4(5)} \approx 6734.28$, because $A = P\left(1+\dfrac{r}{n}\right)^{nt}$.

3. Since $\left(3^x - 9\right)\left(3^x + 8\right) = 0$, then $3^x \neq -8$ and $3^x = 9$. Therefore, $x = 2$.

4. Since $\dfrac{2^{x^2+1}}{2^{x-1}} = 2^{x^2-x+2} = 2^4$, then $x^2 - x + 2 = 4 \rightarrow x^2 - x - 2 = 0$.

   $(x-2)(x+1) = 0$, $x = 2$ or -1.

   Answer: **1.** $12762.82   **2.** $6734.28   **3.** 2   **4.** $x = 2$ or $x = -1$

Tips

TIP 28 — Logarithmic Functions

The function is given by

$$y = \log_a x \quad \left(x = a^y\right), \quad \text{where } x > 0, \ a > 0, \ \text{and } a \neq 1.$$

Properties of Logarithms:

1. $\log_a 1 = 0$

2. $\log_a a = 1$

3. $\log_a a^x = x \log_a a = x$

4. $a^{\log_a x} = x$

5. If $\log_a x = \log_a y$, then $x = y$.

6. $\log_{10} x = \log x$: (Common logarithms)

7. $\log_e x = \ln x$: (Natural logarithms)

8. $\log_a x = \dfrac{\log_b x}{\log_b a}$: (Change of base)

9. $\log_a (xy) = \log_a x + \log_a y$: (Product property)

10. $\log_a \dfrac{x}{y} = \log_a x - \log_a y$: (Quotient property)

11. $\log_a x^n = n \log_a x$: (Power property)

12. $\log_a x = \log_{a^n} x^n$: (All real n except 0)

13. $\log_a x = \dfrac{1}{\log_x a}$: (Reciprocal property)

Graphs of Logarithmic Functions: $y = \log_a x$

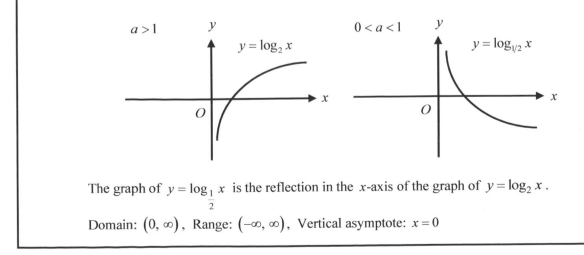

The graph of $y = \log_{\frac{1}{2}} x$ is the reflection in the x-axis of the graph of $y = \log_2 x$.

Domain: $(0, \infty)$, Range: $(-\infty, \infty)$, Vertical asymptote: $x = 0$

Tips

1. If $\ln(x-2)+\ln(2x-3)=2\ln x$, then $x=$

2. \$10,000 is invested in an account at an interest rate of 5%, compounded continuously. The value A, of the investment at any time is given by the equation $A=Pe^{rt}$, where t represents the number of years. How long will it take the balance to double?

3. If $\log_3 x+\log_3(x-8)=2$, then $x=$

4. If $y=3e^x-2$, what is its inverse function?

EXPLANATION

1. $\ln(2x^2-7x+6)=\ln x^2 \rightarrow 2x^2-7x+6=x^2 \rightarrow (x-6)(x-1)=0$

Since $x>2$, the answer is $x=6$ only.

2. $20,000=10,000e^{0.05t} \rightarrow 0.05t=\ln 2 \rightarrow t=\dfrac{\ln 2}{0.05}\approx 13.86$

3. $\log_3(x^2-8x)=2 \rightarrow x^2-8x=3^2 \rightarrow (x-9)(x+1)=0$, $x=9$ or -1

Since domain is $x>8$, $x=-1$ cannot be the solution.

4. $x=3e^y-2 \rightarrow e^y=\dfrac{x+2}{3} \rightarrow f^{-1}:y=\ln\left(\dfrac{x+2}{3}\right)$

Answer: **1.** $x=6$ **2.** 13.86   **3.** 9   **4.** $f^{-1}(x)=\ln\left(\dfrac{x+2}{3}\right)$

Tips

Functions	Domain	Range	Period
$\sin\theta$	All real numbers	$-1 \le \sin\theta \le 1$	$2\pi, 360°$
$\cos\theta$	All real numbers	$-1 \le \cos\theta \le 1$	$2\pi, 360°$
$\tan\theta$	All real numbers except $\theta = 180°n + 90°$	All real numbers	$\pi, 180°$
$\csc\theta$	All real numbers except $180°n$	$\left|\csc\theta\right| \ge 1$	$2\pi, 360°$
$\sec\theta$	All real numbers except $90° + 180°n$	$\left|\sec\theta\right| \ge 1$	$2\pi, 360°$
$\cot\theta$	All real numbers except $180°n$	All real numbers	$\pi, 180°$

Reciprocal Identities

$$\sec\theta = \frac{1}{\cos\theta} \qquad \csc\theta = \frac{1}{\sin\theta} \qquad \cot\theta = \frac{1}{\tan\theta}$$

Quotient Identities

$$\tan\theta = \frac{\sin\theta}{\cos\theta} \qquad \cot\theta = \frac{\cos\theta}{\sin\theta}$$

Pythagorean Identities

$$\sin^2\theta + \cos^2\theta = 1 \qquad 1 + \tan^2\theta = \sec^2\theta \qquad 1 + \cot^2\theta = \csc^2\theta$$

Tips

PRACTICE

1. If $\sin\theta + \cos\theta = \dfrac{1}{2}$, then $\sin\theta\cos\theta =$

2. If $\sin\theta + \cos\theta = \dfrac{1}{4}$, what is the value of $\tan\theta + \cot\theta$?

3. If $\cos\theta = -\dfrac{4}{5}$ and $90^{o} < \theta < 180^{o}$, what is the value of $\tan\theta$?

4. If the roots of the equation $3x^2 + kx - 1 = 0$ are $\sin\theta$ and $\cos\theta$, what is the positive value of k ?

EXPLANATION

1. $(\sin\theta + \cos\theta)^2 = \dfrac{1}{4}$ $\rightarrow$ $\sin^2\theta + \cos^2\theta + 2\sin\theta\cos\theta = \dfrac{1}{4}$ $\rightarrow$ $1 + 2\sin\theta\cos\theta = \dfrac{1}{4}$

   Therefore, $\sin\theta\cos\theta = -\dfrac{3}{8}$.

2. $(\sin\theta + \cos\theta)^2 = \dfrac{1}{16}$ $\rightarrow$ $1 + 2\sin\theta\cos\theta = \dfrac{1}{16}$ $\rightarrow$ $\sin\theta\cos\theta = -\dfrac{15}{32}$

   $\tan\theta + \cot\theta = \dfrac{\sin\theta}{\cos\theta} + \dfrac{\cos\theta}{\sin\theta} = \dfrac{\sin^2\theta + \cos^2\theta}{\cos\theta\sin\theta} = \dfrac{1}{\cos\theta\sin\theta} = -\dfrac{32}{15}$

3. Since $\sec\theta = \dfrac{1}{\cos\theta} = -\dfrac{5}{4}$,

   $1 + \tan^2\theta = \sec^2\theta$ $\rightarrow$ $\tan^2\theta = \sec^2\theta - 1$ $\rightarrow$ $\tan^2\theta = \left(-\dfrac{5}{4}\right)^2 - 1 = \dfrac{9}{16}$.

   $\tan\theta = \pm\sqrt{\dfrac{9}{16}} = \pm\dfrac{3}{4}$. In the second quadrant, $\tan\theta < 0$. Therefore, $\tan\theta = -\dfrac{3}{4}$.

4. Sum and product of the roots. $\sin\theta + \cos\theta = -\dfrac{k}{3}$ and $\sin\theta\cos\theta = -\dfrac{1}{3}$.

   $(\sin\theta + \cos\theta)^2 = 1 + 2\sin\theta\cos\theta = \dfrac{k^2}{9}$

   Therefore, $1 - \dfrac{2}{3} = \dfrac{k^2}{9}$ $\rightarrow$ $\dfrac{1}{3} = \dfrac{k^2}{9}$ $\rightarrow$ $k^2 = 3$. $k = \sqrt{3}$

   Answer: **1.** $-\dfrac{3}{8}$ **2.** $-\dfrac{32}{15}$ **3.** $-\dfrac{3}{4}$ **4.** $\sqrt{3}$

Tips

TIP 30   Circle (Trigonometry)

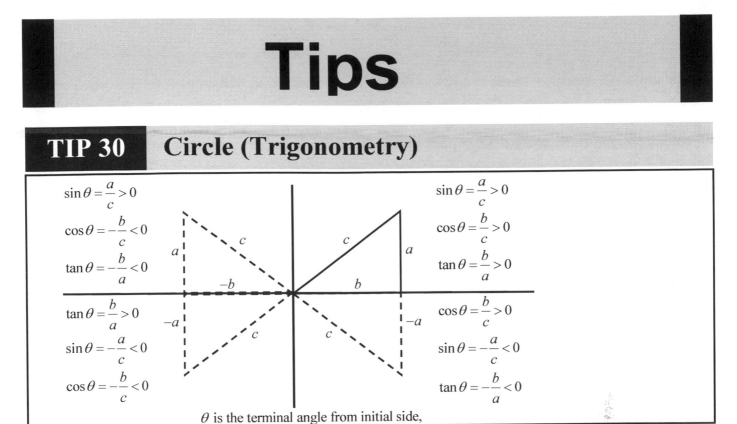

θ is the terminal angle from initial side,

PRACTICE

1. If $\cos\theta = -\dfrac{4}{5}$ and $\tan\theta > 0$, then what is the value of $\sin\theta$?

2. In the interval $0° \le x < 360°$, $\sin x = \cos x$ where x is

3. If $\tan x = -\dfrac{3}{2}$ and $\cos x < 0$, then what is the value of x?

EXPLANATION

1. Since the angle terminates in Quadrant III, $\sin\theta = -\dfrac{3}{5}$.

2. They are equal in Quadrant I and III.

3. The angle is in Quadrant II.

$$x = \tan^{-1}\left(-\frac{3}{2}\right) = -56.3°$$

Therefore, $x = 180° - 56.3° = 123.7°$

Answer: **1.** $-\dfrac{3}{5}$ **2.** $45°, 225°$ **3.** $123.7°$

Tips

If θ is the terminal angle, its **reference angle** is the acute angle θ' formed by **the terminal side** of θ and the **horizontal axis**.

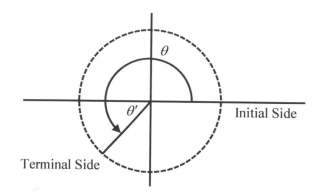

Cofunction: Any trigonometric function of an acute angle is equal to the Cofunction of its complement.

If $A + B = 90°$, then $\sin A = \cos B$, $\sec A = \csc B$, and $\tan A = \cot B$.

PRACTICE

1. Rewrite $\cos 258°$ as a function of a positive acute angle.

2. Write an expression equivalent to $\cot\left(-118°\right)$ as a function of an acute angle whose measure is less than $45°$.

3. If θ is an acute angle and $\csc\left(\theta + 15°\right) = \sec 45°$, then $\sin\theta = $

EXPLANATION

1. $\theta' = 258 - 180 = 78$, $\qquad \cos 258° = \overset{\text{Using reference angle}}{-\cos 78°} = \overset{\text{Using cofunction}}{-\sin 12°}$

2. $\theta' = 180 - 118 = 62$, $\qquad \cot(-118°) = \cot 62° = \tan 28°$

3. Cofunction: $\theta + 15 + 45 = 90 \rightarrow \theta = 30° \rightarrow \sin 30° = \dfrac{1}{2}$

Answer: **1.** $-\cos 78°$ or $-\sin 12°$ **2.** $\tan 28°$ **3.** $\dfrac{1}{2}$

Tips

1. $y = a\sin(bx - c) + d$ and $y = a\cos(bx - c) + d$.

     Amplitude : $|a|$

     Period : $p = \dfrac{2\pi}{b}$

     Middle line : $y = d$

2. $y = \tan(bx - c) + d$

     Amplitude : Does not exist.

     Period : $p = \dfrac{\pi}{b}$

     Middle line : $y = d$

PRACTICE

1. Find the period and amplitude of the function $f(t) = -5\cos\dfrac{\pi t}{12} - 4$.

2. What is the period and amplitude of $y = 4\sin x\cos x - 1$?

3. If the height is given by $h = -30\sin\dfrac{\pi}{15}(t - 25) + 15$, what are the maximum and minimum values of the height?

EXPLANATION

1. $p = \dfrac{2\pi}{\pi/12} = 24$ and amp $= |-5| = 5$.

2. $y = 4\sin x\cos x - 1 = 2\sin 2x - 1$

     Therefore, amp is 2 and $p = \dfrac{2\pi}{2} = \pi$.

3. Since amplitude is 30, maximum $= 30 + 15 = 45$ and minimum $= 15 - 30 = -15$.

1.
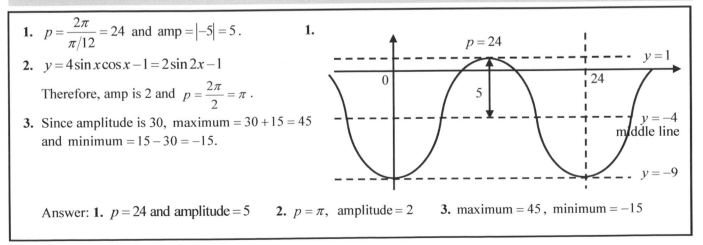

Answer: **1.** $p = 24$ and amplitude $= 5$ **2.** $p = \pi$, amplitude $= 2$ **3.** maximum $= 45$, minimum $= -15$

Tips

TIP 33 — Inverse Trigonometric Functions

Inverse Sine Function

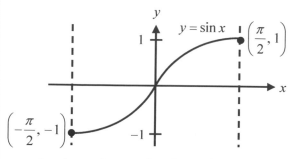

$y = \sin x$ has an inverse function only on this interval.

Inverse Cosine Function

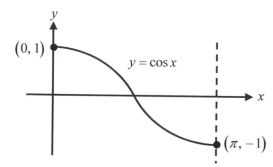

$y = \cos x$ has an inverse function only on this interval.

Inverse Tangent Function

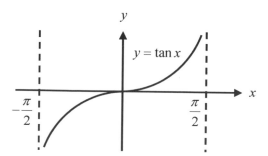

$y = \tan x$ has an inverse function only on this interval.

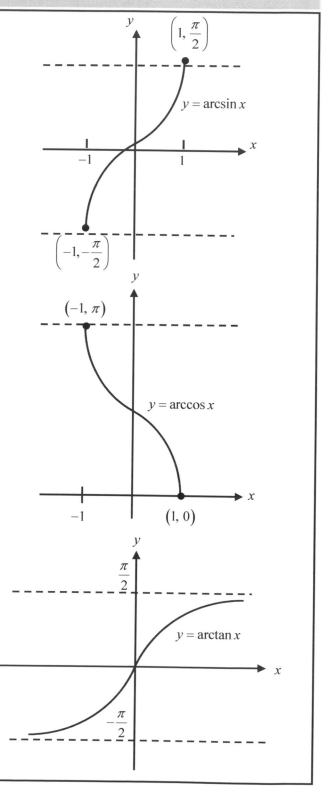

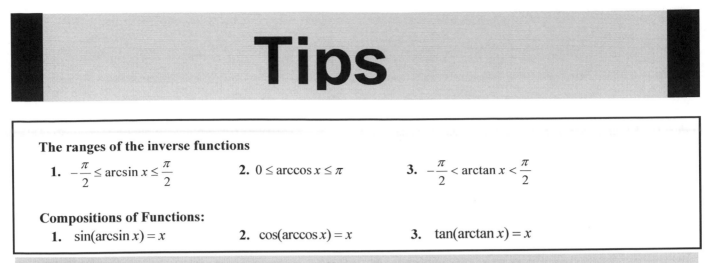

Tips

The ranges of the inverse functions

1. $-\dfrac{\pi}{2} \le \arcsin x \le \dfrac{\pi}{2}$ **2.** $0 \le \arccos x \le \pi$ **3.** $-\dfrac{\pi}{2} < \arctan x < \dfrac{\pi}{2}$

Compositions of Functions:

1. $\sin(\arcsin x) = x$ **2.** $\cos(\arccos x) = x$ **3.** $\tan(\arctan x) = x$

PRACTICE

1. What is the value of $\tan\big(\arctan(-3)\big)$?

2. What is the value of $\arcsin\left(\sin\dfrac{5\pi}{3}\right)$?

3. $\tan\left(\arccos\dfrac{2}{3}\right) =$

4. $\cos\left(\arcsin\left(-\dfrac{3}{5}\right)\right) =$

EXPLANATION

1. Let $\arctan(-3) = x.$ $\rightarrow$ $\tan x = -3$. Therefore $\tan\big(\arctan(-3)\big) = \tan x = -3$.

2. $\sin\dfrac{5\pi}{3} = -\dfrac{\sqrt{3}}{2}$, $\arcsin\left(\sin\left(\dfrac{5\pi}{3}\right)\right) = \arcsin\left(-\dfrac{\sqrt{3}}{2}\right) = -\dfrac{\pi}{3}$

3. $\arccos\dfrac{2}{3} = x$ $\rightarrow$ $\cos x = \dfrac{2}{3}$ $\rightarrow$ Therefore, $\tan\left(\arccos\dfrac{2}{3}\right) = \tan x = \dfrac{\sqrt{5}}{2}.$

4. $\arcsin\left(-\dfrac{3}{5}\right) = x$ $\rightarrow$ $\sin x = -\dfrac{3}{5}$ $\rightarrow$ Therefore, $\cos\left(\arcsin\left(-\dfrac{3}{5}\right)\right) = \cos x = \dfrac{4}{5}.$

Answer: **1.** -3 **2.** $-\dfrac{\pi}{3}$ **3.** $\dfrac{\sqrt{5}}{2}$ **4.** $\dfrac{4}{5}$

Tips

TIP 34 — Sum and Difference of Angles

Functions of the Sum of Two Angles	Functions of the Difference of Two Angles
$\sin(A+B) = \sin A \cos B + \cos A \sin B$	$\sin(A-B) = \sin A \cos B - \cos A \sin B$
$\cos(A+B) = \cos A \cos B - \sin A \sin B$	$\cos(A-B) = \cos A \cos B + \sin A \sin B$
$\tan(A+B) = \dfrac{\tan A + \tan B}{1 - \tan A \tan B}$	$\tan(A-B) = \dfrac{\tan A - \tan B}{1 + \tan A \tan B}$

PRACTICE

1. If $\sin x = \dfrac{1}{2}$ and $\cos y = \dfrac{1}{3}$, where x and y are positive acute angles, what is the value of $\cos(x-y)$?

2. $\tan(180° - y) =$

3. If $\sin A = 0.6$, $\sin B = -0.8$, $\dfrac{\pi}{2} < A < \pi$, and $\pi < B < \dfrac{3\pi}{2}$, what is the value of $\sin(A+B)$?

EXPLANATION

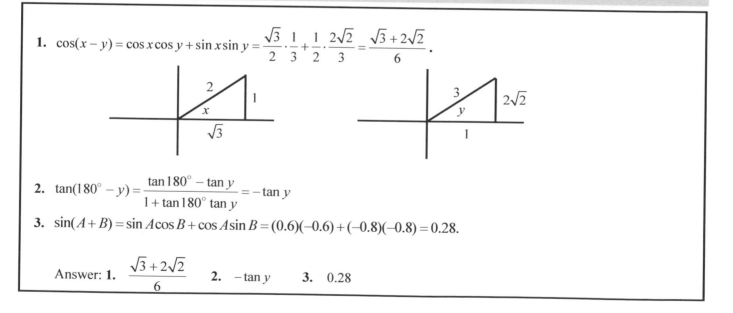

1. $\cos(x-y) = \cos x \cos y + \sin x \sin y = \dfrac{\sqrt{3}}{2} \cdot \dfrac{1}{3} + \dfrac{1}{2} \cdot \dfrac{2\sqrt{2}}{3} = \dfrac{\sqrt{3} + 2\sqrt{2}}{6}$.

2. $\tan(180° - y) = \dfrac{\tan 180° - \tan y}{1 + \tan 180° \tan y} = -\tan y$

3. $\sin(A+B) = \sin A \cos B + \cos A \sin B = (0.6)(-0.6) + (-0.8)(-0.8) = 0.28$.

Answer: **1.** $\dfrac{\sqrt{3} + 2\sqrt{2}}{6}$ **2.** $-\tan y$ **3.** 0.28

Tips

Double Angle Formulas

Functions of the double angle

| $\sin 2A = 2\sin A \cos A$ | $\cos 2A = \cos^2 A - \sin^2 A$

 $\cos 2A = 1 - 2\sin^2 A$

 $\cos 2A = 2\cos^2 A - 1$ | $\tan 2A = \dfrac{2\tan A}{1 - \tan^2 A}$ |

PRACTICE

1. If $\sin\theta = \dfrac{4}{5}$ and $\dfrac{\pi}{2} < \theta < \pi$, what is the value of $\sin 2\theta$?

2. If $\sin x = -\dfrac{5}{13}$, then $\cos 2x =$

3. If $\cos\alpha = -\dfrac{1}{2}$ and $\dfrac{\pi}{2} < \alpha < \pi$, then $\tan 2\alpha =$

EXPLANATION

1. In Quadrant II, $\cos\theta = -\dfrac{3}{5}$. $\sin 2\theta = 2\sin\theta\cos\theta = 2\left(\dfrac{4}{5}\right)\left(-\dfrac{3}{5}\right) = -\dfrac{24}{25}$

2. $\cos 2x = 1 - 2\sin^2 x = 1 - 2\left(-\dfrac{5}{13}\right)^2 = 1 - \dfrac{50}{169} = \dfrac{119}{169}$

3. In Quadrant II, $\tan\alpha = -\sqrt{3}$.
Therefore,

$\tan 2\alpha = \dfrac{2\tan\alpha}{1 - \tan^2\alpha} = \dfrac{2\left(-\sqrt{3}\right)}{1 - \left(-\sqrt{3}\right)^2} = \sqrt{3}$.

Answer: **1.** $-\dfrac{24}{25}$ **2.** $\dfrac{119}{169}$ **3.** $\sqrt{3}$

Tips

TIP 36 — Half Angle formulas

Half Angle Formulas

$\sin\dfrac{A}{2} = \pm\sqrt{\dfrac{1-\cos A}{2}}$	$\cos\dfrac{A}{2} = \pm\sqrt{\dfrac{1+\cos A}{2}}$	$\tan\dfrac{A}{2} = \pm\sqrt{\dfrac{1-\cos A}{1+\cos A}}$

PRACTICE

1. If $\sin A = -\dfrac{4}{5}$ and $\pi < A < \dfrac{3\pi}{2}$, what is the value of $\cos\left(\dfrac{1}{2}A\right)$?

2. If $\cos x = -\dfrac{5}{13}$ and $\dfrac{\pi}{2} < x < \pi$, then what is the value of $\cos\dfrac{x}{2}$?

3. If y is a positive acute angle and $\sin\dfrac{y}{2} = \dfrac{1}{2}$, then what is the value of y?

EXPLANATION

1. Since $\dfrac{\pi}{2} < \dfrac{A}{2} < \dfrac{3\pi}{4}$ (Quadrant II), then $\cos A = -\dfrac{3}{5}$ and $\cos\dfrac{A}{2} = -\sqrt{\dfrac{1+\cos A}{2}} = -\sqrt{\dfrac{1-\dfrac{3}{5}}{2}} = -\dfrac{\sqrt5}{5}$.

2. Since $\dfrac{\pi}{4} < \dfrac{x}{2} < \dfrac{\pi}{2}$, $\cos\dfrac{x}{2} = +\sqrt{\dfrac{1+\cos x}{2}} = \sqrt{\dfrac{1+\left(-\dfrac{5}{13}\right)}{2}} = \dfrac{2\sqrt{13}}{13}$.

3. $\dfrac{y}{2} = 30° \;\rightarrow\; y = 60°$.

Answer: **1.** $-\dfrac{\sqrt5}{5}$ **2.** $\dfrac{2\sqrt{13}}{13}$ **3.** $60°$

Tips

PRACTICE

1. In the interval $0° \leq x < 360°$, what is the value of x that satisfies the equation $4\sin^2 x + 4\cos x - 5 = 0$?

2. In the interval $0° \leq x < 360°$, what is the value of x that satisfies the equation $\cos^2 x + 2\sin x - 1 = 0$?

3. In the interval $0 \leq x < 2\pi$, what is the value of x that satisfies the equation $2\sec^2 x - 3\tan x - 1 = 0$?

4. What is the measure of the positive acute angle that satisfies the equation $1 + \sin x = 2\cos^2 x$?

EXPLANATION

1. $4(1 - \cos^2 x) + 4\cos x - 5 = 0 \rightarrow 4\cos^2 x - 4\cos x + 1 = 0 \rightarrow (2\cos x - 1)^2 = 0$

   $\cos x = \dfrac{1}{2} \rightarrow x = 60°, 300°$

2. $(1 - \sin^2 x) + 2\sin x - 1 = 0 \rightarrow \sin^2 x - 2\sin x = 0 \rightarrow \sin x(\sin x - 2) = 0$

   $\sin x = 0$ or $\sin x = 2$ (reject)   Therefore, $x = 0°, 180°$

3. Since $\sec^2 x = 1 + \tan^2 x$, $2(1 + \tan^2 x) - 3\tan x - 1 = 0 \rightarrow 2\tan^2 x - 3\tan x + 1 = 0$

   $(2\tan x - 1)(\tan x - 1) = 0 \rightarrow \tan x = \dfrac{1}{2}$ or $\tan x = 1$

   If $\tan x = 0.5$, then $x = \tan^{-1}(0.5) \approx 0.46$ or $x = 0.46 + \pi \approx 3.61$.

   If $\tan x = 1$, then $x = \tan^{-1} 1 \approx 0.79$ or $x = 0.79 + \pi \approx 3.93$.

   Therefore, $x = 0.46, \ 3.60, \ 0.79, \ 3.93$

   > Remember: For these questions,
   > You can use a calculator.
   > Graph and find the zeros.

4. $1 + \sin x = 2(1 - \sin^2 x) \rightarrow 2\sin^2 x + \sin x - 1 = 0 \rightarrow (2\sin x - 1)(\sin x + 1) = 0$

   $\sin x = \dfrac{1}{2}$ or $\sin x = -1$. Therefore, the positive acute angle is $30°$.

   Answer: **1.** $60°, 300°$ **2.** $0°, 180°$ **3.** $0.46, \ 0.79, \ 3.61, \ 3.93$ **4.** $30°$

Tips

The Law of Sines

Area of a Triangle:

If ABC is a triangle with sides a, b, and c, then

$$\text{Area} = \frac{bc\sin A}{2} = \frac{ab\sin C}{2} = \frac{ac\sin B}{2}.$$

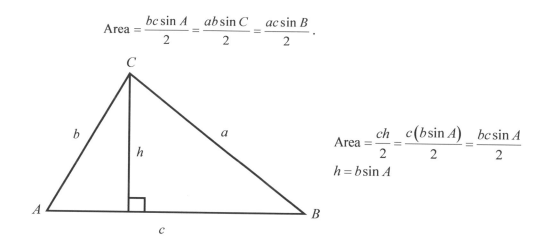

$$\text{Area} = \frac{ch}{2} = \frac{c(b\sin A)}{2} = \frac{bc\sin A}{2}$$

$$h = b\sin A$$

Law of Sines:

If ABC is a triangle with sides a, b, and c, then

$$\frac{a}{\sin A} = \frac{b}{\sin B} = \frac{c}{\sin C}$$

PRACTICE

1. In $\triangle ABC$, what is the ratio $a:b$ if $\angle A = 30°$ and $\angle B = 45°$?

2. How many possible triangles can be constructed if $a = 10$, $b = 12$, and $\angle B = 20°$?

3. How many distinct triangles can be constructed if the measures of two sides are 4 and 6 and the measure of the angle opposite the smaller side is $30°$?

EXPLANATION

1. Law of sines:

$$\frac{a}{\sin 30°} = \frac{b}{\sin 45°} \;\rightarrow\; \frac{a}{1/2} = \frac{b}{\sqrt{2}/2} \;\rightarrow\; \frac{a}{b} = \frac{\frac{1}{2}}{\frac{\sqrt{2}}{2}} = \frac{\sqrt{2}}{2}$$

2. $\dfrac{10}{\sin A} = \dfrac{12}{\sin 20°} \;\rightarrow\; \sin A = \dfrac{10\sin 20°}{12} \approx 0.28$: $\angle A$ lies in Quadrant I or II.

$A = \sin^{-1} 0.28 \approx 16°$ or $164°$

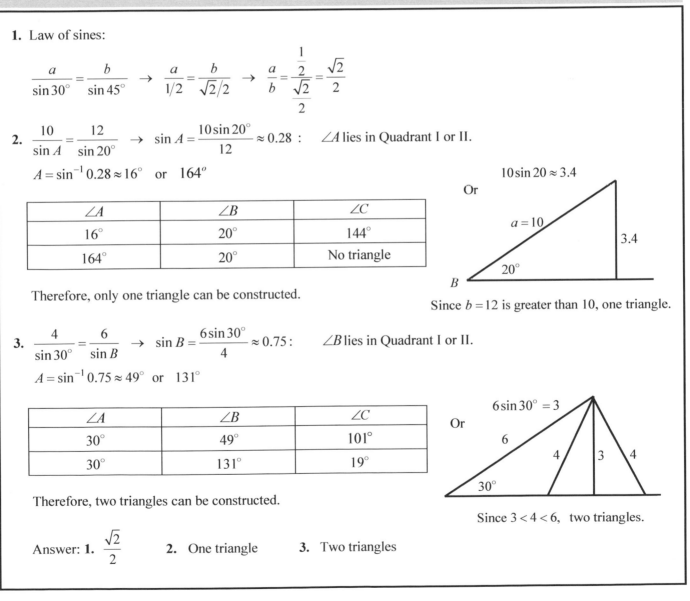

$\angle A$	$\angle B$	$\angle C$
$16°$	$20°$	$144°$
$164°$	$20°$	No triangle

Therefore, only one triangle can be constructed.

Or

$10\sin 20 \approx 3.4$

$a = 10$ 3.4 $20°$ B

Since $b = 12$ is greater than 10, one triangle.

3. $\dfrac{4}{\sin 30°} = \dfrac{6}{\sin B} \;\rightarrow\; \sin B = \dfrac{6\sin 30°}{4} \approx 0.75$: $\angle B$ lies in Quadrant I or II.

$A = \sin^{-1} 0.75 \approx 49°$ or $131°$

$\angle A$	$\angle B$	$\angle C$
$30°$	$49°$	$101°$
$30°$	$131°$	$19°$

Therefore, two triangles can be constructed.

Or

$6\sin 30° = 3$ 6   4   3   4 $30°$

Since $3 < 4 < 6$, two triangles.

Answer: **1.** $\dfrac{\sqrt{2}}{2}$ **2.** One triangle   **3.** Two triangles

Tips

TIP 39   The Law of Cosines

Law of Cosines:

$a^2 = b^2 + c^2 - 2bc\cos A$	$\cos A = \dfrac{b^2 + c^2 - a^2}{2bc}$
$b^2 = a^2 + c^2 - 2ac\cos B$	$\cos B = \dfrac{a^2 + c^2 - b^2}{2ac}$
$c^2 = a^2 + b^2 - 2ab\cos C$	$\cos C = \dfrac{a^2 + b^2 - c^2}{2ab}$

PRACTICE

1. In $\triangle ABC$, if $a = \sqrt{3}$ and $b = 1$, and $\angle C = 30°$, then $c =$

2. If two forces of 30 pounds and 40 pounds act on a body with an angle of $120°$ between them, what is the magnitude of the resultant?

EXPLANATION

1. The Law of cosines:

$$c^2 = \left(\sqrt{3}\right)^2 + (1)^2 - 2\left(\sqrt{3}\right)(1)\cos 30° \quad \rightarrow \quad c^2 = 1 \quad \rightarrow \quad c = 1$$

2. In a parallelogram, two consecutive angles are supplementary and opposite sides are $\cong$.

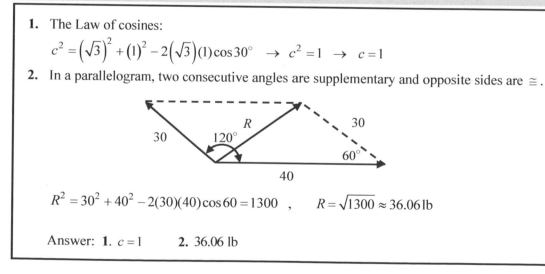

$$R^2 = 30^2 + 40^2 - 2(30)(40)\cos 60 = 1300 \quad, \quad R = \sqrt{1300} \approx 36.06 \, \text{lb}$$

Answer: **1.** $c = 1$ **2.** 36.06 lb

Tips

TIP 40	Permutation

A permutation of a set of values is **an arrangement** where **order is important.**

The number of ways of obtaining an ordered r elements from n elements is given by

$$_nP_r = \frac{n!}{(n-r)!}$$

PRACTICE

1. In how many ways can a class with 15 students choose a president, a vice-president, and a treasurer?

2. In how many different orders can the program for a music concert be arranged if 6 students are to perform?

3. How many 8-letter arrangements can be made from the letters in the word **PARALLEL**?

EXPLANATION

1. $_{15}P_3 = \frac{15!}{12!} = 15 \cdot 14 \cdot 13 = 2730$

2. $_6P_6 = 6! = 720$

3. **Permutations with repetition:**
   This is a permutation of **8** letters taken at a time when 2**A** and 3**L** are identical.

   Therefore, $\frac{_8P_8}{2!3!} = \frac{8!}{2!3!} = 3360$

   Answer: **1.** 2730   **2.** 720   **3.** 3360

Tips

TIP 41 | Combination

A selection in which **order is not important** is called a **combination.**

The number of combinations of n things taken r at a time is

$$_nC_r = \frac{_nP_r}{r!} \quad \text{or} \quad \binom{n}{r} = \frac{_nP_r}{r!}$$

$$_nC_r = \frac{n!}{(n-r)!\,r!}$$

1. $_nC_n = 1$ **2.** $_nC_o = 1$ **3.** $_nC_r = {_nC_{n-r}}$

PRACTICE

1. There are 10 novels and 6 biographies in a book reading list. If a student chose 5 novels and 3 biographies to read, how many different combinations can be chosen?

2. There are 6 boys and 5 girls in a chess club. In how many ways can 2 boys and 3 girls be selected to attend the regional tournament?

3. If $_nP_r = 120$ and $\binom{n}{r} = 20$, then what is the value of r?

EXPLANATION

1. $\binom{10}{5}\binom{6}{3} = 5,040$

2. $\binom{6}{2}\binom{5}{3} = 150$

3. $\binom{n}{r} = \frac{_nP_r}{r!} = \frac{120}{r!} = 20 \quad \rightarrow \quad$ Therefore, $r! = 6 \rightarrow r = 3$.

Answer: **1.** 5040   **2.** 150   **3.** 3

Tips

TIP 42   Dividing Group

When we divide group into several groups,

1) Each group has different number of people

How many ways to divide group of 10 people into one group of 7 people and the other group f 3 people?

$$\text{The number of ways} = {}_{10}C_7 \times {}_3C_3 = 120$$

2) Some groups has same number of people

How many ways to divide of 10 people into two groups of 3 people and one group of 4 people?

$$\text{The number of ways} = \frac{{}_{10}C_3 \times {}_7C_3 \times {}_4C_4}{2!} = 2100$$

Because two groups has the same number of people, ${}_{10}C_3 \times {}_7C_3 \times {}_4C_4$ should be divided by $2!$.

If the number of people $n = a + a + a + b + b + c$, then the number of ways divides into the groups of

a, a, a, b, b and c is

$$\text{The number of ways} = \frac{\binom{n}{a}\binom{n-a}{a}\binom{n-2a}{a}\binom{n-3a}{b}\binom{n-3a-b}{b}\binom{n-3a-2b}{c}}{(3!)(2!)}$$

PRACTICE

1. How many ways are there to divide 8 people into two groups of three people and one group of two people?

2. Eight people are divided into one groups of 5 people and the other group of 3 people. How many ways are there?

EXPLANATION

1. $\binom{8}{3}\binom{5}{3}\binom{2}{2}\dfrac{1}{2!} = \dfrac{(56)(10)(1)}{2} = 280$

2. $\binom{8}{5}\binom{3}{3} = 56$

Tips

TIP 43　Binomial Expansion Theorem

Formula for expanding $(x+y)^n$ **for positive integers** n **is**

$$(x+y)^n = {}_nC_o\,(x)^n\,(y)^0 + {}_nC_1\,(x)^{n-1}\,(y)^1 + {}_nC_2\,(x)^{n-2}\,(y)^2 + \cdots + {}_nC_{n-1}\,(x)^1\,(y)^{n-1} + {}_nC_n\,(x)^0\,(y)^n$$

1. For any binomial expansion of $(x+y)^n$, there are $n+1$ terms.

2. The general term of the expansion is

$$ {}_nC_r\,(x)^{n-r}\,(y)^r \qquad \text{or} \qquad \binom{n}{r}(x)^{n-r}\,(y)^r, \quad \text{where } r=0,1,2,3\cdots n.$$

PRACTICE

1. What is the third term of the expansion of $(a-2b)^4$?

2. What is the middle term of the expansion of $(x-2y)^6$?

3. In the expansion of $\left(x^2 - \dfrac{1}{x^2}\right)^{10}$, what is the value of the constant term?

EXPLANATION

1. The third term is $\binom{4}{2}(a)^2(-2b)^2 = 6(-2)^2\,a^2b^2 = 24a^2b^2$.

2. The middle term is $\binom{6}{3}(x)^3(-2y)^3 = -160x^3y^3$.

3. $\binom{10}{r}\left(x^2\right)^{10-r}\left(-x^{-2}\right)^r = \binom{10}{r}(-1)^r x^{20-2r-2r} = \binom{10}{r}(-1)^r x^{20-4r}$, $\quad 20-4r=0 \;\rightarrow\; r=5$

Therefore, the constant term is $\binom{10}{5}(-1)^5 = -252$.

Answer:　**1.** $24a^2b^2$ 　　**2.** $-160x^3y^3$ 　　**3.** -252

Tips

TIP 44   Sum of Coefficients of a Binomial Expansion

From Binomial Expansion Theorem below

$$(x+y)^n = {}_nC_o(x)^n(y)^0 + {}_nC_1(x)^{n-1}(y)^1 + {}_nC_2(x)^{n-2}(y)^2 + \cdots + {}_nC_{n-1}(x)^1(y)^{n-1} + {}_nC_n(x)^0(y)^n,$$

Sum of Binomial Coefficients (SBC) is

$${}_nC_o + {}_nC_1 + {}_nC_2 + {}_nC_3 + {}_nC_4 + \cdots + {}_nC_{n-1} + {}_nC_n.$$

Since Binomial expansion is true for all real values of x and y, when you put $x=1$ and $y=1$ in the expansion,

$$(1+1)^n = {}_nC_o(1)^n(1)^0 + {}_nC_1(1)^{n-1}(1)^1 + {}_nC_2(1)^{n-2}(1)^2 + \cdots + {}_nC_{n-1}(1)^1(1)^{n-1} + {}_nC_n(1)^0(1)^n$$

or $2^n = {}_nC_o + {}_nC_1 + {}_nC_2 + \cdots + {}_nC_{n-1} + {}_nC_n.$

Therefore, $SBC = 2^n$.

Example 1: What is the sum of coefficients in the binomial expansion of $(2x-3y)^3$?

     Putting $x=1$ and $y=1$, $SBC = (2-3)^3 = -1$.

     Check: $(2x-3y)^3 = 8x^3 - 36x^2y + 54xy^2 - 27y^3 \quad \rightarrow SBC = 8 + (-36) + 54 + (-27) = -1$

PRACTICE

1. What is the sum of coefficients in the binomial expansion of $(1-2x)^8$?

2. What is the value of ${}_nC_o + {}_nC_1 + {}_nC_2 + {}_nC_3 + {}_nC_4 + \cdots + {}_nC_{n-1} + {}_nC_n$?

EXPLANATION

1. Putting $x=1$: $SBC = (1-2)^8 = (-1)^8 = 1$

2. $(x+y)^n = {}_nC_o(x)^n(y)^0 + {}_nC_1(x)^{n-1}(y)^1 + {}_nC_2(x)^{n-2}(y)^2 + \cdots + {}_nC_{n-1}(x)^1(y)^{n-1} + {}_nC_n(x)^0(y)^n$

     Putting $x=1$ and $y=1$: $SBC = (1+1)^n = 2^n$

     Answer: **1.**   1   **2.** 2^n

Tips

TIP 45 Binomial Probability

If the probability of success is p and the probability of failure is $1 - p = q$, then the probability of exactly r successes in n independent trials is:

$$P = {}_nC_r p^r q^{n-r}$$

PRACTICE

1. If a fair coin is tossed 10 times, what is the probability of rolling a head exactly 7 times?

2. If a fair coin is tosses 5 times, what is the probability of obtaining at most 3 heads?

3. A coin is loaded so that the probability of heads on a single throw is three times the probability of tails. What is the probability of at most 3 heads when the coin is tossed 6 times?

EXPLANATION

1. $P = {}_{10}C_7 \left(\dfrac{1}{2}\right)^7 \left(\dfrac{1}{2}\right)^3 = \dfrac{15}{128} \approx 0.12$

2. $P = {}_5C_0 \left(\dfrac{1}{2}\right)^0 \left(\dfrac{1}{2}\right)^5 + {}_5C_1 \left(\dfrac{1}{2}\right)^1 \left(\dfrac{1}{2}\right)^4 + {}_5C_2 \left(\dfrac{1}{2}\right)^2 \left(\dfrac{1}{2}\right)^3 + {}_5C_3 \left(\dfrac{1}{2}\right)^3 \left(\dfrac{1}{2}\right)^2 = \dfrac{26}{32} = 0.8125$

   Or, binomcdf(5, 0.5, 3) = 0.8125 (Graphing Calculator)

3. Since $P(H) = 0.75$ and $P(T) = 0.25$, the probability is:

   ${}_6C_0 (0.75)^0 (0.25)^6 + {}_6C_1 (0.75)^1 (0.25)^5 + {}_6C_2 (0.75)^2 (0.25)^4 + {}_6C_3 (0.75)^3 (0.25)^3$
   $=$ binomcdf (6, 0.75, 3) $= 0.16943359 \approx 0.17$

   Answer: **1.** $\dfrac{15}{128}$ **2.** $\dfrac{13}{16}$ or 0.8125   **3.** 0.17

Tips

If 5 cards are drawn at random from a standard deck, what is the probability that all 5 cards are hearts?

Method 1:

Since there are 13 hearts in the 52-card deck, the probability that the first card drawn is a heart is $\frac{13}{52}$ and the

probability that the second card drawn is a heart is $\frac{12}{51}$. Therefore, continuing in this way, the probability is

$$P(\text{all hearts}) = \frac{13}{52} \cdot \frac{12}{51} \cdot \frac{11}{50} \cdot \frac{10}{49} \cdot \frac{9}{48} \approx 0.000495$$

Method 2:

Using combinations: $P(\text{all hearts}) = \frac{_{13}C_5}{_{52}C_5} \approx 0.000495$

PRACTICE

1. If three marbles are picked at random from a bag containing 4 red marbles and 5 white marbles, what is the probability that exactly 2 marbles are red?

EXPLANATION

1. **Method 1:** There are three ways to pick: *RRW*,   *RWR*,   *WRR*

   The probability of *RRW* : $\frac{4}{9} \cdot \frac{3}{8} \cdot \frac{5}{7} = \frac{5}{42}$. Each has the same probability. Therefore, $\frac{5}{42} \times 3 = \frac{5}{14}$

   Method 2: Using combinations.

   $$P = \frac{_4C_2 \times _5C_1}{_9C_3} = \frac{30}{84} = \frac{5}{14}$$

   Answer: **1.** $\frac{5}{14}$

Tips

TIP 47   Heron's Formula

Given any triangle with sides a, b, and c, the area of the triangle is given by

$$\text{Area} = \sqrt{s(s-a)(s-b)(s-c)} \quad , \text{ where } s = \frac{a+b+c}{2}.$$

PRACTICE

1. Find the area of a triangle having sides of lengths 5, 12, and 15.

EXPLANATION

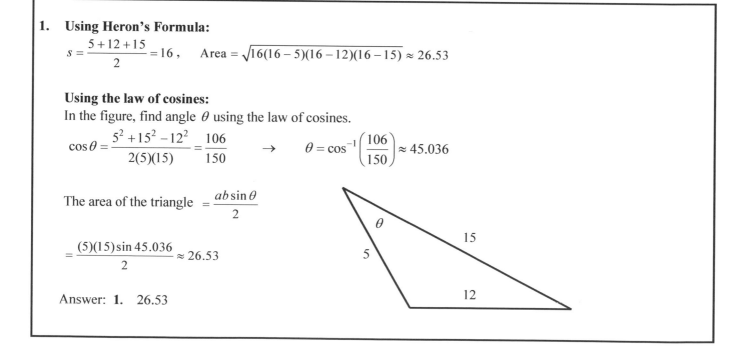

1. **Using Heron's Formula:**

    $s = \dfrac{5+12+15}{2} = 16, \quad \text{Area} = \sqrt{16(16-5)(16-12)(16-15)} \approx 26.53$

    Using the law of cosines:

    In the figure, find angle θ using the law of cosines.

    $\cos\theta = \dfrac{5^2 + 15^2 - 12^2}{2(5)(15)} = \dfrac{106}{150} \quad \rightarrow \quad \theta = \cos^{-1}\left(\dfrac{106}{150}\right) \approx 45.036$

    The area of the triangle $= \dfrac{ab\sin\theta}{2}$

    $= \dfrac{(5)(15)\sin 45.036}{2} \approx 26.53$

    Answer: **1.** 26.53

Tips

For a vector $\vec{V} = \overrightarrow{AB}$

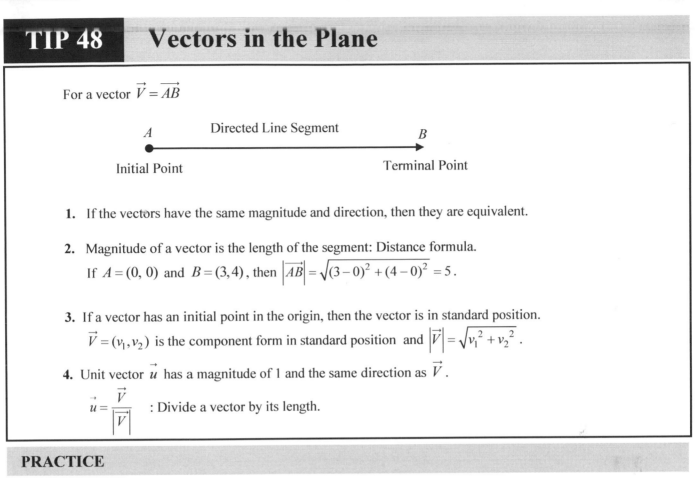

1. If the vectors have the same magnitude and direction, then they are equivalent.

2. Magnitude of a vector is the length of the segment: Distance formula.
   If $A = (0, 0)$ and $B = (3, 4)$, then $\left|\overrightarrow{AB}\right| = \sqrt{(3-0)^2 + (4-0)^2} = 5$.

3. If a vector has an initial point in the origin, then the vector is in standard position.
   $\vec{V} = (v_1, v_2)$ is the component form in standard position and $\left|\vec{V}\right| = \sqrt{v_1^2 + v_2^2}$.

4. Unit vector $\vec{u}$ has a magnitude of 1 and the same direction as $\vec{V}$.

   $\vec{u} = \dfrac{\vec{V}}{\left|\vec{V}\right|}$: Divide a vector by its length.

PRACTICE

1. Find the unit vector in the direction of $\vec{V} = (-3, 4)$.

2. If $\vec{A}$ is represented by the directed line segment from $P = (2, 3)$ to $Q = (-2, 8)$, what is the magnitude of vector $\vec{A}$?

Tips

3. If $\vec{a} = (-2, 3)$ and $\vec{b} = (4, 6)$, then what is the value of $\left| 2\vec{a} + \vec{b} \right|$?

EXPLANATION

1. $\vec{V}$ is in standard position and the initial point is at (0, 0).

   $\left| \vec{V} \right| = \sqrt{(-3)^2 + 4^2} = 5$

   Therefore, $\vec{u} = \dfrac{\vec{V}}{\left| \vec{V} \right|} = \dfrac{(-3,\ 4)}{5} = (-0.6,\ 0.8)$

2. $\overrightarrow{PQ} = (-2, 8) - (2, 3) = (-4, 5)$

   $\left| \overrightarrow{PQ} \right| = \sqrt{(-4)^2 + 5^2} = \sqrt{41}$

   Or, use distance formula:

   $D = \sqrt{(2 - {}^-2)^2 + (3 - 8)^2} = \sqrt{41}$

3. $2\vec{a} + \vec{b} = 2(-2, 3) + (4, 6) = (0, 12)$

   Therefore, $\left| 2\vec{a} + \vec{b} \right| = \sqrt{0^2 + 12^2} = 12$

   Answer: **1.** $(-0.6, 0.8)$ **2.** $\sqrt{41}$ **3.** 12

Tips

TIP 49   Interchange of Inputs

Example 1. If $f(x) = 5x - 2$, what is $f(x-5)$?

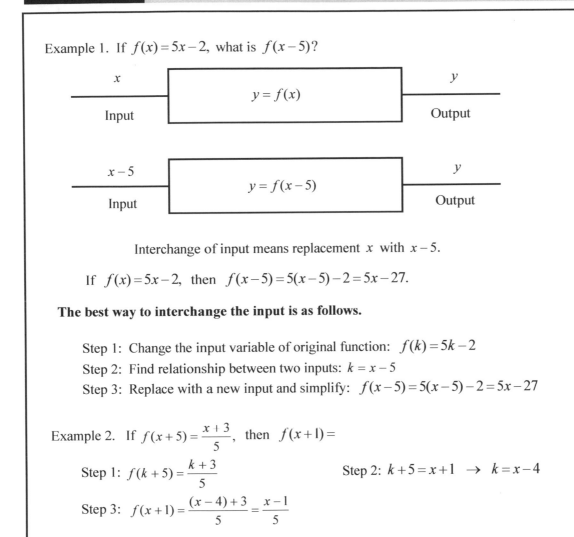

Interchange of input means replacement x with $x - 5$.

If $f(x) = 5x - 2$, then $f(x-5) = 5(x-5) - 2 = 5x - 27$.

The best way to interchange the input is as follows.

    Step 1: Change the input variable of original function: $f(k) = 5k - 2$
    Step 2: Find relationship between two inputs: $k = x - 5$
    Step 3: Replace with a new input and simplify: $f(x-5) = 5(x-5) - 2 = 5x - 27$

Example 2. If $f(x+5) = \dfrac{x+3}{5}$, then $f(x+1) =$

    Step 1: $f(k+5) = \dfrac{k+3}{5}$ Step 2: $k+5 = x+1 \;\rightarrow\; k = x - 4$

    Step 3: $f(x+1) = \dfrac{(x-4)+3}{5} = \dfrac{x-1}{5}$

PRACTICE

1. If $f(2x) = x^2 + 5$, what is $f\left(\dfrac{x}{2}\right)$?

2. If $f\left(\dfrac{x-1}{4}\right) = 2x + 3$, then $f(x) =$

3. If $f\left(\dfrac{x}{2}+5\right)=x^2-1,$ then $f(2x+1)=$

1. Step 1: $f(2x)=x^2+5$ $\rightarrow$ $f(2k)=k^2+5$

Step 2: $2k=\dfrac{x}{2}$ $\rightarrow$ $k=\dfrac{x}{4}$

Step 3: $f\left(\dfrac{x}{2}\right)=\left(\dfrac{x}{4}\right)^2+5$ $\rightarrow$ $f\left(\dfrac{x}{2}\right)=\dfrac{x^2}{16}+5$

2. Step 1: $f\left(\dfrac{k-1}{4}\right)=2k+3$

Step 2: $\dfrac{k-1}{4}=x$ $\rightarrow$ $k-1=4x$ $\rightarrow$ $k=4x+1$

Step 3: $f(x)=2(4x+1)+3$ $\rightarrow$ $f(x)=8x+5$

3. Step 1: $f\left(\dfrac{x}{2}+5\right)=x^2-1$ $\rightarrow$ $f\left(\dfrac{k}{2}+5\right)=k^2-1$

Step 2: $\dfrac{k}{2}+5=2x+1$ $\rightarrow$ $\dfrac{k}{2}=2x-4$ $\rightarrow$ $k=4x-8$

Step 3: $f(2x+1)=\left(4x-8\right)^2-1$ $\rightarrow$ $f(2x+1)=16x^2-64x+63$

Answer: 1. $f\left(\dfrac{x}{2}\right)=\dfrac{x^2}{16}+5$ **2.** $f(x)=8x+5$ **3.** $f(2x+1)=16x^2-64x+63$

Tips

TIP 50   Polynomial Inequalities

Graphical Solution:

1. Solve $(x-4)(x-2)(x+2) > 0$.

    Step 1. Find critical points. $(x-4)(x-2)(x+2) = 0 \rightarrow x = 4, \ 2, \ -2$

    Step 2. Graph $y = (x-4)(x-2)(x+2)$.

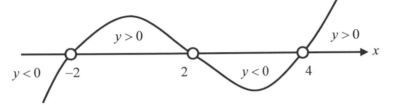

    Step 3) From the graph above, find the intervals for $y > 0$.

         The solution is $-2 < x < 2$ or $x > 4$.

2. Solve $(x-4)(x-2)^2(x+2) < 0$.

    Step 1. Find the critical points. $(x-4)(x-2)^2(x+2) = 0 \rightarrow x = 4, \ 2, \ -2$

    Step 2. Graph $y = (x-4)(x-2)^2(x+2)$.

         Zeros: $x = 4$, $x = 2$ (two equal roots), and $x = -2$.

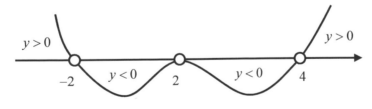

    Step 3. Find the intervals for $y < 0$.

         The solution is $-2 < x < 2$ or $2 < x < 4$.

Tips

1. Solve the inequality $(x-1)(x-2)^2(x+1)(x+2)^2 \geq 0$.

2. What is the solution set of $2x^3 - 3x^2 - 24x > -12$?

EXPLANATION

1. Graphical solution: use graphing utility.

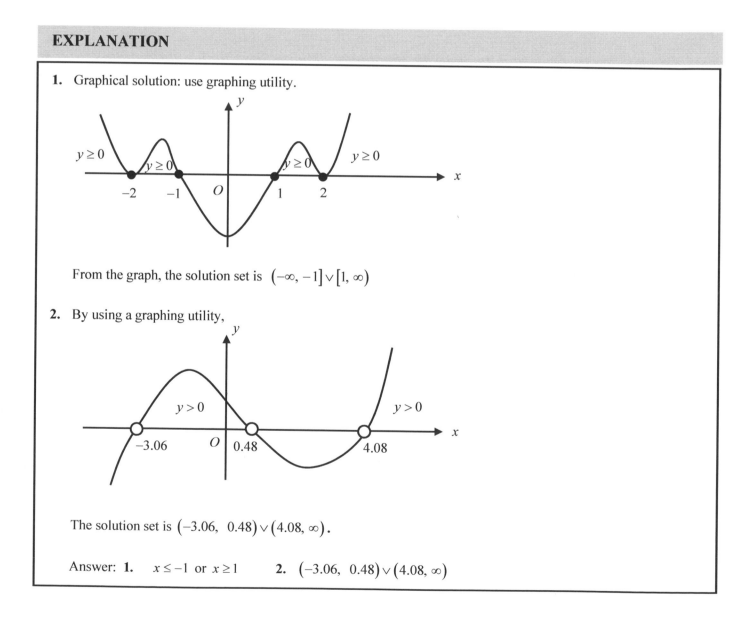

From the graph, the solution set is $(-\infty, -1] \vee [1, \infty)$

2. By using a graphing utility,

The solution set is $(-3.06, \ 0.48) \vee (4.08, \infty)$.

Answer: **1.** $x \leq -1$ or $x \geq 1$ **2.** $(-3.06, \ 0.48) \vee (4.08, \infty)$

Tips

TIP 51   Rational Inequalities

Graphic Solution:

1. Solve the rational inequality $\dfrac{(x-1)(x+2)}{x-2} \geq 0$.

Method 1. Test value using critical points

Critical points from the equation: $\dfrac{(x-1)(x+2)}{x-2} = 0 \rightarrow x = 1$ and $x = -2$ (closed)

Critical points from undefined: $x = 2$ (open)
There are four possible solution set

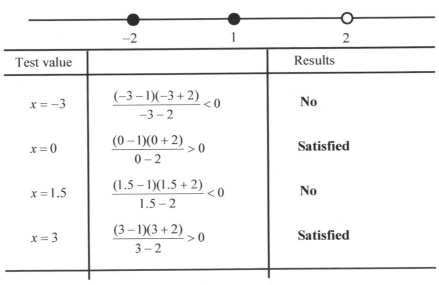

Test value		Results
$x = -3$	$\dfrac{(-3-1)(-3+2)}{-3-2} < 0$	**No**
$x = 0$	$\dfrac{(0-1)(0+2)}{0-2} > 0$	**Satisfied**
$x = 1.5$	$\dfrac{(1.5-1)(1.5+2)}{1.5-2} < 0$	**No**
$x = 3$	$\dfrac{(3-1)(3+2)}{3-2} > 0$	**Satisfied**

Solution: $-2 \leq x \leq 1$ or $x > 2$

Method 2. Using the graph

Since $(x-2)^2 > 0$, multiply both sides by $(x-2)^2$.

$$(x-2)^2 \frac{(x-1)(x+2)}{x-2} \geq 0 \cdot (x-2)^2 \rightarrow (x-2)(x-1)(x+2) \geq 0$$

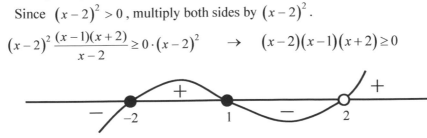

From the graph above, the solution set is $[-2,\ 1] \vee (2,\ \infty)$.

Tips

1. Solve the inequality $\dfrac{(x-2)^2(x-3)}{(x-1)(x+2)} \le 0$.

EXPLANATION

1. **Method 1)** Multiply both sides by $(x-1)^2(x+2)^2$ which is positive.

   $(x-1)(x+2)(x-2)^2(x-3) \le 0$ and $x \ne 1$, $x \ne -2$

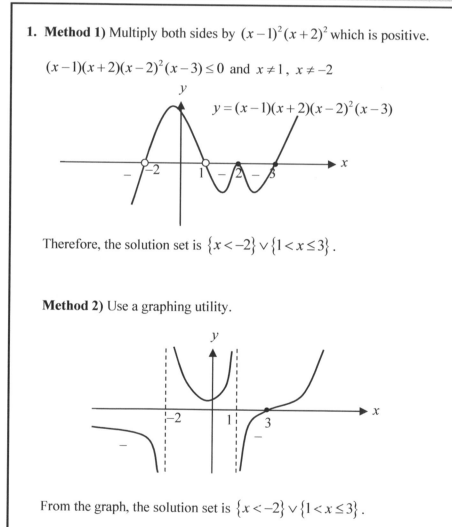

   Therefore, the solution set is $\{x < -2\} \vee \{1 < x \le 3\}$.

   Method 2) Use a graphing utility.

   From the graph, the solution set is $\{x < -2\} \vee \{1 < x \le 3\}$.

Tips

$$\lim_{x \to c} f(x) = L$$

The limit of $f(x)$ is L as x approaches c.

1. If $f(x)$ is a polynomial function, then $\lim_{x \to c} f(x) = f(c)$: direct substitution.

2. If $f(x)$ is a rational function given by $\dfrac{N(x)}{D(x)}$ such that $D(c) \neq 0$, then

$$\lim_{x \to c} f(x) = \lim_{x \to c} \frac{N(x)}{D(x)} = \frac{N(c)}{D(c)}$$

3. If $f(x) = \dfrac{1}{x}$, then $\lim_{x \to 0} \dfrac{1}{x} = +\infty$ or $-\infty$: the limit does not exist.

4. $\lim_{x \to 1} \dfrac{x^3 - x}{x^2 - 1} = \lim_{x \to 1} \dfrac{x(x^2 - 1)}{x^2 - 1} = \lim_{x \to 1} x = 1$

5. $e = \lim_{x \to 0} (1 + x)^{\frac{1}{x}}$ or $e = \lim_{x \to \infty} \left(1 + \dfrac{1}{x} \right)^x$

PRACTICE

1. $\lim_{x \to -1} \dfrac{x^2 + x - 6}{x + 2} =$

2. $\lim_{x \to 2} \dfrac{x^2 + x - 6}{x - 2} =$

3. $\lim_{x \to 1} \dfrac{x^2 + 2x - 3}{\sqrt{x} - 1} =$

4. $\lim_{x \to 3} \dfrac{x - 3}{x^2 - 9} =$

5. $\lim\limits_{x\to 0}\dfrac{\sqrt{x+4}-2}{x}=$

EXPLANATION

1. Since $D(1)\neq 0$, $\lim\limits_{x\to -1}\dfrac{x^2+x-6}{x+2}=\dfrac{1-1-6}{-1+2}=-6$: (direct substitution)

2. Since $D(2)=0$ and $N(2)=0$, $\lim\limits_{x\to 2}\dfrac{(x+3)(x-2)}{(x-2)}=\lim\limits_{x\to 2}(x+3)=5$

3. Rationalizing Skill:

Since $D(1)=0$ and $N(1)=0$, then

$$\lim\limits_{x\to 1}\frac{(x+3)(x-1)\left(\sqrt{x}+1\right)}{\left(\sqrt{x}-1\right)\left(\sqrt{x}+1\right)}=\lim\limits_{x\to 1}\frac{(x+3)(x-1)\left(\sqrt{x}+1\right)}{(x-1)}=\lim\limits_{x\to 1}(x+3)\left(\sqrt{x}+1\right)=8\,.$$

4. Since $D(3)=0$ and $N(3)=0$, then $\lim\limits_{x\to 3}\dfrac{(x-3)}{(x+3)(x-3)}=\lim\limits_{x\to 3}\dfrac{1}{x+3}=\dfrac{1}{6}.$

5. Rationalizing Skill:

$D(0)=0$ and $N(0)=0$

$$\lim\limits_{x\to 0}\frac{\left(\sqrt{x+4}-2\right)\left(\sqrt{x+4}+2\right)}{x\left(\sqrt{x+4}-2\right)}=\lim\limits_{x\to 0}\frac{\left(\sqrt{x+4}\right)^2-2^2}{x\left(\sqrt{x+4}+2\right)}=\lim\limits_{x\to 0}\frac{x}{x\left(\sqrt{x+4}+2\right)}=\lim\limits_{x\to 0}\frac{1}{\left(\sqrt{x+4}+2\right)}=\frac{1}{4}$$

Answer: 1. -6 **2.** 5 **3.** 8 **4.** $\dfrac{1}{6}$ **5.** $\dfrac{1}{4}$

Tips

Rational Function and Asymptote

A **rational function** can be written in the form $R(x) = \dfrac{N(x)}{D(x)}$, where $N(x)$ and $D(x)$ are polynomials and $D(x) \neq 0$.

1. The line $x = a$ is a vertical asymptote of the graph if $D(a) = 0$.

2. The line $y = b$ is a horizontal asymptote of the graph if $R(x) \to b$ as $x \to \infty$ or $x \to -\infty$.

    Example 1: $R(x) = \dfrac{1}{x}$

        Domain: $(-\infty, 0) \vee (0, +\infty)$ or $x \neq 0$

        Range: $(-\infty, 0) \vee (0, +\infty)$ or $y \neq 0$

        Vertical asymptote: $x = 0$

        Horizontal asymptote: $y = 0$

    Example 2: $f(x) = \dfrac{2x}{x-1}$

        $D(x) = 0$, vertical asymptote: $x = 1$

        $\lim\limits_{x \to \infty} \dfrac{2x}{x-1} = 2$, horizontal asymptote: $y = 2$

        Domain: $x \neq 1$

        Range: $y \neq 2$

    Example 3: $g(x) = \dfrac{2x}{x^2 + 1}$

        $D(x) = 0 \to x^2 + 1 \neq 0$, no vertical asymptote.

        $\lim\limits_{x \to \infty} \dfrac{2x}{x^2 + 1} = 0$, horizontal asymptote: $y = 0$.

        Domain: all real x

        Range: $-1 \leq y \leq 1$ (using graphing utility)

3. **Slant asymptote** (or, oblique asymptote): If the degree in the numerator is greater than the degree in denominator, the original function should be rearranged by long division.

$$f(x) = \frac{2x^2 - 3x + 1}{x+1} = \boxed{2x - 5} + \frac{6}{x+1} \quad \to \quad \text{The slant asymptote is } y = 2x - 5.$$

Tips

Example 4: $h(x) = \dfrac{x^2 + 2x - 3}{x^2 - 1}$

$h(x) = \dfrac{(x+3)\,\cancel{(x-1)}}{(x+1)\,\cancel{(x-1)}} = \dfrac{(x+3)}{(x+1)}$

$D(x) = 0 \quad \rightarrow \quad x = -1 : \text{vertical asymptote}$

$y = \lim\limits_{x \to \infty} \dfrac{x+3}{x+1} = 1 \quad \rightarrow \quad y = 1 : \text{horizontal asymptote}$

$f(1)$ is still undefined.

Domain: $(-\infty, -1) \vee (-1, 1) \vee (1, \infty)$

Range : $(-\infty, 1) \vee (1, 2) \vee (2, \infty)$

(1, 2)

$y = 1$

O

$x = -1$

Example 5: $f(x) = \dfrac{x^2 - x}{x + 1}$

$f(x) = x - 2 + \dfrac{2}{x+1}$ (Use long division)

$D(x) = 0 \quad \rightarrow \quad x = -1 : \text{vertical asymptote}$

$y = \lim\limits_{x \to \infty} (x - 2) + \dfrac{2}{x+1} = (x - 2) \quad \rightarrow \quad y = x - 2 : \text{slant asymptote}$

Domain: $(-\infty, -1) \vee (-1, \infty)$

Range: $(-\infty, -5.82] \vee [-0.17, \infty)$ (using graphing utility)

$y = x - 2$

O

$x = -1$

74

Tips

PRACTICE

1. Find all asymptotes of the rational function $f(x) = \dfrac{2x^2 + 1}{x}$?

2. If $g(x) = \dfrac{x^2 + x - 2}{x^2 + 2x - 3}$, then its vertical asymptote(s) is(are)

3. If the vertical asymptote of the rational function $R(x) = \dfrac{x^2 - 3x + b}{(x-1)(x+1)}$ is $x = -1$, what is the value of b ?

EXPLANATION

1. Since $f(x) = 2x + \dfrac{1}{x}$, vertical asymptote: $x = 0$, and slant asymptote: $y = 2x$.

2. $g(x) = \dfrac{(x+2)\,(x-1)}{(x+3)\,(x-1)} = \dfrac{(x+2)}{(x+3)}$ $\rightarrow$ vertical asymptote: $D(x) = 0$ $\rightarrow$ $x = -3$

3. Since $x = 1$ is not asymptote, the numerator must have a factor of $(x-1)$. Therefore,

$$f(1) = 0 \quad \rightarrow \quad 1 - 3 + b = 0 \quad \rightarrow \quad b = 2$$

Answer: **1.** $x = 0$, $y = 2x$ **2.** $x = -3$ **3.** $b = 2$

Tips

TIP 54   Parametric Equations

Parametric equations define a relation using parameters.

Conversion from two parametric equations to a single equation:
Eliminating the parameter from the simultaneous equations.

| Parametric equations | $\Rightarrow$ | Solve for t in one equation | $\Rightarrow$ | Substitute in second equation | $\Rightarrow$ | Rectangular equation |

Example 1:

If $x = a\cos t$ and $y = b\sin t$, what is the graph of the parametric equations?

$$\cos t = \frac{x}{a} \quad \text{and} \quad \sin t = \frac{y}{b}$$

To eliminate the parameter t,

$$\cos^2 t + \sin^2 t = 1 \quad \rightarrow \quad \frac{x^2}{a^2} + \frac{y^2}{b^2} = 1 \quad : \quad \text{Ellipse}$$

PRACTICE

1. What is the curve given by the parametric equations $x = \sqrt{t}$ and $y = t + 2$?

2. What is the graph given by the parametric equations $x = \sec\theta$ and $y = \tan\theta$?

EXPLANATION

1. $t = x^2 \rightarrow y = x^2 + 2$, $x \geq 0$ (Domain is restricted because $x = \sqrt{t}$)

2. Since $1 + \tan^2\theta = \sec^2\theta$, $\quad 1 + y^2 = x^2 \rightarrow x^2 - y^2 = 1$: hyperbola

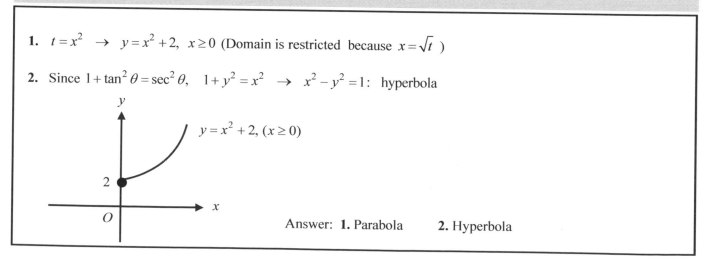

$y = x^2 + 2, (x \geq 0)$

Answer: **1.** Parabola   **2.** Hyperbola

Tips

Polar Coordinates

Polar Coordinates and Rectangular Coordinates Conversions

$$x = r\cos\theta$$
$$y = r\sin\theta$$
$$\tan\theta = \frac{y}{x} \quad \rightarrow \quad \theta = \tan^{-1}\frac{y}{x}$$
$$r^2 = x^2 + y^2 \quad \rightarrow \quad r = \sqrt{x^2 + y^2}$$

PRACTICE

1. If the coordinates of a polar point are $\left(5, \dfrac{\pi}{2}\right)$, what are its rectangular coordinates?

2. If the rectangular coordinates are $(\sqrt{3}, -1)$, what are its polar coordinates?

Equation Conversion:

3. What is the graph of the polar equation $r = 5$?

4. What is the graph of the polar equation $r = \sec\theta$?

5. Convert the polar equation $r = \dfrac{6}{2 - 3\sin\theta}$ to rectangular form.

6. Convert the rectangular equation $3x - 6y + 2 = 0$ to polar form.

Tips

7. Convert the rectangular equation $x^2 + y^2 - 6x = 0$ to polar form.

EXPLANATION

1. $x = r\cos\theta = 5\cos\dfrac{\pi}{2} = 0$ and $y = r\sin\theta = 5\sin\dfrac{\pi}{2} = 1$. Therefore, $(0, 5)$.

2. $r = \sqrt{\left(\sqrt{3}\right)^2 + 1^2} = 2$, $\theta = \tan^{-1}\left(\dfrac{-1}{\sqrt{3}}\right) = -30° = -\dfrac{\pi}{6}$. Therefore, $\left(2, -\dfrac{\pi}{6}\right)$.

3. $r = \sqrt{x^2 + y^2} = 5 \;\rightarrow\; x^2 + y^2 = 25$

4. $r = \sec\theta \;\rightarrow\; \sec\theta = \dfrac{1}{\cos\theta}$, $\cos\theta = \dfrac{x}{r} \;\rightarrow\; \sec\theta = \dfrac{r}{x}$

Therefore, $r = \dfrac{r}{x} \;\rightarrow\; x = 1$.

5. $r = \dfrac{6}{2 - 3\sin\theta} \;\rightarrow\; r = \dfrac{6}{2 - 3\dfrac{y}{r}} \;\rightarrow\; 2r - 3y = 6 \;\rightarrow\; 2r = 3y + 6$

$2\sqrt{x^2 + y^2} = 3y + 6 \;\rightarrow\; 4\left(x^2 + y^2\right) = \left(3y + 6\right)^2 \;\rightarrow\; 4x^2 + 4y^2 = 9y^2 + 36y + 36$

Therefore,
$4x^2 - 5y^2 - 36y - 36 = 0$. Hyperbola

6. $3x - 6y + 2 = 0 \;\rightarrow\; 3(r\cos\theta) - 6(r\sin\theta) + 2 = 0 \;\rightarrow\; r(3\cos\theta - 6\sin\theta) = -2$

$r = \dfrac{-2}{3\cos\theta - 6\sin\theta}$

7. $x^2 + y^2 = r^2$ and $x = r\cos\theta$. Therefore, $r^2 = 6r\cos\theta \;\rightarrow\; r = 6\cos\theta$.

Answer: **1.** $(0, 5)$ **2.** $\left(2, -\dfrac{\pi}{6}\right)$ or $\left(2, \dfrac{11\pi}{6}\right)$ **3.** $x^2 + y^2 = 25$, circle   **4.** $x = 1$

5. $4x^2 - 5y^2 - 36y - 36 = 0$, Hyperbola   **6.** $r = -\dfrac{2}{3\cos\theta - 6\sin\theta}$ **7.** $r = 6\cos\theta$

Tips

TIP 56 Matrix

A. Order of Matrix:

An $m \times n$ (m by n) matrix is a rectangular array of numbers arranged in m rows (horizontal lines) and n columns (vertical lines).

$$\begin{bmatrix} 5 & 2 \\ 2 & 1 \\ 1 & 5 \end{bmatrix}$$

This matrix has three rows and two columns.
The order of the matrix is 3×2 (3 by 2).

B. Addition of Matrices:

If two matrices have the same order, then you can add two matrices by adding their corresponding entries.

$$\begin{bmatrix} -1 & 3 \\ 2 & 4 \end{bmatrix} + \begin{bmatrix} 2 & -2 \\ 1 & -3 \end{bmatrix} = \begin{bmatrix} -1+2 & 3-2 \\ 2+1 & 4-3 \end{bmatrix} = \begin{bmatrix} 1 & 1 \\ 3 & 1 \end{bmatrix}$$

C. Scalar Multiplication:

$$3\begin{bmatrix} 1 & -3 \\ -2 & 4 \end{bmatrix} = \begin{bmatrix} 3 & -9 \\ -6 & 12 \end{bmatrix}$$

D. Scalar Multiplication and Matrix Subtraction:

If $A = \begin{bmatrix} -1 & 2 \\ 2 & 3 \end{bmatrix}$ and $B = \begin{bmatrix} -2 & 4 \\ -3 & 2 \end{bmatrix}$, then $2A - 3B$ is

$$2\begin{bmatrix} -1 & 2 \\ 2 & 3 \end{bmatrix} - 3\begin{bmatrix} -2 & 4 \\ -3 & 2 \end{bmatrix} = \begin{bmatrix} -2 & 4 \\ 4 & 6 \end{bmatrix} - \begin{bmatrix} -6 & 12 \\ -9 & 6 \end{bmatrix} = \begin{bmatrix} 4 & -8 \\ 13 & 0 \end{bmatrix}$$

E. Multiplication of Matrices:

Row by Column Multiplication
The number of columns of the first matrix must equal to the number of rows of the second matrix.

$$\begin{bmatrix} 2 & -3 \\ -1 & 2 \end{bmatrix}\begin{bmatrix} 1 \\ 3 \end{bmatrix} = \begin{bmatrix} 2 \cdot 1 + (-3) \cdot 3 \\ (-1) \cdot 1 + 2 \cdot 3 \end{bmatrix} = \begin{bmatrix} -7 \\ 5 \end{bmatrix}$$

Tips

$$A \quad \times \quad B \quad = \quad AB$$

$$\underbrace{m \times n}_{\text{Order of } A} \quad \underbrace{n \times p}_{\text{Order of } B} \quad \underbrace{m \times p}_{\text{Order of } AB}$$

F. Determinant of a 2×2 matrix:

$$\begin{vmatrix} a & b \\ c & d \end{vmatrix} = ad - bc$$

PRACTICE

1. What is the determinant of the matrix $A = \begin{bmatrix} 2 & -3 \\ -1 & 2 \end{bmatrix}$?

2. If matrices $A, B, C,$ and D have orders of $2 \times 3,\ 2 \times 3,\ 3 \times 2,$ and 2×2, respectively, what are the orders of following operations?

   I) $A(2B)$ II) $D(A - 3B)$ III) $(BC - D)A$

EXPLANATION

1. $\begin{vmatrix} 2 & -3 \\ -1 & 2 \end{vmatrix} = 2 \cdot 2 - (-3)(-1) = 4 - 3 = 1$

2. **1)** $A(2B) \rightarrow (2 \times 3)(2 \times 3)$: Invalid

   2) $D(A - 3B) \rightarrow (2 \times 2)(2 \times 3) = (2 \times 3)$

   3. $(BC - D)A \rightarrow BC: \rightarrow (2 \times 3)(3 \times 2) = (2 \times 2),\quad BC - D: \rightarrow (2 \times 2)$
   $$(BC - D)A: \rightarrow (2 \times 2)(2 \times 3) = (2 \times 3)$$

Tips

TIP 57	Inclination Angle

Inclination angle is the angle measured counterclockwise from the x-axis to the line.

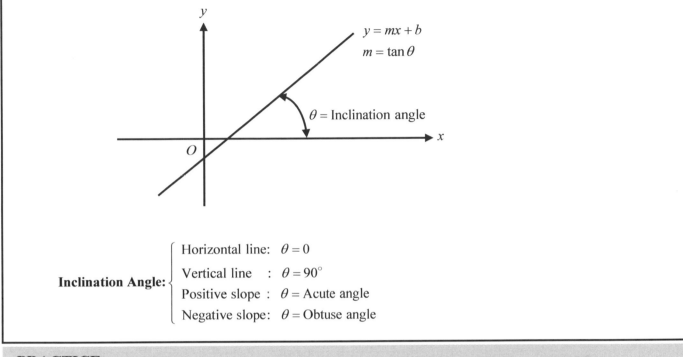

$$
\textbf{Inclination Angle:} \begin{cases} \text{Horizontal line:} & \theta = 0 \\ \text{Vertical line} \quad : & \theta = 90° \\ \text{Positive slope} : & \theta = \text{Acute angle} \\ \text{Negative slope:} & \theta = \text{Obtuse angle} \end{cases}
$$

PRACTICE

1. If a line has an equation of $2x - 3y = 5$, what is the inclination angle of the line?

EXPLANATION

1. $2x - 3y = 5 \quad \rightarrow \quad y = \dfrac{2}{3}x - \dfrac{5}{3} \quad \rightarrow \quad m = \dfrac{2}{3}$

$\tan\theta = \dfrac{2}{3} \quad \rightarrow \quad \theta = \tan^{-1}\dfrac{2}{3} = 33.69006753 \approx 33.7°$

Answer: **1.** $33.7°$

Tips

Angle between Two Lines

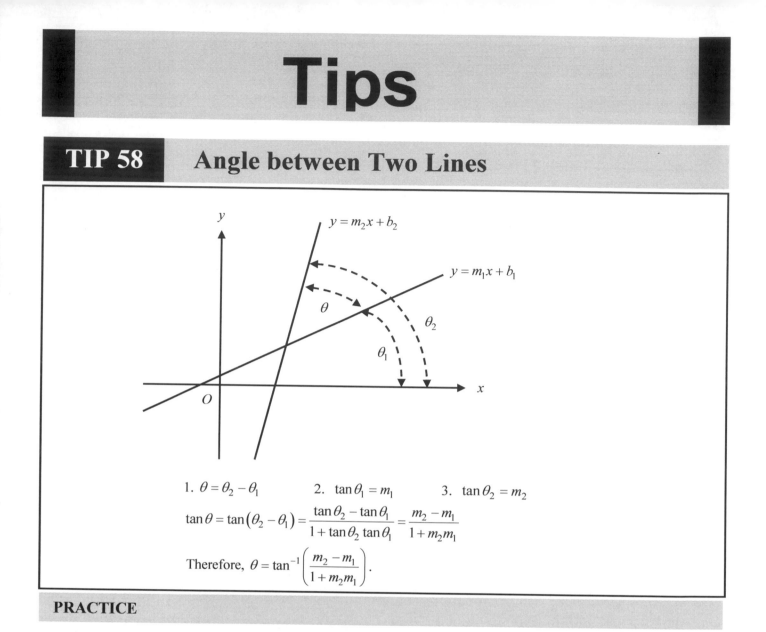

1. $\theta = \theta_2 - \theta_1$ 2. $\tan\theta_1 = m_1$ 3. $\tan\theta_2 = m_2$

$$\tan\theta = \tan(\theta_2 - \theta_1) = \frac{\tan\theta_2 - \tan\theta_1}{1 + \tan\theta_2 \tan\theta_1} = \frac{m_2 - m_1}{1 + m_2 m_1}$$

Therefore, $\theta = \tan^{-1}\left(\dfrac{m_2 - m_1}{1 + m_2 m_1}\right)$.

PRACTICE

1.   Find the angle between the two lines $y = -x + 2$ and $y = 2x - 1$.

EXPLANATION

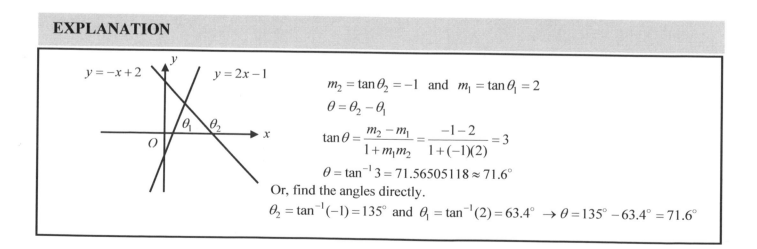

$m_2 = \tan\theta_2 = -1$ and $m_1 = \tan\theta_1 = 2$

$\theta = \theta_2 - \theta_1$

$\tan\theta = \dfrac{m_2 - m_1}{1 + m_1 m_2} = \dfrac{-1 - 2}{1 + (-1)(2)} = 3$

$\theta = \tan^{-1} 3 = 71.56505118 \approx 71.6°$

Or, find the angles directly.

$\theta_2 = \tan^{-1}(-1) = 135°$ and $\theta_1 = \tan^{-1}(2) = 63.4°$ $\rightarrow \theta = 135° - 63.4° = 71.6°$

Tips

Intermediate Value Theorem

If f is continuous on a closed interval $[a,b]$ and k is any number between $f(a)$ and $f(b)$, then there is at least one number c in $[a,b]$ such that $f(c) = k$.

1. If $f(a) > 0$ and $f(b) < 0$ on a closed interval $[a,b]$, then there are at least one real zeros somewhere between a and b.

PRACTICE

1. If $P(x) = x^3 - 4x^2 + 6$, what are the intervals needed to guarantee real zeros?

(Use the Intermediate Value Theorem to find intervals of length 1.)

PRACTICE

1. Using a graphic utility,

Since $f(-2) = -18 < 0$ and $f(-1) = 1 > 0$, there is a zero between -2 and -1.

$f(1) = 3 > 0$ and $f(2) = -2 < 0$, there is a zero between 1 and 2.

$f(3) = -3 < 0$ and $f(4) = 6 > 0$, there is a zero between 3 and 4.

Answer: **1.** $(-2, -1), (1, 2), (3, 4)$

Tips

If the polynomial $f(x) = a_n x^n + a_{n-1} x^{n-1} + \cdots + a_1 x + a_o$ has integer coefficients,

the possible rational zeros of f are

$$\text{Possible Rational Zeros} = \frac{\text{factors of constant term}}{\text{factors of leading coefficient}}$$

PRACTICE

1. What is all possible rational zeros of $f(x) = x^3 - x + 1$?

2. Find the possible rational zeros of $f(x) = 2x^3 + 3x^2 - 8x + 3$.

PRACTICE

1. $\dfrac{\text{Factors of constant term}}{\text{Factors of leading coefficients}} = \dfrac{\pm 1}{\pm 1} = \pm 1$

By testing these zeros, you can see that neither works.
$f(1) = 1$ and $f(-1) = 1$
Therefore, you can conclude that the polynomial function has no rational zeros.
The real zero is $x = -1.324718 \cdots$ irrational root.

2. $\dfrac{\pm 1, \ \pm 3}{\pm 1, \ \pm 2} = \pm 1, \ \pm 3, \ \pm \dfrac{1}{2}, \ \pm \dfrac{3}{2}$

By using a graphing utility, you can find the real rational zeros of f are

$x = 1$, $x = \dfrac{1}{2}$, and $x = -3$.

Answer: 1. ± 1 **2.** $\pm 1, \ \pm 3, \ \pm \dfrac{1}{2}, \ \pm \dfrac{3}{2}$

Tips

If $f(x) = a_n x^n + a_{n-1} x^{n-1} + \cdots + a_1 x + a_o$ with real coefficients and $a_0 \neq 0$,

1. The number of **positive zeros** of f is either equal to the number of variations in sign of $f(x)$ or less than the number by an even integer.

2. The number of **negative zeros** of f is either equal to the number of variations in sign of $f(-x)$ or less than the number by an even integer.

PRACTICE

1. Find the possible real zeros of $f(x) = 4x^3 - 6x^2 + 3x - 3$?

PRACTICE

1. Check the number of variations in sign of $f(x) = 4x^3 - 6x^2 + 3x - 3$

$$\overbrace{+4 \quad -6}^{+\text{ to }-} \quad \overbrace{-6 \quad +3}^{-\text{ to }+} \quad \overbrace{+3 \quad -3}^{+\text{ to }-}$$

Three variations in sign.

Check the number of variations in sign of $f(-x) = -4x^3 - 6x^2 - 3x - 3$

No variations in sign.

Conclusion: 1) Three positive zeros and no negative zeros.
       or
       2) One positive real zero and no negative zeros. (One positive real zero and two imaginary roots)

Answer: **1.** Three positive real zeros or one positive real zero
       and has no negative real zeros.

No Test Material on This Page

Test 1

Dr. John Chung's

SAT II Mathematics Level 2

MATHEMATICS LEVEL 2 TEST

REFERENCE INFORMATION

THE FOLLOWING INFORMATION IS FOR YOUR REFERENCE IN ANSWERING SOME OF THE QUESTIONS IN THIS TEST

Volume of a right circular cone with radius r and height h: $V = \dfrac{1}{3}\pi r^2 h$

Lateral Area of a right circular cone with circumference of the base c and slant height ℓ: $S = \dfrac{1}{2}c\ell$

Volume of a sphere with radius r: $V = \dfrac{4}{3}\pi r^3$

Surface Area of a sphere with radius r: $S = 4\pi r^2$

Volume of a pyramid with base area B and height h: $V = \dfrac{1}{3}Bh$

Dr. John Chung's SAT II Math Level 2

Answer Sheet

01 Ⓐ Ⓑ Ⓒ Ⓓ Ⓔ   26 Ⓐ Ⓑ Ⓒ Ⓓ Ⓔ
02 Ⓐ Ⓑ Ⓒ Ⓓ Ⓔ   27 Ⓐ Ⓑ Ⓒ Ⓓ Ⓔ
03 Ⓐ Ⓑ Ⓒ Ⓓ Ⓔ   28 Ⓐ Ⓑ Ⓒ Ⓓ Ⓔ
04 Ⓐ Ⓑ Ⓒ Ⓓ Ⓔ   29 Ⓐ Ⓑ Ⓒ Ⓓ Ⓔ
05 Ⓐ Ⓑ Ⓒ Ⓓ Ⓔ   30 Ⓐ Ⓑ Ⓒ Ⓓ Ⓔ
06 Ⓐ Ⓑ Ⓒ Ⓓ Ⓔ   31 Ⓐ Ⓑ Ⓒ Ⓓ Ⓔ
07 Ⓐ Ⓑ Ⓒ Ⓓ Ⓔ   32 Ⓐ Ⓑ Ⓒ Ⓓ Ⓔ
08 Ⓐ Ⓑ Ⓒ Ⓓ Ⓔ   33 Ⓐ Ⓑ Ⓒ Ⓓ Ⓔ
09 Ⓐ Ⓑ Ⓒ Ⓓ Ⓔ   34 Ⓐ Ⓑ Ⓒ Ⓓ Ⓔ
10 Ⓐ Ⓑ Ⓒ Ⓓ Ⓔ   35 Ⓐ Ⓑ Ⓒ Ⓓ Ⓔ
11 Ⓐ Ⓑ Ⓒ Ⓓ Ⓔ   36 Ⓐ Ⓑ Ⓒ Ⓓ Ⓔ
12 Ⓐ Ⓑ Ⓒ Ⓓ Ⓔ   37 Ⓐ Ⓑ Ⓒ Ⓓ Ⓔ
13 Ⓐ Ⓑ Ⓒ Ⓓ Ⓕ   38 Ⓐ Ⓑ Ⓒ Ⓓ Ⓔ
14 Ⓐ Ⓑ Ⓒ Ⓓ Ⓔ   39 Ⓐ Ⓑ Ⓒ Ⓓ Ⓔ
15 Ⓐ Ⓑ Ⓒ Ⓓ Ⓔ   40 Ⓐ Ⓑ Ⓒ Ⓓ Ⓔ
16 Ⓐ Ⓑ Ⓒ Ⓓ Ⓔ   41 Ⓐ Ⓑ Ⓒ Ⓓ Ⓔ
17 Ⓐ Ⓑ Ⓒ Ⓓ Ⓔ   42 Ⓐ Ⓑ Ⓒ Ⓓ Ⓔ
18 Ⓐ Ⓑ Ⓒ Ⓓ Ⓔ   43 Ⓐ Ⓑ Ⓒ Ⓓ Ⓔ
19 Ⓐ Ⓑ Ⓒ Ⓓ Ⓔ   44 Ⓐ Ⓑ Ⓒ Ⓓ Ⓔ
20 Ⓐ Ⓑ Ⓒ Ⓓ Ⓔ   45 Ⓐ Ⓑ Ⓒ Ⓓ Ⓔ
21 Ⓐ Ⓑ Ⓒ Ⓓ Ⓔ   46 Ⓐ Ⓑ Ⓒ Ⓓ Ⓔ
22 Ⓐ Ⓑ Ⓒ Ⓓ Ⓔ   47 Ⓐ Ⓑ Ⓒ Ⓓ Ⓔ
23 Ⓐ Ⓑ Ⓒ Ⓓ Ⓔ   48 Ⓐ Ⓑ Ⓒ Ⓓ Ⓔ
24 Ⓐ Ⓑ Ⓒ Ⓓ Ⓔ   49 Ⓐ Ⓑ Ⓒ Ⓓ Ⓔ
25 Ⓐ Ⓑ Ⓒ Ⓓ Ⓔ   50 Ⓐ Ⓑ Ⓒ Ⓓ Ⓔ

The number of right answers: ☐

The number of wrong answers: ☐

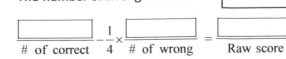

$$\underbrace{\boxed{}}_{\text{\# of correct}} - \frac{1}{4} \times \underbrace{\boxed{}}_{\text{\# of wrong}} = \underbrace{\boxed{}}_{\text{Raw score}}$$

Score Conversion Table

Raw Score	Scaled Score	Raw Score	Scaled Score	Raw Score	Scaled Score
50	800	28	640	6	480
49	800	27	630	5	470
48	800	26	620	4	470
47	800	25	620	3	460
46	800	24	610	2	460
45	800	23	610	1	450
44	800	22	600	0	450
43	800	21	600		
42	800	20	590		
41	800	19	590		
40	780	18	580		
39	760	17	570		
38	750	16	560		
37	740	15	550		
36	720	14	540		
35	710	13	530		
34	700	12	520		
33	690	11	510		
32	680	10	500		
31	670	9	490		
30	660	8	490		
29	650	7	480		

MATHEMATICS LEVEL 2 TEST

For each of the following problems, decide which is the BEST of the choices given. If the exact numerical value is not one of the choices, select the choice that best approximates this value. Then fill in the corresponding circle on the answer sheet

Note: (1) A scientific or graphing calculator will be necessary for answering some (but not all) of the questions in this test. For each question you will have to decide whether or not you should use a calculator.

(2) For some questions in this test you may have to decide whether your calculator should be in the radian mode or the degree mode.

(3) Figures that accompany problems in this test are intended to provide information useful in solving the problems. They are drawn as accurately as possible EXCEPT when it is stated in a specific problem that its figure is not drawn to scale. All figures lie in a plane unless otherwise indicated.

(4) Unless otherwise specified, the domain of any function f is assumed to be the set of all real numbers x for which $f(x)$ is a real number. The range of f is assumed to be the set of all real numbers $f(x)$, where x is in the domain of f.

(5) Reference information that may be useful in answering the questions in this test can be found on the page preceding Question 1.

USE THIS SPACE FOR SCRATCHWORK

1. If $a(x+2)+b(x-1)=3$ for all x, then $a=$

    (A) -1 (B) 0 (C) 1 (D) 2 (E) 3

2. If $a+b=2$ and $ab=-1$, then $a^2+b^2=$

    (A) 4 (B) 5 (C) 6 (D) 8 (E) 10

3. If the graph of $3x+4y=5$ is perpendicular to the graph of $kx+2y=5$, then $k=$

    (A) -2
    (B) -2.67
    (C) 2.15
    (D) 3.20
    (E) 4

GO ON TO THE NEXT PAGE

USE THIS SPACE FOR SCRATCHWORK.

4. If $K = \dfrac{AB}{A+B}$, then $B =$

(A) $\dfrac{A}{1-A}$

(B) $\dfrac{AK}{A-K}$

(C) $\dfrac{AK}{K-A}$

(D) $\dfrac{A+k}{A}$

(E) $\dfrac{A-K}{AK}$

5. If $\log 3 = a$, then $\log 90 =$

(A) $1+2a$

(B) $10a^2$

(C) $10+2a$

(D) $30a$

(E) $10+3a$

6. If $f(x) = 3\ln x$ and $g(x) = e^x$, then $g(f(x)) =$

(A) $3x$

(B) e^x

(C) e^{2x}

(D) x^3

(E) $x^2 + 1$

7. In Figure 1, the slant height of a regular circular cone is 20 cm and the radius of the base is 10 cm . Find the volume of the cone?

(A) 1813.8 cm^3 (B) 3000.5 cm^3 (C) 4120.4 cm^3

(D) 7024.8 cm^3 (D) 7046.6 cm^3

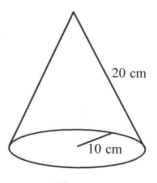

20 cm

10 cm

Figure 1

GO ON TO THE NEXT PAGE

MATHEMATICS LEVEL 2 TEST - *Continued*

8. If $2 - i$ is one of the zeros of the polynomial $p(x)$, then a factor of $p(x)$ could be

(A) $x^2 - 2$
(B) $x^2 - 4$
(C) $x^2 - 4x + 4$
(D) $x^2 - 4x + 5$
(E) $x^2 + 4x + 3$

9. When a polynomial function $f(x) = x^2 + 5x - k$ is divided by $(x - 2)$, the remainder is 5. What is the value of k?

(A) 19
(B) 18
(C) 16
(D) 10
(E) 9

10. Figure 2 shows a cube with edge of length 6, what is the length of diagonal $\overline{PQ}$?

(A) 18
(B) 15
(C) $6\sqrt{6}$
(D) $6\sqrt{3}$
(E) $6\sqrt{2}$

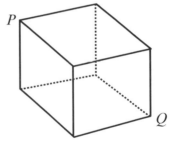

Figure 2

11. An equation of line ℓ in figure 3 is

(A) $3x - 4y - 4 = 0$
(B) $3x + 4y - 4 = 0$
(C) $4x - 3y - 4 = 0$
(D) $4x + 3y + 12 = 0$
(E) $4x + 3y - 12 = 0$

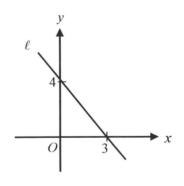

Figure 3

GO ON TO THE NEXT PAGE

USE THIS SPACE FOR SCRATCHWORK.

12. The mean score of 10 students of an algebra class was 85. When two new students enrolled, the mean increased to 86. What was the average of the new students?

(A) 88
(B) 89
(C) 90
(D) 91
(E) 92

13. If $\sin\theta + \cos\theta = \dfrac{1}{2}$, then $\tan\theta + \cot\theta =$

(A) −4.12
(B) −2.67
(C) −1.35
(D) 2.67
(E) 4.12

14. What is the period of the function f, where $f(x) = -5 - \cos\left(\dfrac{3x - \pi}{2}\right)$?

(A) $\dfrac{\pi}{3}$

(B) $\dfrac{2\pi}{3}$

(C) $\dfrac{4\pi}{3}$

(D) 2π

(E) $\dfrac{3\pi}{2}$

15. Find all of the asymptotes of $y = \dfrac{x^2 - 3x + 2}{x^2 - 1}$.

(A) $x = 1$
(B) $x = 1, \ x = -1$
(C) $x = 1, \ y = 1$
(D) $x = -1, \ y = 1$
(E) $x = -1, x = 1,$ and $y = 1$

GO ON TO THE NEXT PAGE

16. If $f(2x) = \dfrac{x}{3}$, then $f(x) =$

(A) $\dfrac{2x}{3}$ (B) $\dfrac{x}{3}$ (C) $\dfrac{x}{6}$ (D) $3x$ (E) $6x$

17. If three numbers $\log a,$ $\log b,$ and $\log c$ in that order form an arithmetic progression, which of the following is true?

(A) $b = ac$

(B) $c = ab$

(C) $b = \dfrac{a+c}{2}$

(D) $b^2 = ac$

(E) $b^2 = a + c$

18. The point of set (x, y) such that $x^2 - y^2 = 0$ is

(A) A circle
(B) An ellipse
(C) A hyperbola
(D) A point
(E) Two lines

19. What is the sum of the geometric series
$$10 + 5 + \frac{5}{2} + \frac{5}{4} + \frac{5}{8} + \cdots ?$$

(A) 30
(B) 25
(C) 20
(D) 19
(E) 18

20. Which of the following is an equation whose graph is the set of points equidistant from the point $(0, 4)$ and $(2, 2)$?

(A) $y = 2$ (B) $x = 2$ (C) $y = x$ (D) $y = x + 2$
(E) $y = -x - 2$

GO ON TO THE NEXT PAGE

MATHEMATICS LEVEL 2 TEST - *Continued*

USE THIS SPACE FOR SCRATCHWORK.

21. The solution set of $|3x-5|<10$ is

(A) $\{x>5\}$

(B) $\{x>-5\}$

(C) $\left\{-\dfrac{5}{3}<x<5\right\}$

(D) $\left\{x>5 \text{ or } x<-\dfrac{5}{3}\right\}$

(E) $\{x<-5 \text{ or } x>15\}$

22. In the graph in Figure 4, which of the following could be the equation of the graph?

(A) $y=\sin x+3$

(B) $y=\sin 2x$

(C) $y=3\sin x+3$

(D) $y=3\sin 2x+3$

(E) $y=3\sin\dfrac{1}{2}x+3$

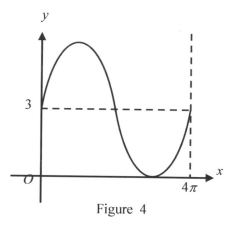

Figure 4

23. What is the range of $f(x)=x^2-5x+6$?

(A) $y\geq 0$
(B) $y\geq -0.25$
(C) $2\leq y\leq 3$
(D) $y\leq 5$
(E) All real numbers

24. If $\sin(x-10)^\circ=\cos(2x+28)^\circ$, then which of the following could be the value of x?

(A) 0
(B) 10
(C) 20
(D) 24
(E) 30

GO ON TO THE NEXT PAGE

USE THIS SPACE FOR SCRATCHWORK.

25. Which of the following is the equation of the inverse of $y = 3^{x+1}$?

    (A) $y = \log_{x+1} 3$

    (B) $y = \log(x) - 1$

    (C) $y = \log_3 \left(\dfrac{x}{3} \right)$

    (D) $y = \log_3 (x) + 1$

    (E) $y = \log_3 (x - 1)$

26. If $f(x) = x^2 + kx + 9$ is always greater than 0 for all real x, which of the following could be the value of k ?

    (A) -10 (B) -5 (C)   10   (D)   12   (E)   13

27. Which of the following is the center of a circle $x^2 + y^2 + 10x + 6y = 10$?

    (A) $(-5, -3)$

    (B) $(5, 3)$

    (C) $(10, 6)$

    (D) $(-10, -6)$

    (E) $(10, -10)$

28. What is the domain of the function defined by $f(x) = \dfrac{\sqrt{2x - 10}}{x^2 - 3x + 2}$?

    (A)   All real numbers except 1
    (B)   All real number except 2
    (C)   All real numbers except 1 and 2
    (D) $x > 5$
    (E) $x \geq 5$

GO ON TO THE NEXT PAGE

USE THIS SPACE FOR SCRATCHWORK.

29. If $x^2 + y^2 = 20$ and $x^2 = y$, then $x =$

    (A) $\{-3\}$
    (B) $\{-2, 2\}$
    (C) $\{4\}$
    (D) $\{10\}$
    (E) $\{4, 10\}$

30. If $f(x) = \log_2 (x-1) + 2$, then $f^{-1}(x) =$

    (A) 2^{x-1}
    (B) $x^2 + 1$
    (C) 2^{x-2}
    (D) $2^{x-2} + 1$
    (E) $2^{2x} + 2^x + 1$

31. Figure 5 shows a right triangle. If the length of $\overline{AD}$ is 8 and the length of $\overline{BD}$ is 4, then the length of $\overline{AC}$ is

    (A) 15.23
    (B) 16.42
    (C) 17.89
    (D) 18.44
    (E) 20.25

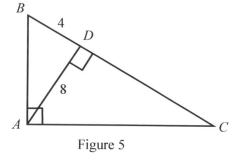

Figure 5

32. If complex number $z = 4 - 6i$, then $|z - 2| =$

    (A) 5.87
    (B) 6.32
    (C) 6.38
    (D) 7.21
    (E) 7.31

33. The coefficient of the middle term of the expansion of $(x - 3y)^6$ is

    (A) −540   (B) −270   (C) 135   (D) 270   (E) 540

GO ON TO THE NEXT PAGE

USE THIS SPACE FOR SCRATCHWORK.

34. If $\sqrt{x^2 + 6x + 9} = x$, which of the following is the solution?

(A) $x = -\dfrac{3}{2}$

(B) $x = \dfrac{1}{2}$

(C) $x = -\dfrac{1}{4}$

(D) $x = \dfrac{1}{4}$

(E) No solution

35. A sequence is defined as $a_1 = 1$ and $a_{n+1} = a_n + 3$.
Which of the following is the nth term of this sequence?

(A) $3n - 2$

(B) $4n - 3$

(C) $5n - 4$

(D) $6n - 5$

(E) $n^2 - n + 1$

36. If $f(x) = x^2 + 2x - 4$ for $x \geq 0$, what is the value of
$f^{-1}(4)$?

(A) 2
(B) 4
(C) 5
(D) 8
(E) 10

37. In triangle ABC, $a = 6$, $b = 6\sqrt{3}$, and $\angle A = 30°$. What is
the measure of $\angle C$?

(A) $30°$ only

(B) $90°$ only

(C) $30°$ or $90°$

(D) $120°$ only

(E) $60°$ or $120°$

GO ON TO THE NEXT PAGE

USE THIS SPACE FOR SCRATCHWORK.

38. If $\log_2 5 = a$ and $\log_2 3 = b$, then $\log_2 \sqrt{75} =$

(A) $\sqrt{2a + b}$

(B) $2a + b$

(C) $\frac{1}{2}(a + b)$

(D) $\frac{1}{2}(a + 2b)$

(E) $a + \frac{1}{2}b$

39. Which of the following could be the graph of the parametric equations represented by $x = 3\sin\theta$ and $y = 4\cos\theta$?

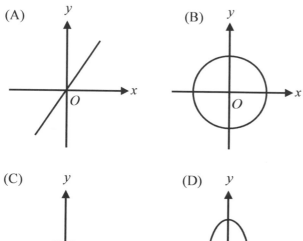

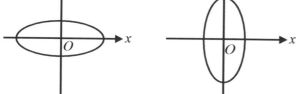

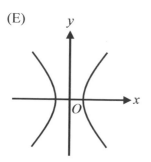

MATHEMATICS LEVEL 2 TEST - *Continued*

USE THIS SPACE FOR SCRATCHWORK.

40. If the three sides of a triangle are 4, 5, and 7, then the area of the triangle is

(A) 9.80   (B) 9.92   (C) 10.2   (D) 11.43   (E) 11.56

41. If $\dfrac{(n+1)!}{(n-1)!} = 56$, what is the value of n?

(A) 6
(B) 7
(C) 8
(D) 10
(E) 12

42. The radius of the base of a right circular cone is 5 and the slant height of the cone is 10. What is the surface area of the cone?

(A) 50π
(B) 68π
(C) 70π
(D) 75π
(E) 80π

43. If the 11th term of an arithmetic sequence is 30 and the 21st term is 0, what is the 10th term of the sequence?

(A) 30
(B) 33
(C) 36
(D) 39
(E) 42

44. $\displaystyle\lim_{n \to 1} \dfrac{n^2 - 1}{\sqrt{n} - 1} =$

(A) 0   (B) 1   (C) 2   (D) 4   (E) Limit does not exist.

GO ON TO THE NEXT PAGE

MATHEMATICS LEVEL 2 TEST - *Continued*

USE THIS SPACE FOR SCRATCHWORK.

45. If one of the roots of a polynomial function $f(x) = 0$ is

$1 + \dfrac{\sqrt{3}}{2}i$, which of the following could be $f(x)$?

(A) $2x^2 - 4x + 6$

(B) $x^2 - 2x + 10$

(C) $3x^2 + 6x - 4$

(D) $4x^2 - 8x + 7$

(E) $5x^2 - 10x + 7$

46. If $p(x) = x^3 - 2x^2 + mx + n$ is divisible by $x^2 - 3x + 2$, what is the value of m?

(A) -2

(B) -1

(C) 0

(D) 1

(E) 2

47. If $f(x) = \cos x$ and $g(x) = x^2 + 3$, which of the following is not true?

(A) $f(x) \cdot g(x) + 2$ is an even function.

(B) $f(x) + g(x)$ is an even function.

(C) $g(f(x))$ is an even function.

(D) $f(x) - g(x) + 2$ is an even function.

(E) $f(x-1) + g(x-1)$ is an even function

48. Under which of the following conditions is

$\dfrac{x}{(x-1)(x+2)} < 0$?

(A) $x < 0$ or $x > 2$

(B) $x < -2$ or $x > 1$

(C) $x < 1$ or $x > 0$

(D) $x < -2$ or $0 < x < 1$

(E) $-2 < x < 0$ or $x > 1$

USE THIS SPACE FOR SCRATCHWORK.

49. What are the asymptotes of the hyperbola whose equation is
$16x^2 - 25y^2 - 400 = 0$?

(A) $y = \pm \dfrac{16}{25}x$

(B) $y = \pm \dfrac{25}{16}x$

(C) $y = \pm \dfrac{4}{5}x$

(D) $y = \pm \dfrac{5}{4}x$

(E) $y = \pm \dfrac{16}{5}x$

50. If $kx^2 + 4x - 2 = 0$ have two different real roots, which of the following is the values of k ?

(A) $k > -2$

(B) $k < -2$

(C) $-2 < k < 0$ or $k > 0$

(D) $-2 < k < 2$

(E) $-1 < k < 3$

STOP

IF YOU FINISH BEFORE TIME IS CALLED, YOU MAY CHECK YOUR WORK ON THIS TEST ONLY.

DO NOT TURN TO ANY OTHER TEST IN THIS BOOK.

No Test Material on This Page

#	answer	#	answer	#	answer	#	answer	#	answer
1	C	11	E	21	C	31	C	41	B
2	C	12	D	22	E	32	B	42	D
3	B	13	B	23	B	33	A	43	B
4	B	14	C	24	D	34	E	44	D
5	A	15	D	25	C	35	A	45	D
6	D	16	C	26	B	36	A	46	B
7	A	17	D	27	A	37	C	47	E
8	D	18	E	28	E	38	E	48	D
9	E	19	C	29	B	39	D	49	C
10	D	20	D	30	D	40	A	50	C

TEST 1   ANSWERS

Explanations: Test 1

1. (C) $a(x+2)+b(x-1)=3 \rightarrow (a+b)x+2a-b=3$

To be equal for all numbers x: $a+b=0$ and $2a-b=3$.
Therefore,

$$a+b=0$$
$$\frac{2a-b=3}{3a=\quad 3} \rightarrow a=1$$

2. (C) $(a+b)^2 = a^2+b^2+2ab = 2^2$ and $ab=-1$.

Therefore, $a^2+b^2 = 4-2ab = 4-2(-1)=6$.

3. (B) $3x+4y=5 \rightarrow y=-\frac{3}{4}x+\frac{5}{4}$ and $kx+2y=5 \rightarrow y=-\frac{k}{2}x+\frac{5}{2}$.

To be perpendicular, the product of the two slopes should be -1.

Therefore, $\left(-\frac{3}{4}\right)\left(-\frac{k}{2}\right)=\frac{3k}{8}=-1$. $k=\frac{-8}{3}=-2.67$.

4. (B) Since $K=\frac{AB}{A+B}$, $KA+KB=AB$ or $KA=AB-KB=(A-K)B$.

Therefore, $B=\frac{AK}{A-K}$.

5. (A) Since $\log 90 = \log(3\times3\times10)=\log3+\log3+\log10$, $\log3=a$ and $\log10=1$,
$\log 90 = a+a+1=2a+1$.

6. (D) $g(f(x))=e^{3\ln x}=e^{\ln x^3}=x^3$

7. **(A)** By Pythagorean Theorem the height of the cone is $\sqrt{20^2 - 10^2} = \sqrt{300} = 10\sqrt{3}$.

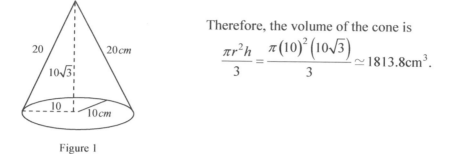

Therefore, the volume of the cone is

$$\frac{\pi r^2 h}{3} = \frac{\pi (10)^2 \left(10\sqrt{3}\right)}{3} \simeq 1813.8\text{cm}^3.$$

Figure 1

8. **(D)** Since $2 - i$ is one of the roots, the other root must be $2 + i$ (conjugate). Therefore, the equation with these two roots is $\left[x - (2-i)\right]\left[x - (2+i)\right] = \left[(x-2)+i\right]\left[(x-2)-i\right] = 0$.

$(x-2)^2 - i^2 = 0 \;\rightarrow\; x^2 - 4x + 4 + 1 = 0 \;\rightarrow\; x^2 - 4x + 5 = 0$

9. **(E)** Remainder Theorem

$x^2 + 5x - k = (x-2)Q(x) + R$, where $Q(x)$ is quotient and $R = 5$. When $x = 2$, both sides have the same number. Since $2^2 + 5(2) - k = 5$, $\;\rightarrow\; k = 9$

Or, (1) use long division.

$$
\begin{array}{r}
x + 7 \\
x-2\overline{\smash{)}\,x^2 + 5x - k} \\
\underline{x^2 - 2x} \\
7x - k \\
\underline{7x - 14} \\
-k + 14 = 5
\end{array}
$$

Therefore, $k = 9$.

(2) Synthetic Division.

$$
\begin{array}{r|rrr}
2 & 1 & 5 & -k \\
  &   & 2 & 14 \\
\hline
  & 1 & 7 & 14-k
\end{array}
$$

Therefore, the remainder is $14 - k = 5 \;\rightarrow\; k = 9$.

10. **(D)** The length of diagonal $\overline{PQ}$ is $\sqrt{6^2 + 6^2 + 6^2} = \sqrt{108} = 6\sqrt{3}$.

11. **(E)** If a and b are x- and y-intercept respectively, the equation of the line is $\dfrac{x}{a} + \dfrac{y}{b} = 1$.

Since $\dfrac{x}{3} + \dfrac{y}{4} = 1$, the equation is $4x + 3y = 12$. Therefore, $4x + 3y - 12 = 0$.

12. **(D)** The sum of scores of 10 students is $85 \times 10 = 850$. Let the average of score of two student be x.

Since $\dfrac{850 + 2x}{12} = 86 \;\rightarrow\; 850 + 2x = 12(86) \;\rightarrow\; 2x = 182$, $x = 91$.

13. (B) $\tan\theta + \cot\theta = \dfrac{\sin\theta}{\cos\theta} + \dfrac{\cos\theta}{\sin\theta} = \dfrac{\sin^2\theta + \cos^2\theta}{\sin\theta\cos\theta} = \dfrac{1}{\sin\theta\cos\theta}$ ------- (1)

$\left(\sin\theta + \cos\theta\right)^2 = 1 + 2\sin\theta\cos\theta = \dfrac{1}{4} \;\rightarrow\; \sin\theta\cos\theta = \dfrac{-3}{8}$ ------- (2)

Substitute (2) into (1)

$\dfrac{1}{-\dfrac{3}{8}} = -\dfrac{8}{3}$

14. (C)   The frequency of the periodic function is $\dfrac{3}{2}$, because the function can be expressed as follow.

$f(x) = -5 - \cos\dfrac{3}{2}\left(x - \dfrac{\pi}{3}\right)$, where the coefficient of x is the frequency.

Therefore, the period of the function is $\dfrac{2\pi}{f} = \dfrac{2\pi}{3/2} = \dfrac{4\pi}{3}$.

15. (D)   Since $y = \dfrac{(x-2)(x-1)}{(x-1)(x+1)} = \dfrac{x-2}{x+1}$, there is no asymptote at $x = 1$.

Denominator : $x + 1 = 0 \;\rightarrow\; x = -1$ (vertical asymptote)

For other asymptote: $y = \lim\limits_{x\to\infty} \dfrac{x-2}{x+1} = 1$ (horizontal asymptote)

16. (C)   Since $f(2x) = \dfrac{x}{3} = \dfrac{(2x)}{6}, \;\rightarrow\; f(x) = \dfrac{x}{6}$.

Or, to avoid confusion, change the function to $f(2k) = \dfrac{k}{3}$. Let $2k = x$, then $k = \dfrac{x}{2}$.

Substitute the function in terms of x . $f(x) = \dfrac{\dfrac{x}{2}}{3} = \dfrac{x}{6}$.

17. (D)   Since $\log a, \log b$, and $\log c$ are arithmetic progression, $\log c - \log b = \log b - \log a$.

By log operation, $\log\dfrac{c}{b} = \log\dfrac{b}{a} \;\rightarrow\; \dfrac{c}{b} = \dfrac{b}{a} \;\rightarrow\; b^2 = ac$.

18. (E) $x^2 - y^2 = 0 \;\rightarrow\; (x+y)(x-y) = 0 \;\rightarrow\; y = -x$ or $y = x$. That represent two lines.

19. (C)   The sum of geometric series is $S = \lim\limits_{n\to\infty} \dfrac{a(1-r^n)}{1-r}$, where a is the first term and r is the

common ratio. When $|r| < 1$, the sum is $S = \dfrac{a}{1-r}$. Therefore, $S = \dfrac{10}{1-\dfrac{1}{2}} = \dfrac{10}{\dfrac{1}{2}} = 20$.

20. (D) Line m which is equidistant from two points must be perpendicular bisector of the line segment.

The midpoint is $\left(\dfrac{0+2}{2}, \dfrac{4+2}{2}\right) = (1,3)$ and the slope of the segment is $\dfrac{4-2}{0-2} = -1$

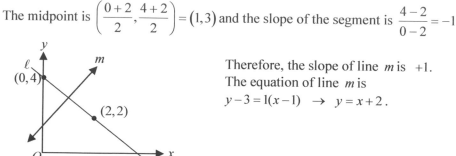

Therefore, the slope of line m is $+1$.
The equation of line m is
$y - 3 = 1(x - 1) \;\rightarrow\; y = x + 2$.

21. (C) $|3x - 5| < 10 \;\rightarrow\; -10 < 3x - 5 < 10 \;\rightarrow\; -5 < 3x < 15 \;\rightarrow\; \dfrac{-5}{3} < x < 5$

22. (E) From the graph, the middle line is 3, amplitude is 3, and period is 4π. The frequency is $\dfrac{2\pi}{4\pi} = \dfrac{1}{2}$.

$y = A\sin(Bx) + C$　　A : amplitude　　B : frequency　　C : middle line　　Period $= \dfrac{2\pi}{B}$

Therefore, the equation of the trigonometric graph is $y = 3\sin\dfrac{1}{2}x + 3$.

23. (B) The graph of $y = x^2 - 5x + 6$ is concave up which has a minimum on axis of symmetry.

The axis of symmetry is $x = \dfrac{-b}{2a} = \dfrac{5}{2} = 2.5$. Therefore, the minimum of y is

$f(2.5) = (2.5)^2 - 5(2.5) + 6 = -0.25$. The range is $y \geq -0.25$.

Or, by completing squared form, $y = (x - 2.5)^2 - 0.25$. You can use a graphing calculator.

24. (D) Cofunction: Since $\sin(x - 10)$ and $\cos(2x + 28)$ are cofunctions,
$x - 10 + 2x + 28 = 90$. Therefore, $3x = 72 \;\rightarrow\; x = 24$.

25. (C) Switch x and y, then express y in terms of x. Therefore,

$x = 3^{y+1} \;\rightarrow\; y + 1 = \log_3 x \;\rightarrow\; y = \log_3 x - 1 = \log_3 x - \log_3 3 = \log_3 \dfrac{x}{3}$.

26. (B) Since $f(x)$ is greater than 0 for all x, $f(x) = 0$ cannot have x-intercept (zeros).
Therefore, discriminant must be negative (imaginary roots).
$D = b^2 - 4ac = k^2 - 4(1)(9) < 0 \;\rightarrow\; (k + 6)(k - 6) < 0 \;\rightarrow\; -6 < k < 6$

27. (A) Complete squared form: $x^2 + 10x + \boxed{25} + y^2 + 6y + \boxed{9} = 10 + \boxed{25} + \boxed{9}$
$\rightarrow\; (x + 5)^2 + (y + 3)^2 = 44$
Therefore, the center is $(-5, -3)$.

28. (E)   Domain of the polynomial function is $2x - 10 \geq 0$ and $(x-2)(x-1) \neq 0$.

Therefore, $\{x \geq 5\} \cap \{x \neq 2,1\} = \{x \geq 5\}$.

29. (B)   Substitute $y = x^2$ into $x^2 + y^2 = 20$. Then $x^4 + x^2 - 20 = 0 \;\rightarrow\; (x^2 + 5)(x^2 - 4) = 0$

Since $x^2 + 5 \neq 0$, $x^2 - 4 = 0 \;\rightarrow\; x = 2$ or $x = -2$.

30. (D)   Switch x and y: $x = \log_2(y-1) + 2 \;\rightarrow\; x - 2 = \log_2(y-1)$

Therefore, $y - 1 = 2^{x-2} \;\rightarrow\; y = 2^{x-2} + 1$.

31. (C)   By the formula, $BD \cdot DC = 8^2 \;\rightarrow\; DC = \dfrac{64}{4} = 16$

$AC^2 = CD \cdot CB \;\rightarrow\; AC^2 = 16 \cdot 20 = 320 \;\rightarrow\; AC = \sqrt{320} \simeq 17.89$

32. (B) $|z - 2| = |4 - 6i - 2| = |2 - 6i|$, $|2 - 6i| = \sqrt{2^2 + (-6)^2} = \sqrt{40} \simeq 6.32$

33. (A)   The middle term is the 4th term.

The 4th term is $_6C_3(x)^3(-3y)^3 = -540x^3y^3$.

34. (E) $\left(\sqrt{x^2 + 6x + 9}\right)^2 = x^2 \;\rightarrow\; x = -1.5$ But $x \geq 0$. No solution.

Or, since $\sqrt{x^2 + 6x + 9} = \sqrt{(x+3)^2} = |x+3|$, then $|x+3| = x$.

If $x \geq -3$, $x + 3 = x \;\rightarrow\; 3 = 0$ No solution

If $x < -3$, $-x - 3 = x \;\rightarrow\; x = \dfrac{-3}{2}$ But $\dfrac{-3}{2}$ is not less than -3. No solution

35. (A)   From the recursive equation $a_{n+1} - a_n = 3$, it is arithmetic sequence with common difference 3 and the first term 1.

Therefore, $a_n = a_1 + (n-1)d = 1 + (n-1)(3) = 3n - 2$.

36. (A)   From original function, you can find $f^{-1}(4)$. The input of f^{-1} was the output of f.

Since, $x^2 + 2x - 4 = 4 \;\rightarrow\; x^2 + 2x - 8 = 0 \;\rightarrow\; (x+4)(x-2) = 0$, $x = 2$ $(x \geq 0)$.

This value of x is the output of f^{-1}. Therefore, $f^{-1}(4) = 2$.

37. (C)   The law of sines: $\dfrac{\sin 30}{6} = \dfrac{\sin B}{6\sqrt{3}} \;\rightarrow\; \sin B = \dfrac{6\sqrt{3}\sin 30}{6} = \dfrac{\sqrt{3}}{2}$

Therefore, $B = 60$ or 120.   Now find $\angle C$.

$$
\begin{array}{ll}
A: 30 & 30 \\
B: 60 & 120 \qquad \angle C = 90 \text{ or } 30. \\
C: 90 & 30
\end{array}
$$

38. (E)   Since $\log_2 5 = a$ and $\log_2 3 = b$,

$$\log_2 \sqrt{75} = \frac{1}{2}\log_2 75 = \frac{1}{2}\left(\log_2 5 \times 5 \times 3\right) = \frac{1}{2}\left(\log_2 5 + \log_2 5 \times \log_2 3\right)$$

$$= \frac{1}{2}\left(2a + b\right) = a + \frac{1}{2}b$$

39. (D)   Parametric equation: $x = 3\sin\theta$ and $y = 4\cos\theta$

From $\cos^2\theta + \sin^2\theta = 1$ (Pythagorean identity), $\sin\theta = \frac{x}{3}$, and $\cos\theta = \frac{y}{4}$

$\dfrac{x^2}{3^2} + \dfrac{y^2}{4^2} = 1$ $\rightarrow$ It is ellipse and major axis is on the y-axis. Graph (D) is correct.

40. (A)   Three sides of a triangle are given. Heron's formula: The area of the triangle is

$$A = \sqrt{s(s-a)(s-b)(s-c)}, \text{ where } s = \frac{a+b+c}{2}$$

Therefore, $s = \dfrac{4+5+7}{2} = 8$ and the area is $\sqrt{8(8-4)(8-5)(8-7)} \simeq 9.80$.

41. (B) $\dfrac{(n+1)!}{(n-1)!} = \dfrac{(n+1)n\,\cancel{(n-1)}!}{\cancel{(n-1)}!} = (n+1)n$, $n^2 + n = 56$ $\rightarrow$ $(n+8)(n-7) = 0$

Since $n \neq -8$, $n = 7$.

42. (D)

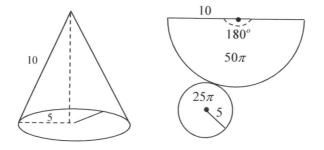

Since the circumference of the base is 10π and the circumference of the lateral side is 20π, lateral side is exactly a semicircle which has a central angle $180°$. Therefore, the surface area is $25\pi + 50\pi = 75\pi$.

Or, use the formula $S_f = \pi rs + \pi r^2$, s is a slant height. $\pi(5)(10) + \pi(5^2) = 75\pi$

43. (B)   Since $a_{11} = a + 10d = 30$ and $a_{21} = a + 20d = 0$,

$a + 10d = 30$

$\dfrac{a + 20d = 0}{-10d = 30}$ $\rightarrow$ $d = -3$ and $a = 60$.

Therefore, $a_{10} = a + 9d = 60 - 27 = 33$. Or, since $a_{10} + (-3) = a_{11}$, then $a_{11} = 30 - (-3) = 33$.

44. (D) $\displaystyle\lim_{n\to 1}\frac{n^2-1}{\left(\sqrt{n}-1\right)}=\lim_{n\to 1}\frac{(n-1)(n+1)(\sqrt{n}+1)}{(\sqrt{n}-1)(\sqrt{n}+1)}=\lim_{x\to 1}\frac{(n-1)(n+1)(\sqrt{n}+1)}{(n-1)}=\frac{2\times 2}{1}=4$

45. (D) Since $1+\dfrac{i\sqrt{3}}{2}$, the other root mist be $1-\dfrac{i\sqrt{3}}{2}$ (conjugate). Therefore,

$$0=\left[x-\left(1+\frac{i\sqrt{3}}{2}\right)\right]\left[x-\left(1-\frac{i\sqrt{3}}{2}\right)\right]=\left(x-1-\frac{i\sqrt{3}}{2}\right)\left(x-1+\frac{i\sqrt{3}}{2}\right)=(x-1)^2-\left(\frac{i\sqrt{3}}{2}\right)^2$$

When simplified, $x^2-2x+\dfrac{7}{4}=0$ is equivalent to $4x^2-8x+7=0$.

Therefore, $f(x)=4x^2-8x+7$.

Or,

1) Use sum and product of two root.

The equation is defined by $ax^2+bx+c=0 \;\rightarrow\; x^2+\dfrac{b}{a}x+\dfrac{c}{a}=0$.

Sum of roots $=\dfrac{-b}{a}=\left(1+\dfrac{i\sqrt{3}}{2}\right)+\left(1-\dfrac{i\sqrt{3}}{2}\right)=2 \;\rightarrow\; \dfrac{b}{a}=-2$

Product of roots $=\dfrac{c}{a}=\left(1+\dfrac{i\sqrt{3}}{2}\right)\left(1-\dfrac{i\sqrt{3}}{2}\right)=\dfrac{7}{4}$

When substitute, $x^2-2x+\dfrac{7}{4}=0 \;\rightarrow\; 4x^2-8x+7=0$.

2) Because the coefficients of the equation is real, let $x=1+\dfrac{i\sqrt{3}}{2}$.

$$x-1=\frac{i\sqrt{3}}{2} \;\rightarrow\; (x-1)^2=\left(\frac{i\sqrt{3}}{2}\right)^2 \;\rightarrow\; x^2-2x+1=-\frac{3}{4}$$

Therefore, the equation is $x^2-2x+\dfrac{7}{4}=0 \;\rightarrow\; 4x^2-8x+7=0$.

46. (B) Remainder Theorem:

Let $x^3-2x^2+mx+n=(x-1)(x-2)Q(x)$, where $Q(x)$ is the quotient.

When $x=1$, $1-2(1)+m(1)+n=0 \;\rightarrow\; m+n=1$ ----- (1)

When $x=2$, $8-2(4)+m(2)+n=0 \;\rightarrow\; 2m+n=0$ ------ (2)

$(2)-(1)$

$m=-1$ and $n=2$.

Or, you can solve it using long-division and synthetic division.

$$\begin{array}{r}
x+1 \\
x^2-3x+2\overline{\smash{\big)}\, x^3-2x^2+mx+n}
\end{array}$$

$$\begin{array}{r}
x^3-3x^2+2x \\
\hline
x^2+(m-2)x+n
\end{array}$$

Therefore, $m=-1$ and $n=2$.

$$\begin{array}{r}
x^2-3x+2 \\
\hline
(m+1)x+(n-2)
\end{array}$$

47. (E) If $f(x)$ and $g(x)$ are even, $f\times g=$ even, $f+g=$ even, and $f-g=$ even.
(E) is not even, because it is translated to the right by 1.

48. (D) Multiplying both sides by $(x-1)^2(x+2)^2\dfrac{-b\pm\sqrt{b^2-4ac}}{2a}$, it will be simplified as follows.

$$(x-1)^2(x+2)^2\dfrac{x}{(x-1)(x+2)}<0\times(x-1)^2(x+2)^2$$

$y=x(x-1)(x+2)<0$

Using graphic solution,

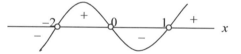

From the graph, the value of y is negative for $x<-2$ or $0<x<1$.

49. (C) Asymptote of hyperbola:

$$16x^2-25y^2=400 \quad\rightarrow\quad \dfrac{16x^2}{400}-\dfrac{25y^2}{400}=1 \quad\rightarrow\quad \dfrac{x^2}{25}+\dfrac{y^2}{16}=1$$

Since $a=5$ and $b=4$, the asymptote is $y=\pm\dfrac{4}{5}x.$

50. (C) In order to have two different real roots, discriminant $D=b^2-4ac>0$.
Since $16-4k(-2)>0$, $k>-2$. But the leading coefficient of quadratic equation cannot be zero.
$k\neq 0$. Therefore, $-2<k<0$ or $k>0$.

END

Test 2

Dr. John Chung's

SAT II Mathematics Level 2

MATHEMATICS LEVEL 2 TEST

REFERENCE INFORMATION

THE FOLLOWING INFORMATION IS FOR YOUR REFERENCE IN ANSWERING SOME OF THE QUESTIONS IN THIS TEST

Volume of a right circular cone with radius r and height h: $V = \dfrac{1}{3}\pi r^2 h$

Lateral Area of a right circular cone with circumference of the base c and slant height ℓ: $S = \dfrac{1}{2}c\ell$

Volume of a sphere with radius r: $V = \dfrac{4}{3}\pi r^3$

Surface Area of a sphere with radius r: $S = 4\pi r^2$

Volume of a pyramid with base area B and height h: $V = \dfrac{1}{3}Bh$

Dr. John Chung's SAT II Math Level 2

Answer Sheet

01 Ⓐ Ⓑ Ⓒ Ⓓ Ⓔ   26 Ⓐ Ⓑ Ⓒ Ⓓ Ⓔ
02 Ⓐ Ⓑ Ⓒ Ⓓ Ⓔ   27 Ⓐ Ⓑ Ⓒ Ⓓ Ⓔ
03 Ⓐ Ⓑ Ⓒ Ⓓ Ⓔ   28 Ⓐ Ⓑ Ⓒ Ⓓ Ⓔ
04 Ⓐ Ⓑ Ⓒ Ⓓ Ⓔ   29 Ⓐ Ⓑ Ⓒ Ⓓ Ⓔ
05 Ⓐ Ⓑ Ⓒ Ⓓ Ⓔ   30 Ⓐ Ⓑ Ⓒ Ⓓ Ⓔ
06 Ⓐ Ⓑ Ⓒ Ⓓ Ⓔ   31 Ⓐ Ⓑ Ⓒ Ⓓ Ⓔ
07 Ⓐ Ⓑ Ⓒ Ⓓ Ⓔ   32 Ⓐ Ⓑ Ⓒ Ⓓ Ⓔ
08 Ⓐ Ⓑ Ⓒ Ⓓ Ⓔ   33 Ⓐ Ⓑ Ⓒ Ⓓ Ⓔ
09 Ⓐ Ⓑ Ⓒ Ⓓ Ⓔ   34 Ⓐ Ⓑ Ⓒ Ⓓ Ⓔ
10 Ⓐ Ⓑ Ⓒ Ⓓ Ⓔ   35 Ⓐ Ⓑ Ⓒ Ⓓ Ⓔ
11 Ⓐ Ⓑ Ⓒ Ⓓ Ⓔ   36 Ⓐ Ⓑ Ⓒ Ⓓ Ⓔ
12 Ⓐ Ⓑ Ⓒ Ⓓ Ⓔ   37 Ⓐ Ⓑ Ⓒ Ⓓ Ⓔ
13 Ⓐ Ⓑ Ⓒ Ⓓ Ⓔ   38 Ⓐ Ⓑ Ⓒ Ⓓ Ⓔ
14 Ⓐ Ⓑ Ⓒ Ⓓ Ⓔ   39 Ⓐ Ⓑ Ⓒ Ⓓ Ⓔ
15 Ⓐ Ⓑ Ⓒ Ⓓ Ⓔ   40 Ⓐ Ⓑ Ⓒ Ⓓ Ⓔ
16 Ⓐ Ⓑ Ⓒ Ⓓ Ⓔ   41 Ⓐ Ⓑ Ⓒ Ⓓ Ⓔ
17 Ⓐ Ⓑ Ⓒ Ⓓ Ⓔ   42 Ⓐ Ⓑ Ⓒ Ⓓ Ⓔ
18 Ⓐ Ⓑ Ⓒ Ⓓ Ⓔ   43 Ⓐ Ⓑ Ⓒ Ⓓ Ⓔ
19 Ⓐ Ⓑ Ⓒ Ⓓ Ⓔ   44 Ⓐ Ⓑ Ⓒ Ⓓ Ⓔ
20 Ⓐ Ⓑ Ⓒ Ⓓ Ⓔ   45 Ⓐ Ⓑ Ⓒ Ⓓ Ⓔ
21 Ⓐ Ⓑ Ⓒ Ⓓ Ⓔ   46 Ⓐ Ⓑ Ⓒ Ⓓ Ⓔ
22 Ⓐ Ⓑ Ⓒ Ⓓ Ⓔ   47 Ⓐ Ⓑ Ⓒ Ⓓ Ⓔ
23 Ⓐ Ⓑ Ⓒ Ⓓ Ⓔ   48 Ⓐ Ⓑ Ⓒ Ⓓ Ⓔ
24 Ⓐ Ⓑ Ⓒ Ⓓ Ⓔ   49 Ⓐ Ⓑ Ⓒ Ⓓ Ⓔ
25 Ⓐ Ⓑ Ⓒ Ⓓ Ⓔ   50 Ⓐ Ⓑ Ⓒ Ⓓ Ⓔ

The number of right answers: ☐

The number of wrong answers: ☐

$$\underbrace{\boxed{}}_{\text{\# of correct}} - \frac{1}{4} \times \underbrace{\boxed{}}_{\text{\# of wrong}} = \underbrace{\boxed{}}_{\text{Raw score}}$$

Score Conversion Table

Raw Score	Scaled Score	Raw Score	Scaled Score	Raw Score	Scaled Score
50	800	28	640	6	480
49	800	27	630	5	470
48	800	26	620	4	470
47	800	25	620	3	460
46	800	24	610	2	460
45	800	23	610	1	450
44	800	22	600	0	450
43	800	21	600		
42	800	20	590		
41	800	19	590		
40	780	18	580		
39	760	17	570		
38	750	16	560		
37	740	15	550		
36	720	14	540		
35	710	13	530		
34	700	12	520		
33	690	11	510		
32	680	10	500		
31	670	9	490		
30	660	8	490		
29	650	7	480		

MATHEMATICS LEVEL 2 TEST

For each of the following problems, decide which is the BEST of the choices given. If the exact numerical value is not one of the choices, select the choice that best approximates this value. Then fill in the corresponding circle on the answer sheet

Note: (1) A scientific or graphing calculator will be necessary for answering some (but not all) of the questions in this test. For each question you will have to decide whether or not you should use a calculator.

(2) For some questions in this test you may have to decide whether your calculator should be in the radian mode or the degree mode.

(3) Figures that accompany problems in this test are intended to provide information useful in solving the problems. They are drawn as accurately as possible EXCEPT when it is stated in a specific problem that its figure is not drawn to scale. All figures lie in a plane unless otherwise indicated.

(4) Unless otherwise specified, the domain of any function f is assumed to be the set of all real numbers x for which $f(x)$ is a real number. The range of f is assumed to be the set of all real numbers $f(x)$, where x is in the domain of f.

(5) Reference information that may be useful in answering the questions in this test can be found on the page preceding Question 1.

USE THIS SPACE FOR SCRATCHWORK

1. If $\dfrac{x^2-1}{x+1} = 3x+5$, then $x+3 =$

    (A) −3
    (B) −2
    (C)   0
    (D)   2
    (E)   4

2. The slope of a line which contains the points $(a+3, -4)$
    and $(6a-2, 6)$ is $-\dfrac{1}{2}$. What is the value of a?

    (A) −3
    (B) −2
    (C)   2
    (D)   3
    (E)   5

GO ON TO THE NEXT PAGE

USE THIS SPACE FOR SCRATCHWORK.

3. What is the equation of a line whose x-intercept is 5 and y-intercept is -4?

(A) $4x + 5y = 15$
(B) $5x + 4y = 20$
(C) $4x - 5y = 15$
(D) $4x + 5y = 20$
(E) $4x - 5y = 20$

4. If $c - 5 = \sqrt{4c + 1}$, what is the value of c?

(A) 2
(B) 12
(C) 2 or 12
(D) -2
(E) -12

5. If $(a + b) + (a - b)i = 1 + 5i$, where a and b are real numbers, then $a =$

(A) 0
(B) 1
(C) 2
(D) 3
(E) 4

6. If $z_1 = 1 + 2i$ and $z_2 = 3 - 5i$, then $|z_1 + z_2| =$

(A) 10
(B) 5
(C) 4
(D) 3
(E) 2

7. If $90° \le \theta < 180°$ and $\sin \theta = \dfrac{1}{2}$, then $\sin(2\theta) =$

(A) -0.87
(B) -0.94
(C) -0.60
(D) 0.87
(E) 0.94

GO ON TO THE NEXT PAGE

MATHEMATICS LEVEL 2 TEST - *Continued*

8. If figure 1 shows the graph of $y = f(x)$, then which of the following is the graph of $y = f(-x)$?

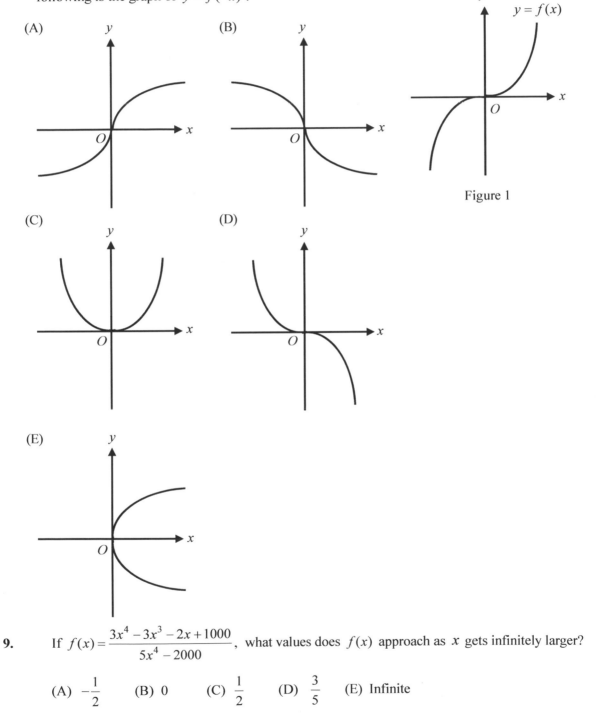

Figure 1

9. If $f(x) = \dfrac{3x^4 - 3x^3 - 2x + 1000}{5x^4 - 2000}$, what values does $f(x)$ approach as x gets infinitely larger?

(A) $-\dfrac{1}{2}$ (B) 0 (C) $\dfrac{1}{2}$ (D) $\dfrac{3}{5}$ (E) Infinite

GO ON TO THE NEXT PAGE

MATHEMATICS LEVEL 2 TEST - *Continued*

USE THIS SPACE FOR SCRATCHWORK.

10. In the graph of Figure 2, the equation of the graph is $y = A\cos(Bx + C) + D$. What is the value of B?

    (A) 6

    (B) 3

    (C) $\dfrac{\pi}{6}$

    (D) $\dfrac{\pi}{3}$

    (E) 6π

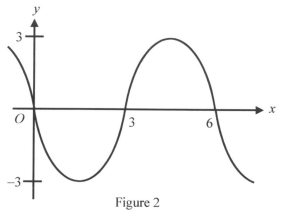

Figure 2

11. $\cos\left(\dfrac{3\pi}{2} - \theta\right) =$

    (A) $\sin\theta$
    (B) $\cos\theta$
    (C) $-\sin\theta$
    (D) $-\cos\theta$
    (E) $2\sin\theta\cos\theta$

12. In how many ways can 15 people be divided into two groups, one group with 10 and the other with 5 people?

    (A) 3003
    (B) 6006
    (C) 12000
    (D) 48600
    (E) 9018009

13. If the polar equation is $r = \sin\theta$, which of the following represents the graph?

    (A) An ellipse
    (B) A circle
    (C) A line
    (D) A parabola
    (E) A hyperbola

GO ON TO THE NEXT PAGE

MATHEMATICS LEVEL 2 TEST - *Continued*

14. Figure 3 shows a parallelogram with sides 10 and 15. If $\angle Q = 135°$, what is the area of the parallelogram?

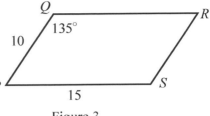

Figure 3

(A) 53.03
(B) 66.02
(C) 83.33
(D) 106.07
(E) 121.67

15. Figure 4 shows a rectangular solid. If the area of face I is 15, the area of face II is 20, and the area of face III is 18, then what is the volume of the solid?

(A) 67.48
(B) 73.48
(C) 88.98
(D) 96.76
(E) 101.44

Figure 4

16. If $180° < \theta < 270°$ and $\cos\theta = -0.707$, what is the value of $\tan\left(\dfrac{\theta}{2}\right)$?

(A) 2.414
(B) −2.414
(C) 3.424
(D) −3.424
(E) 1.414

17. What is the smallest positive value of x, in radian that satisfies the equation $3\sin x + \sin 2x = 0$?

(A) 0.01
(B) 2.14
(C) 3.14
(D) 6.28
(E) 9.42

GO ON TO THE NEXT PAGE

USE THIS SPACE FOR SCRATCHWORK.

18. Figure 5 shows the graph of $y = \log_2(2x)$. What is the sum of the areas of the three shaded rectangles?

   (A) 24
   (B) 32
   (C) 36
   (D) 42
   (E) 48

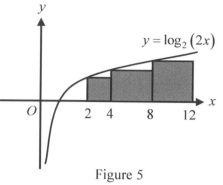

Figure 5

<u>Note</u>: Figure not drawn to scale.

19. The current population of Lake Pond is 50,000. The population at any time t can be calculated by the function $P(t) = Ae^{-0.025t}$, where A is initial population and t is the time in years. How many years would it take for the population to reach half the present population?

   (A) 12.4
   (B) 15.5
   (C) 18.4
   (D) 24.6
   (E) 27.7

20. Which of the following are asymptotes of the graph of $y = \dfrac{x^2 - 1}{x(x-1)}$?

   I. $x = 0$
   II. $x = 1$
   III. $y = 1$

   (A) I only
   (B) II only
   (C) I and II only
   (D) I and III only
   (E) I, II, and III

GO ON TO THE NEXT PAGE

USE THIS SPACE FOR SCRATCHWORK.

21. What is the range of the function defined by

$$f(x) = \begin{cases} \sqrt{x-1} & , \ x \geq -1 \\ 1-x^2 & , \ x < -1 \end{cases}$$

(A) $y \geq -1$

(B) $y < 0$

(C) $y \neq 0$

(D) $-1 < y < 1$

(E) All real numbers

22. If $|x-3| - y + 2 = 0$ and $x - y + 2 = 0$, then $x =$

(A) 0.5

(B) 1.0

(C) 1.5

(D) 2.0

(E) 2.5

23. If the 5th term of a geometric sequence is 24, and the 7th term is 144, what is the first term of the sequence?

(A) 2

(B) $\dfrac{3}{2}$

(C) $\dfrac{2}{3}$

(D) $\dfrac{1}{3}$

(E) $\dfrac{1}{4}$

24. If a cube is inscribed inside a sphere of radius 10, what is the volume of the cube?

(A) 1539.60

(B) 1450.56

(C) 1300.48

(D) 1148.04

(E) 1200

GO ON TO THE NEXT PAGE

USE THIS SPACE FOR SCRATCHWORK.

25. If $\sin x + 2\cos x = 0$, where $0 \le x < 2\pi$, then x could equal

(A) 1.017
(B) 1.107
(C) 2.034
(D) 2.412
(E) 3.003

26. Figure 6 shows a cube with edge 10. What is the area of triangle *ABC* ?

(A) 129.90
(B) 88.83
(C) 86.60
(D) 82.37
(E) 50.00

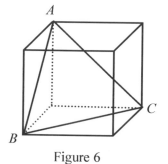

Figure 6

27. $\dfrac{\left[(n+1)!\right]^2}{\left[(n-1)!\right]^2} =$

(A) $n+1$

(B) n^2

(C) $n^2 - n$

(D) $n^2(n+1)^2$

(E) $(n+1)(n-1)$

28. For all θ, $\sin(90° - \theta) + \cos(180° - \theta) - \tan(180° - \theta) =$

(A) $\sin\theta$
(B) $\cos\theta$
(C) $\tan\theta$
(D) $\sin\theta - \cos\theta$
(E) $\cos\theta - \sin\theta$

GO ON TO THE NEXT PAGE

MATHEMATICS LEVEL 2 TEST - *Continued*

USE THIS SPACE FOR SCRATCHWORK.

29.   If $f(2x-3)=4x-2$, $f(x)=$

   (A) $x+4$
   (B) $x-4$
   (C) $2x+4$
   (D) $3x+5$
   (E) $3x-5$

30.   If a circle is defined by the equation $x^2-10x+y^2-2y=10$,
      what are the coordinates of the center of the circle?

   (A) $(5,1)$
   (B) $(5,-1)$
   (C) $(-5,1)$
   (D) $(-5,-1)$
   (E) $(-10,-2)$

31.   If x, 12, $3x-6$,… are the first three terms in a geometric
      progression, then the 5th term could be

   (A) 1.5
   (B) 36.5
   (C) 40.5
   (D) 60
   (E) 96

32.   The multiplicative inverse of $\dfrac{1-i}{3+i}$ is

   (A) $\dfrac{1-2i}{10}$
   (B) $2-i$
   (C) $1+2i$
   (D) $2+i$
   (E) $\dfrac{3-i}{2}$

GO ON TO THE NEXT PAGE

MATHEMATICS LEVEL 2 TEST - *Continued*

USE THIS SPACE FOR SCRATCHWORK.

33. The value of $\sin\left(2\cos^{-1}\left(\dfrac{1}{2}\right)\right) =$

(A) $\dfrac{1}{3}$

(B) $\dfrac{\sqrt{3}}{2}$

(C) $-\dfrac{\sqrt{3}}{2}$

(D) $\dfrac{2\sqrt{2}}{3}$

(E) $-\dfrac{2\sqrt{2}}{3}$

34. Figure 7 shows the graph of $p(x) = ax^3 + bx^2 + cx + d$.
    Which of the following must be true.

(A) $b > 0$
(B) $a < 0$
(C) $b = 0$
(D) $b < 0$
(E) $d > 0$

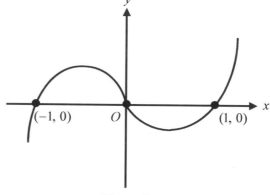

Figure 7

35. A solution for the equation $\cos^2 x + 2\sin x + 7 = 0$, where
    $0 < x \le 2\pi$, is

(A) 4   (B) -2 (C) $\dfrac{\pi}{4}$ (D) $-\dfrac{\pi}{2}$ (E) No solution

36. What is the period of the graph of $y = 2\sin(3\pi x - \pi) + 1$?

(A) π

(B) $\dfrac{2\pi}{3}$

(C) $\dfrac{2}{3}$

(D) $\dfrac{\pi}{3}$

(E) 2π

GO ON TO THE NEXT PAGE

MATHEMATICS LEVEL 2 TEST - *Continued*

37.   Which of the following could be the graph of $f(x) = x - [x]$?

(A)   (B)

(C)   (D)

(D)

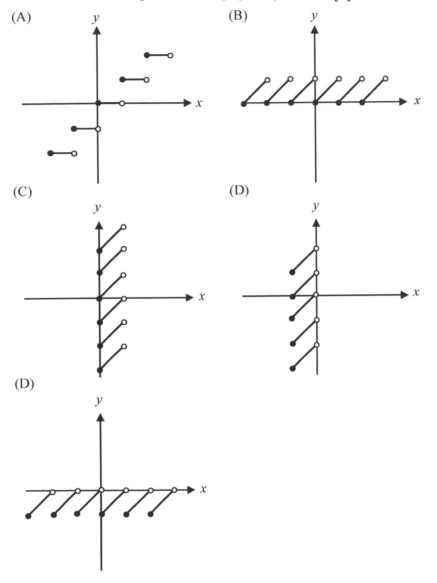

38.   If a function f has the property of the fundamental period such that $f(x) = f(x+2)$, which of the following could be f ?

    (A) $2\sin x + 1$

    (B) $\sin 2x$

    (C) $\cos 2x - 1$

    (D) $3\tan 2x$

    (E) $4\tan \dfrac{\pi}{2} x$

GO ON TO THE NEXT PAGE

USE THIS SPACE FOR SCRATCHWORK.

39. $\lim\limits_{h \to 0} \dfrac{h}{\sqrt{4+h}-2} =$

    (A) 0
    (B) 2
    (C) 4
    (D) Infinite
    (E) Undefined

40. In Figure 8, if $BD = 10$, what is the length of $\overline{AC}$?

    (A) 20
    (B) 25.12
    (C) 34.64
    (D) 36
    (E) 36.56

Figure 8

41. Which of the following is the equation of the common chord of the circles with equations $x^2 + y^2 = 16$ and $x^2 + y^2 - 8x - 8y + 16 = 0$?

    (A) $y = x$
    (B) $y = -x$
    (C) $y = x + 4$
    (D) $y = x - 4$
    (E) $y = -x + 4$

42. Which of the following functions are odd?

    I. $f(x) = x^4 + 5x^2 - 3$

    II. $f(x) = 3x^3 + 5x + 1$

    III. $f(x) = x^3 + x$

    (A) I only
    (B) II only
    (C) III only
    (D) II and III
    (E) I, II, and III

GO ON TO THE NEXT PAGE

MATHEMATICS LEVEL 2 TEST - *Continued*

USE THIS SPACE FOR SCRATCHWORK.

43. Figure 9 is a tetrahedron such that $\overline{OB} \perp \overline{OA} \perp \overline{OC}$ and $OA = 4$, $OB = 3$, and $OC = 4$. What is the area of $\triangle ABC$?

(A) 11.66
(B) 16.42
(C) 18.44
(D) 20.25
(E) 21.32

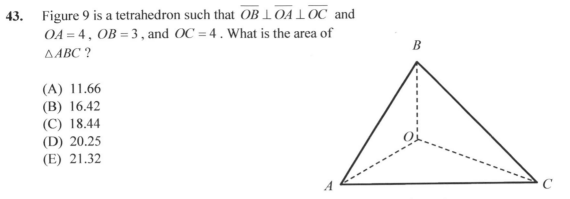

Figure 9

44. $3^{\log_9 18} =$

(A) $3\sqrt{2}$
(B) $3\sqrt{3}$
(C) $2\sqrt{5}$
(D) $2\sqrt{6}$
(E) $2\sqrt{7}$

45. If $\sin x = t$ for all x in the interval $\frac{\pi}{2} < x < \pi$,

then $\sin 2x =$

(A) $\dfrac{t}{\sqrt{1-t^2}}$

(B) $\dfrac{t^2}{1-t^2}$

(C) $\dfrac{1}{t\sqrt{1-t}}$

(D) $-2t\sqrt{1-t^2}$

(E) $2t\sqrt{t^2-1}$

GO ON TO THE NEXT PAGE

USE THIS SPACE FOR SCRATCHWORK.

46. If a vector $\vec{a} = (5, -12)$, then which of the following is the unit vector of $\vec{a}$?

   (A) $(1, -1)$

   (B) $\left(\dfrac{1}{5}, \dfrac{-1}{12}\right)$

   (C) $(0.38, -0.92)$

   (D) $(0.5, -1)$

   (E) $(0.25, -0.75)$

47. In Figure 10, if $\overline{OH}$ is perpendicular to the line $3x - 4y = 28$, what is the length of $\overline{OH}$?

   (A) 5.6
   (B) 6.5
   (C) 8.0
   (D) 8.5
   (E) 8.7

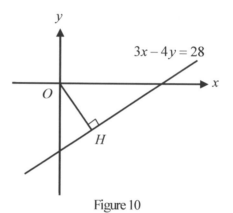

Figure 10

48. If matrix A has dimension $m \times n$, matrix B has dimension $p \times m$, and matrix C has dimension $n \times p$, which of the following must be true?

   (A) The product AB exists.
   (B) The product BC exists.
   (C) The product ABC exists.
   (D) The product CBA exists.
   (E) The product BCA exists.

49. If the height of a cylinder is increased by 10 percent, by what percent must the radius of the circular base be increased so that the volume of the cylinder is increased by 25 percent?

   (A) 5.6%
   (B) 6.2%
   (C) 6.6%
   (D) 7.5%
   (E) 7.7%

GO ON TO THE NEXT PAGE

USE THIS SPACE FOR SCRATCHWORK.

50.   If the binomial expansion is defined by

$$(x+y)^n = {}_nC_0 x^n y^o + {}_nC_1 x^{n-1} y^1 + {}_nC_2 x^{n-2} y^2 + ... + {}_nC_n x^o y^n,$$

then ${}_nC_1 + {}_nC_2 + {}_nC_3 + ... + {}_nC_n =$

(A) $\dfrac{n(n+1)}{2}$

(B) $n^2 + n$

(C) 2^{n+1}

(D) $2^n - 1$

(E) $2^n + 2^{n-1}$

STOP

IF YOU FINISH BEFORE TIME IS CALLED, YOU MAY CHECK YOUR WORK ON THIS TEST ONLY.

DO NOT TURN TO ANY OTHER TEST IN THIS BOOK.

No Test Material on This Page

TEST 2			ANSWERS						
#	answer	#	answer	#	answer	#	answer	#	answer
1	C	11	C	21	E	31	C	41	E
2	A	12	A	22	C	32	C	42	C
3	E	13	B	23	C	33	B	43	A
4	B	14	D	24	A	34	C	44	A
5	D	15	B	25	C	35	E	45	D
6	B	16	B	26	C	36	C	46	C
7	A	17	C	27	D	37	B	47	A
8	D	18	B	28	C	38	E	48	D
9	D	19	E	29	C	39	C	49	C
10	D	20	D	30	A	40	C	50	D

Explanations: Test 2

1. (C)   Since $\dfrac{x^2-1}{x+1} = \dfrac{(x-1)(x+1)}{(x+1)} = x-1$, then $x-1 = 3x+5 \;\rightarrow\; x=-3$.

Therefore, $x+3 = -3+3 = 0$.

2. (A)   Since $\dfrac{6-\,^-4}{6a-2-(a+3)} = \dfrac{10}{5a-5} = \dfrac{2}{a-1}$, then $\dfrac{2}{a-1} = -\dfrac{1}{2}$. Therefore, $a=-3$.

3. (E)   The equation is $\dfrac{x}{5} + \dfrac{y}{(-4)} = 1$. Therefore, $4x-5y=20$.

Or, $y = mx-4$ passes through a point $(4,0)$. Therefore, by substitution, $m = \dfrac{4}{5}$.

4. (B) $(c-5)^2 = \left(\sqrt{4c+1}\right)^2 \;\rightarrow\; c^2-14c+24=0 \;\rightarrow\; (c-2)(c-12)=0$

$c=2$, 12.   From the equation, $c \ge 5$.   Hence $c=12$.

5. (D)   Complex number identity:

$a+b=1$

$\dfrac{a-b=5}{2a\;\;=6}$ Hence $a=3$.

6. (B) $z_1 + z_2 = 1+2i+3-5i = 4-3i$, $|z_1+z_2| = |4-3i| = \sqrt{4^2+(-3)^2} = 5$

7. (A) $\sin\theta = \dfrac{1}{2}$ in the second quadrant $(90 \le \theta < 180)$, then $\cos\theta = \dfrac{-\sqrt{3}}{2}$.

Therefore, $\sin(2\theta) = 2\sin\theta\cos\theta = 2\left(\dfrac{1}{2}\right)\left(\dfrac{-\sqrt{3}}{2}\right) = \dfrac{-\sqrt{3}}{2} = -0.87$.

8. (D) $y = f(-x)$ is a reflection with y-axis. (D) is correct.

9. (D) $\lim\limits_{x \to \infty} \dfrac{3x^4 - 3x^3 - 2x + 1000}{5x^4 - 2000} = \dfrac{3}{5}$

10. (D)   From the graph, period is 6. Frequency $B = \dfrac{2\pi}{P(\text{period})} = \dfrac{2\pi}{6} = \dfrac{\pi}{3}$.

11. (C) $\cos\left(\dfrac{3\pi}{2} - \theta\right) = \cos\left(\dfrac{3\pi}{2}\right)\cos\theta + \sin\left(\dfrac{3\pi}{2}\right)\sin\theta = 0 \cdot \cos\theta + (-1)\sin\theta = -\sin\theta$

12. (A) $_{15}C_{10} = \;_{15}C_5 \quad \rightarrow \quad _{15}C_5 = \dfrac{15 \times 14 \times 13 \times 12 \times 11}{5!} = 3003$

13. (B)   Since $\sin\theta = \dfrac{y}{r}$, $r = \sin\theta \;\rightarrow\; r = \dfrac{y}{r} \;\rightarrow\; r^2 = y$. $r^2 = x^2 + y^2$ in rectangular coordinates.

Therefore, $x^2 + y^2 = y \;\rightarrow\; x^2 + y^2 - y = 0$ represents a circle.

The equation of the circle is $x^2 + \left(y - \dfrac{1}{2}\right)^2 = \dfrac{1}{4}$.

14. (D)   The area $= 10 \times 15 \times \sin 135 \simeq 106.07$

15. (B)   Let the dimensions of the solid be $a, b,$ and c. The volume of the solid is $V = abc$.
Therefore, the areas of each face are as follows. Multiply both sides and find the volume.

$\quad ab = 15$

$\quad bc = 20$

$\quad \dfrac{ca = 18}{(abc)^2 = 5400} \qquad \therefore V = abc = \sqrt{5400} = 73.48.$

16. (B) $\theta = \cos^{-1}(-0.707) = 135°$, but $\theta = 225°$ where $180° < \theta < 270°$. Therefore,

$\tan\dfrac{225}{2} \simeq -2.414.$

17. (C) $3\sin x + \sin 2x = 0 \;\rightarrow\; 3\sin x + 2\sin x \cos x = 0 \;\rightarrow\; \sin x(3 + 2\cos x) = 0$

Therefore, $\sin x = 0 \;\rightarrow\; x = \pi, 2\pi, \ldots$ and $\cos x \neq \dfrac{-3}{2} \;(-1 < \cos x < 1)$.

The smallest positive number is $\pi \simeq 3.14$.

18. (B)   Sum of the areas:

$2(\log_2 4) + 4(\log_2 8) + 4(\log_2 16) = 2(\log_2 2^2) + 4(\log_2 2^3) + 4(\log_2 2^4)$

$= 4 + 12 + 16 = 32$

19. (E) Calculator will be needed.

$$25,000 = 50,000e^{-0.025t} \rightarrow \frac{1}{2} = e^{-0.025t} \rightarrow t = \frac{\ln 0.5}{-0.025} \simeq 27.7$$

20. (D) Since $y = \dfrac{(x-1)(x+1)}{x(x-1)} = \dfrac{x+1}{x}$, then

Denominator: $x = 0$ (Vertical asymptote)

$y = \lim\limits_{x \to \infty} \dfrac{x+1}{x} = 1$ (Horizontal asymptote).

21. (E) The range of $f(x)$ is all real from the graph below. $R_y = (-\infty, +\infty)$

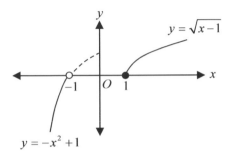

22. (C) If $x \geq 3$,

$$x - 3 - y + 2 = 0 \rightarrow x - y - 1 = 0$$
$$\underline{-)\ x - y + 2 = 0} \qquad \text{No solution.}$$
$$-3 = 0$$

If $x < 3$,

$$-x + 3 - y + 2 = 0 \rightarrow -x - y + 5 = 0$$
$$\underline{-)\ x - y + 2 = 0} \qquad \text{Therefore, } x = \frac{3}{2} = 1.5.$$
$$-2x + 3 = 0$$

23. (C) Geometric sequence:

$\begin{matrix} a_5 = ar^4 = 24 \\ a_7 = ar^6 = 144 \end{matrix}$, $\dfrac{a_7}{a_5} = \dfrac{ar^6}{ar^4} = r^2 = 6$. Therefore, $a(6)^2 = 24 \rightarrow a = \dfrac{24}{36} = \dfrac{2}{3}$.

24. (A) Let the length of a side of the cube be x. Since the length of the diagonal of the cube is equal to the diameter of the sphere, $\sqrt{x^2 + x^2 + x^2} = x\sqrt{3} \rightarrow x\sqrt{3} = 20 \rightarrow x = \dfrac{20}{\sqrt{3}}$.

Therefore, the volume of the cube is $x^3 = \left(\dfrac{20}{\sqrt{3}}\right)^3 \simeq 1539.60$.

25. (C) $\sin x + 2\cos x = 0 \rightarrow \sin x = -2\cos x \rightarrow \dfrac{\sin x}{\cos x} = -2 \rightarrow \tan x = -2$

$x = \tan^{-1}(-2) \simeq -1.1071$. Therefore $x \simeq 2.035$ or 5.176 in the interval $[0, 2\pi)$.

Or, use your graphing calculator.

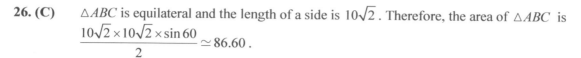

26. (C) $\triangle ABC$ is equilateral and the length of a side is $10\sqrt{2}$. Therefore, the area of $\triangle ABC$ is
$$\frac{10\sqrt{2}\times 10\sqrt{2}\times\sin 60}{2}\simeq 86.60.$$

27. (D) $\dfrac{\left[(n+1)!\right]^2}{\left[(n-1)!\right]^2}=\left((n+1)n\right)^2=(n+1)^2n^2$

28. (C)   Trigonometry identities:
$\sin(90-\theta)+\cos(180-\theta)-\tan(180-\theta)$

$=\left(\sin 90\cos\theta-\cos 90\sin\theta\right)+\left(\cos 180\cos\theta+\sin 180\sin\theta\right)-\left(\dfrac{\tan 180-\tan\theta}{1+\tan 180\tan\theta}\right)$

$=\cos\theta+(-\cos\theta)-(-\tan\theta)=\tan\theta$

29. (C)   Since $f(2x-3)=2(2x-3)+4$, then $f(x)=2x+4$.

Or, change variable : $f(2k-3)=4k-2$ and let $x=2k-3$ and $k=\dfrac{x+3}{2}$. Then replace with x.

Therefore, $f(x)=4\left(\dfrac{x+3}{2}\right)-2=2x+4$.

30. (A) $x^2-10x+y^2-2y=10\ \rightarrow\ (x-5)^2+(y-1)^2=36$
Center is at (5, 1).

31. (C)   The common ratio between two consecutive terms of geometric progress is equal.
hence $\dfrac{12}{x}=\dfrac{3x-6}{12}$. From the equation

$3x^2-6x-144=0\ \rightarrow\ x^2-2x-48=0\ \rightarrow\ (x-8)(x+6)=0\ \rightarrow\ x=8$ or -6.

If $x=8$, then $r=\dfrac{3}{2}$ and $a_5=8\left(\dfrac{3}{2}\right)^4=40.5$.

If $x=-6$, then $r=\dfrac{12}{-6}=-2$ and $a_5=(-6)(-2)^4=-96$.

32. (C)   The multiplicative inverse of $\dfrac{1-i}{3+i}$ is $\dfrac{3+i}{1-i}\ \rightarrow\ \dfrac{(3+i)(1+i)}{(1-i)(1+i)}=\dfrac{2+4i}{2}=1+2i$.

33. (B)   Use your calculator.
Or, $\theta=\cos^{-1}\dfrac{1}{2}\ \rightarrow\ \cos\theta=\dfrac{1}{2}$, where $0<\theta<\pi$.

Because $\sin\theta=\dfrac{\sqrt{3}}{2}$, $\sin 2\theta=2\sin\theta\cos\theta=2\left(\dfrac{\sqrt{3}}{2}\right)\left(\dfrac{1}{2}\right)=\dfrac{\sqrt{3}}{2}$.

Or, $\theta=60$ and $\sin 2\theta=\sin 120=\dfrac{\sqrt{3}}{2}$.

34. (C) From the graph, $a > 0$ and the sum of the roots is $\dfrac{-b}{a} = (-1 + 0 + 1) = 0 \;\rightarrow\; b = 0$.

And product of the root is $\dfrac{-d}{a} = (-1)(0)(1) = 0 \;\rightarrow\; d = 0$.

Or, find $p(0) = d = 0$, $p(1) = a + b + c = 0$, and $p(-1) = -a + b - c = 0$, and solve it.

35. (E) $\cos^2 x + 2\sin x + 7 = 0 \;\rightarrow\; (1 - \sin^2 x) + 2\sin x + 7 = 0 \;\rightarrow\; \sin^2 x - 2\sin x - 8 = 0$
$(\sin x - 4)(\sin x + 2) = 0 \;\rightarrow\; \sin x \neq 4$ or $\sin x \neq -2$. No solution.

36. (C) $y = 2\sin(3\pi x - \pi) + 1 \;\rightarrow\; y = 2\sin 3\pi\left(x - \dfrac{1}{3}\right) + 1$

From the equation frequency is 3π and period is $P = \dfrac{2\pi}{3\pi} = \dfrac{2}{3}$.

37. (B) $f(x) = x - [x]$. For the following intervals,

$$\begin{cases} 0 \le x < 1, & f(x) = x \\ 1 \le x < 2, & f(x) = x - 1 \\ 2 \le x < 3, & f(x) = x - 2 \\ \ldots \end{cases}$$

(B) is correct.

38. (E) $f(x) = f(x + 2)$ is a periodic function with the fundamental period 2.

(A) period $= 2\pi$ (B) period $= \dfrac{2\pi}{2} = \pi$ (C) period $= \dfrac{2\pi}{2} = \pi$

(D) period $= \dfrac{\pi}{2}$ (E) period $= \dfrac{\pi}{\pi/2} = 2$

39. (C) $\displaystyle\lim_{h \to 0} \frac{h}{\sqrt{4+h} - 2} = \lim_{h \to 0} \frac{h(\sqrt{4+h} + 2)}{(\sqrt{4+h} - 2)(\sqrt{4+h} + 2)} = \lim_{h \to 0} \frac{h(\sqrt{4+h} + 2)}{h} = 4$

40. (C)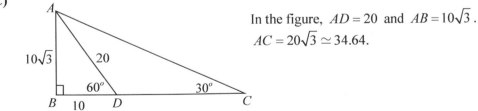

In the figure, $AD = 20$ and $AB = 10\sqrt{3}$.
$AC = 20\sqrt{3} \simeq 34.64$.

41. (E) From the equation $x^2 + y^2 - 8x - 8y + 16 = 0$ and $x^2 + y^2 = 16$
$16 - 8x - 8y + 16 = 0 \;\rightarrow\; 8x + 8y - 32 = 0 \;\rightarrow\; y = -x + 4$

42. (C) $f(x) = x^3 + x$: odd function + odd function = odd function

43. (A) By Pythagorean Theorem, $AC = 5$, $BC = 5$, and $4\sqrt{2}$.

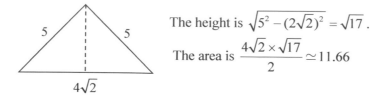

The height is $\sqrt{5^2 - (2\sqrt{2})^2} = \sqrt{17}$.

The area is $\dfrac{4\sqrt{2} \times \sqrt{17}}{2} \simeq 11.66$

Or, use Heron's formula. $A = \sqrt{s(s-a)(s-b)(s-c)}$, where $s = \dfrac{a+b+c}{2}$.

44. (A) By the logarithmic operation : $\log_a b = \log_{\sqrt{a}} \sqrt{b} = \log_{a^2} b^2$

$3^{\log_9 18} = 3^{\log_3 \sqrt{18}} = \sqrt{18} = 3\sqrt{2}$

45. (D) If $\sin x = t$ on $\dfrac{\pi}{2} < x < \pi$, then $\cos x = \dfrac{-\sqrt{1-t^2}}{1}$.

Therefore, $\sin 2x = 2\sin x \cos x = 2(t)(-\sqrt{1-t^2}) = -2t\sqrt{1-t^2}$.

46. (C) Since unit vector $\vec{u} = \dfrac{\vec{a}}{|\vec{a}|}$ and $|\vec{a}| = \sqrt{5^2 + (-12)^2} = 13$, then

$\vec{u} = \dfrac{(5,-12)}{13} = \left(\dfrac{5}{13}, \dfrac{-12}{13}\right) \simeq (0.38, -0.92)$.

47. (A) The distance from $(0,0)$ to the line $3x - 4y - 28 = 0$ is $D = \dfrac{|3(0) - 4(0) - 28|}{\sqrt{3^2 + 4^2}} = \dfrac{28}{5} = 5.6$.

48. (D) (A) $AB = [m \times n][p \times m]$ doesn't exist

(B) $BC = [p \times m][n \times p]$ doesn't exist

(C) $ABC = [m \times n][p \times m][n \times p]$ doesn't exist

(D) $CBA = [n \times p][p \times m][m \times n]$ exist

(E) $BCA = [p \times m][n \times p][m \times n]$ doesn't exist

49. (C) Let the volume be $V = \pi r^2 h$ and new radius be R. Since h increased by 10% and

V increased by 25%, $1.25V = \pi R^2 (1.1h)$ $\rightarrow$ $1.25\pi r^2 h = \pi R^2 (1.1h)$ $\rightarrow$ $\dfrac{R^2}{r^2} = \dfrac{1.25\pi h}{1.1\pi h}$

$\dfrac{R}{r} = \sqrt{\dfrac{1.25}{1.1}} = 1.066 = 1 + 0.066$ Therefore, the radius is increased by 6.6%.

50. (D)   In order to find the sum of the coefficients of the binomial expansion, substitute $x = y = 1$.

$$(1+1)^n = {}_nC_0 + {}_nC_1 + {}_nC_2 + \ldots\ldots + {}_nC_n$$

$$2^n = 1 + {}_nC_1 + {}_nC_2 + \ldots\ldots + {}_nC_n$$

$$2^n - 1 = {}_nC_1 + {}_nC_2 + \ldots\ldots + {}_nC_n$$

END

No Test Material on This Page

Test 3

Dr. John Chung's

SAT II Mathematics Level 2

MATHEMATICS LEVEL 2 TEST

REFERENCE INFORMATION

THE FOLLOWING INFORMATION IS FOR YOUR REFERENCE IN ANSWERING SOME OF THE QUESTIONS IN THIS TEST

Volume of a right circular cone with radius r and height h: $V = \dfrac{1}{3}\pi r^2 h$

Lateral Area of a right circular cone with circumference of the base c and slant height ℓ: $S = \dfrac{1}{2}c\ell$

Volume of a sphere with radius r: $V = \dfrac{4}{3}\pi r^3$

Surface Area of a sphere with radius r: $S = 4\pi r^2$

Volume of a pyramid with base area B and height h: $V = \dfrac{1}{3}Bh$

Dr. John Chung's SAT II Math Level 2

Answer Sheet

01 Ⓐ Ⓑ Ⓒ Ⓓ Ⓔ		26 Ⓐ Ⓑ Ⓒ Ⓓ Ⓔ
02 Ⓐ Ⓑ Ⓒ Ⓓ Ⓔ		27 Ⓐ Ⓑ Ⓒ Ⓓ Ⓔ
03 Ⓐ Ⓑ Ⓒ Ⓓ Ⓔ		28 Ⓐ Ⓑ Ⓒ Ⓓ Ⓔ
04 Ⓐ Ⓑ Ⓒ Ⓓ Ⓔ		29 Ⓐ Ⓑ Ⓒ Ⓓ Ⓔ
05 Ⓐ Ⓑ Ⓒ Ⓓ Ⓔ		30 Ⓐ Ⓑ Ⓒ Ⓓ Ⓔ
06 Ⓐ Ⓑ Ⓒ Ⓓ Ⓔ		31 Ⓐ Ⓑ Ⓒ Ⓓ Ⓔ
07 Ⓐ Ⓑ Ⓒ Ⓓ Ⓔ		32 Ⓐ Ⓑ Ⓒ Ⓓ Ⓔ
08 Ⓐ Ⓑ Ⓒ Ⓓ Ⓔ		33 Ⓐ Ⓑ Ⓒ Ⓓ Ⓔ
09 Ⓐ Ⓑ Ⓒ Ⓓ Ⓔ		34 Ⓐ Ⓑ Ⓒ Ⓓ Ⓔ
10 Ⓐ Ⓑ Ⓒ Ⓓ Ⓔ		35 Ⓐ Ⓑ Ⓒ Ⓓ Ⓔ
11 Ⓐ Ⓑ Ⓒ Ⓓ Ⓔ		36 Ⓐ Ⓑ Ⓒ Ⓓ Ⓔ
12 Ⓐ Ⓑ Ⓒ Ⓓ Ⓔ		37 Ⓐ Ⓑ Ⓒ Ⓓ Ⓔ
13 Ⓐ Ⓑ Ⓒ Ⓓ Ⓔ		38 Ⓐ Ⓑ Ⓒ Ⓓ Ⓔ
14 Ⓐ Ⓑ Ⓒ Ⓓ Ⓔ		39 Ⓐ Ⓑ Ⓒ Ⓓ Ⓔ
15 Ⓐ Ⓑ Ⓒ Ⓓ Ⓔ		40 Ⓐ Ⓑ Ⓒ Ⓓ Ⓔ
16 Ⓐ Ⓑ Ⓒ Ⓓ Ⓔ		41 Ⓐ Ⓑ Ⓒ Ⓓ Ⓔ
17 Ⓐ Ⓑ Ⓒ Ⓓ Ⓔ		42 Ⓐ Ⓑ Ⓒ Ⓓ Ⓔ
18 Ⓐ Ⓑ Ⓒ Ⓓ Ⓔ		43 Ⓐ Ⓑ Ⓒ Ⓓ Ⓔ
19 Ⓐ Ⓑ Ⓒ Ⓓ Ⓔ		44 Ⓐ Ⓑ Ⓒ Ⓓ Ⓔ
20 Ⓐ Ⓑ Ⓒ Ⓓ Ⓔ		45 Ⓐ Ⓑ Ⓒ Ⓓ Ⓔ
21 Ⓐ Ⓑ Ⓒ Ⓓ Ⓔ		46 Ⓐ Ⓑ Ⓒ Ⓓ Ⓔ
22 Ⓐ Ⓑ Ⓒ Ⓓ Ⓔ		47 Ⓐ Ⓑ Ⓒ Ⓓ Ⓔ
23 Ⓐ Ⓑ Ⓒ Ⓓ Ⓔ		48 Ⓐ Ⓑ Ⓒ Ⓓ Ⓔ
24 Ⓐ Ⓑ Ⓒ Ⓓ Ⓔ		49 Ⓐ Ⓑ Ⓒ Ⓓ Ⓔ
25 Ⓐ Ⓑ Ⓒ Ⓓ Ⓔ		50 Ⓐ Ⓑ Ⓒ Ⓓ Ⓔ

The number of right answers: ☐

The number of wrong answers: ☐

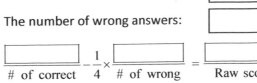

$$\underset{\text{\# of correct}}{\boxed{}} - \frac{1}{4} \times \underset{\text{\# of wrong}}{\boxed{}} = \underset{\text{Raw score}}{\boxed{}}$$

Score Conversion Table

Raw Score	Scaled Score	Raw Score	Scaled Score	Raw Score	Scaled Score
50	800	28	640	6	480
49	800	27	630	5	470
48	800	26	620	4	470
47	800	25	620	3	460
46	800	24	610	2	460
45	800	23	610	1	450
44	800	22	600	0	450
43	800	21	600		
42	800	20	590		
41	800	19	590		
40	780	18	580		
39	760	17	570		
38	750	16	560		
37	740	15	550		
36	720	14	540		
35	710	13	530		
34	700	12	520		
33	690	11	510		
32	680	10	500		
31	670	9	490		
30	660	8	490		
29	650	7	480		

MATHEMATICS LEVEL 2 TEST

For each of the following problems, decide which is the BEST of the choices given. If the exact numerical value is not one of the choices, select the choice that best approximates this value. Then fill in the corresponding circle on the answer sheet

Note: (1) A scientific or graphing calculator will be necessary for answering some (but not all) of the questions in this test. For each question you will have to decide whether or not you should use a calculator.

(2) For some questions in this test you may have to decide whether your calculator should be in the radian mode or the degree mode.

(3) Figures that accompany problems in this test are intended to provide information useful in solving the problems. They are drawn as accurately as possible EXCEPT when it is stated in a specific problem that its figure is not drawn to scale. All figures lie in a plane unless otherwise indicated.

(4) Unless otherwise specified, the domain of any function f is assumed to be the set of all real numbers x for which $f(x)$ is a real number. The range of f is assumed to be the set of all real numbers $f(x)$, where x is in the domain of f.

(5) Reference information that may be useful in answering the questions in this test can be found on the page preceding Question 1.

USE THIS SPACE FOR SCRATCHWORK

1. If $a(x+1) + b(x-1) - 2 = 0$ for all real x,
   then $a =$

   (A) −2
   (B) −1
   (C) 0
   (D) 1
   (E) 2

2. If $i = \sqrt{-1}$, which of the following is a negative integer?

   (A) i^{24} (B) i^{33} (C) i^{46} (D) i^{55} (E) i^{72}

3. If $f(2) = 0$ and $f(-1) = 0$, which of the following must be
   a factor of $f(x)$?

   (A) $x+2$ (B) $x-1$ (C) $x^2 + x - 2$
   (D) $x^2 - x - 2$ (E) None of these

GO ON TO THE NEXT PAGE

USE THIS SPACE FOR SCRATCHWORK.

4. If $\sqrt{x^2} = |x|$, then the solution consists of

(A) Zero only
(B) Positive real numbers only
(C) Negative real numbers only
(D) All real numbers
(E) No real numbers

5. If $|x| < \dfrac{2}{3}$, then $\left|9x^2 - 4\right|$ is equivalent to

(A) $9x^2 - 4$

(B) $9x^2 + 4$

(C) $4 - 9x^2$

(D) $-4 - 9x^2$

(E) $3x - 2$

6. If -1 is a root of the equation $kx^2 + 6x - 4 = 0$, then the other root is

(A) 4   (B) 2   (C) 0.4   (D) -0.4 (E) -2.5

7. Figure 1 shows the graph of the equation $2x - 3y + 9 = 0$. What is the value of θ ?

(A) $33.7°$

(B) $34.2°$

(C) $37.8°$

(D) $38.1°$

(E) $40.6°$

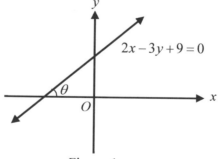

Figure 1

8. If $f(x) = x + 1$ and $(f \circ g)(x) = x^2 + 3x + 2$, which of the following is $g(x)$?

(A) $x + 2$

(B) $x^2 + 3x$

(C) $x^2 + 3x - 1$

(D) $x^2 + 3x + 1$

(E) $(x + 1)^2(x + 2)$

GO ON TO THE NEXT PAGE

MATHEMATICS LEVEL 2 TEST - *Continued*

9.   If $x - 3$ is a factor of $2x^3 - kx - 3$, then $k =$

(A) 3
(B) 7
(C) 9
(D) 15
(E) 17

10.   If $f(x) = x^{-\frac{2}{3}}$, then $f\left(\dfrac{1}{8}\right) =$

(A) 4   (B) -4 (C) $\dfrac{1}{4}$ (D) $-\dfrac{1}{4}$ (E) 8

11.   If the pendulum of a clock swings through an angle of 2.8 radians and the length of the arc that its tip travels is 40, then the length of the pendulum is

(A) 12.54
(B) 13.58
(C) 14.29
(D) 52
(E) 112

12.   If $y = 10 + 5\sin(2x)$, what is the minimum value of y?

(A)   5
(B)   10
(C) -5
(D) -10
(E) -15

13.   The period of the graph of $y = 3\cos^2(2x)$ is

(A) $\dfrac{\pi}{8}$ (B) $\dfrac{\pi}{4}$ (C) $\dfrac{\pi}{2}$ (D) π (E) 2π

14.   If $-2 - \sqrt{7}$ is a root of the equation $x^2 + 4x + 3k = 0$, then $k =$

(A) 1   (B) -1 (C) 2   (D) -2 (E) 4

GO ON TO THE NEXT PAGE

USE THIS SPACE FOR SCRATCHWORK.

15. If $ax^2 + bx + c < 0$ for all real numbers x, then which of the following must be true?

(A) $a > 0$ and $b^2 - 4ac < 0$

(B) $a > 0$ and $b^2 - 4ac > 0$

(C) $a < 0$ and $b^2 - 4ac > 0$

(D) $a < 0$ and $b^2 - 4ac < 0$

(E) $a < 0$ and $b^2 - 4ac = 0$

16. If the roots of the equation $x^2 + x - 3 = 0$ are α and β, then $\dfrac{1}{\alpha} + \dfrac{1}{\beta} =$

(A) $\dfrac{1}{3}$ (B) $\dfrac{2}{3}$ (C) $\dfrac{-2}{3}$ (D) $\dfrac{2}{5}$ (E) $\dfrac{3}{5}$

17. If the points $(3, 7)$, $(1, k)$, and $(-1, 1)$ are collinear, what is the value of k?

(A) 2   (B) 4   (C) 5   (D) 7   (E) 8

18. The graph of the function $f(x) = \dfrac{x^2 - x - 2}{x^2 + 3x + 2}$ has a vertical asymptote at $x =$

(A) -1 only

(B) 2 only

(C) -2 only

(D) -1 and -2 only

(E) $-1, -2$, and 2

GO ON TO THE NEXT PAGE

MATHEMATICS LEVEL 2 TEST - *Continued*

USE THIS SPACE FOR SCRATCHWORK.

19. Which of the following is the length of the radius of the sphere $x^2 + 2x + y^2 - 2y + z^2 = 3$

   (A) $\sqrt{3}$
   (B) $\sqrt{5}$
   (C) 3
   (D) 5
   (E) $2\sqrt{5}$

20. Which of the following is the equation whose graph is the set of points equidistant from points $(0, 4)$ and $(2, 0)$?

   (A) $y = x + 1$

   (B) $y = 2x + 1$

   (C) $y = \frac{1}{2}x + \frac{1}{2}$

   (D) $y = \frac{1}{2}x + \frac{3}{2}$

   (E) $y = \frac{1}{4}x - \frac{3}{2}$

21. $\lim\limits_{n \to \infty} \sum\limits_{i=1}^{n} \dfrac{1}{2^i} =$

   (A) 0
   (B) 1
   (C) 5
   (D) 10
   (E) Infinite

22. Which of the following is equivalent to $\dfrac{x-1}{x} < 0$?

   (A) $x < 0$
   (B) $0 < x < 1$
   (C) $x > 0$
   (D) $0 < x < 5$
   (E) $x < 1$

GO ON TO THE NEXT PAGE

USE THIS SPACE FOR SCRATCHWORK.

23. A school committee of 5 is to be chosen from a group consisting of 5 boys and 6 girls. How many ways can the committee be made up of 3 boys and 2 girls?

(A) 100
(B) 150
(C) 600
(D) 1200
(E) 1800

24. The interquartile range of a data set is 12. If the first quartile is 65, which of the following could be the median?

(A) 50
(B) 64
(C) 70
(D) 77
(E) 80

25. What is the range of the function defined by $f(x) = \dfrac{1}{x} - 2$?

(A) All real numbers
(B) All real numbers except -2
(C) All real numbers except 0
(D) All real numbers except 2
(E) All real numbers between -2 and 3

26. The formula $A = P\left(1 + \dfrac{r}{n}\right)^{nt}$ gives the amount A in a savings account with initial investment P which is compounded monthly at an annual interest rate of 6 percent for t years. How many years will it take the initial investment to double?

(A) 5.3
(B) 6.5
(C) 8.3
(D) 11.6
(E) 13.1

150

USE THIS SPACE FOR SCRATCHWORK.

27. A line has parametric equations $x = 5 - t$ and $y = 7 + 2t$, where t is the parameter. The slope of the line is

(A) $\dfrac{5}{7}$ (B) 2   (C) $\dfrac{7 + 2t}{5 - t}$ (D) $\dfrac{7}{5}$ (E) -2

28. $\displaystyle\lim_{n \to 0}\left(\dfrac{\ln(n+1)^2}{n}\right) =$

(A) 0
(B) 1
(C) 2
(D) 5
(E) Undefined

29. If the graph of f in Figure 2 is a polynomial of degree 7, which of the following could be f?

(A) $x^3(x+3)^2(x-2)(x-4)$

(B) $x^2(x+3)(x-2)(x-4)(x-1)^2$

(C) $x^2(x+3)(x-2)(x-3)(x+1)^2$

(D) $x^2(x+3)^2(x-3)^2(x-4)$

(E) $x^2(x+3)(x-2)(x-4)(x^2+1)$

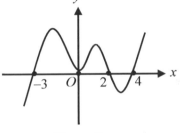

Figure 2

30. If $a_1 = 1$, $a_2 = 3$, and $a_{n+1} = \dfrac{a_n + a_{n+2}}{2}$, then what is the 20th term of this sequence?

(A) 36
(B) 39
(C) 41
(D) 43
(E) 60

GO ON TO THE NEXT PAGE

USE THIS SPACE FOR SCRATCHWORK.

31. If $f(x) = 2x^3 - 3x + 2$, which of the following statements is true?

    (A) The function is increasing for all real x.
    (B) The function is increasing for $x > 0$
    (C) The equation $f(x) = 0$ have three real roots.
    (D) The equation $f(x) = 0$ have two imaginary roots.
    (E) The inverse of the function is also a function.

32. If $f(x) = x^2 + 1$, where $x \geq 0$, then $\left(f \circ f^{-1}\right)(x)$ could equal

    (A) 1   (B) x (C) x^2 (D) $x^2 + 1$ (E) $\dfrac{1}{x^2 + 1}$

33. If $\log_a x = 3$ and $\log_b x = 4$, then $\log_{ab} x =$

    (A) 12   (B) $\dfrac{8}{3}$ (C) $\dfrac{12}{7}$ (D) $\dfrac{7}{12}$ (E) $\dfrac{3}{8}$

34. If a cylinder whose height is equal to the diameter of its base is inscribed in a sphere, then the ratio of the volume of the cylinder to the volume of the sphere is

    (A) $\dfrac{1}{2}$

    (B) $\dfrac{\sqrt{2}}{3}$

    (C) $\dfrac{2\sqrt{2}}{3}$

    (D) $\sqrt{2}$

    (E) $\dfrac{3\sqrt{2}}{8}$

MATHEMATICS LEVEL 2 TEST - *Continued*

35. Which of the following is the graph of $\dfrac{|x|}{2} + \dfrac{|y|}{3} = 1$?

(A)

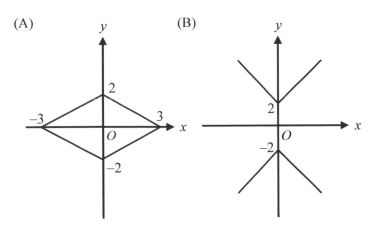

(B)

(C)

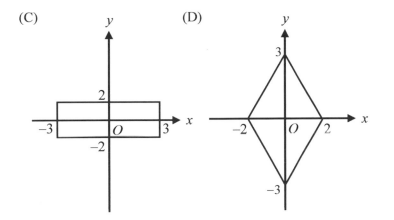

(D)

(E)

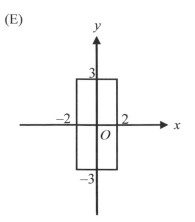

GO ON TO THE NEXT PAGE

USE THIS SPACE FOR SCRATCHWORK.

36. Figure 3 shows the part of a circle with a radius r and central angle θ in radians. What is the area of the figure?

(A) $r\theta$

(B) $r^2\theta$

(C) $\dfrac{r^2\theta}{2}$

(D) $\dfrac{\pi r^2\theta}{360}$

(E) $\dfrac{\pi r^2}{\theta}$

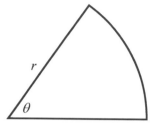

Figure 3

37. When a fair coin is tossed 4 times, what is the probability of tossing at least 3 heads?

(A) $\dfrac{5}{16}$

(B) $\dfrac{1}{2}$

(C) $\dfrac{9}{16}$

(D) $\dfrac{3}{4}$

(E) $\dfrac{5}{8}$

38. If $\left|\vec{a}\right|=10$ and $\left|\vec{b}\right|=18$, then which of the following could NOT be $\left|\vec{a}+\vec{b}\right|$?

(A) 7
(B) 8
(C) 15
(D) 22
(E) 28

MATHEMATICS LEVEL 2 TEST - *Continued*

39. If $\left(\dfrac{1}{2}\right)^{2a} = \left(\dfrac{1}{3}\right)^{b}$, what is the value of $\dfrac{a}{b}$?

(A) 0.33
(B) 0.67
(C) 0.79
(D) 0.81
(E) 0.87

40. If the equation $\sin^2\theta + 8\cos\theta + 5 = 0$, where $0° \leq \theta < 360°$, how many solutions are there in the interval?

(A) 1   (B) 2   (C) 3   (D) 4   (E) 0

41. If $(n!)^2 - 118n! - 240 = 0$, what is the value of n?

(A) 2   (B) 3   (C) 4   (D) 5   (E) 6

42. If the equation of an ellipse is $18x^2 + 5y^2 - 90 = 0$, what is the length of the major axis of the ellipse?

(A) 2.24
(B) 5.00
(C) 8.49
(D) 9.00
(E) 10.0

43. If $2^x + 4^x = 4 \cdot 2^x$, then $x =$

(A) 2
(B) $\sqrt{3}$
(C) 5
(D) $\log_2 3$
(E) $\log_4 3$

GO ON TO THE NEXT PAGE

MATHEMATICS LEVEL 2 TEST - *Continued*

USE THIS SPACE FOR SCRATCHWORK.

44. Which of the following intervals contain a root of
$x^3 - 3x^2 + 3x + 2 = 0$

(A) $-2 < x < -1$
(B) $-1 < x < 0$
(C) $0 < x < 1$
(D) $2 < x < 3$
(E) $3 < x < 4$

45. If the statement is "If $xy = 0$, then $x = 0$ or $y = 0$", an indirect proof of the statement begins with the assumption that

(A) $x = 0$ or $y = 0$
(B) $x = 0$ and $y = 0$
(C) $xy \neq 0$
(D) $x \neq 0$ or $y \neq 0$
(E) $x \neq 0$ and $y \neq 0$

46. By the rational zero theorem, which of the following could not be a possible rational zero of the equation
$y = 2x^4 - 3x^2 - 2x + 10$?

(A) $-\dfrac{1}{2}$ (B) $\dfrac{1}{5}$ (C) $-\dfrac{5}{2}$ (D) $\dfrac{5}{2}$ (E) 5

47. Matrix $A = \begin{bmatrix} 1 & 2 \\ 3 & 4 \end{bmatrix}$ and matrix $B = \begin{bmatrix} a \\ b \end{bmatrix}$. If $AB = \begin{bmatrix} 3 \\ 4 \end{bmatrix}$,
then $a =$

(A) 3   (B) 2   (C) 1   (D) –1   (E) –2

48. If a set $A = \{1, 2, 3, 4, 5, 6, 7, 8, 9, 10\}$, how many subsets are there containing the elements 3, 4, and 5?

(A) 64
(B) 128
(C) 256
(D) 512
(E) 1024

USE THIS SPACE FOR SCRATCHWORK.

49. If a cone with a slant height equal to the diameter of the base is inscribed in a sphere with a radius of 10, what is the volume of the cone?

   (A) 375π
   (B) 300π
   (C) 250π
   (D) 200π
   (E) 160π

50. Given the parametric equations $x = \sec\theta$ and $y = \tan\theta$, which of the following is the graph of the points (x, y)?

   (A) Circle
   (B) Ellipse
   (C) Parabola
   (D) Hyperbola
   (E) None of these

STOP

IF YOU FINISH BEFORE TIME IS CALLED, YOU MAY CHECK YOUR WORK ON THIS TEST ONLY.

DO NOT TURN TO ANY OTHER TEST IN THIS BOOK.

No Test Material on This Page

TEST 3					ANSWERS				
#	answer	#	answer	#	answer	#	answer	#	answer
1	D	11	C	21	B	31	D	41	D
2	C	12	A	22	B	32	B	42	C
3	D	13	C	23	B	33	C	43	D
4	D	14	B	24	C	34	E	44	B
5	C	15	D	25	B	35	D	45	E
6	C	16	A	26	D	36	C	46	B
7	A	17	B	27	E	37	A	47	E
8	D	18	C	28	C	38	A	48	B
9	E	19	B	29	E	39	C	49	A
10	A	20	D	30	B	40	B	50	D

Explanations: Test 3

1. (D) $a(x+1)+b(x-1)-2=0 \rightarrow (a+b)x+a-b-2=0$ must be true for all real x.
Therefore, $a+b=0$ and $a-b=2$. By addition $a=1$ and $b=-1$.

2. (C) $i^{46}=i^{44}\times i^2=-1$

3. (D)   Since $(x-2)$ and $(x+1)$ are factors of $f(x)$, $f(x)=(x-2)(x+1)Q(x)$.
Therefore, $f(x)=\left(x^2-x-2\right)Q(x)$.

4. (D) $\sqrt{x^2}=|x|$ is always true for any value of x.

5. (C)   Since $|x|<\dfrac{2}{3}$, then $-\dfrac{2}{3}<x<\dfrac{2}{3}$.
For this interval: $9x^2<9\left(\dfrac{4}{9}\right) \rightarrow 9x^2<4 \rightarrow 9x^2-4<0$.
Therefore, $\left|9x^2-4\right|=-(9x^2-4)=4-9x^2$.

6. (C)   The product of the roots is $\dfrac{-4}{k}$ and the sum of the roots is $\dfrac{-6}{k}$. Let the other root be r.

$\dfrac{-6}{k}=-1+r \rightarrow k=\dfrac{-6}{r-1} ---(1)$

$\dfrac{-4}{k}=-1r \rightarrow k=\dfrac{4}{r} ---(2)$

From (1) and (2), $\dfrac{-6}{r-1}=\dfrac{4}{r} \rightarrow 4r-4=-6r \rightarrow r=0.4$

7. (A) $\tan\theta=$ slope of the line. $3y=2x+9 \rightarrow y=\dfrac{2}{3}x+3$ The slope is $\dfrac{2}{3}$.

Therefore, $\tan\theta = \dfrac{2}{3} \ \rightarrow \ \theta = \tan^{-1}\dfrac{2}{3} \ \rightarrow \ \theta \simeq 33.7^o$

8. (D) Since $f\big(g(x)\big) = g(x) + 1 = x^2 + 3x + 2$, then $g(x) = x^2 + 3x + 1$.

9. (E) By factor theorem: $f(3) = 2(3)^3 - k(3) - 3 = 0 \ \rightarrow \ 51 = 3k \ \rightarrow \ k = 17$

10. (A) $f(x) = x^{-\frac{2}{3}} \ \rightarrow \ f\left(\dfrac{1}{8}\right) = \left(\dfrac{1}{8}\right)^{-\frac{2}{3}} = \left(2^{-3}\right)^{-\frac{2}{3}} = 2^2 = 4$. Or use a calculator.

11. (C) The length of a arc $s = r\theta$, where r is a radius(the length of the pendulum) and θ is the central angle in radian.

Therefore, $40 = r \times 2.8 \ \rightarrow \ r = \dfrac{40}{2.8} \simeq 14.29$.

12. (A) Since $-5 \le 5\sin(2x) \le 5$, the minimum will be $10 - 5 = 5$.

13. (C) The period of $y = \cos(2x)$ is $\dfrac{2\pi}{2} = \pi$. Therefore, the period of $y = 3\cos^2(2x)$ is $\dfrac{\pi}{2}$ as follows.

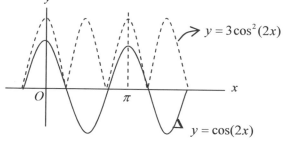

14. (B) If $-2 - \sqrt{7}$ is one of the roots, then the other root is $-2 + \sqrt{7}$. The product of the roots is $3k$.
Therefore, $3k = (-2 + \sqrt{7})(-2 - \sqrt{7}) = (-2)^2 - (\sqrt{7})^2 = -3 \ \rightarrow \ k = -1$.

15. (D) The graph must be as follows. Therefore, the graph is concave down and the function do not have real roots (Imaginary).

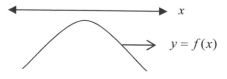

16. (A) Since sum of the roots $\alpha + \beta = \dfrac{-1}{1} = -1$ and product of the roots $\alpha\beta = \dfrac{-3}{1} = -3$,

$\dfrac{1}{\alpha} + \dfrac{1}{\beta} = \dfrac{\alpha + \beta}{\alpha\beta} = \dfrac{-1}{-3} = \dfrac{1}{3}$.

17. (B) Because the three point on the same line, the slope between any two points are equal.

$$\frac{k-7}{1-3}=\frac{k-1}{1-(-1)} \rightarrow \frac{k-7}{-2}=\frac{k-1}{2} \rightarrow k=4.$$

18. (C) Since $f(x)=\dfrac{(x-2)\cancel{(x+1)}}{(x+2)\cancel{(x+1)}}=\dfrac{(x-2)}{(x+2)}$, $f(x)$ has a vertical asymptote at $x=-2$.

19. (B) $x^2+2x+y^2-2y+z^2=3 \rightarrow (x+1)^2+(y-1)^2+z^2=5$

Therefore, the radius is $r=\sqrt{5}$.

20. (D) The equation which pass through $(0,4)$ and $(2,0)$: $y=-2x+4$

$$\text{slope}=\frac{4-0}{0-2}=-2, \quad \text{midpoint}=\left(\frac{0+2}{2},\frac{4+0}{2}\right)=(1,2)$$

Therefore, the line of equidistance is perpendicular to the line and pass through $(1, 2)$.

$$y=\frac{1}{2}x+b \rightarrow 2=\frac{1}{2}(1)+b \rightarrow b=\frac{3}{2}$$

The equation is $y=\dfrac{1}{2}x+\dfrac{3}{2}$.

21. (B) Series: $S=\dfrac{a}{1-r}$

$$\lim_{n\to\infty}\sum_{i=1}^{n}\frac{1}{2^i}=\frac{1}{2}+\frac{1}{4}+\frac{1}{8}+\frac{1}{16}+...=\frac{\dfrac{1}{2}}{1-\dfrac{1}{2}}=1.$$

22. (B) Because $x^2>0$, $x^2\times\dfrac{x-1}{x}<0\times x^2 \rightarrow x(x-1)<0 \rightarrow 0<x<1$

Or, you can use the test value method.

23. (B) $_5C_3\times{}_6C_2=150.$

24. (C) Interquartile range = upper quartile – lower quartile = 12
Since Interquartile has the range $[65, 77]$, the median must be in this range.

25. (B) $y=-2$ is an asymptote.

26. (D) Since the interest is compounded monthly, $n=12$.

$$2P=p\left(1+\frac{0.06}{12}\right)^{12t} \rightarrow 2=1.005^{12t}$$

$$12t=\log_{1.005}2 \rightarrow t=\frac{\log 2}{12\log 1.005}\simeq 11.6$$

27. (E) $t = 5 - x \rightarrow$ substitute $\rightarrow y = 7 + 2(5 - x) \rightarrow y = -2x + 17$
Slope is -2.

28. (C) Since $e = \lim_{n \to 0}(1 + n)^{\frac{1}{n}}$, $\lim_{n \to 0}\frac{2\ln(n+1)}{n} = \lim_{n \to 0} 2\ln(1+n)^{\frac{1}{n}} = 2\ln e = 2$.

29. (E) At $x = 0$, the graph is bounced on x-axis and pass at $x = -3, 2,$ and 4.
Therefore, the polynomial have factors as follows.
$P(x) = x^m(x+3)^n(x-2)^n(x-4)^n$ (imaginary roots), where $m =$ even and $n =$ odd.
(E) could be the polynomial function.

30. (B) Since $2a_{n+1} = a_n + a_{n+2} \rightarrow a_{n+1} - a_n = a_{n+2} - a_{n+1}$, the sequence is arithmetic progress.
$a_1 = 1$ and $d = 2$. Therefore, $a_{20} = a_1 + (20 - 1)d = 1 + 19 \times 2 = 39$.
Or, find the pattern. You can find $a_1 = 1$, $a_2 = 3$, $a_3 = 5$, $a_4 = 7, \ldots$, which is arithmetic sequence.

31. (D) Use your graphic calculator. The graph will be as follows.

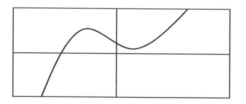

(D) is correct. $f(x)$ have one real root and two imaginary roots.

(E) is incorrect. Use horizontal line test to check whether it's inverse is a function. When the function is both increasing and decreasing, it's inverse is not a function.

32. (B) $f(f^{-1}(x)) = f^{-1}(f(x)) = x$

33. (C) $\log_{ab} x = \dfrac{\log x}{\log ab} = \dfrac{\log x}{\log a + \log b}$ -------- (1)

$\dfrac{\log x}{\log a} = 3 \rightarrow \log a = \dfrac{\log x}{3}$ and $\dfrac{\log x}{\log b} = 4 \rightarrow \log b = \dfrac{\log x}{4}$

Substitute into (1)
$\log_{ab} x = \dfrac{\log x}{\dfrac{\log x}{3} + \dfrac{\log x}{4}} = \dfrac{12}{7}$

Or, use the formula: $\log_{ab} x = \dfrac{1}{\log_x ab} \rightarrow \dfrac{1}{\log_x a + \log_x b} = \dfrac{1}{\dfrac{1}{3} + \dfrac{1}{4}} = \dfrac{1}{\dfrac{7}{12}} = \dfrac{12}{7}$

34. (E) $V_c = \pi\left(\dfrac{d}{2}\right)^2 d = \dfrac{\pi d^3}{4}$ and $V_s = \dfrac{4\pi\left(\dfrac{d\sqrt{2}}{2}\right)^3}{3} = \dfrac{\pi d^3 \sqrt{2}}{3}$, where the diameter of the sphere

is $d\sqrt{2}$.

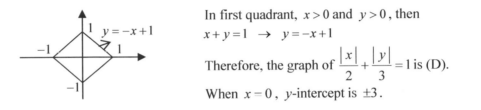

$\dfrac{V_c}{V_s} = \dfrac{\dfrac{\pi d^3}{4}}{\dfrac{\pi d^3 \sqrt{2}}{3}} = \dfrac{3}{4\sqrt{2}} = \dfrac{3\sqrt{2}}{8}$

Or, you can use a convenient number for d.
Use $d = 2$.

35. (D)   Memorize the graph of $|x| + |y| = 1$ is as follows.

In first quadrant, $x > 0$ and $y > 0$, then

$x + y = 1 \;\rightarrow\; y = -x + 1$

Therefore, the graph of $\dfrac{|x|}{2} + \dfrac{|y|}{3} = 1$ is (D).

When $x = 0$, y-intercept is ± 3.

36. (C) $A = \dfrac{r^2 \theta}{2}$ because $A = \pi r^2 \times \dfrac{\theta}{2\pi}$.

37. (A)   At least 3 heads is greater than or equal to 3 heads. Therefore,

$P = {}_4C_3 \left(\dfrac{1}{2}\right)^3 \left(\dfrac{1}{2}\right) + {}_4C_4 \left(\dfrac{1}{2}\right)^4 = \dfrac{4}{16} + \dfrac{1}{16} = \dfrac{5}{16}$.

38. (A)   If $\vec{a}$ and $\vec{b}$ are in the same direction, $|\vec{a} + \vec{b}| = |\vec{a}| + |\vec{b}| = 18$. If $\vec{a}$ and $\vec{b}$ are in the opposite

direction, then $|\vec{a} + \vec{b}| = |\vec{b}| - |\vec{a}| = 8$. Therefore, $8 \le |\vec{a} + \vec{b}| \le 18$. It cannot be 7.

39. (C) $\left(\dfrac{1}{2}\right)^{\frac{2a}{b}} = \left(\dfrac{1}{3}\right)^{\frac{b}{b}} \;\rightarrow\; \left(\dfrac{1}{2}\right)^{\frac{2a}{b}} = \dfrac{1}{3} \;\rightarrow\; \dfrac{2a}{b} = \log_{\frac{1}{2}} \dfrac{1}{3} = \dfrac{\log \dfrac{1}{3}}{\log \dfrac{1}{2}} = \dfrac{\log 3}{\log 2}$

Therefore, $\dfrac{a}{b} = \dfrac{\log 3}{2\log 2} \simeq 0.79$.

40. (B)   Use graphic utility.

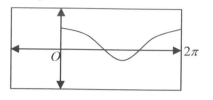

Or algebraically as follows.

Since $\sin^2\theta = 1 - \cos^2\theta$, the equation is

$1 - \cos^2\theta + 8\cos\theta + 5 = 0 \;\rightarrow\; \cos^2\theta - 8\cos\theta - 6 = 0$.

Therefore, $\cos\theta = \dfrac{8 \pm \sqrt{64 + 24}}{2} \;\rightarrow\; \cos\theta \simeq 8.69$ or $\cos\theta \simeq -0.69$. $\cos\theta \neq 8.69$ and

$\cos\theta \simeq -0.69$. Therefore, $\theta \simeq 2.3328$ or $\theta \simeq 3.9503$.

41. (D)   The equation can be factored as follow.

$(n! - 120)(n! + 2) = 0 \qquad\rightarrow\qquad$ Since $n! \neq -2$, then $n! = 120 \quad\rightarrow\quad 5! = 120 \quad\rightarrow\quad n = 5$.

42. (C)   Change the equation into a standard form. $\dfrac{18x^2}{90} + \dfrac{5y^2}{90} = \dfrac{90}{90} \;\rightarrow\; \dfrac{x^2}{90\!\big/18} + \dfrac{y^2}{90\!\big/5} = 1$

Since $\dfrac{90}{5} > \dfrac{90}{18}$, major axis is on y-axis. Therefore, $a^2 = \dfrac{90}{5} \;\rightarrow\; a = \sqrt{18}$.

Major axis is $2a = 2\sqrt{18} \simeq 8.49$.

43. (D)   Since $2^x + 2^{2x} = 4 \cdot 2^x \;\rightarrow\; 2^{2x} - 3 \cdot 2^x = 0 \;\rightarrow\; 2^x(2^x - 3) = 0$ and $2^x \neq 0$,

the solution is $2^x - 3 = 0 \;\rightarrow\; 2^x = 3 \;\rightarrow\; x = \log_2 3$.

44. (B)   If $f(a) \times f(b) < 0$, then $f(x) = 0$ has at least one solution on interval (a,b).

Since $f(-1) = -5 < 0$ and $f(0) = 2 > 0$, then $f(-1) \cdot f(0) < 0$. Therefore, the equation has a

solution on interval $(-1, 0)$.

Or, use a graph calculator to find the zeros. The graph will be as follow.

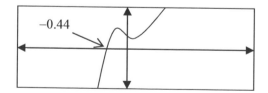

45. (E)   Indirect proof is a proof in which a statement to be proved is assumed false and if the

assumption leads to impossibility, then the statement assumed false has been proved true.

Therefore, $\sim(x = 0 \text{ or } y = 0)$ is $x \neq 0$ and $y \neq 0$. In symbolic notation is as follows.

$\sim(x = 0 \cup y = 0) \;\rightarrow\; \sim(x = 0) \cap \sim(y = 0)$: De Morgan's Law

46. (B) The possible rational zeros are obtained as follows.

$$\frac{\text{factors of } 10}{\text{factors of } 2} = \frac{+1, \ +2, \ +5, \ +10}{\pm 1, \ \pm 2}$$

Therefore, $\frac{1}{5}$ cannot be the rational root of the equation.

47. (E) From matrix equation

$$\begin{bmatrix} 1 & 2 \\ 3 & 4 \end{bmatrix}\begin{bmatrix} a \\ b \end{bmatrix} = \begin{bmatrix} 3 \\ 4 \end{bmatrix}$$

$a + 2b = 3$ and $3a + 4b = 4$

Therefore, $\dfrac{\begin{aligned} 3a + 4b &= 4 \\ 2a + 4b &= 6 \end{aligned}}{a \quad\;\; = -2}$

48. (B) Number of subsets of $\{1,2,6,7,8,9,10\}$ is $2^7 = 128$.

Now add elements 3, 4, and 5 to those subsets.
Therefore, number of subsets containing 3, 4, and 5 is also 128.

49. (A)

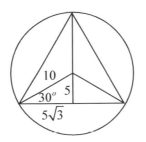

From the figure above, the radius of the cone is $5\sqrt{3}$ and the height is 15.

Therefore, the volume of the cone is $V = \dfrac{\pi(5\sqrt{3})^2 \times 15}{3} = 375\pi$.

50. (D) Parametric equation: eliminate θ. Since $1 + \tan^2\theta = \sec^2\theta$, substitute x and y.

Therefore, $1 + y^2 = x^2 \;\to\; x^2 - y^2 = 1$, which represents hyperbola.

END

No Test Material on This Page

Test 4

Dr. John Chung's

SAT II Mathematics Level 2

MATHEMATICS LEVEL 2 TEST

REFERENCE INFORMATION

THE FOLLOWING INFORMATION IS FOR YOUR REFERENCE IN ANSWERING SOME OF THE QUESTIONS IN THIS TEST

Volume of a right circular cone with radius r and height h: $V = \dfrac{1}{3}\pi r^2 h$

Lateral Area of a right circular cone with circumference of the base c and slant height ℓ: $S = \dfrac{1}{2}c\ell$

Volume of a sphere with radius r: $V = \dfrac{4}{3}\pi r^3$

Surface Area of a sphere with radius r: $S = 4\pi r^2$

Volume of a pyramid with base area B and height h: $V = \dfrac{1}{3}Bh$

Dr. John Chung's SAT II Math Level 2

Answer Sheet

01 Ⓐ Ⓑ Ⓒ Ⓓ Ⓔ   26 Ⓐ Ⓑ Ⓒ Ⓓ Ⓔ
02 Ⓐ Ⓑ Ⓒ Ⓓ Ⓔ   27 Ⓐ Ⓑ Ⓒ Ⓓ Ⓔ
03 Ⓐ Ⓑ Ⓒ Ⓓ Ⓔ   28 Ⓐ Ⓑ Ⓒ Ⓓ Ⓔ
04 Ⓐ Ⓑ Ⓒ Ⓓ Ⓔ   29 Ⓐ Ⓑ Ⓒ Ⓓ Ⓔ
05 Ⓐ Ⓑ Ⓒ Ⓓ Ⓔ   30 Ⓐ Ⓑ Ⓒ Ⓓ Ⓔ
06 Ⓐ Ⓑ Ⓒ Ⓓ Ⓔ   31 Ⓐ Ⓑ Ⓒ Ⓓ Ⓔ
07 Ⓐ Ⓑ Ⓒ Ⓓ Ⓔ   32 Ⓐ Ⓑ Ⓒ Ⓓ Ⓔ
08 Ⓐ Ⓑ Ⓒ Ⓓ Ⓔ   33 Ⓐ Ⓑ Ⓒ Ⓓ Ⓔ
09 Ⓐ Ⓑ Ⓒ Ⓓ Ⓔ   34 Ⓐ Ⓑ Ⓒ Ⓓ Ⓔ
10 Ⓐ Ⓑ Ⓒ Ⓓ Ⓔ   35 Ⓐ Ⓑ Ⓒ Ⓓ Ⓔ
11 Ⓐ Ⓑ Ⓒ Ⓓ Ⓔ   36 Ⓐ Ⓑ Ⓒ Ⓓ Ⓔ
12 Ⓐ Ⓑ Ⓒ Ⓓ Ⓔ   37 Ⓐ Ⓑ Ⓒ Ⓓ Ⓔ
13 Ⓐ Ⓑ Ⓒ Ⓓ Ⓔ   38 Ⓐ Ⓑ Ⓒ Ⓓ Ⓔ
14 Ⓐ Ⓑ Ⓒ Ⓓ Ⓔ   39 Ⓐ Ⓑ Ⓒ Ⓓ Ⓔ
15 Ⓐ Ⓑ Ⓒ Ⓓ Ⓔ   40 Ⓐ Ⓑ Ⓒ Ⓓ Ⓔ
16 Ⓐ Ⓑ Ⓒ Ⓓ Ⓔ   41 Ⓐ Ⓑ Ⓒ Ⓓ Ⓔ
17 Ⓐ Ⓑ Ⓒ Ⓓ Ⓔ   42 Ⓐ Ⓑ Ⓒ Ⓓ Ⓔ
18 Ⓐ Ⓑ Ⓒ Ⓓ Ⓔ   43 Ⓐ Ⓑ Ⓒ Ⓓ Ⓔ
19 Ⓐ Ⓑ Ⓒ Ⓓ Ⓔ   44 Ⓐ Ⓑ Ⓒ Ⓓ Ⓔ
20 Ⓐ Ⓑ Ⓒ Ⓓ Ⓔ   45 Ⓐ Ⓑ Ⓒ Ⓓ Ⓔ
21 Ⓐ Ⓑ Ⓒ Ⓓ Ⓔ   46 Ⓐ Ⓑ Ⓒ Ⓓ Ⓔ
22 Ⓐ Ⓑ Ⓒ Ⓓ Ⓔ   47 Ⓐ Ⓑ Ⓒ Ⓓ Ⓔ
23 Ⓐ Ⓑ Ⓒ Ⓓ Ⓔ   48 Ⓐ Ⓑ Ⓒ Ⓓ Ⓔ
24 Ⓐ Ⓑ Ⓒ Ⓓ Ⓔ   49 Ⓐ Ⓑ Ⓒ Ⓓ Ⓔ
25 Ⓐ Ⓑ Ⓒ Ⓓ Ⓔ   50 Ⓐ Ⓑ Ⓒ Ⓓ Ⓔ

The number of right answers: ☐

The number of wrong answers: ☐

$$\frac{\boxed{}}{\text{\# of correct}} - \frac{1}{4} \times \boxed{}_{\text{\# of wrong}} = \boxed{}_{\text{Raw score}}$$

Score Conversion Table

Raw Score	Scaled Score	Raw Score	Scaled Score	Raw Score	Scaled Score
50	800	28	640	6	480
49	800	27	630	5	470
48	800	26	620	4	470
47	800	25	620	3	460
46	800	24	610	2	460
45	800	23	610	1	450
44	800	22	600	0	450
43	800	21	600		
42	800	20	590		
41	800	19	590		
40	780	18	580		
39	760	17	570		
38	750	16	560		
37	740	15	550		
36	720	14	540		
35	710	13	530		
34	700	12	520		
33	690	11	510		
32	680	10	500		
31	670	9	490		
30	660	8	490		
29	650	7	480		

MATHEMATICS LEVEL 2 TEST

For each of the following problems, decide which is the BEST of the choices given. If the exact numerical value is not one of the choices, select the choice that best approximates this value. Then fill in the corresponding circle on the answer sheet

Note: (1) A scientific or graphing calculator will be necessary for answering some (but not all) of the questions in this test. For each question you will have to decide whether or not you should use a calculator.

(2) For some questions in this test you may have to decide whether your calculator should be in the radian mode or the degree mode.

(3) Figures that accompany problems in this test are intended to provide information useful in solving the problems. They are drawn as accurately as possible EXCEPT when it is stated in a specific problem that its figure is not drawn to scale. All figures lie in a plane unless otherwise indicated.

(4) Unless otherwise specified, the domain of any function f is assumed to be the set of all real numbers x for which $f(x)$ is a real number. The range of f is assumed to be the set of all real numbers $f(x)$, where x is in the domain of f.

(5) Reference information that may be useful in answering the questions in this test can be found on the page preceding Question 1.

USE THIS SPACE FOR SCRATCHWORK

1.　$\left(a-\dfrac{1}{a}\right)^2-\left(a+\dfrac{1}{a}\right)^2=$

(A)　4
(B)　−4
(C)　2
(D)　−2
(E)　2a

2.　If $\cos x=\dfrac{1}{3}$ for $0<x<\dfrac{\pi}{2}$, then $\sin 2x=$

(A)　0.25
(B)　0.30
(C)　0.50
(D)　0.63
(E)　0.75

GO ON TO THE NEXT PAGE

USE THIS SPACE FOR SCRATCHWORK.

3. The inverse of which of the following graphs is also a function?

(A)

(B)

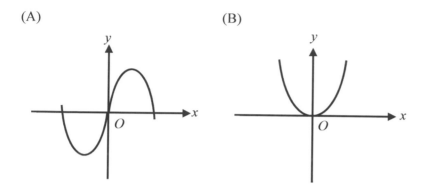

(C)

(D)

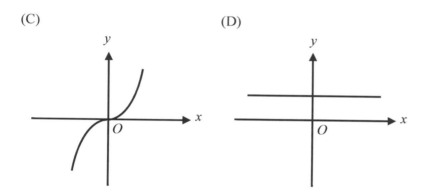

(E)

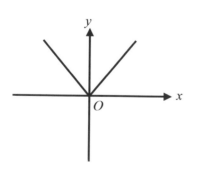

GO ON TO THE NEXT PAGE

MATHEMATICS LEVEL 2 TEST - *Continued*

USE THIS SPACE FOR SCRATCHWORK.

4. If $\sqrt{x^2} = 5$, then $x =$

    (A) 5 only
    (B) −5 only
    (C) 5 and −5
    (D) 25 and −15
    (E) −25 only

5. The radius of the circle $x^2 - 2x + y^2 - 4y = 9$ is

    (A) 3.00
    (B) 3.74
    (C) 4.12
    (D) 5.43
    (E) 6.15

6. If $f(x) = \sqrt{9x^2 - x}$ and $g(x) = \dfrac{x-1}{x+1}$, then $f\big(g(2)\big) =$

    (A) $\dfrac{\sqrt{2}}{3}$ (B) $\dfrac{\sqrt{3}}{3}$ (C) $\dfrac{\sqrt{5}}{3}$ (D) $\dfrac{\sqrt{6}}{3}$ (E) $\dfrac{2\sqrt{2}}{3}$

7. If $f(x) = 5$ for all real numbers x, then
    $f(x-2) + f(x+2) =$

    (A) 0   (B) 2   (C) 5   (D) 10   (E) 20

8. $\dfrac{(10! \times 10!)}{(9!)^2} =$

    (A) $\dfrac{100!}{81!}$

    (B) $\dfrac{100}{81}$

    (C) 100

    (D) $\dfrac{1000}{81}$

    (E) $\dfrac{10000}{9}$

 **GO ON TO THE NEXT PAGE**

MATHEMATICS LEVEL 2 TEST - *Continued*

USE THIS SPACE FOR SCRATCHWORK.

9. The set of all real numbers of x such that $\left|x^2 - 1\right| < 1$ consists of

(A) $\left\{x < -\sqrt{2}\right\}$

(B) $\left\{-\sqrt{2} < x < 0\right\} \vee \left\{0 < x < \sqrt{2}\right\}$

(C) $\left\{0 < x < \sqrt{2}\right\}$

(D) $\left\{x < -\sqrt{2}\right\} \vee \left\{x > \sqrt{2}\right\}$

(E) $\left\{x > \sqrt{2}\right\}$

10. If the line $y = x + k$ is tangent to the graph of the circle $x^2 + y^2 = 4$, then $k =$

(A) $2\sqrt{2}$ only

(B) $3\sqrt{2}$ only

(C) $4\sqrt{2}$ only

(D) $\pm 2\sqrt{2}$

(E) $\pm 4\sqrt{2}$

11. If $f(x) = 2\ln(x+1)$ and $g(x) = e^x$, then $(g \circ f)(x) =$

(A) e^{x+1}

(B) $e^{x^2 + 2x + 1}$

(C) $x + 1$

(D) $2(x + 1)$

(E) $x^2 + 2x + 1$

12. If $f(x) = x^3 + 3x + 1$, then $f^{-1}(f(x)) =$

(A) x

(B) x^2

(C) $x^3 + 3x + 1$

(D) $\sqrt[3]{x^3 + 3x + 1}$

(E) $\left(x^3 + 3x + 1\right)^3$

GO ON TO THE NEXT PAGE

MATHEMATICS LEVEL 2 TEST - *Continued*

USE THIS SPACE FOR SCRATCHWORK.

13. $\log_{16} 81 - \log_2 3 =$

(A) -2 (B) -1 (C) 0 (D) 1 (E) 3

14.   Three numbers have a sum of 36, a product of 1680, and form an arithmetic sequence. What is the largest number?

(A) 10
(B) 12
(C) 14
(D) 16
(E) 18

15.   If $a + bi = \dfrac{3+i}{1+i}$, which of the following is true?

(A) $a = 1, \ b = 2$
(B) $a = 2, \ b = 1$
(C) $a = 2, \ b = -1$
(D) $a = -2, \ b = 1$
(E) $a = -2, \ b = -1$

16.   If $\sin(A + B) = 0.25$, $\sin A = \dfrac{\sqrt{3}}{2}$, and

$90° < A + B < 180°$, then B could be

(A) $65°$
(B) $80.5°$
(C) $105.5°$
(D) $120.5°$
(E) $125.4°$

GO ON TO THE NEXT PAGE

MATHEMATICS LEVEL 2 TEST - *Continued*

USE THIS SPACE FOR SCRATCHWORK.

17. If the equation of a parabola is $y = 2x^2$, then the directrix of the graph is

(A) $y = 2$

(B) $y = \dfrac{1}{2}$

(C) $y = \dfrac{1}{8}$

(D) $y = -\dfrac{1}{8}$

(E) $y = -\dfrac{1}{2}$

18. Which of the following is symmetric with respect to the origin?

(A) $y = x^2 - x$

(B) $y = x + 5$

(C) $y = x^5 + 3x^3 + x$

(D) $y = x^6 + x^4 + x^2$

(E) $y = x^7 + x^5 + 1$

19. What is the x-intercept of the hyperbola

$$\frac{(x-1)^2}{10} - \frac{(y+2)^2}{4} = 1 \,?$$

(A) $(4.16, 0)$ and $(-4.16, 0)$

(B) $(3.12, 0)$ and $(-3.12, 0)$

(C) $(4.16, 0)$ and $(-2.16, 0)$

(D) $(5.47, 0)$ and $(-3.47, 0)$

(E) $(5.12, 0)$ and $(-5.12, 0)$

GO ON TO THE NEXT PAGE

MATHEMATICS LEVEL 2 TEST - *Continued*

USE THIS SPACE FOR SCRATCHWORK.

20. $\sin\left(\theta - \dfrac{\pi}{2}\right) =$

(A) $\sin\theta$
(B) $-\sin\theta$
(C) $\cos\theta$
(D) $-\cos\theta$
(E) $\sin\theta\cos\theta$

21. Which of the following is the solution set of

$$\dfrac{(x-2)(x-1)^2}{x+2} \le 0$$

(A) $x < -2$
(B) $x \ge 0$
(C) $-2 \le x \le 1$
(D) $-2 < x \le 2$
(E) $-2 \le x \le 1$ or $x > 2$

22. There are 4 boys and 5 girls in a chess club. In how many ways could 3 boys and 3 girls be selected to attend the school tournament?

(A)   40
(B)   80
(C)   120
(D)   360
(E)   720

23. If the probability that a light bulb is defective is $\dfrac{1}{10}$, what is the probability that a package of 10 light bulbs has exactly two defective bulbs?

(A) 0.01   (B) 0.10   (C) 0.19   (D) 0.25   (E) 0.33

GO ON TO THE NEXT PAGE

USE THIS SPACE FOR SCRATCHWORK.

24. A polynomial $P(x)$ has remainder of three when divided by $(x-1)$ and remainder of five when divided by $(x-2)$. If $P(x)$ is divided by $(x-1)(x-2)$, then the remainder is

(A) 8
(B) $x+8$
(C) $2x-1$
(D) $2x+1$
(E) $3x+1$

25. In Figure 1, a triangle is inscribed in a semicircle. If $BC=10$, what is the area of $\triangle ABC$ in terms of θ?

(A) $50\sin\theta$

(B) $50\cos\theta$

(C) $50\sin\theta\cos\theta$

(D) $50\tan\theta$

(E) $\dfrac{50}{\tan\theta}$

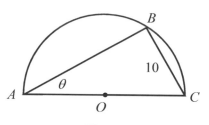

Figure 1

26. If a rectangular prism has dimensions a, b, and c, which of the following represents the length of its diagonal?

(A) $\sqrt{a+b+c}$

(B) $\sqrt[3]{a^2+b^2+c^2}$

(C) $\sqrt{a^2+b^2+c^2}$

(D) $\sqrt{a^3+b^3+c^3}$

(E) $\sqrt[3]{a^3+b^3+c^3}$

GO ON TO THE NEXT PAGE

USE THIS SPACE FOR SCRATCHWORK.

27. If vectors $\vec{a} = (3, -4)$ and $\vec{b} = (-2, 3)$, then $\left| \vec{a} - \vec{b} \right| =$

    (A) 5.68
    (B) 7.07
    (C) 8.60
    (D) 9.13
    (E) 10.87

28. If $3 + 4i$ is a root of $2x^2 + ax + b = 0$, then $b =$

    (A) 25
    (B) −25
    (C) 50
    (D) −50
    (E) It cannot be determined from the information given.

29. If $\cos\theta = -\dfrac{1}{3}$ and $90° < \theta < 180°$, then $\sin(2\theta)$ equals

    (A) $\dfrac{3\sqrt{3}}{8}$

    (B) $-\dfrac{3\sqrt{2}}{8}$

    (C) $\dfrac{4\sqrt{2}}{9}$

    (D) $-\dfrac{4\sqrt{2}}{9}$

    (E) $-\dfrac{5\sqrt{2}}{11}$

30. What is the distance from the plane $3x - 4y - 5z + 10 = 0$ to the point $(0, 0, 0)$?

    (A) $\sqrt{2}$
    (B) 2
    (C) $2\sqrt{2}$
    (D) 4
    (E) $4\sqrt{2}$

GO ON TO THE NEXT PAGE

USE THIS SPACE FOR SCRATCHWORK.

31. If $x_0 = 1$ and $x_{n+1} - x_n = 2n$, then $x_{10} =$

   (A) 20
   (B) 91
   (C) 162
   (D) 268
   (E) 381

32. The line $ax + by - 4 = 0$ forms a triangular region with the
   x-axis and y-axis. What is the area of the region in terms
   of a and b?

   (A) $\dfrac{2}{|ab|}$ (B) $\dfrac{4}{|ab|}$ (C) $\dfrac{|ab|}{8}$ (D) $\dfrac{|ab|}{16}$ (E) $\dfrac{8}{|ab|}$

33. Which of the following is equivalent to the expression
   $\dfrac{\tan 70^\circ - \tan 20^\circ}{1 + \tan 70^\circ \tan 20^\circ}$?

   (A) $\tan 90^\circ$

   (B) $\tan 50^\circ$

   (C) $\dfrac{\tan 90^\circ}{\tan 50^\circ}$

   (D) $\dfrac{\tan 50^\circ}{1 - \tan 50^\circ}$

   (E) $\dfrac{1 - \tan 50^0}{\tan 50^o}$

34. In $\triangle ABC$, $\angle B$ is an obtuse angle, $AB = 15$, $BC = 20$, and
   the area of the triangle is 90. What is the measure of $\angle B$?

   (A) 0.36
   (B) 0.64
   (C) 2.50
   (D) 5.48
   (C) 5.63

GO ON TO THE NEXT PAGE

MATHEMATICS LEVEL 2 TEST - *Continued*

35. The constant term of the expansion of $\left(x+\dfrac{1}{x}\right)^{10}$ is

    (A) 1   (B) 45   (C) 150   (D) 210   (E) 252

36. The lateral surface area of a right cylinder in Figure 2 is 80. If the height of the cylinder is 10, what is the volume of the cylinder?

    (A) 48.4
    (B) 50.9
    (C) 54.8
    (D) 60.3
    (E) 61.4

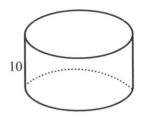

10

Figure 2

37. Figure 3 shows the graph of $y = ax^2 + bx + c$. Which of the following could NOT be true?

    (A) $ab > 0$
    (B) $bc < 0$
    (C) $ac < 0$
    (D) $b^2 > 4ac$
    (E) $b^2 < 4ac$

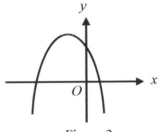

Figure 3

38. Which of the following is an odd function?

    (A) $f(x) = x^2 - 5$

    (B) $f(x) = x + \sin x$

    (C) $f(x) = x + |x|$

    (D) $f(x) = 3$

    (E) $f(x) = \dfrac{1}{x^2 - 1}$

39. If $\theta = \operatorname{Arc\,cos} \dfrac{1}{2}$, what is the value of $\sin \dfrac{\theta}{2}$?

    (A) $\dfrac{1}{2}$ (B) $-\dfrac{1}{2}$ (C) $\dfrac{\sqrt{3}}{2}$ (D) $-\dfrac{\sqrt{3}}{2}$ (E) $\dfrac{\sqrt{3}}{3}$

GO ON TO THE NEXT PAGE

USE THIS SPACE FOR SCRATCHWORK.

40. If $f(x) = (x-1)(x^2 + x + 1)$, which of the following statements are true?

    I. The function f is increasing for $x \geq 1$

    II. The function $f(x) = 0$ has three real solutions.

    III. The domain of the function $f(x)$ is all real numbers.

  (A) I only
  (B) II only
  (C) I and III only
  (D) II and III only
  (E) I, II, and III

41. If $\angle A$ is obtuse and $\cos A = -\dfrac{3}{5}$, $\cos\dfrac{1}{2}A$ is

  (A) $-\dfrac{3}{5}$

  (B) $-\dfrac{1}{5}$

  (C) $\dfrac{1}{5}$

  (D) $\dfrac{\sqrt{5}}{5}$

  (E) $\dfrac{2\sqrt{5}}{5}$

42. What is the length of the major axis of an ellipse whose equation is $4x^2 - 16x + y^2 - 4y + 16 = 0$?

  (A) 1
  (B) 2
  (C) 4
  (D) 6
  (E) 8

GO ON TO THE NEXT PAGE

USE THIS SPACE FOR SCRATCHWORK.

43. Which of the following is an even function?

 (A) $f(x) = \sin x$
 (B) $f(x) = \tan x$
 (C) $f(x) = e^{2x}$
 (D) $f(x) = 2x^2 - 3$
 (E) $f(x) = \log x$

44. What is the sum of the infinite series

 $$1 - \frac{2}{3} + \frac{4}{9} - \frac{8}{27} + ...?$$

 (A) 0
 (B) 0.2
 (C) 0.4
 (D) 0.6
 (D) Infinite

45. $\lim\limits_{n \to \infty} \dfrac{2}{\sqrt{n^2 + n} - n} =$

 (A) 0
 (B) 2
 (C) 4
 (D) 10
 (E) Infinite

46. If $y = \log_5 \left(x^2 - 6x + 14 \right)$, what is the minimum value of the equation ?

 (A) -2
 (B) -1
 (C) $\;\;1$
 (D) $\;\;2$
 (E) $\;\;5$

47. If $_{n+1}P_2 - {}_nP_2 = 12$, what is the integer value of n ?

 (A) 5   (B) 6   (C) 7   (D) 8   (E) 10

GO ON TO THE NEXT PAGE

USE THIS SPACE FOR SCRATCHWORK.

48.   The middle term of the expansion of $(x-2y)^4$ is

(A) $12x^2y^2$

(B) $-12x^2y^2$

(C) $24x^2y^2$

(D) $-24x^2y^2$

(E) $32x^2y^2$

49.   If $f(x)=\sqrt{9-x^2}$ and $x\le 0$, what is the inverse of $f(x)$?

(A) $f^{-1}(x)=\sqrt{x^2-3}$

(B) $f^{-1}(x)=\sqrt{9-x^2}$ and $x\le 0$

(C) $f^{-1}(x)=-\sqrt{9-x^2}$ and $x\ge 0$

(D) $f^{-1}(x)=-\sqrt{9-x^2}$ and $x\le 0$

(E) $f^{-1}(x)=\sqrt{x^2-9}$ and $x\le 0$

50.   In Figure 4, what is the equation of line ℓ that is tangent to
the circle $x^2+y^2=1$ and passes through the point $(0, 2)$?

(A) $y=-x+2$

(B) $y=-\sqrt{2}x+2$

(C) $y=-\sqrt{3}x+2$

(D) $y=-2x+2$

(E) $y=-3x+2$

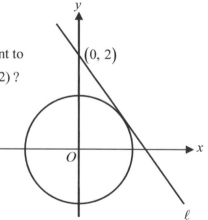

Figure 4

S T O P

IF YOU FINISH BEFORE TIME IS CALLED, YOU MAY CHECK YOUR WORK ON THIS TEST ONLY.

DO NOT TURN TO ANY OTHER TEST IN THIS BOOK.

No Test Material on This Page

TEST 4 ANSWERS

#	answer	#	answer	#	answer	#	answer	#	answer
1	B	11	E	21	D	31	B	41	D
2	D	12	A	22	A	32	E	42	C
3	C	13	C	23	C	33	B	43	D
4	C	14	C	24	D	34	C	44	D
5	B	15	C	25	E	35	E	45	C
6	D	16	C	26	C	36	B	46	C
7	D	17	D	27	C	37	E	47	B
8	C	18	C	28	C	38	B	48	C
9	B	19	D	29	D	39	A	49	C
10	D	20	D	30	A	40	C	50	C

Explanations: Test 4

1. **(B)** Since $\left(a-\dfrac{1}{a}\right)^2 = a^2 + \dfrac{1}{a^2} - 2$ and $\left(a+\dfrac{1}{a}\right)^2 = a^2 + \dfrac{1}{a^2} + 2$,

then $\left(a-\dfrac{1}{a}\right)^2 - \left(a+\dfrac{1}{a}\right)^2 = -4$.

2. **(D)** In Quadrant I:

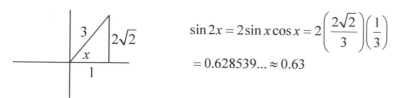

$$\sin 2x = 2\sin x \cos x = 2\left(\dfrac{2\sqrt{2}}{3}\right)\left(\dfrac{1}{3}\right)$$
$$= 0.628539... \approx 0.63$$

3. **(C)** Only choice (C) passed a horizontal line test.
Only one-to-one functions have an inverse function.

4. **(C)** Since $\sqrt{x^2} = |x|$, $|x| = 5$. Therefore, $x = \pm 5$.

5. **(B)** $x^2 - 2x + y^2 - 4y = 9 \rightarrow (x-1)^2 + (y-2)^2 = 14$
$r^2 = 14 \rightarrow r = 3.74165... \approx 3.74$

6. **(D)** $g(2) = \dfrac{2-1}{2+1} = \dfrac{1}{3}$, $f\left(\dfrac{1}{3}\right) = \sqrt{9\left(\dfrac{1}{3}\right)^2 - \dfrac{1}{3}} = \sqrt{\dfrac{2}{3}} = \dfrac{\sqrt{6}}{3}$

7. **(D)** $f(x) = 5$ is a constant function for any real x. Therefore, $5 + 5 = 10$.

8. (C) Since $10! = 10 \cdot 9!$, $\dfrac{10 \cdot 9! \cdot 10 \cdot 9!}{9! \, 9!} = 100$.

9. (B) $\left|x^2 - 1\right| < 1 \quad \rightarrow \quad -1 < x^2 - 1 < 1 \quad \rightarrow \quad \left\{x^2 > 0\right\} \cap \left\{x^2 - 2 < 0\right\}$

$\rightarrow \quad \left\{x \neq 0\right\} \cap \left\{-\sqrt{2} < x < \sqrt{2}\right\}$

10. (D) Substitute $y = x + k$. $x^2 + (x + k)^2 = 4$

$x^2 + x^2 + 2kx + k^2 = 4 \quad \rightarrow \quad 2x^2 + 2kx + k^2 - 4 = 0$

Since the line is tangent to the ellipse, its discriminant should be 0.

$D = 4k^2 - 4(2)(k^2 - 4) = 0 \quad \rightarrow \quad k^2 = 8 \quad \rightarrow \quad k = \pm 2\sqrt{2}$

Or, since $OM = 2$, $\overline{OM} \perp \overline{MP}$,
$\triangle OPR$ is an isosceles triangle,
and $MP = 2$,
$OP = \sqrt{2^2 + 2^2} = 2\sqrt{2}$.
Therefore, the values of
k are $2\sqrt{2}$ or $-2\sqrt{2}$.

11. (E) $g\left(f(x)\right) = e^{2\ln(x+1)} = e^{\ln(x+1)^2} = (x+1)^2 = x^2 + 2x + 1$

12. (A) $f^{-1}\left(f(x)\right) = x$ and $f\left(f^{-1}(x)\right) = x$.

13. (C) Since $\log_2 3 = \log_{2^4} 3^4 = \log_{16} 81$, then $\log_{16} 81 - \log_{16} 81 = 0$.

14. (C) Let three numbers be $a - d$, a, $a + d$, where $d > 0$.

$(a - d) + a + (a + d) = 3a = 36 \quad \rightarrow \quad a = 12$

$(12 - d)12(12 + d) = 1680 \quad \rightarrow \quad 144 - d^2 = 140 \quad \rightarrow \quad d^2 = 4 \quad \rightarrow \quad d = 2$

Therefore, the largest number is $12 + 2 = 14$.

15. (C) $\dfrac{3 + i}{1 + i} = \dfrac{(3 + i)(1 - i)}{(1 + i)(1 - i)} = \dfrac{4 - 2i}{2} = 2 - i$

Since $a + bi = 2 - i$, $a = 2$ and $b = -1$.

16. (C) Since $\sin(A + B) = 0.2$, $A + B = 165.5224... \approx 165.5°$ in Quadrant II.

$\sin A = \dfrac{\sqrt{3}}{2} \quad \rightarrow \quad A = 60°$ or $120°$

Therefore, $165.5° - 60° = 105.5°$ or $165.5° - 120° = 45.5°$.

17. (D) The standard form of the parabola is $x^2 = \dfrac{1}{2}y = 4\left(\dfrac{1}{8}\right)y$.

Therefore, the focus is at $\left(0, \dfrac{1}{8}\right)$ and the directrix is $y = -\dfrac{1}{8}$.

18. (C) Odd functions are symmetric with respect to the origin.
(C) is odd function.

19. (D) Let $y = 0$. $\dfrac{(x-1)^2}{10} - 1 = 1 \;\rightarrow\; (x-1)^2 = 20 \;\rightarrow\; (x-1) = \pm\sqrt{20}$

$x = 1 \pm 2\sqrt{5} \;\rightarrow\; x \approx 5.47 \text{ or } -3.47$

20. (D) $\sin\left(\theta - \dfrac{\pi}{2}\right) = \sin\theta\cos\dfrac{\pi}{2} - \cos\theta\sin\dfrac{\pi}{2} = -\cos\theta$

21. (D) Method 1) Graphic Solution: multiply by $(x+2)^2 > 0$.

$(x+2)^2 \dfrac{(x-2)(x-1)^2}{(x+2)} \le 0 \cdot (x+2)^2 \qquad \rightarrow \quad (x+2)(x-2)(x-1)^2 \le 0 \text{ and } x \ne -2$

$y = (x+2)(x-2)(x-1)^2$

Therefore, $y \le 0$ in the interval $-2 < x \le 2$.

Method 2) Test value:

Test value $\quad -3 \qquad 0 \qquad 1.5 \qquad 3$

At $x = -2 \;\rightarrow\; \dfrac{(-)(+)}{(-)} \le 0 \;(F)$

At $x = 0 \;\rightarrow\; \dfrac{(-)(+)}{(+)} \le 0 \;(T)$

At $x = 1.5 \;\rightarrow\; \dfrac{(-)(+)}{(+)} \le 0 \;(T)$ $\qquad -2 \le x < 2$

At $x = 3 \;\rightarrow\; \dfrac{(+)(+)}{(+)} \le 0 \;(F)$

Method 3) Use graphic utility directly.

22. (A) $\binom{4}{3} \times \binom{5}{3} = 4 \cdot 10 = 40$ $\binom{4}{3} = {}_4C_3$

23. (C) $\binom{10}{2}\left(\frac{1}{10}\right)^2\left(\frac{9}{10}\right)^8 = 0.1937... \approx 0.19$

24. (D) $P(x) = (x-1)Q_1(x) + 3$ -------(1) $P(x) = (x-2)Q_2(x) + 5$ ------(2)
$P(x) = (x-1)(x-2)Q(x) + ax + b$ -------(3)
From equations (1) and (3)
$P(1) = 3 = a + b$ --------(4)
From equations (2) and (3)
$P(2) = 5 = 2a + b$ ------(5)
From (4) and (5)
$a = 2$ and $b = 1$. Therefore, the remainder is $2x + 1$.

25. (E)   Since $\tan\theta = \dfrac{10}{AB}$, $AB = \dfrac{10}{\tan\theta}$.

The area of $\triangle ABC = \dfrac{1}{2}(10)\left(\dfrac{10}{\tan\theta}\right) = \dfrac{50}{\tan\theta}$.

26. (C)   The length of the diagonal $= \sqrt{a^2 + b^2 + c^2}$

27. (C) $\vec{z} = \vec{a} - \vec{b} = \big(3 - (-2), -4 - 3\big) = (5, -7)$, $|\vec{z}| = \sqrt{5^2 + (-7)^2} = 8.602325 \approx 8.60$

28. (C)   Since $3 + 4i$ is a root of the equation, then its conjugate $3 - 4i$ is also the root of the equation.
The product of the roots is $\dfrac{b}{2}$.

$(3 + 4i)(3 - 4i) = 25 = \dfrac{b}{2} \ \rightarrow \ b = 50$

29. (D) $\sin 2\theta = 2\sin\theta\cos\theta = 2\left(\dfrac{2\sqrt{2}}{3}\right)\left(-\dfrac{1}{3}\right) = -\dfrac{4\sqrt{2}}{9}$

30. (A) $D = \dfrac{|3(0) - 4(0) - 5(0) + 10|}{\sqrt{3^2 + (-4)^2 + (-5)^2}} = \dfrac{10}{5\sqrt{2}} = \dfrac{2}{\sqrt{2}} = \sqrt{2}$

31. (B)

$$n=1, \quad x_2 - x_1 = 2 \quad x_2 = x_1 + 2 = 1 + 2$$
$$n=2, \quad x_3 - x_2 = 4 \quad x_3 = x_2 + 4 = 1 + 2 + 4$$
$$n=3, \quad x_4 - x_3 = 6 \quad x_4 = x_3 + 6 = 1 + 2 + 4 + 6$$
$$\cdots\cdots$$
$$n=9, \quad x_{10} - x_9 = 18 \quad x_{10} = x_9 + 18 = 1 + 2 + 4 + 6 + \cdots + 18$$

Therefore, $x_{10} = 1 + (2 + 4 + 6 + \cdots + 18) = 1 + \dfrac{(2+18)\cdot 9}{2} = 91$

32. (E) x-intercept: $ax = 4 \rightarrow x = \dfrac{4}{a}$, y-intercept: $by = 4 \rightarrow y = \dfrac{4}{b}$

The area of the triangle $A = \dfrac{1}{2}\left(\dfrac{4}{|a|}\right)\left(\dfrac{4}{|b|}\right) = \dfrac{8}{|ab|}$: area cannot be negative.

33. (B) Since $\tan(A - B) = \dfrac{\tan A - \tan B}{1 + \tan A \tan B}$, $\tan(70° - 20°) = \dfrac{\tan 70° - \tan 20°}{1 + \tan 70° \tan 20°}$.

34. (C) Area of $\triangle ABC = \dfrac{15 \cdot 20 \cdot \sin B}{2} = 90 \rightarrow \sin B = \dfrac{3}{5} \rightarrow B = \sin^{-1}\left(\dfrac{3}{5}\right) = 0.6435\cdots$

Since $\angle B$ is obtuse, $\angle B = \pi - 0.6435 \approx 2.50$.

35. (E) Since the general term is $_{10}C_r (x)^r \left(\dfrac{1}{x}\right)^{10-r} = {}_{10}C_r x^r \cdot x^{-10+r} = {}_{10}C_r x^{2r-10}$,

the constant term is $_{10}C_5 x^°$ when $r = 5$. That is $_{10}C_5 = 252$.

36. (B) The lateral area: $2\pi rh = 80 \rightarrow r = \dfrac{80}{2\pi h} = \dfrac{80}{20r} = \dfrac{4}{\pi}$

$V = \pi r^2 h = \pi\left(\dfrac{4}{\pi}\right)^2 \cdot 10 = \dfrac{160}{\pi} = 50.9295\cdots \approx 50.9$

37. (E) From the graph, (1) Concave down ----- $a < 0$

(2) Axis of symmetry ----- $-\dfrac{b}{2a} < 0 \rightarrow b < 0$

(3) y-intercept ----- $f(0) = c > 0$

(4) Two unequal roots ---- $D = b^2 - 4ac > 0 \rightarrow b^2 > 4ac$

(E) is not true because $y = f(x)$ has two real roots.

38. (B) Since $y = x$ and $y = \sin x$ are odd functions, then $f(x) = x + \sin x$ is an odd function.

39. (A) Since $\theta = \arccos\left(\dfrac{1}{2}\right) = 60°$, $\sin\left(\dfrac{60°}{2}\right) = \sin 30° = \dfrac{1}{2}$.

40. (C)   Graphic utility: The graph of $f(x) = (x-1)(x^2+x+1)$ is as follows.

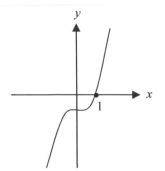

i) The function is increasing for $x \geq 1$.
ii) The domain of the function is all real x.

Algebraically: $x^2 + x + 1$ is positive for all real x, because its discriminant $D < 0$.
Therefore, for the interval $x \geq 1$, $f(x)$ is always positive.

41. (D)   Since $\cos A = -\dfrac{3}{5}$ and A is obtuse, $A = 126.8698976$. $\dfrac{A}{2} = 63.4349 = $ acute angle

Therefore, $\cos\dfrac{A}{2} = +\sqrt{\dfrac{1+\cos A}{2}} = \sqrt{\dfrac{1+\left(-\dfrac{3}{5}\right)}{2}} = \sqrt{\dfrac{1}{5}} = \dfrac{\sqrt{5}}{5}$.

Or, $\cos(63.4349) = 0.447214 \approx \dfrac{\sqrt{5}}{5}$.

42. (C)   The standard expression of the ellipse: $4(x^2 - 4x + 4) + (y^2 - 4y + 4) = -16 + 16 + 4$

$4(x-2)^2 + (y-2)^2 = 4 \;\to\; \dfrac{(x-2)^2}{1} + \dfrac{(y-2)^2}{4} = 1 \;\to\; a^2 = 4 \;\to\; a = 2$

Therefore, the length of the major axis $= 2a = 4$

43. (D) $f(x) = 2x^2 - 3$, because $f(x) = f(-x)$.

44. (D)   Since $r = -\dfrac{2}{3}$ and $\left|-\dfrac{3}{4}\right| < 1$, the sum of the series $= \dfrac{a}{1-r} = \dfrac{1}{1-\left(-\dfrac{2}{3}\right)} = \dfrac{3}{5}$.

45. (C) $\displaystyle\lim_{x\to\infty} \dfrac{2\left(\sqrt{n^2+n}+n\right)}{\left(\sqrt{n^2+n}-n\right)\left(\sqrt{n^2+n}+n\right)} = \lim_{x\to\infty} \dfrac{2\left(\sqrt{n^2+n}+n\right)}{n^2+n-n^2} = \lim_{x\to\infty} \dfrac{2\left(\sqrt{n^2+n}+n\right)}{n}$

$\displaystyle\lim_{x\to\infty} 2\left(\sqrt{1+\dfrac{1}{n}}+1\right) = 4$

46. (C) The graph of $f(x) = x^2 - 6x + 14$ has a minimum of 23 at $x = 3$ (axis of symmetry).

Therefore, the minimum of $y = \log_5 5 = 1$.

Or using graphic utility: Trace the minimum.

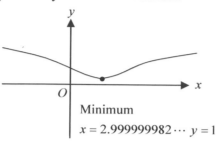

Minimum
$x = 2.999999982 \cdots \ y = 1$

47. (B) $_{n+1}P_2 - {}_nP_2 = 12 \quad \rightarrow \quad (n+1)n - n(n-1) = 1 \quad \rightarrow \quad n^2 + n - n^2 + n = 12$

$n = 6$

48. (C) The middle term is the third term: $\binom{4}{2}(x)^2(-2y)^2 = 24x^2y^2$

$\binom{4}{0}(x)^4(-2y)^0$ is the first term.

49. (C) The domain of function $f : x \leq 0 \quad \rightarrow \quad$ The range of $f^{-1}(x): y \leq 0$

The range of function $f : y \geq 0 \quad \rightarrow \quad$ The domain of $f^{-1}(x): x \geq 0$

Therefore, the inverse can be obtained as follows,

$y = \sqrt{9-x^2} \ \ (\text{switch } x \text{ and } y) \ \rightarrow \ x = \sqrt{9-\left(f^{-1}\right)^2} \ \rightarrow \ \left(f^{-1}\right)^2 = 9 - x^2$

$f^{-1} = \pm\sqrt{9-x^2}$

Since the range of the inverse is $y \leq 0$ and its domain is $x \geq 0$, $f^{-1}(x) = -\sqrt{9-x^2}$ and $x \geq 0$.

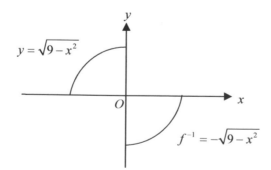

50. (C) Let the equation of line ℓ be $y = mx + 2$. Since the line is tangent to the circle, the discriminant of the equation $x^2 + (mx + 2)^2 = 1$ must be 0.

$x^2 + m^2 x^2 + 4mx + 4 - 1 = 0 \rightarrow (1 + m^2)x^2 + 4mx + 3 = 0$

$D = (4m)^2 - 4(1 + m^2)(3) = 0 \rightarrow 16m^2 - 12 - 12m^2 = 0 \rightarrow 4m^2 = 12$

$m^2 = 3 \rightarrow m = \pm\sqrt{3}$, Since the line ℓ has a negative slope, the equation of line ℓ is

$y = -\sqrt{3}x + 2$.

END

No Test Material on This Page

Test 5

Dr. John Chung's

SAT II Mathematics Level 2

MATHEMATICS LEVEL 2 TEST

REFERENCE INFORMATION

THE FOLLOWING INFORMATION IS FOR YOUR REFERENCE IN ANSWERING SOME OF THE QUESTIONS IN THIS TEST

Volume of a right circular cone with radius r and height h: $V = \dfrac{1}{3}\pi r^2 h$

Lateral Area of a right circular cone with circumference of the base c and slant height ℓ: $S = \dfrac{1}{2}c\ell$

Volume of a sphere with radius r: $V = \dfrac{4}{3}\pi r^3$

Surface Area of a sphere with radius r: $S = 4\pi r^2$

Volume of a pyramid with base area B and height h: $V = \dfrac{1}{3}Bh$

Dr. John Chung's SAT II Math Level 2

Answer Sheet

01 Ⓐ Ⓑ Ⓒ Ⓓ Ⓔ　　26 Ⓐ Ⓑ Ⓒ Ⓓ Ⓔ
02 Ⓐ Ⓑ Ⓒ Ⓓ Ⓔ　　27 Ⓐ Ⓑ Ⓒ Ⓓ Ⓔ
03 Ⓐ Ⓑ Ⓒ Ⓓ Ⓔ　　28 Ⓐ Ⓑ Ⓒ Ⓓ Ⓔ
04 Ⓐ Ⓑ Ⓒ Ⓓ Ⓔ　　29 Ⓐ Ⓑ Ⓒ Ⓓ Ⓔ
05 Ⓐ Ⓑ Ⓒ Ⓓ Ⓔ　　30 Ⓐ Ⓑ Ⓒ Ⓓ Ⓔ
06 Ⓐ Ⓑ Ⓒ Ⓓ Ⓔ　　31 Ⓐ Ⓑ Ⓒ Ⓓ Ⓔ
07 Ⓐ Ⓑ Ⓒ Ⓓ Ⓔ　　32 Ⓐ Ⓑ Ⓒ Ⓓ Ⓔ
08 Ⓐ Ⓑ Ⓒ Ⓓ Ⓔ　　33 Ⓐ Ⓑ Ⓒ Ⓓ Ⓔ
09 Ⓐ Ⓑ Ⓒ Ⓓ Ⓔ　　34 Ⓐ Ⓑ Ⓒ Ⓓ Ⓔ
10 Ⓐ Ⓑ Ⓒ Ⓓ Ⓔ　　35 Ⓐ Ⓑ Ⓒ Ⓓ Ⓔ
11 Ⓐ Ⓑ Ⓒ Ⓓ Ⓔ　　36 Ⓐ Ⓑ Ⓒ Ⓓ Ⓔ
12 Ⓐ Ⓑ Ⓒ Ⓓ Ⓔ　　37 Ⓐ Ⓑ Ⓒ Ⓓ Ⓔ
13 Ⓐ Ⓑ Ⓒ Ⓓ Ⓔ　　38 Ⓐ Ⓑ Ⓒ Ⓓ Ⓔ
14 Ⓐ Ⓑ Ⓒ Ⓓ Ⓔ　　39 Ⓐ Ⓑ Ⓒ Ⓓ Ⓔ
15 Ⓐ Ⓑ Ⓒ Ⓓ Ⓔ　　40 Ⓐ Ⓑ Ⓒ Ⓓ Ⓔ
16 Ⓐ Ⓑ Ⓒ Ⓓ Ⓔ　　41 Ⓐ Ⓑ Ⓒ Ⓓ Ⓔ
17 Ⓐ Ⓑ Ⓒ Ⓓ Ⓔ　　42 Ⓐ Ⓑ Ⓒ Ⓓ Ⓔ
18 Ⓐ Ⓑ Ⓒ Ⓓ Ⓔ　　43 Ⓐ Ⓑ Ⓒ Ⓓ Ⓔ
19 Ⓐ Ⓑ Ⓒ Ⓓ Ⓔ　　44 Ⓐ Ⓑ Ⓒ Ⓓ Ⓔ
20 Ⓐ Ⓑ Ⓒ Ⓓ Ⓔ　　45 Ⓐ Ⓑ Ⓒ Ⓓ Ⓔ
21 Ⓐ Ⓑ Ⓒ Ⓓ Ⓔ　　46 Ⓐ Ⓑ Ⓒ Ⓓ Ⓔ
22 Ⓐ Ⓑ Ⓒ Ⓓ Ⓔ　　47 Ⓐ Ⓑ Ⓒ Ⓓ Ⓔ
23 Ⓐ Ⓑ Ⓒ Ⓓ Ⓔ　　48 Ⓐ Ⓑ Ⓒ Ⓓ Ⓔ
24 Ⓐ Ⓑ Ⓒ Ⓓ Ⓔ　　49 Ⓐ Ⓑ Ⓒ Ⓓ Ⓔ
25 Ⓐ Ⓑ Ⓒ Ⓓ Ⓔ　　50 Ⓐ Ⓑ Ⓒ Ⓓ Ⓔ

The number of right answers: ☐

The number of wrong answers: ☐

$$\underline{\hspace{2cm}} - \frac{1}{4} \times \underline{\hspace{2cm}} = \underline{\hspace{2cm}}$$
# of correct　　# of wrong　　Raw score

Score Conversion Table

Raw Score	Scaled Score	Raw Score	Scaled Score	Raw Score	Scaled Score
50	800	28	640	6	480
49	800	27	630	5	470
48	800	26	620	4	470
47	800	25	620	3	460
46	800	24	610	2	460
45	800	23	610	1	450
44	800	22	600	0	450
43	800	21	600		
42	800	20	590		
41	800	19	590		
40	780	18	580		
39	760	17	570		
38	750	16	560		
37	740	15	550		
36	720	14	540		
35	710	13	530		
34	700	12	520		
33	690	11	510		
32	680	10	500		
31	670	9	490		
30	660	8	490		
29	650	7	480		

MATHEMATICS LEVEL 2 TEST

For each of the following problems, decide which is the BEST of the choices given. If the exact numerical value is not one of the choices, select the choice that best approximates this value. Then fill in the corresponding circle on the answer sheet

Note: (1) A scientific or graphing calculator will be necessary for answering some (but not all) of the questions in this test. For each question you will have to decide whether or not you should use a calculator.

(2) For some questions in this test you may have to decide whether your calculator should be in the radian mode or the degree mode.

(3) Figures that accompany problems in this test are intended to provide information useful in solving the problems. They are drawn as accurately as possible EXCEPT when it is stated in a specific problem that its figure is not drawn to scale. All figures lie in a plane unless otherwise indicated.

(4) Unless otherwise specified, the domain of any function f is assumed to be the set of all real numbers x for which $f(x)$ is a real number. The range of f is assumed to be the set of all real numbers $f(x)$, where x is in the domain of f.

(5) Reference information that may be useful in answering the questions in this test can be found on the page preceding Question 1.

USE THIS SPACE FOR SCRATCHWORK

1. Which is the negation of the statement "Some numbers are even"?

   (A) All numbers are even.
   (B) Some numbers are not even.
   (C) All numbers are not even.
   (D) All numbers are odd.
   (E) Some numbers are not odd.

2. In how many ways can 2 juniors and 2 seniors be selected from a group of 8 juniors and 6 seniors?

   (A) 4
   (B) 48
   (C) 420
   (D) 480
   (E) 840

USE THIS SPACE FOR SCRATCHWORK.

3. Find the largest integral value of k such that the roots of
$x^2 + 5x + k = 0$ are real?

(A) 4   (B) 6   (C) 7   (D) 8   (E) 10

4. In Figure 1, $\overline{BD}$ is the altitude to the hypotenuse $\overline{AC}$. If
$BD = 8$ and $BC = 10$, which is the area of $\triangle ABC$?

(A) 66.67
(B) 112.45
(C) 125.36
(D) 133.33
(E) 150

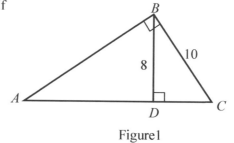

Figure1

5. If a and b are positive numbers, and $a^2 + b^2 = 29$ and
$ab = 10$, then $a + b =$

(A) $\sqrt{7}$ (B) 7   (C) 8   (D) $5\sqrt{2}$ (E) $7\sqrt{2}$

6. If $x = 2i$ is a solution to the equation $x^3 + kx = 0$, what is the
value of k ?

(A) 8
(B) 6
(C) 4
(D) 2
(E) 1

7. If $f(x) = \dfrac{1}{x}$ and $g(x) = \sqrt{x+5}$, what is the domain of
$f(g(x))$?

(A) All x such that $x > -5$
(B) All x such that $x > 0$
(C) All x such that $x \geq 0$
(D) All x such that $x \neq 0$ and $x > -5$
(E) All x such that $x \neq 0$ and $x \geq -5$

GO ON TO THE NEXT PAGE

USE THIS SPACE FOR SCRATCHWORK.

8.   Which of the following graphs best describes the set of points

(a, b) for which $\left|\dfrac{a}{2}\right| + |b| = 2$ in the xy-plane ?

(A)   (B)

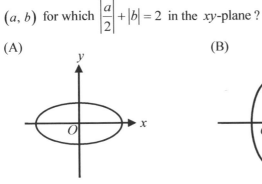

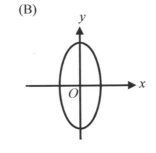

(C)   (D)

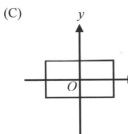

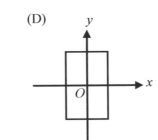

(E)

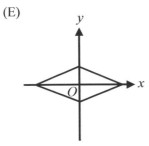

9.   Which of the following is symmetric with respect to
      the y-axis ?

(A) $y = (x-1)^2$

(B) $x = y^2$

(C) $x^2 + 4y^2 = 4$

(D) $x^2 - 2x + y^2 = 3$

(E) $y = |x - 2|$

GO ON TO THE NEXT PAGE

USE THIS SPACE FOR SCRATCHWORK.

10. If $x^{0.4} = 10$, then what is the value of $x^{0.6}$?

    (A) $10\sqrt{10}$
    (B) $15\sqrt{5}$
    (C) $\sqrt{100}$
    (D) $15\sqrt{10}$
    (E) $\sqrt{10000}$

11. If $e^x = 3$, what is the value of $\left(\dfrac{1}{e^3}\right)^{-2x}$?

    (A) 729   (B) 64   (C) 27   (D) $\dfrac{1}{64}$ (E) $\dfrac{1}{729}$

12. If $\dfrac{x - \dfrac{1}{x}}{1 - \dfrac{1}{x^2}} = 5$, what is the value of x?

    (A) -5 (B) -3 (C) -1.25 (D) 1.25   (E) 5

13. Figure 2 shows a hemisphere with a radius of 4. Find the surface area of that figure.

    (A) 20π
    (B) 32π
    (C) 36π
    (D) 42π
    (E) 48π

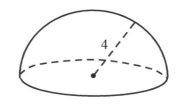

Figure 2

14. If two forces of 10 pounds and 15 pounds act on a body with an angle of $60°$ between them, what is the magnitude of the resultant?

    (A) 16.80
    (B) 18.21
    (C) 20.42
    (D) 21.80
    (E) 24.92

GO ON TO THE NEXT PAGE

MATHEMATICS LEVEL 2 TEST - *Continued*

15. If the matrix equation $\begin{pmatrix} 2 & -3 \\ 2 & 5 \end{pmatrix}\begin{pmatrix} x \\ y \end{pmatrix} = \begin{pmatrix} 2 \\ 3 \end{pmatrix}$, what is the value of y?

(A) -0.625
(B) -0.505
(C) 0.125
(D) 3.500
(E) 4.254

16. In the arithmetic progression $\{a_n\}$, $a_2 = 50$ and $a_4 = 44$. Which is the first term that is a negative number?

(A) 17th
(B) 18th
(C) 19th
(D) 20th
(E) 21th

17. If $\log_2 x + \log_2(x-1) < 1$, which of the following is the solution set of the inequality?

(A) $\{x \mid x < -1\}$
(B) $\{x \mid -1 < x < 2\}$
(C) $\{x \mid 0 < x < 2\}$
(D) $\{x \mid 1 < x < 2\}$
(E) $\{x \mid x > 2\}$

18. In a game, the probability of winning is $\dfrac{1}{4}$ and the probability of losing is $\dfrac{3}{4}$. If 3 games are played, what is the probability of winning at least 2 games?

(A) $\dfrac{3}{64}$ (B) $\dfrac{5}{64}$ (C) $\dfrac{5}{32}$ (D) $\dfrac{10}{27}$ (E) $\dfrac{5}{16}$

GO ON TO THE NEXT PAGE

USE THIS SPACE FOR SCRATCHWORK.

19. The graph of a polynomial function is shown in Figure 3. Which of the following could be the equation of the polynomial function?

(A) $P(x) = x(x+1)(x-3)(x^2-1)$

(B) $P(x) = x(x-1)(x^2-9)$

(C) $P(x) = x(x-1)(x+3)(x^2+5)$

(D) $P(x) = x(x+1)(x-3)(x^2+5x+10)$

(E) $P(x) = x(x+1)(x-3)^2(x^2+1)$

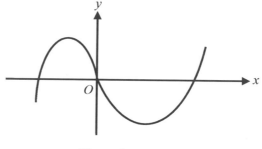

Figure 3

20. If $\sin(A-60) = \cos 40$, the measure of $\angle A$ is

(A) 110   (B) 90   (C) 80   (D) 45   (E) 20

21. If $\tan A = 4$ and $\tan B = 3$, what is the value of $\tan(A-B)$?

(A) 0.065
(B) 0.077
(C) 0.126
(D) 0.245
(E) 0.333

22. If $\dfrac{(x^2-3x-4)}{x^2} < 0$, which of the following is the solution of the inequality?

(A) $x < -1$
(B) $x > -1$
(C) $-1 < x < 4$
(D) $-1 < x < 0$ or $0 < x < 4$
(E) All real x

GO ON TO THE NEXT PAGE

MATHEMATICS LEVEL 2 TEST - *Continued*

USE THIS SPACE FOR SCRATCHWORK.

23. In Figure 4, line ℓ is the perpendicular bisector of $\overline{AB}$ at point E. What is the area of $\triangle ADE$?

(A) 2
(B) 3
(C) 4
(D) 5
(E) 10

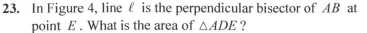

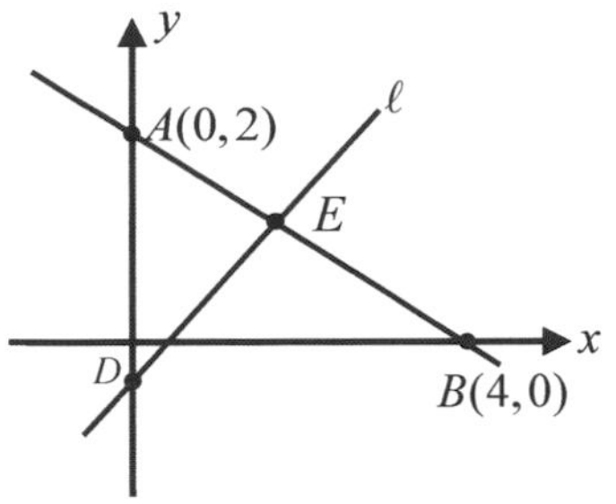

Note: Figure not drawn to scale.

Figure 4

24. In Figure 5, if the radius of the semicircle is 5, what is the area of the inscribed square?

(A) 9 (B) 16 (C) 20 (D) 25 (E) 36

Figure 5

25. What is the value of $\sec\left(\arctan\dfrac{1}{\sqrt{3}}\right)$?

(A) $\dfrac{\sqrt{3}}{2}$ (B) $\dfrac{2\sqrt{3}}{3}$ (C) $\dfrac{2\sqrt{2}}{3}$ (D) $\dfrac{3}{5}$ (E) $\dfrac{4}{7}$

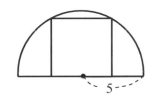

26. If two lines $y = 2x - 4$ and $y = mx + 5$ are parallel, where m is a constant, then the distance between the two lines is

(A) 4.02
(B) 5
(C) 5.4
(D) 6.25
(E) 8

27. If the parametric equations are $x = 4\sin 2\theta$ and $y = 2\cos 2\theta$, which of the following represents the graph of point (x, y)?

(A) Line
(B) Parabola
(C) Hyperbola
(D) Ellipse
(E) Circle

GO ON TO THE NEXT PAGE

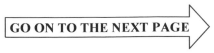

USE THIS SPACE FOR SCRATCHWORK.

28. If the equation of a circle is $x^2 - 2x + y^2 - 4y = 1$, then the area of the circle is

(A) 5π
(B) 6π
(C) 25π
(D) 36π
(E) 42π

29. In Figure 6, the graph of plane $2x + 3y + 4z = 12$ in three dimensions forms a triangular pyramid with base $\triangle AOC$. What is the volume of the pyramid?

(A) 12
(B) 18
(C) 36
(D) 48
(E) 72

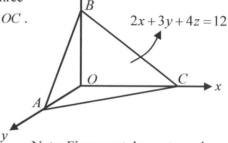

Note: Figure not drawn to scale.

Figure 6

30. $\sin^2\theta + \sin^2\theta \cdot \tan^2\theta =$

(A) $\sin^2\theta$
(B) $\cos^2\theta$
(C) $\tan^2\theta$
(D) $\cot^2\theta$
(E) $\sec^2\theta$

31. If the value of $f(x) = x^2 - 3x - k$ is always positive for any x, which of the following could be the value of k?

(A) -3
(B) -2
(C) 0
(D) 2
(E) 3

GO ON TO THE NEXT PAGE

USE THIS SPACE FOR SCRATCHWORK.

32. In Figure 7, $AB = 5$ and $BC = 10$. What is the area of the quadrilateral?

(A) 25.6
(B) 28.4
(C) 32.5
(D) 42.6
(E) 62.9

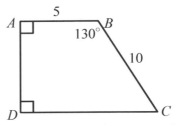

Note: Figure not drawn to scale.

Figure 7

33. If $a(x+1) + b(x-1) - (x+2) = 0$ for all real x, where a and b are constants, what is the value of a?

(A) 1.5　(B) 2.0　(C) 2.5　(D) 3.5　(E) 4.5

34. When polynomial $f(x) = 2x^2 + 5x + k$ is divided by $2x + 3$, the remainder is 5. What is the value of constant k?

(A) 1
(B) 3
(C) 5
(D) 7
(E) 8

35. What is the value of $(\sin x + \cos x)^2 - \sin 2x$?

(A) −1　(B) 0　(C) 1　(D) 2　(E) 3

36. What is the value of θ in the interval $0 \le \theta \le \dfrac{\pi}{2}$ that satisfies the equation $6\cos\theta + 1 = 5\sec\theta$?

(A) 0.45
(B) 0.59
(C) 0.62
(D) 0.78
(E) 0.82

GO ON TO THE NEXT PAGE

USE THIS SPACE FOR SCRATCHWORK.

37. If the ratio of the two roots of the equation $x^2 - kx + 18 = 0$ is $1:2$, which of the following is all the values of constant k?

(A) $\{3,6\}$

(B) $\{-9, 9\}$

(C) $\{9\}$

(D) $\{10,12\}$

(E) $\{6, 9\}$

38. If $f(x) = \dfrac{2x+1}{x-1}$ and $f^{-1}(x)$ is the inverse of $f(x)$, then $f^{-1}(3) =$

(A) -3 (B) 2 (C) 4 (D) 6 (E) 10

39. Figure 8 shows a triangle in a circle with center O. If the radius of circle O is 2, what is the area of the triangle in terms of θ?

(A) $\sin 2\theta$

(B) $2\sin\theta$

(C) $2\sin 2\theta$

(D) $2\cos\theta$

(E) $2\cos 2\theta$

Figure 8

40. In five years, the population of Spring Lake decreased steadily from 50,000 to 45,000. Find the rate of decrease per year?

(A) 1.2%

(B) 2.1%

(C) 2.4%

(D) 2.5%

(E) 3.0%

GO ON TO THE NEXT PAGE

USE THIS SPACE FOR SCRATCHWORK.

41. Find the measure of the angle between two forces of 10 pounds and 20 pounds if the magnitude of their resultant is 25 pounds.

   (A) $45.3°$
   (B) $71.8°$
   (C) $108.2°$
   (D) $123.5°$
   (E) $135.7°$

42. Find the asymptotes of $\dfrac{x^2}{8} - \dfrac{y^2}{18} = 1$.

   (A) $y = \pm\dfrac{3}{2}x$

   (B) $y = \pm\dfrac{2}{3}x$

   (C) $y = \pm\dfrac{2}{9}x$

   (D) $y = \pm\dfrac{9}{2}x$

   (E) $y = \pm\dfrac{9}{4}x$

43. If $x = \left(\log_{27} 3\right)^{\log_3 27}$, then $\log_3 x =$

   (A) 3   (B) -3 (C) $\dfrac{1}{3}$ (D) $\dfrac{1}{9}$ (E) $\dfrac{1}{27}$

44. In Figure 9, the volume of the right circular cone is 12π and the radius of the base is 3. What is the lateral area of the cone?

   (A) 4π
   (B) 6π
   (C) 15π
   (D) 18π
   (E) 36π

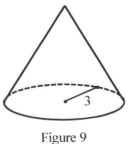

Figure 9

USE THIS SPACE FOR SCRATCHWORK.

45. The area of a triangle whose sides are of lengths 7, 20, and 23 is

   (A) $20\sqrt{5}$
   (B) 25
   (C) $25\sqrt{5}$
   (D) 30
   (E) $30\sqrt{5}$

46. What is the value of $(1+i)^{10}$?

   (A) $8i$
   (B) $16i$
   (C) $32i$
   (D) -32
   (E) -64

47. In how many ways can 10 people be divided into three groups, one group with 4 people and the other two groups with 3 people each?

   (A) 210
   (B) 420
   (C) 2100
   (D) 4200
   (E) 326000

48. Which of the following equations could be the graph shown in Figure 10?

   (A) $\dfrac{x^2}{16}+\dfrac{y^2}{6}=1$

   (B) $\dfrac{(x-8)^2}{8}+\dfrac{(y-3)^2}{3}=1$

   (C) $\dfrac{(x-8)^2}{16}+\dfrac{(y-3)^2}{9}=1$

   (D) $\dfrac{(x-8)^2}{64}+\dfrac{(y-3)^2}{9}=1$

   (E) $\dfrac{(x+8)^2}{64}+\dfrac{(y+3)^2}{9}=1$

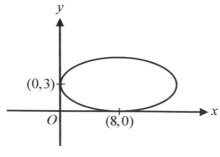

Figure 10

GO ON TO THE NEXT PAGE

MATHEMATICS LEVEL 2 TEST - *Continued*

USE THIS SPACE FOR SCRATCHWORK.

49.

	Day 1	Day 2	Day 3
16GB	10	15	20
64GB	5	9	13
128GB	11	17	18

The table above shows the number of smart phones that were sold during a three-day sale. The prices of models 16GB, 64GB, and 128GB were $300, $400, and $500, respectively. Which of the following matrix representations gives the total daily income, in dollars, received from the sale of the smart phones for each of the three days?

(A) $\begin{bmatrix} 10 & 15 & 20 \\ 5 & 9 & 13 \\ 11 & 17 & 18 \end{bmatrix} \begin{bmatrix} 300 & 400 & 500 \end{bmatrix}$

(B) $\begin{bmatrix} 10 & 15 & 20 \\ 5 & 9 & 13 \\ 11 & 17 & 18 \end{bmatrix} \begin{bmatrix} 300 \\ 400 \\ 500 \end{bmatrix}$

(C) $\begin{bmatrix} 10 & 5 & 11 \\ 15 & 9 & 17 \\ 20 & 13 & 18 \end{bmatrix} \begin{bmatrix} 300 \\ 400 \\ 500 \end{bmatrix}$

(D) $\begin{bmatrix} 300 \\ 400 \\ 500 \end{bmatrix} \begin{bmatrix} 10 & 5 & 11 \\ 15 & 9 & 17 \\ 20 & 13 & 18 \end{bmatrix}$

(E) $300\begin{bmatrix} 10 & 5 & 11 \end{bmatrix} + 400\begin{bmatrix} 15 & 9 & 17 \end{bmatrix} + 500\begin{bmatrix} 20 & 13 & 18 \end{bmatrix}$

GO ON TO THE NEXT PAGE

USE THIS SPACE FOR SCRATCHWORK.

50. From the binomial expansion of $(2x-3)^6$, what is the coefficient of x^4 ?

   (A)   −60
   (B)   68
   (C)   720
   (D) 2160
   (E) 4320

STOP

IF YOU FINISH BEFORE TIME IS CALLED, YOU MAY CHECK YOUR WORK ON THIS TEST ONLY.

DO NOT TURN TO ANY OTHER TEST IN THIS BOOK.

No Test Material on This Page

No Test Material on This Page

| TEST 5 | | | | ANSWERS | | | | | |

#	answer	#	answer	#	answer	#	answer	#	answer
1	C	11	A	21	B	31	A	41	B
2	C	12	E	22	D	32	E	42	A
3	B	13	E	23	D	33	A	43	B
4	A	14	D	24	C	34	E	44	C
5	B	15	C	25	B	35	C	45	E
6	C	16	C	26	A	36	B	46	C
7	A	17	D	27	D	37	B	47	C
8	E	18	C	28	B	38	C	48	D
9	C	19	D	29	A	39	C	49	C
10	A	20	A	30	C	40	B	50	D

Explanations: Test 5

1. (C) Remember the negation of the word "some" is "all."
Therefore, the negation is "All numbers are not even."

2. (C) $\binom{8}{2} \cdot \binom{6}{2} = 28 \cdot 15 = 420$

3. (B) Discriminant: $D = 25 - 4k \geq 0 \rightarrow 4k \leq 25 \rightarrow \rightarrow k \leq 6.25$
The largest integer value of k is 6.

4. (A) $DC = 6$

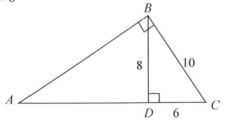

$BD^2 = AD \cdot DC \rightarrow 64 = AD \cdot 6 \rightarrow AD = \dfrac{32}{3}$

The area of $\triangle ABC = \dfrac{1}{2}\left(6 + \dfrac{32}{3}\right)(8) = 66.6666\cdots \approx 66.7$.

5. (B) $(a+b)^2 = a^2 + b^2 + 2ab = 29 + 2(10) = 49 \rightarrow a + b = 7$ (a and b are positive.)

6. (C) Substitution: $(2i)^3 + k(2i) = 0 \rightarrow -8i + 2ki = 0 \rightarrow \rightarrow 2k = 8 \rightarrow \rightarrow k = 4$

7. (A) Since $f\big(g(x)\big) = \dfrac{1}{\sqrt{x+5}}$, the domain is $x + 5 > 0 \rightarrow x > -5$.

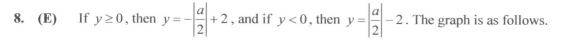

8. (E) If $y \geq 0$, then $y = -\left|\dfrac{a}{2}\right| + 2$, and if $y < 0$, then $y = \left|\dfrac{a}{2}\right| - 2$. The graph is as follows.

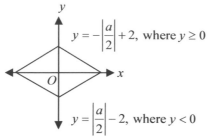

9. (C) (A) is symmetric with respect to $x = 1$. (B) is symmetric with respect to the x-axis. (C) is symmetric with respect to the x-axis or y-axis.

(D) is symmetric with respect to $x = 1$ or the y-axis. $(x-1)^2 + y^2 = 4$

(E) is symmetric with respect to $x = 2$.

10. (A) $x^{0.6} = \left(x^{0.4}\right)^{\frac{3}{2}} = 10^{\frac{3}{2}} = 10\sqrt{10}$

11. (A) $\left(\dfrac{1}{e^3}\right)^{-2x} = \left(e^{-3}\right)^{-2x} = e^{6x} = \left(e^x\right)^6 = 3^6 = 729$

Or, since $e^x = 3 \;\rightarrow\; x = \ln 3$, then $e^{6x} = e^{6\ln 3} = e^{\ln 3^6} = 3^6$.

12. (E) Compound fraction: multiply common denominator by x^2.

$$\dfrac{\left(x - \dfrac{1}{x}\right)x^2}{\left(1 - \dfrac{1}{x^2}\right)x^2} = \dfrac{x^3 - x}{x^2 - 1} = \dfrac{x\left(x^2 - 1\right)}{x^2 - 1} = x$$

Therefore, $x = 5$.

13. (E) Since the surface area of a sphere is $4\pi r^2 = 4\pi(4)^2 = 64\pi$, the surface area of a hemisphere is 32π. The area of the circular base is 16π. Therefore, the entire surface area is 48π.

14. (D) In a parallelogram, two consecutive angles are supplementary.

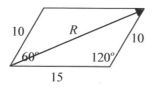

Law of cosine: $R = \sqrt{10^2 + 15^2 - 2(10)(15)\cos 120^\circ} = 21.79441\cdots \approx 21.8$

15. (C) From the matrix equation:

$$2x - 3y = 2$$
$$-\underline{|\ 2x + 5y = 3\ } \qquad , \qquad y = 0.125$$
$$-8y = -1$$

16. (C) Since $a_2 = a_1 + d = 50$ and $a_4 = a_1 + 3d = 44$, then $d = -3$ and $a_1 = 53$.
$a_n = a_1 + (n-1)d \ \rightarrow \ a_n = 53 + (n-1)(-3) < 0 \ \rightarrow \ 3n < 56$
Therefore, $n < 18.666\cdots$ and the first negative term is the 19th term.

17. (D) $\log_2 x + \log_2(x-1) < 1 \ \rightarrow \ \log_2\left(x^2 - x\right) < 1 \ \rightarrow \ \log_2\left(x^2 - x\right) < \log_2 2$

Since base 2 is greater than 1, $x^2 - x < 2 \ \rightarrow \ x^2 - x - 2 < 0 \ \rightarrow \ (x-2)(x+1) < 0$.
The solution of the inequality is $-1 < x < 2$, but $x > 1$ from the logarithmic equation.
Therefore, $1 < x < 2$.

18. (C) $\dbinom{3}{2}\left(\dfrac{1}{4}\right)^2\left(\dfrac{3}{4}\right)^1 + \dbinom{3}{3}\left(\dfrac{1}{4}\right)^3\left(\dfrac{3}{4}\right)^0 = \dfrac{9}{64} + \dfrac{1}{64} = \dfrac{5}{32}$

19. (D) The function has one zero at $x = 0$, one negative zero, and one positive zero.
Choice (D) has one zero at $x = 0$, one negative zero, and one positive zero.
$x^2 + 5x + 10$ has imaginary roots.

20. (A) Cofunction: $A - 60 + 40 = 90 \ \rightarrow \ A = 110$

21. (B) $\tan(A - B) = \dfrac{\tan A - \tan B}{1 + \tan A \tan B} = \dfrac{4 - 3}{1 + 4 \cdot 3} = \dfrac{1}{13} = 0.07692\cdots \approx 0.077$

22. (D) Test value: Graphing utility:
$\dfrac{x^2 - 3x - 4}{x^2} < 0 \ \rightarrow \ x^2 - 3x - 4 < 0 \ \rightarrow \ (x-4)(x+1) < 0 \ \rightarrow \ -1 < x < 4$ and $x \neq 0.$
Therefore, the solution set is $\{-1 < x < 0\} \cup \{0 < x < 4\}$

23. (D) The slope of $\overline{AB} = -\dfrac{2}{4} = -\dfrac{1}{2}$ and the midpoint E is $\left(\dfrac{0+4}{2}, \dfrac{2+0}{2}\right) = (2, 1)$.

The slope of the perpendicular line is 2 and passes through (2,1).
The equation of line ℓ is $y = 2x - 3$.

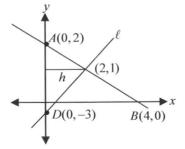

Since $AD = 5$ and the height $h = 2$,
the area of $\triangle ADE$ is $\dfrac{5 \cdot 2}{2} = 5$.

24. (C)   From the figure below: $5^2 = x^2 + (2x)^2. \rightarrow 25 = 5x^2 \rightarrow x = \sqrt{5}$

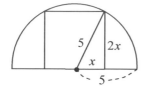

The length of an edge is $2\sqrt{5}$.

The area of the square is $\left(2\sqrt{5}\right)^2 = 20$.

25. (B)   Use calculator: $\dfrac{1}{\cos\left(\tan^{-1}\left(\dfrac{1}{\sqrt{3}}\right)\right)} = 1.1547\cdots = \dfrac{2\sqrt{3}}{3}$

Or, algebraically

Let $X = \tan^{-1}\dfrac{1}{\sqrt{3}}$. $\tan X = \dfrac{1}{\sqrt{3}}$ and $-90° < X < 90°$.

Therefore, $\sec X = \dfrac{1}{\cos X} = \dfrac{2}{\sqrt{3}} = \dfrac{2\sqrt{3}}{3}$.

26. (A)   Choose one point on $y = 2x - 4$: that is $\rightarrow$ $(0, -4)$. Two lines are parallel: $m = 2$.

The distance between a point $(0, -4)$ and the line $2x - y + 5 = 0$ is

$$D = \frac{|2(0) - (-4) + 5|}{\sqrt{2^2 + (-1)^2}} = \frac{9}{\sqrt{5}} = 4.02492\cdots \approx 4.02$$

27. (D)   Since $\sin 2\theta = \dfrac{x}{4}$ and $\cos 2\theta = \dfrac{y}{2}$, $\sin^2(2\theta) + \cos^2(2\theta) = 1 \rightarrow \dfrac{x^2}{16} + \dfrac{y^2}{4} = 1$.

The graph of the parametric equations is an ellipse.

28. (B) $x^2 - 2x + y^2 - 4y = 1 \rightarrow (x-1)^2 + (y-2)^2 = 6 \rightarrow r = \sqrt{6}$

Therefore, the area of the circle are, $\pi r^2 = 6\pi$.

29. (A)   The coordinates of each intercept is: $C(x, 0, 0)$, $A(0, y, 0)$, and $B(0, 0, z)$

When $y = 0$ and $z = 0$, $2x + 3(0) + 4(0) = 12 \rightarrow x = 6$.

           $x = 0$ and $z = 0$, $2(0) + 3y + 4(0) = 12 \rightarrow y = 4$

           $x = 0$ and $y = 0$, $2(0) + 3(0) + 4z = 12 \rightarrow z = 3$

The volume of the cone: $\dfrac{Bh}{3} = \dfrac{\left(\dfrac{6 \times 4}{2}\right) \cdot 3}{3} = 12$

30. (C) $\sin^2\theta + \sin^2\theta \tan^2\theta = \sin^2\theta\left(1 + \tan^2\theta\right) = \sin^2\theta \cdot \sec^2\theta = \sin^2\theta \cdot \dfrac{1}{\cos^2\theta} = \tan^2\theta$

31. (A) Since $f(x)$ is always positive, $f(x) = 0$ must have imaginary roots

$$D = b^2 - 4ac = (-3)^2 - 4(1)(-k) < 0 \quad \rightarrow \quad k < -\frac{9}{4}$$

Choice (A) : $-3 < -\frac{9}{4}$

32. (E) $EC = 10\sin 40$, $BE = 10\cos 40$, and $DC = 5 + EC\sin 40$.

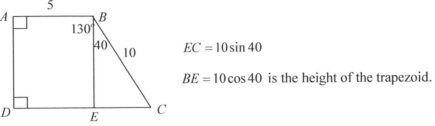

$EC = 10\sin 40$

$BE = 10\cos 40$ is the height of the trapezoid.

The area of the trapezoid:

$$A = \frac{h(b_1 + b_2)}{2} = \frac{10\cos 40 \cdot (5 + 5 + 10\sin 40)}{2} = 62.922415\cdots \approx 62.9$$

33. (A) $a(x+1) + b(x-1) - (x+2) = 0 \quad \rightarrow \quad (a+b-1)x + (a-b-2) = 0$

To be identical, $a+b-1 = 0$ and $a-b-2 = 0$.

Therefore, $2a = 3 \quad \rightarrow \quad a = \frac{3}{2}$.

34. (E) Remainder theorem: (or, long division)

$$f(x) = 2x^2 + 5x + k = (2x+3)Q(x) + 5 \quad \rightarrow \quad f\left(-\frac{3}{2}\right) = \frac{9}{2} - \frac{15}{2} + k = 5 \quad \rightarrow \quad k = 8$$

35. (C) $(\sin x + \cos x)^2 - \sin 2x \quad \rightarrow \quad \sin^2 x + 2\sin x\cos x + \cos^2 x - 2\sin x\cos x = 1$

36. (B) Use a graphic utility. Graph $y = \dfrac{5}{\cos x} - 6\cos x - 1$ and find the zero.

Or algebraically,

$$6\cos\theta + 1 = 5\sec\theta \quad \rightarrow \quad 6\cos\theta + 1 = \frac{5}{\cos\theta} \quad \rightarrow \quad 6\cos^2\theta + \cos\theta - 5 = 0$$

$$(6\cos\theta - 5)(\cos + 1) = 0$$

Therefore, $\cos\theta = \dfrac{5}{6}$ and $\cos\theta = -1$. Since $0 \le \theta \le \dfrac{\pi}{2}$, (calculator must be in radian mode)

$$\cos\theta = \frac{5}{6} \quad \rightarrow \quad \theta = \cos^{-1}\frac{5}{6} = 0.58568\cdots \approx 0.58$$

37. (B) Define the two roots as n and $2n$. The product of the two roots: $2n^2 = 18 \quad \rightarrow \quad n = \pm 3$

The sum of the roots: $n + 2n = 3n = \pm 9$

38. (C) From the inverse: $x = \dfrac{2y+1}{y-1}$ → $f^{-1} : y = \dfrac{x+1}{x-2}$ → $f^{-1}(3) = \dfrac{4}{1} = 4$

$\qquad\qquad\qquad\qquad$ Or, $3 = \dfrac{2y+1}{y-1}$ → $y = 4$

39. (C) Since $AB = 2\cos\theta$ and $OB = 2\sin\theta$,

$\qquad$ the area of $\triangle OAC = \dfrac{4\cos\theta \cdot 2\sin\theta}{2} = 4\sin\theta\cos\theta = 2\sin(2\theta)$

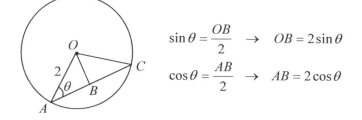

$$\sin\theta = \dfrac{OB}{2} \quad\rightarrow\quad OB = 2\sin\theta$$

$$\cos\theta = \dfrac{AB}{2} \quad\rightarrow\quad AB = 2\cos\theta$$

40. (B) $45000 = 50000(1-r)^5$ → $0.9 = (1-r)^5$ → $1-r = 0.9^{\frac{1}{5}}$

$\qquad r = 1 - 0.9^{\frac{1}{5}} = 0.0208516376 \approx 2.1\%$

41. (B) The Law of Cosines: $\angle ABC$ and θ are supplementary.

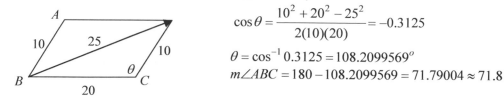

$\qquad\qquad\qquad\qquad\qquad \cos\theta = \dfrac{10^2 + 20^2 - 25^2}{2(10)(20)} = -0.3125$

$\qquad\qquad\qquad\qquad\qquad \theta = \cos^{-1} 0.3125 = 108.2099569^o$

$\qquad\qquad\qquad\qquad\qquad m\angle ABC = 180 - 108.2099569 = 71.79004 \approx 71.8$

42. (A) $\dfrac{x^2}{8} - \dfrac{y^2}{18} = 1$ → $a = \sqrt{8}$ and $b = \sqrt{18}$

$\qquad$ Therefore, the asymptotes are : $y = \pm\dfrac{b}{a}x = \pm\dfrac{\sqrt{18}}{\sqrt{8}}x = \pm\dfrac{3}{2}x$

43. (B) Since $\log_{27} 3 = \dfrac{\log 3}{3\log 3} = \dfrac{1}{3}$ and $\log_3 27 = 3$, then $x = \left(\log_{27} 3\right)^{\log_3 27} = \left(3^{-1}\right)^3 = 3^{-3}$.

$\qquad$ Therefore, $\log_3 3^{-3} = -3$.

44. (C) $A = \pi r s$, where r is a radius and s is a slant height.

$\qquad\qquad\qquad\qquad\qquad V = \dfrac{\pi r^2 h}{3} = \dfrac{\pi \cdot 9 \cdot h}{3} = 3\pi h$ → $3\pi h = 12\pi$ → $h = 4$

$\qquad\qquad\qquad\qquad\qquad$ Therefore, $s = 5$.

$\qquad\qquad\qquad\qquad\qquad A = \pi \cdot 3 \cdot 5 = 15\pi$

45. (E) Heron's Formula: $s = \dfrac{a+b+c}{2}$

$s = \dfrac{7+20+23}{2} = \dfrac{50}{2} = 25$

The area is $\sqrt{s(s-a)(s-b)(s-c)} = \sqrt{25(25-7)(25-20)(25-23)} = 30\sqrt{5}$

46. (C) Since $(1+i)^2 = 1 + 2i + i^2 = 2i$, $(1+i)^{10} = (2i)^5 = 2^5 i^5 = 32i$.

47. (C) $\dfrac{{}_{10}C_4 \times {}_6C_3 \times {}_3C_3}{2!} = 2100$

48. (D) From the graph: center $(8,3)$, $a = 8$, and $b = 3$.

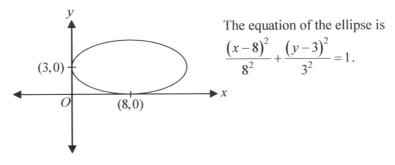

The equation of the ellipse is

$$\dfrac{(x-8)^2}{8^2} + \dfrac{(y-3)^2}{3^2} = 1.$$

49. (C) Total income each day:
Day 1: $10 \times (300) + 5 \times (400) + 11 \times (500)$
Day 2: $15 \times (300) + 9 \times (400) + 17 \times (500)$
Day 3: $20 \times (300) + 13 \times (400) + 18 \times (500)$
Its matrix form is choice (C).

50. (D) $\dbinom{6}{r}(2x)^{n-r}(-3)^r \;\rightarrow\; \dbinom{6}{r}(2)^{6-r}(-3)^r x^{6-r}$

Since $x^{6-r} = x^4$, $r = 2$.

The coefficient of x^4 is $\dbinom{6}{2} \cdot 2^4 \cdot (-3)^2 = 2160$.

END

No Test Material on This Page

Test 6

Dr. John Chung's

SAT II Mathematics Level 2

MATHEMATICS LEVEL 2 TEST

REFERENCE INFORMATION

THE FOLLOWING INFORMATION IS FOR YOUR REFERENCE IN ANSWERING SOME OF THE QUESTIONS IN THIS TEST

Volume of a right circular cone with radius r and height h: $V = \dfrac{1}{3}\pi r^2 h$

Lateral Area of a right circular cone with circumference of the base c and slant height ℓ: $S = \dfrac{1}{2}c\ell$

Volume of a sphere with radius r: $V = \dfrac{4}{3}\pi r^3$

Surface Area of a sphere with radius r: $S = 4\pi r^2$

Volume of a pyramid with base area B and height h: $V = \dfrac{1}{3}Bh$

Dr. John Chung's SAT II Math Level 2

Answer Sheet

01 Ⓐ Ⓑ Ⓒ Ⓓ Ⓔ   26 Ⓐ Ⓑ Ⓒ Ⓓ Ⓔ
02 Ⓐ Ⓑ Ⓒ Ⓓ Ⓔ   27 Ⓐ Ⓑ Ⓒ Ⓓ Ⓔ
03 Ⓐ Ⓑ Ⓒ Ⓓ Ⓔ   28 Ⓐ Ⓑ Ⓒ Ⓓ Ⓔ
04 Ⓐ Ⓑ Ⓒ Ⓓ Ⓔ   29 Ⓐ Ⓑ Ⓒ Ⓓ Ⓔ
05 Ⓐ Ⓑ Ⓒ Ⓓ Ⓔ   30 Ⓐ Ⓑ Ⓒ Ⓓ Ⓔ
06 Ⓐ Ⓑ Ⓒ Ⓓ Ⓔ   31 Ⓐ Ⓑ Ⓒ Ⓓ Ⓔ
07 Ⓐ Ⓑ Ⓒ Ⓓ Ⓔ   32 Ⓐ Ⓑ Ⓒ Ⓓ Ⓔ
08 Ⓐ Ⓑ Ⓒ Ⓓ Ⓔ   33 Ⓐ Ⓑ Ⓒ Ⓓ Ⓔ
09 Ⓐ Ⓑ Ⓒ Ⓓ Ⓔ   34 Ⓐ Ⓑ Ⓒ Ⓓ Ⓔ
10 Ⓐ Ⓑ Ⓒ Ⓓ Ⓔ   35 Ⓐ Ⓑ Ⓒ Ⓓ Ⓔ
11 Ⓐ Ⓑ Ⓒ Ⓓ Ⓔ   36 Ⓐ Ⓑ Ⓒ Ⓓ Ⓔ
12 Ⓐ Ⓑ Ⓒ Ⓓ Ⓔ   37 Ⓐ Ⓑ Ⓒ Ⓓ Ⓔ
13 Ⓐ Ⓑ Ⓒ Ⓓ Ⓔ   38 Ⓐ Ⓑ Ⓒ Ⓓ Ⓔ
14 Ⓐ Ⓑ Ⓒ Ⓓ Ⓔ   39 Ⓐ Ⓑ Ⓒ Ⓓ Ⓔ
15 Ⓐ Ⓑ Ⓒ Ⓓ Ⓔ   40 Ⓐ Ⓑ Ⓒ Ⓓ Ⓔ
16 Ⓐ Ⓑ Ⓒ Ⓓ Ⓔ   41 Ⓐ Ⓑ Ⓒ Ⓓ Ⓔ
17 Ⓐ Ⓑ Ⓒ Ⓓ Ⓔ   42 Ⓐ Ⓑ Ⓒ Ⓓ Ⓔ
18 Ⓐ Ⓑ Ⓒ Ⓓ Ⓔ   43 Ⓐ Ⓑ Ⓒ Ⓓ Ⓔ
19 Ⓐ Ⓑ Ⓒ Ⓓ Ⓔ   44 Ⓐ Ⓑ Ⓒ Ⓓ Ⓔ
20 Ⓐ Ⓑ Ⓒ Ⓓ Ⓔ   45 Ⓐ Ⓑ Ⓒ Ⓓ Ⓔ
21 Ⓐ Ⓑ Ⓒ Ⓓ Ⓔ   46 Ⓐ Ⓑ Ⓒ Ⓓ Ⓔ
22 Ⓐ Ⓑ Ⓒ Ⓓ Ⓔ   47 Ⓐ Ⓑ Ⓒ Ⓓ Ⓔ
23 Ⓐ Ⓑ Ⓒ Ⓓ Ⓔ   48 Ⓐ Ⓑ Ⓒ Ⓓ Ⓔ
24 Ⓐ Ⓑ Ⓒ Ⓓ Ⓔ   49 Ⓐ Ⓑ Ⓒ Ⓓ Ⓔ
25 Ⓐ Ⓑ Ⓒ Ⓓ Ⓔ   50 Ⓐ Ⓑ Ⓒ Ⓓ Ⓔ

The number of right answers: ☐

The number of wrong answers: ☐

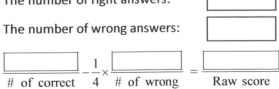

$$\underbrace{\boxed{}}_{\text{\# of correct}} - \frac{1}{4} \times \underbrace{\boxed{}}_{\text{\# of wrong}} = \underbrace{\boxed{}}_{\text{Raw score}}$$

Score Conversion Table

Raw Score	Scaled Score	Raw Score	Scaled Score	Raw Score	Scaled Score
50	800	28	640	6	480
49	800	27	630	5	470
48	800	26	620	4	470
47	800	25	620	3	460
46	800	24	610	2	460
45	800	23	610	1	450
44	800	22	600	0	450
43	800	21	600		
42	800	20	590		
41	800	19	590		
40	780	18	580		
39	760	17	570		
38	750	16	560		
37	740	15	550		
36	720	14	540		
35	710	13	530		
34	700	12	520		
33	690	11	510		
32	680	10	500		
31	670	9	490		
30	660	8	490		
29	650	7	480		

MATHEMATICS LEVEL 2 TEST

For each of the following problems, decide which is the BEST of the choices given. If the exact numerical value is not one of the choices, select the choice that best approximates this value. Then fill in the corresponding circle on the answer sheet

Note: (1) A scientific or graphing calculator will be necessary for answering some (but not all) of the questions in this test. For each question you will have to decide whether or not you should use a calculator.

(2) For some questions in this test you may have to decide whether your calculator should be in the radian mode or the degree mode.

(3) Figures that accompany problems in this test are intended to provide information useful in solving the problems. They are drawn as accurately as possible EXCEPT when it is stated in a specific problem that its figure is not drawn to scale. All figures lie in a plane unless otherwise indicated.

(4) Unless otherwise specified, the domain of any function f is assumed to be the set of all real numbers x for which $f(x)$ is a real number. The range of f is assumed to be the set of all real numbers $f(x)$, where x is in the domain of f.

(5) Reference information that may be useful in answering the questions in this test can be found on the page preceding Question 1.

USE THIS SPACE FOR SCRATCHWORK

1.   If $\dfrac{1}{x} - x = \dfrac{1}{x} + x$, then $x =$

(A) –1   (B) 0   (C) 1   (D) 2   (E) undefined

2.   If $\dfrac{1}{1 - \dfrac{1}{x}} = 2$, what is the value of x?

(A) –2   (B) 2   (C) $-\dfrac{1}{2}$ (D) $\dfrac{1}{2}$ (E) $\dfrac{1}{4}$

3.   If $3^x = 5^y$, then $\dfrac{x}{y} =$

(A) $\dfrac{3}{5}$ (B) $\dfrac{5}{3}$ (C) $\log_3 5$ (D) $\log_5 3$ (E) 3^5

GO ON TO THE NEXT PAGE

USE THIS SPACE FOR SCRATCHWORK.

4. What is the number of arrangements of letters that can be formed from the letters of the word "abscissa"?

    (A) 40320
    (B) 20160
    (C) 6720
    (D) 3360
    (E) 1680

5. If $\left(\log x\right)^2 + \log x^2 = 3$, then which of the following could be the value of x?

    (A) -10 (B) 3   (C) 5   (D) 8   (E) 10

6. What is the minimum value of $y = \sin|x| + 3$?

    (A) 0   (B) 1   (C) 2   (D) 3   (E) 4

7. If $\dfrac{1}{x^2-1} = \dfrac{A}{x+1} + \dfrac{B}{x-1}$ for all real x, what is the value of constant B?

    (A) -1 (B) $-\dfrac{1}{2}$ (C) $\dfrac{1}{2}$ (D) 1   (E) 2

8. If $x + \sqrt{\left(1-\sqrt{3}\right)^2} = 3$, then $x =$

    (A) $1-\sqrt{3}$
    (B) $4-\sqrt{3}$
    (C) $2+\sqrt{3}$
    (D) $\sqrt{3}-2$
    (E) $\sqrt{3}-4$

9. In Figure 1, if $\triangle ABC$ is equilateral, what is the slope of $\overline{BC}$?

    (A) $-\sqrt{3}$ (B) $-\sqrt{2}$ (C) -1 (D) 1   (E) $\sqrt{3}$

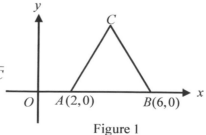

Figure 1

MATHEMATICS LEVEL 2 TEST - *Continued*

USE THIS SPACE FOR SCRATCHWORK.

10. If $\tan\theta = \dfrac{1}{2}$, then $(\sin\theta + \cos\theta)^2 =$

(A) 1.8   (B) 2.0   (C) 2.2   (D) 2.4   (E) 2.6

11. The graph of $y = f(x)$ is shown in Figure 2. Which of the following is the equation of the graph?

(A) $y = |x| + 3$

(B) $y = |x + 3| + 3$

(C) $y = -|x + 3| + 3$

(D) $y = -|x - 3| + 3$

(E) $y = -|x - 3| - 3$

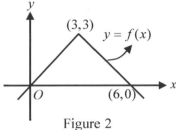

Figure 2

12. If $f(x) = \log_2\left(x^2 + 7\right)$ and $f\left(g(1)\right) = 4$, which of the following could be $g(x)$?

(A) $g(x) = x^2 + x + 2$

(B) $g(x) = 2x^2 + x - 1$

(C) $g(x) = \cos(\pi x) + 4$

(D) $g(x) = \sin(\pi x) + 2$

(E) $g(x) = 3^x - 1$

13. If the roots of $2x^2 - kx + 14 = 0$ are integers, then which of the following could be the value of constant k?

(A) 6   (B) 8   (C) 10   (D) 12   (E) 16

14. Which of the following is an equation with roots 0 and $2 - \sqrt{3}$?

(A) $0 = x^3 - 3x^2 + x$

(B) $0 = x^3 + 4x^2 - x$

(C) $0 = x^3 - 4x^2 + x$

(D) $0 = x^2 - 2x - 2$

(E) $0 = x^3 + 2x^2 + 2x$

GO ON TO THE NEXT PAGE

USE THIS SPACE FOR SCRATCHWORK.

15. How far is the point $(2,1)$ from the line $3x - y = 4$?

(A) 0.316
(B) 0.542
(C) 1.358
(D) 2.855
(E) 3.282

16. If the polar coordinates of point A are $\left(10, \dfrac{2\pi}{3}\right)$, which of

the following are the rectangular coordinates of point A?

(A) $\left(-5\sqrt{3}, 5\right)$

(B) $\left(5, 5\sqrt{3}\right)$

(C) $\left(5, -5\sqrt{3}\right)$

(D) $\left(-5, 5\sqrt{3}\right)$

(E) $\left(-5, -5\sqrt{3}\right)$

17. In Figure 3, $AD = 20$ and $\overline{BD}$ is perpendicular to $\overline{AC}$. What is the length of $\overline{CD}$?

(A) 10.35
(B) 12.07
(C) 13.06
(D) 14.85
(E) 15.50

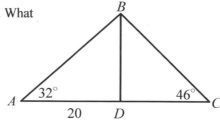

Note: Figure not drawn to scale.

Figure 3

18. If $\left(\sqrt{3}\right)^{4-6x} = 27^{x}$, then $x =$

(A) $\dfrac{1}{3}$ (B) $\dfrac{1}{2}$ (C) $\dfrac{2}{3}$ (D) $\dfrac{3}{4}$ (E) $\dfrac{3}{2}$

GO ON TO THE NEXT PAGE

MATHEMATICS LEVEL 2 TEST - *Continued*

USE THIS SPACE FOR SCRATCHWORK.

19. Which of the following is the solution of $\dfrac{x}{(x-1)(x-2)} < 0$?

    (A) $-\infty < x < 1$
    (B) $-5 < x < 2$
    (C) $-\infty < x < 2$
    (D) $-\infty < x < 0$ or $1 < x < 2$
    (E) $-\infty < x < 1$ or $x > 2$

20. What are the asymptotes of $f(x) = \dfrac{x}{x^3 + x}$?

    (A) $x = 0$
    (B) $x = 0$ and $x = -1$
    (C) $x = -1$ and $y = 0$
    (D) $y = 0$
    (E) $x = 0$ and $y = 0$

21. If $f(x) = \log_3\left(\sqrt{x}\right) + 3$ and $g(x)$ is the inverse of $f(x)$, what is the value of $g(2)$?

    (A) $\dfrac{1}{27}$ (B) $\dfrac{1}{9}$ (C) $\dfrac{1}{3}$ (D) 3   (E) 9

22. If $\sin 2\theta = \dfrac{1}{4}$, what is the value of $(\cos\theta - \sin\theta)^2$?

    (A) 1.25
    (B) 0.75
    (C) 0.50
    (D) 0.25
    (E) 0.15

USE THIS SPACE FOR SCRATCHWORK.

23. Which of the following is a horizontal tangent to the ellipse
$$\frac{(x-3)^2}{49} + \frac{(y-2)^2}{25} = 1?$$

(A) $y = 2$

(B) $y = 3$

(C) $y = 5$

(D) $y = 7$

(E) $y = 10$

24. Which of the following is true of the graph of the function
$xy = x^2 + 1?$

(A) Even function

(B) Odd function

(C) Symmetric with respect to x-axis

(D) Symmetric with respect to y-axis

(E) Symmetric with respect to $y = x$

25. What is the value of $\left| \dfrac{2+i}{i-2} \right|$?

(A) 1 (B) $\sqrt{2}$ (C) $\sqrt{3}$ (D) 2 (E) $2\sqrt{3}$

26. In $\triangle ABC$, if $\angle A = 30°$, $a = 5$ and $b = 10$, then $\triangle ABC$ in Figure 5 is

(A) An acute triangle

(B) A right triangle

(C) An obtuse triangle

(D) An acute or an obtuse triangle

(E) An isosceles triangle

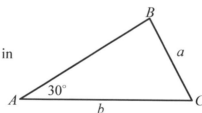

Note: Figure not drawn to scale.

Figure 5

27. If $\cos^2 \theta + \cos \theta = 1$, then $\sin^4 \theta + \sin^2 \theta =$

(A) 1 (B) $\sqrt{2}$ (C) $\sqrt{3}$ (D) $\dfrac{1}{2}$ (E) $\dfrac{\sqrt{3}}{2}$

GO ON TO THE NEXT PAGE

USE THIS SPACE FOR SCRATCHWORK.

28. What is the period of the function $y = -2\tan\left(\dfrac{x}{3} - 1\right) + 4$?

(A) $\dfrac{1}{3}$ (B) 2π (C) 3π (D) 6π (E) 8π

29. In Figure 6, point P is on the x-axis. What is the minimum length of $\overline{AP} + \overline{PB}$?

(A) 7.48
(B) 8.60
(C) 9.25
(D) 9.75
(E) 13.75

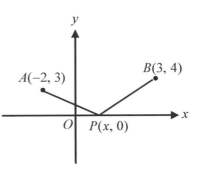

Note: Figure not drawn to scale.

Figure 6

30. The roots of $x^2 + kx + 1 = 0$ are p and q, where k is a constant. If $\dfrac{1}{p} + \dfrac{1}{q} = 10$, what is the value of k?

(A) -10
(B) -5
(C) 5
(D) 10
(E) 15

31. If $(x - 1)$ is a factor of $x^6 - 5x^4 + 4x^3 - x + k$, then what is the value of k?

(A) 1   (B) 2   (C) 3   (D) 4   (E) 5

32. If the quadratic equation $x^2 + 2ax + 2a^2 + 2a - 3 = 0$ has real roots, then which of the following could NOT be the value of a?

(A) -2
(B) -1
(C) 0
(D) 1
(E) 2

GO ON TO THE NEXT PAGE

USE THIS SPACE FOR SCRATCHWORK.

33. What is the distance from the plane $x - 2y + 3z = 5$ to the point $(2, 2, 0)$?

(A) 1.871
(B) 2.225
(C) 2.786
(D) 3.125
(E) 4.750

34. If the line through $(5, 4)$ and $(2, k)$ is perpendicular to the line with equation $3x - 4y = 4$, what is the value of k?

(A) 2
(B) 4
(C) 6
(D) 8
(E) 10

35. If the radius of a right circular cone is 6 and the height of the cone is 8, what is the lateral surface area of the cone?

(A) 20π
(B) 40π
(C) 60π
(D) 96π
(E) 120π

36. If $y = 3\log(10x - x^2)$, what is the maximum value of y?

(A) 3.56
(B) 4.19
(C) 5.25
(D) 6.32
(E) 7.41

37. What is the length of the major axis of the ellipse whose equation is $5x^2 + 18y^2 - 90 = 0$?

(A) 6.25   (B) 7.25   (C) 8.49   (D) 9.34   (E) 10.25

 GO ON TO THE NEXT PAGE

USE THIS SPACE FOR SCRATCHWORK.

38. In Figure 7, $A, B,$ and $C,$ the vertices of the squares, are collinear. What is the value of k?

(A) 8.45
(B) 10.38
(C) 12.25
(D) 13.12
(E) 13.74

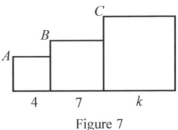

Figure 7

39. If $\theta = \text{Arc}\cos\left(-\dfrac{\sqrt{3}}{2}\right),$ then $\theta =$

(A) $-\dfrac{5\pi}{6}$　(B) $-\dfrac{\pi}{6}$　(C) $\dfrac{\pi}{6}$　(D) $\dfrac{\pi}{2}$　(E) $\dfrac{5\pi}{6}$

40. In a box there are 4 red marbles and 5 white marbles. If marbles are drawn one at a time and replaced after each drawing, what is the probability of drawing exactly 2 red marbles when 3 marbles are drawn?

(A) 0.329
(B) 0.235
(C) 0.198
(D) 0.110
(E) 0.102

41. In Figure 8, P is a point in the square of side-length 10 such that it is equally distant from two consecutive vertices and from the opposite side $\overline{AD}$. What is the length of $\overline{BP}$?

(A) 5
(B) 5.25
(C) 5.78
(D) 6.25
(E) 7.07

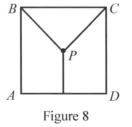

Figure 8

GO ON TO THE NEXT PAGE

MATHEMATICS LEVEL 2 TEST - *Continued*

USE THIS SPACE FOR SCRATCHWORK.

42. If $\log_2\left(\log_3\left(\log_2 x\right)\right)=1$, what is the value of x?

(A) 126
(B) 256
(C) 512
(D) 1024
(E) 2048

43. If matrix $A = \begin{pmatrix} 1 & a \\ 2 & 1 \end{pmatrix}$, $B = \begin{pmatrix} 2 \\ b \end{pmatrix}$, $C = \begin{pmatrix} -1 \\ 3 \end{pmatrix}$, and $AB = C$,

where a and b are constants, what is the value of a?

(A) 1
(B) 2
(C) 3
(D) 4
(E) 5

44. In the arithmetic progression, the first term is 5 and the common difference is 3. What is the sum of the first 20 terms?

(A) 300
(B) 475
(C) 670
(D) 850
(E) 925

45. The sum of the infinite series $\displaystyle\sum_{k=1}^{\infty}\left(\frac{1}{2}\right)^k + \sum_{k=1}^{\infty}\left(\frac{1}{3}\right)^k$ is

(A) 1
(B) 1.5
(C) 2
(D) 3
(E) 4.5

GO ON TO THE NEXT PAGE

MATHEMATICS LEVEL 2 TEST - *Continued*

USE THIS SPACE FOR SCRATCHWORK.

46. $\lim\limits_{n\to\infty}\dfrac{1+2+3+\cdots+n}{n^2}=$

(A) 0.5
(B) 1
(C) 2
(D) 3
(E) 4

47. A committee of 5 is to be chosen from 8 men and 5 women. What is the probability that the committee consists of 2 men and 3 women?

(A) 0.185
(B) 0.218
(C) 0.302
(D) 0.387
(E) 0.425

48. From the expansion of the binomial $(ax-y)^6$, where a is a positive constant, the coefficient of x^2y^4 is 60. What is the value of a?

(A) 2   (B) 3   (C) 4   (D) 6   (E) 8

49. If $f(x)=e^{2x}$ and $g(x)=\ln(x^2+1)$, then $(f\circ g)(x)=$

(A) x^2+1
(B) x^3+x
(C) $2x(x^2+1)$
(D) x^4+2x^2+1
(E) $2x\ln(x^2+1)$

GO ON TO THE NEXT PAGE

MATHEMATICS LEVEL 2 TEST - *Continued*

USE THIS SPACE FOR SCRATCHWORK.

50. If $\dfrac{ab}{a-b} > 0$, then which of the following could be true?

   I. $0 < b < a$
   II. $b < a < 0$
   III. $a < b < 0$

(A) I only
(B) I and II only
(C) II and III only
(D) I and III only
(E) I, II, and III

STOP
**IF YOU FINISH BEFORE TIME IS CALLED, YOU MAY CHECK YOUR WORK ON THIS TEST ONLY.
DO NOT TURN TO ANY OTHER TEST IN THIS BOOK.**

No Test Material on This Page

TEST 6			ANSWERS						

#	answer	#	answer	#	answer	#	answer	#	answer
1	E	11	D	21	B	31	A	41	D
2	B	12	C	22	B	32	E	42	C
3	C	13	E	23	D	33	A	43	C
4	D	14	C	24	B	34	D	44	C
5	E	15	A	25	A	35	C	45	B
6	C	16	D	26	B	36	B	46	A
7	C	17	B	27	A	37	C	47	B
8	B	18	A	28	C	38	C	48	A
9	A	19	D	29	B	39	E	49	D
10	A	20	D	30	A	40	A	50	B

Explanations: Test 6

1. **(E)** $\dfrac{1}{x} - x = \dfrac{1}{x} + x \rightarrow x = 0$

But $x = 0$ is extraneous. The solution is undefined.

2. **(B)** $\dfrac{1(x)}{\left(1 - \dfrac{1}{x}\right)(x)} = \dfrac{x}{x-1} \rightarrow \dfrac{x}{x-1} = 2 \rightarrow x = 2x - 2 \rightarrow x = 2$

3. **(C)** $3^x = 5^y \rightarrow \left(3^x\right)^{\frac{1}{y}} = \left(5^y\right)^{\frac{1}{y}} \rightarrow 3^{\frac{x}{y}} = 5 \rightarrow \dfrac{x}{y} = \log_3 5$

4. **(D)** Permutation with repetition: $\dfrac{8!}{2!3!} = 3360$

5. **(E)** $\left(\log x\right)^2 + \log x^2 = 3 \rightarrow \left(\log x\right)^2 + 2\log x - 3 = 0 \rightarrow \left(\log x + 3\right)\left(\log x - 1\right) = 0$

Since $\log x = -3$ and $\log x = 1$, $x = 10^{-3}$ or 10.

6. **(C)** The graph is symmetric with respect to y-axis. Therefore, the minimum of the function is $-1 + 3 = 2$.

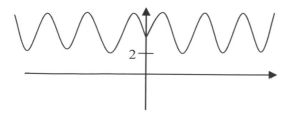

7. (C) $\dfrac{1}{x^2-1}=\dfrac{A}{x+1}+\dfrac{B}{x-1}$ $\rightarrow$ $\dfrac{1}{x^2-1}=\dfrac{A(x-1)}{x^2-1}+\dfrac{B(x+1)}{x^2-1}$ $\rightarrow$ $\dfrac{1}{x^2-1}=\dfrac{(A+B)x+B-A}{x^2-1}$

To be identical, $A+B=0$ and $-A+B=1$. Therefore, $B=\dfrac{1}{2}$.

8. (B) $x+\sqrt{\left(1-\sqrt{3}\right)^2}=3$ $\rightarrow$ $\sqrt{\left(1-\sqrt{3}\right)^2}=3-x$ $\rightarrow$ $\left|1-\sqrt{3}\right|=3-x$ $\rightarrow$ $\sqrt{3}-1=3-x$

Therefore, $x=4-\sqrt{3}$.

9. (A) Since $BM=2$, $\angle A=60°$, and $CM=2\sqrt{3}$, then the slope of $\overleftrightarrow{BC}=-\dfrac{CM}{MB}=-\dfrac{2\sqrt{3}}{2}=-\sqrt{3}$.

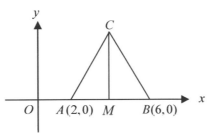

10. (A) Since $\tan\theta=\dfrac{1}{2}$, then

$\begin{cases} (1)\ \sin\theta=\dfrac{1}{\sqrt{5}}\ \text{and}\ \cos\theta=\dfrac{2}{\sqrt{5}} \\ \text{or} \\ (2)\ \sin\theta=-\dfrac{1}{\sqrt{5}}\ \text{and}\ \cos\theta=-\dfrac{2}{\sqrt{5}} \end{cases}$

(1) $\left(\sin\theta+\cos\theta\right)^2=\left(\dfrac{1}{\sqrt{5}}+\dfrac{2}{\sqrt{5}}\right)^2=\dfrac{9}{5}=1.8$

(2) $\left(\sin\theta+\cos\theta\right)^2=\left(-\dfrac{1}{\sqrt{5}}-\dfrac{2}{\sqrt{5}}\right)^2=\dfrac{9}{5}=1.8$

11. (D) Translations: $y=-|x|$ $\xrightarrow{\ T_{3,3}\ }$ $y=-|x-3|+3$

12. (C) Let $g(1)$ be k, then $f(k)=\log_2\left(k^2+7\right)=4$.

$k^2+7=2^4=16$ $\rightarrow$ $k^2=9$ $\rightarrow$ $k=\pm3$

(A) $g(1)=4$ (B) $g(1)=2$ (C) $g(1)=3$

(D) $g(1)=2$ (E) $g(1)=2$

13. (E) Sum of the roots: $r_1 + r_2 = \dfrac{k}{2}$, Product of the roots: $r_1 \cdot r_2 = \dfrac{14}{2} = 7$

Therefore, the roots are 7 and 1, or -7 and -1 . $\rightarrow k = 16$ and -16 .

(Check) Choice (E): $2x^2 - 16x + 14 = 0 \rightarrow x^2 - 8x + 7 = 0 \rightarrow (x-1)(x-7) = 0$

The roots are 1 and 7.

14. (C) The polynomial equation is $x\left[x - \left(2 - \sqrt{3}\right)\right]\left[x - \left(2 + \sqrt{3}\right)\right] = 0$.

$x(x - 2 + \sqrt{3})(x - 2 - \sqrt{3}) = 0 \rightarrow x\left[(x-2)^2 - (\sqrt{3})^2\right] = 0$

Therefore, $x(x^2 - 4x + 1) = 0 \rightarrow 0 = x^3 - 4x^2 + x$

Or, use sum and product of the roots:

Let the quadratic equation be $x^2 + \dfrac{b}{a}x + \dfrac{c}{a} = 0$.

$\text{SUM} = 2 - \sqrt{3} + 2 + \sqrt{3} = 4 \rightarrow \dfrac{b}{a} = -4$, $\text{PRODUCT} = \left(2 - \sqrt{3}\right)\left(2 + \sqrt{3}\right) = 1 \rightarrow \dfrac{c}{a} = 1$

The equation is $x^2 - 4x + 1 = 0$. Because of zero at $x = 0$, the equation is $x(x^2 - 4x + 1) = 0$.

15. (A) Distance from a point $(2, 1)$ to a line $3x - y - 4 = 0$: $D = \dfrac{|3(2) - 1 - 4|}{\sqrt{3^2 + (-1)^2}} = 0.316227766 \approx 0.316$

16. (D) $x = r\cos\theta \rightarrow x = 10\cos\left(\dfrac{2\pi}{3}\right) = -5$

$y = r\sin\theta \rightarrow y = 10\sin\left(\dfrac{2\pi}{3}\right) = 5\sqrt{3}$

17. (B) $BD = 20\tan 32°$ and $CD = \dfrac{BD}{\tan 46°} = \dfrac{20\tan 32°}{\tan 46°} = 12.06858\cdots \approx 12.07$

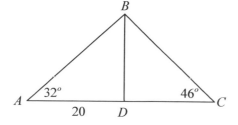

18. (A) $\left(\sqrt{3}\right)^{4-6x} = 27^x \rightarrow \left(3^{\frac{1}{2}}\right)^{4-6x} = 3^{3x} \rightarrow 3^{2-3x} = 3^{3x}$

Exponents: $2 - 3x = 3x \rightarrow 6x = 2 \rightarrow x = \dfrac{1}{3}$

19. (D)   Test value: $\dfrac{x}{(x-1)(x-2)} < 0$

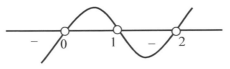

At $x=-1$, $\dfrac{(-)}{(-)(-)} < 0$ (Ok).   At $x=-0.5$, $\dfrac{(-)}{(+)(-)} > 0$. At $x=1.5$, $\dfrac{(+)}{(+)(-)} < 0$

At $x=3$, $\dfrac{(+)}{(+)(+)} > 0$. Therefore, the solution set is $\{-\infty < x < 0\} \cup \{1 < x < 2\}$.

Or, multiply by $(x-1)^2(x-1)^2$ $\rightarrow$ $x(x-1)(x-2) < 0$

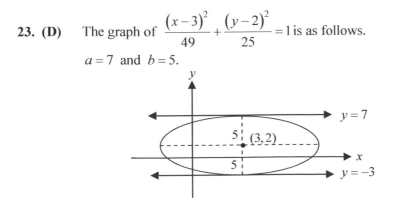

The solution set is $x < 0$ or $1 < x < 2$.

20. (D) $f(x) = \dfrac{x}{x^3 + x} = \dfrac{1}{x^2 + 1}$

$x^2 + 1 \neq 0$ $\rightarrow$ No vertical asymptote

$y = \lim\limits_{x \to \infty} \dfrac{1}{x^2 + 1} = 0$ $\rightarrow$ $y = 0$: Horizontal asymptote

21. (B)   Since $g(x) = f^{-1}(x) = 3^{2(x-3)}$, $g(2) = \dfrac{1}{9}$.

22. (B) $\left(\cos\theta - \sin\theta\right)^2 = \cos^2\theta + \sin^2\theta - 2\cos\theta\sin\theta = 1 - \sin 2\theta = 1 - \dfrac{1}{4} = \dfrac{3}{4}$

23. (D)   The graph of $\dfrac{(x-3)^2}{49} + \dfrac{(y-2)^2}{25} = 1$ is as follows.

$a = 7$ and $b = 5$.

There are two horizontal tangent lines: $y = 7$ and $y = -3$

24. (B) $xy = x^2 + 1 \rightarrow y = \dfrac{x^2+1}{x}$

Choice (A): $f(x) \neq f(-x)$: not even function

Choice (B): $f(x) = -f(-x)$: odd function

Choice (C): $f(x) \neq -f(x)$: not symmetric with respect to x-axis

Choice (D): $f(x) \neq f(-x)$: not symmetric with respect to y-axis

Choice (E): not symmetric with respect to $y = x$

25. (A) $\left|\dfrac{2+i}{i-2}\right| \rightarrow \dfrac{|2+i|}{|-2+i|} = \dfrac{\sqrt{2^2+1^2}}{\sqrt{(-2)^2+1^2}} = \dfrac{\sqrt{5}}{\sqrt{5}} = 1$

26. (B) The law of sines: $\dfrac{\sin 30°}{5} = \dfrac{\sin B}{10} \rightarrow \sin B = \dfrac{10\sin 30°}{5} = 1 \rightarrow B = 90°$

27. (A) $\cos^2 \theta + \cos \theta = 1 \rightarrow \cos \theta = 1 - \cos^2 \theta \rightarrow \cos \theta = \sin^2 \theta$

Since $\sin^4 \theta = \cos^2 \theta$, then $\sin^4 \theta + \sin^2 \theta = \cos^2 \theta + \sin^2 \theta = 1$.

28. (C) Since the frequency is $\dfrac{1}{3}$, the period is $\dfrac{\pi}{\frac{1}{3}} = 3\pi$.

29. (B) To have a minimum length point $P(x, 0)$ should be on the segment $A'B$.

Since $AP = A'P$, the minimum of $\overline{APB}$ is equal to the length of $\overline{A'B}$.

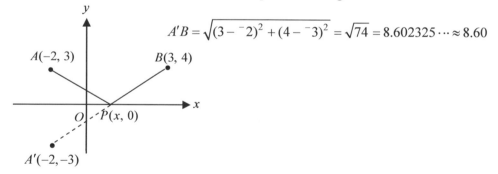

$$A'B = \sqrt{(3 - {}^-2)^2 + (4 - {}^-3)^2} = \sqrt{74} = 8.602325\cdots \approx 8.60$$

30. (A) Since $p + q = -k$ and $pq = 1$, $\dfrac{1}{p} + \dfrac{1}{q} = \dfrac{p+q}{pq} = \dfrac{-k}{1}$. $\quad -k = 10 \rightarrow k = -10$.

31. (A) Factor Theorem: $f(1) = 1 - 5 + 4 - 1 + k = 0 \rightarrow k = 1$

32. (E) Discriminant: $D = (2a)^2 - 4(1)(2a^2 + 2a - 3) \geq 0 \rightarrow (a+3)(a-1) \leq 0$

The solution is: $-3 \leq a \leq 1$

33. (A) Distance from a point to a line: $D = \dfrac{\left|2 - 2(2) + 3(0) - 5\right|}{\sqrt{1^2 + (-2)^2 + 3^2}} = \dfrac{7}{\sqrt{14}} = 1.870828\cdots \approx 1.871$

34. (D) Since the slope of $3x - 4y = 4$ is $\dfrac{3}{4}$, the slope perpendicular to the line is $-\dfrac{4}{3}$.

$$\dfrac{k-4}{2-5} = -\dfrac{4}{3} \;\rightarrow\; \dfrac{k-4}{-3} = \dfrac{4}{-3} \;\rightarrow\; k = 8$$

35. (C) The slant height is $\sqrt{6^2 + 8^2} = 10$. The lateral surface area is $\pi r s = \pi(6)(10) = 60\pi$.

36. (B) $y = 3\log(10x - x^2)$ has a maximum at $x = 5$ [Axis of symmetric of $(f(x) = 10x - x^2)$]

Therefore, the minimum of y is $3\log(10 \cdot 5 - 5^2) = 3\log 25 = 4.193820026\cdots \approx 4.19$

37. (C) $5x^2 + 18y^2 - 90 = 0 \;\rightarrow\; \dfrac{x^2}{18} + \dfrac{y^2}{5} = 1$

The length of the major axis is $2\sqrt{18} = 8.485281374 \approx 8.49$

38. (C) The slopes of $\overline{AB}$ and $\overline{BC}$ are equal.

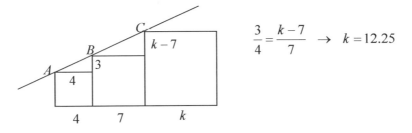

$$\dfrac{3}{4} = \dfrac{k-7}{7} \;\rightarrow\; k = 12.25$$

39. (E) 1) Using calculator:

2) Algebraic solution:

Let $\theta = \text{Arccos}\left(-\dfrac{\sqrt{3}}{2}\right)$, where $0 \le \theta \le \pi$. $\cos\theta = -\dfrac{\sqrt{3}}{2} \;\rightarrow\; \theta = \dfrac{5\pi}{6}$

40. (A) $_3C_2 \left(\dfrac{4}{9}\right)^2 \left(\dfrac{5}{9}\right) = 0.329218107 \approx 0.329$

Or, the ways to draw two red marbles: *WRR, RWR, RRW*

For *WRR*, the probability is $\dfrac{5}{9} \cdot \dfrac{4}{9} \cdot \dfrac{4}{9} = \dfrac{80}{729}$. Therefore, $3 \cdot \left(\dfrac{80}{729}\right) \approx 0.329$.

41. (D) If $PM = x$, then $BN = 10 - x$.

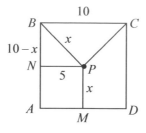

Pythagorean Theorem:
$$x^2 = (10 - x)^2 + 5^2 \quad \rightarrow \quad x = 6.25$$

42. (C) $\log_2\left(\log_3\left(\log_2 x\right)\right) = 1 \quad \rightarrow \quad \log_3\left(\log_2 x\right) = 2 \quad \rightarrow \quad \log_2 x = 9 \quad \rightarrow \quad x = 2^9 = 512$

43. (C) $\begin{pmatrix} 1 & a \\ 2 & 1 \end{pmatrix}\begin{pmatrix} 2 \\ b \end{pmatrix} = \begin{pmatrix} -1 \\ 3 \end{pmatrix} \quad \rightarrow \quad 2 + ab = -1 \quad$ and $\quad 4 + b = 3 \quad \rightarrow \quad b = -1$

Therefore, $2 + a(-1) = -1 \quad \rightarrow \quad a = 3$.

44. (C) $a_{20} = 5 + (20 - 1)3 = 62$, $\quad S_{20} = \dfrac{n(a_1 + a_{20})}{2} = \dfrac{20(5 + 62)}{2} = 670$

45. (B) $\displaystyle\sum_{k=1}^{\infty}\left(\frac{1}{2}\right)^k = \dfrac{\frac{1}{2}}{1 - \frac{1}{2}} = 1 \quad$ and $\quad \displaystyle\sum_{k=1}^{\infty}\left(\frac{1}{3}\right)^k = \dfrac{\frac{1}{3}}{1 - \frac{1}{3}} = 0.5$

Therefore, the sum is $1 + 0.5 = 1.5$.

46. (A) $\displaystyle\lim_{n\to\infty}\frac{1 + 2 + 3 + \cdots + n}{n^2} = \lim_{n\to\infty}\frac{\frac{n(1+n)}{2}}{n^2} = \lim_{n\to\infty}\frac{n^2 + n}{2n^2} = \frac{1}{2}$

47. (B) $P = \dfrac{{}_8C_2 \times {}_5C_3}{{}_{13}C_5} = 0.2175602176 \approx 0.218$

48. (A) Since ${}_6C_r\left(ax\right)^{6-r}\left(-y\right)^r = 60x^2y^4$, ${}_6C_r a^{6-r} x^{6-r}\left(-1\right)^r y^r = {}_6C_r a^{6-r}\left(-1\right)^r x^{6-r}y^r$.

r must be 4. Therefore, ${}_6C_4 a^2\left(-1\right)^4 = 60 \quad \rightarrow \quad 15a^2 = 60 \quad \rightarrow \quad a = 2$

49. (D) $\left(f \circ g\right)(x) = e^{2\ln\left(x^2+1\right)} = e^{\ln\left(x^2+1\right)^2} = \left(x^2 + 1\right)^2 = x^4 + 2x^2 + 1$

50. (B) $\dfrac{ab}{a-b} > 0$

Method 1:

$$\begin{cases} ab > 0 \\ a > b \end{cases} \rightarrow \begin{cases} a > b \text{ and } a > 0, b > 0 \rightarrow a > b > 0 \\ a > b \text{ and } a < 0, b < 0 \rightarrow 0 > a > b \end{cases}$$

$$\begin{cases} ab < 0 \\ a < b \end{cases} \rightarrow \begin{cases} a < b \text{ and } a > 0, b < 0 \rightarrow a > b > 0 \text{ (Not working)} \\ a < b \text{ and } a < 0, b > 0 \rightarrow b > 0 > b \end{cases}$$

Method 2: Plug-in test number

I. $a = 2, b = 1 \rightarrow \dfrac{2 \cdot 1}{2-1} = 2 > 0$ (OK)

II. $b = -2, a = -1 \rightarrow \dfrac{(-1)(-2)}{(-1)-(-2)} = 1 < 0$ (OK)

III. $a = -2, b = -1 \rightarrow \dfrac{(-2)(-1)}{(-2)-(-1)} = -2 < 0$ (NO)

END

No Test Material on This Page

Test 7

Dr. John Chung's

SAT II Mathematics Level 2

MATHEMATICS LEVEL 2 TEST

REFERENCE INFORMATION

THE FOLLOWING INFORMATION IS FOR YOUR REFERENCE IN ANSWERING SOME OF THE QUESTIONS IN THIS TEST

Volume of a right circular cone with radius r and height h : $V = \dfrac{1}{3}\pi r^2 h$

Lateral Area of a right circular cone with circumference of the base c and slant height ℓ : $S = \dfrac{1}{2} c\ell$

Volume of a sphere with radius r : $V = \dfrac{4}{3}\pi r^3$

Surface Area of a sphere with radius r : $S = 4\pi r^2$

Volume of a pyramid with base area B and height h : $V = \dfrac{1}{3} Bh$

Dr. John Chung's SAT II Math Level 2

Answer Sheet

01 Ⓐ Ⓑ Ⓒ Ⓓ Ⓔ   26 Ⓐ Ⓑ Ⓒ Ⓓ Ⓔ
02 Ⓐ Ⓑ Ⓒ Ⓓ Ⓔ   27 Ⓐ Ⓑ Ⓒ Ⓓ Ⓔ
03 Ⓐ Ⓑ Ⓒ Ⓓ Ⓔ   28 Ⓐ Ⓑ Ⓒ Ⓓ Ⓔ
04 Ⓐ Ⓑ Ⓒ Ⓓ Ⓔ   29 Ⓐ Ⓑ Ⓒ Ⓓ Ⓔ
05 Ⓐ Ⓑ Ⓒ Ⓓ Ⓔ   30 Ⓐ Ⓑ Ⓒ Ⓓ Ⓔ
06 Ⓐ Ⓑ Ⓒ Ⓓ Ⓔ   31 Ⓐ Ⓑ Ⓒ Ⓓ Ⓔ
07 Ⓐ Ⓑ Ⓒ Ⓓ Ⓔ   32 Ⓐ Ⓑ Ⓒ Ⓓ Ⓔ
08 Ⓐ Ⓑ Ⓒ Ⓓ Ⓔ   33 Ⓐ Ⓑ Ⓒ Ⓓ Ⓔ
09 Ⓐ Ⓑ Ⓒ Ⓓ Ⓔ   34 Ⓐ Ⓑ Ⓒ Ⓓ Ⓔ
10 Ⓐ Ⓑ Ⓒ Ⓓ Ⓔ   35 Ⓐ Ⓑ Ⓒ Ⓓ Ⓔ
11 Ⓐ Ⓑ Ⓒ Ⓓ Ⓔ   36 Ⓐ Ⓑ Ⓒ Ⓓ Ⓔ
12 Ⓐ Ⓑ Ⓒ Ⓓ Ⓔ   37 Ⓐ Ⓑ Ⓒ Ⓓ Ⓔ
13 Ⓐ Ⓑ Ⓒ Ⓓ Ⓔ   38 Ⓐ Ⓑ Ⓒ Ⓓ Ⓔ
14 Ⓐ Ⓑ Ⓒ Ⓓ Ⓔ   39 Ⓐ Ⓑ Ⓒ Ⓓ Ⓔ
15 Ⓐ Ⓑ Ⓒ Ⓓ Ⓔ   40 Ⓐ Ⓑ Ⓒ Ⓓ Ⓔ
16 Ⓐ Ⓑ Ⓒ Ⓓ Ⓔ   41 Ⓐ Ⓑ Ⓒ Ⓓ Ⓔ
17 Ⓐ Ⓑ Ⓒ Ⓓ Ⓔ   42 Ⓐ Ⓑ Ⓒ Ⓓ Ⓕ
18 Ⓐ Ⓑ Ⓒ Ⓓ Ⓔ   43 Ⓐ Ⓑ Ⓒ Ⓓ Ⓔ
19 Ⓐ Ⓑ Ⓒ Ⓓ Ⓔ   44 Ⓐ Ⓑ Ⓒ Ⓓ Ⓔ
20 Ⓐ Ⓑ Ⓒ Ⓓ Ⓔ   45 Ⓐ Ⓑ Ⓒ Ⓓ Ⓔ
21 Ⓐ Ⓑ Ⓒ Ⓓ Ⓔ   46 Ⓐ Ⓑ Ⓒ Ⓓ Ⓔ
22 Ⓐ Ⓑ Ⓒ Ⓓ Ⓔ   47 Ⓐ Ⓑ Ⓒ Ⓓ Ⓔ
23 Ⓐ Ⓑ Ⓒ Ⓓ Ⓔ   48 Ⓐ Ⓑ Ⓒ Ⓓ Ⓔ
24 Ⓐ Ⓑ Ⓒ Ⓓ Ⓔ   49 Ⓐ Ⓑ Ⓒ Ⓓ Ⓔ
25 Ⓐ Ⓑ Ⓒ Ⓓ Ⓔ   50 Ⓐ Ⓑ Ⓒ Ⓓ Ⓔ

The number of right answers: ☐

The number of wrong answers: ☐

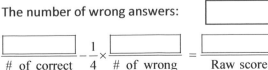

Score Conversion Table

Raw Score	Scaled Score	Raw Score	Scaled Score	Raw Score	Scaled Score
50	800	28	640	6	480
49	800	27	630	5	470
48	800	26	620	4	470
47	800	25	620	3	460
46	800	24	610	2	460
45	800	23	610	1	450
44	800	22	600	0	450
43	800	21	600		
42	800	20	590		
41	800	19	590		
40	780	18	580		
39	760	17	570		
38	750	16	560		
37	740	15	550		
36	720	14	540		
35	710	13	530		
34	700	12	520		
33	690	11	510		
32	680	10	500		
31	670	9	490		
30	660	8	490		
29	650	7	480		

MATHEMATICS LEVEL 2 TEST

For each of the following problems, decide which is the BEST of the choices given. If the exact numerical value is not one of the choices, select the choice that best approximates this value. Then fill in the corresponding circle on the answer sheet

Note: (1) A scientific or graphing calculator will be necessary for answering some (but not all) of the questions in this test. For each question you will have to decide whether or not you should use a calculator.

(2) For some questions in this test you may have to decide whether your calculator should be in the radian mode or the degree mode.

(3) Figures that accompany problems in this test are intended to provide information useful in solving the problems. They are drawn as accurately as possible EXCEPT when it is stated in a specific problem that its figure is not drawn to scale. All figures lie in a plane unless otherwise indicated.

(4) Unless otherwise specified, the domain of any function f is assumed to be the set of all real numbers x for which $f(x)$ is a real number. The range of f is assumed to be the set of all real numbers $f(x)$, where x is in the domain of f.

(5) Reference information that may be useful in answering the questions in this test can be found on the page preceding Question 1.

USE THIS SPACE FOR SCRATCHWORK

1. If $x = 10$, then $\dfrac{x^{x+1} - x^x}{x^x} =$

   (A) 5   (B) 9   (C) 10   (D) 100   (E) 1000

2. If x and y are positive integers and $x^2 - y^2 = 21$, then which of the following could be the value of x?

   (A) 13
   (B) 11
   (C) 10
   (D) 9
   (E) 4

GO ON TO THE NEXT PAGE

USE THIS SPACE FOR SCRATCHWORK.

3. If $f(x) = 4x - 2$, then the inverse function $f^{-1}(x)$ is

(A) $\dfrac{x+8}{4}$

(B) $\dfrac{2x+1}{2}$

(C) $\dfrac{x+2}{4}$

(D) $\dfrac{2x-1}{2}$

(E) $\dfrac{x-2}{4}$

4. In how many points do the graphs of $x^2 - y^2 = 1$ and $y^2 - x^2 = 1$ intersect?

(A) 0
(B) 1
(C) 2
(D) 4
(E) 8

5. If $f(x) = |3x|$ and $g(x) = [2x]$, then $f(g(-5.4)) =$

(A) 33
(B) 30
(C) 25
(D) 20
(E) 3

6. In Figure 1, $AD = CD$ and $AB = 5$. Which of the following is the value of $\tan \angle ACD$?

(A) 0.201
(B) 0.309
(C) 0.407
(D) 0.414
(E) 0.500

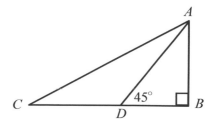

Note: Figure not drawn to scale.

Figure 1

GO ON TO THE NEXT PAGE

MATHEMATICS LEVEL 2 TEST - *Continued*

7. If $\sin\theta\cos\theta = \dfrac{1}{4}$, then which of the following is the value(s) of

$\sin\theta - \cos\theta$?

(A) $\left\{\dfrac{1}{2}\right\}$

(B) $\left\{-\dfrac{1}{2}\right\}$

(C) $\left\{\dfrac{\sqrt{2}}{2}\right\}$

(D) $\left\{-\dfrac{\sqrt{2}}{2}\right\}$

(E) $\left\{\dfrac{\sqrt{2}}{2}, -\dfrac{\sqrt{2}}{2}\right\}$

8. If x increases from $-\dfrac{\pi}{2}$ to $\dfrac{\pi}{2}$, then the value of $\sec x$

(A) decreases, then increases.
(B) increases, then decreases.
(C) increases.
(D) decreases.
(E) none of these

9. If $f\left(\dfrac{3x}{x-1}\right) = x^2 + 1$, what is the value of $f(6)$?

(A) 3
(B) 5
(C) 18
(D) 37
(E) 42

GO ON TO THE NEXT PAGE

MATHEMATICS LEVEL 2 TEST - *Continued*

USE THIS SPACE FOR SCRATCHWORK.

10. If $f(x) = \dfrac{x+1}{x-1}$ and $f(g(x)) = \dfrac{1}{x}$, then which of the following could be $g(x)$?

(A) $x-1$

(B) $\dfrac{1}{x+1}$

(C) $x+1$

(D) $\dfrac{1}{x-1}$

(E) $\dfrac{x+1}{1-x}$

11. What is the range of the function defined by

$$f(x) = \begin{cases} x^2 & , x \geq 0 \\ \dfrac{1}{x} & , x < 0 \end{cases}$$

(A) $y > 0$
(B) $y < 0$
(C) $y \neq 0$
(D) $y \geq 0$
(E) All real numbers

12. If $2\log x = \log(2x+3)$, then which of the following is the solution set of x?

(A) $\{-1\}$
(B) $\{-1, 3\}$
(C) $\{3\}$
(D) $\{3, 4\}$
(E) All real numbers

GO ON TO THE NEXT PAGE

USE THIS SPACE FOR SCRATCHWORK.

13. Which of the following could be the graph of $y = -\dfrac{|x|}{x}$?

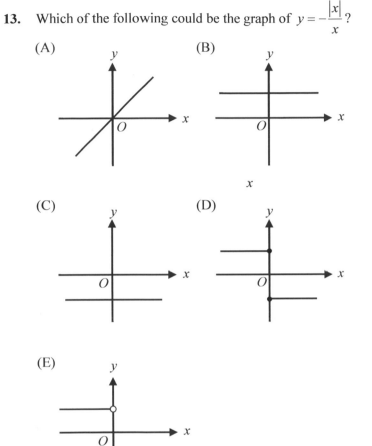

(A)

(B)

(C)

(D)

(E)

14. Which of the following is the equation of the polynomial
with roots $1 - \sqrt{2}$ and i?

(A) $x^3 + x + 1$

(B) $x^3 - 2$

(C) $x^4 - 2$

(D) $x^4 - 3x^2 + 2$

(E) $x^4 - 2x^3 - 2x - 1$

15. If $a = \log_5 9$, then 25^{2a} is

(A) 81   (B) 729   (C) 2187   (D) 6561   (E) 13122

GO ON TO THE NEXT PAGE

USE THIS SPACE FOR SCRATCHWORK.

16. If the volume of a cube is 6^{3a}, then the surface area of the cube is

(A) 6^{2a}

(B) $6(6^a)$

(C) $6(3^{2a})$

(D) 6^{2a+1}

(E) 6^{2a+3}

17. If $\cos 2x = \dfrac{1}{2}$, then $\sin x =$

(A) $-\dfrac{\sqrt{3}}{2}$

(B) $-\dfrac{1}{2}$ or $\dfrac{1}{2}$

(C) $\dfrac{\sqrt{3}}{2}$

(D) $\sqrt{3}$

(E) $-\dfrac{\sqrt{2}}{2}$ or $\dfrac{\sqrt{2}}{2}$

18. If $\text{Arc} \sin\left(-\dfrac{\sqrt{3}}{2}\right) = k$, then $\tan k =$

(A) -1 (B) $-\sqrt{3}$ (C) $\sqrt{3}$ (D) $\dfrac{1}{2}$ (E) 2

19. Which of the following is the domain of $f(x) = \dfrac{\sqrt{x-1}}{x-2}$?

(A) All real numbers
(B) All real numbers except 2
(C) All real numbers greater than or equal to 1
(D) All real numbers greater than or equal to 2
(E) All real numbers greater than or equal to 1 except 2

GO ON TO THE NEXT PAGE

USE THIS SPACE FOR SCRATCHWORK.

20. If $_xC_{x-2} = 21$, then $x =$

(A) 4
(B) 5
(C) 6
(D) 7
(E) 8

21. On a multiple- choice test, there are 5 choices for each question. What is the probability that a student who guesses every answer will have exactly 10 correct answers on a test that consists of 20 questions?

(A) 0.002
(B) 0.02
(C) 0.2
(D) 0.25
(E) 0.5

22. What is the sum of the numerical coefficients of $(x - 2y)^4$?

(A) 0
(B) 1
(C) 16
(D) 32
(E) 48

23. What is the value of $\sum_{n=1}^{100} i^n$?

(A) 0
(B) 1
(C) i
(D) $-i$
(E) -1

GO ON TO THE NEXT PAGE

USE THIS SPACE FOR SCRATCHWORK.

24. If $3 - i\sqrt{2}$ is the root of the quadratic equation $ax^2 - 12x + c = 0$, what is the value of c ?

(A) 11
(B) 22
(C) 25
(D) 33
(E) 44

25. In Figure 2, which of the following is the equation of the graph?

(A) $y = 3\sin 2\theta$

(B) $y = 3\sin 4\theta$

(C) $y = 3\sin 8\theta$

(D) $y = 3\sin\dfrac{\pi\theta}{2}$

(E) $y = 3\sin\dfrac{\pi\theta}{4}$

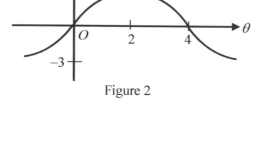

Figure 2

26. What is the length of the major axis of an ellipse whose equation is $x^2 + 4y^2 + 4x - 8y = 8$?

(A) 4　(B) 8　(C) 12　(D) 16　(E) 20

27. What is the slope of the line tangent to the circle $(x-1)^2 + (y-1)^2 = 25$ at the point $(4,5)$?

(A) $-\dfrac{4}{3}$

(B) $-\dfrac{3}{4}$

(C) $-\dfrac{5}{4}$

(D) $-\dfrac{4}{5}$

(E) $\dfrac{4}{5}$

GO ON TO THE NEXT PAGE

28. If $f(x) = f\left(x + \dfrac{\pi}{2}\right)$, then which of the following could be $f(x)$?

    (A) $f(x) = \sin x$
    (B) $f(x) = 2\sin 2x$
    (C) $f(x) = \cos x$
    (D) $f(x) = 2\cos 2x$
    (E) $f(x) = 2\tan 2x$

29. In Figure 3, $ABCD$ is a rectangle and $\tan \angle CBE = \dfrac{1}{7}$ and $\tan \angle EAD = \dfrac{1}{3}$. What is the value of $\tan \angle BDA$?

    (A) 0.488
    (B) 0.476
    (C) 0.434
    (D) 0.421
    (E) 0.306

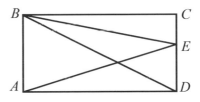

Note: Figure not drawn to scale.

Figure 3

30. If $f(x) = \dfrac{1}{x-3} + 2$, what is the range of the function?

    (A) $y \geq 2$
    (B) $y \leq 2$
    (C) $y \neq 3$
    (D) $y \neq 2$
    (E) All real

31. Figure 4 shows the graph of $f(x)$. Which of the following could be the function $f(x)$?

    (A) $y = |x| + |x-1|$
    (B) $y = |x+1| + |x-1|$
    (C) $y = |x-1| - |x+1|$
    (D) $y = |x+1| - |x-1|$
    (E) $y = |x+1| - |x|$

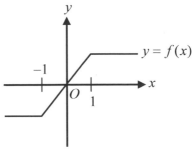

Note: Figure not drawn to scale.

Figure 4

GO ON TO THE NEXT PAGE

MATHEMATICS LEVEL 2 TEST - *Continued*

USE THIS SPACE FOR SCRATCHWORK.

32. The right circular cone is sliced horizontally forming two pieces, each of which has the same height. What is the ratio of the volume of the smaller piece to the volume of the larger piece?

(A) $\dfrac{1}{2}$

(B) $\dfrac{1}{4}$

(C) $\dfrac{1}{5}$

(D) $\dfrac{1}{7}$

(E) $\dfrac{1}{8}$

33. How many possible rational zeros does
$f(x) = 2x^3 + 3x^2 - 8x + 4$ have?

(A) 6
(B) 8
(C) 10
(D) 12
(E) 14

34. What is the polar form of the rectangular equation
$x^2 + y^2 - 4x = 0$?

(A) $r = \sin\theta$
(B) $r^2 = 4\sin\theta$
(C) $r = 4\cos\theta$
(D) $r = 4\sin\theta$
(E) $r = 2\cos\theta$

35. $\displaystyle\lim_{x \to 1} \frac{x-1}{x^3 - x^2 + x - 1} =$

(A) $\dfrac{1}{4}$ (B) $\dfrac{1}{2}$ (C) $\dfrac{2}{3}$ (D) 2   (E) 5

 GO ON TO THE NEXT PAGE

36. If the demand equation for a graphic utility is given by
$D(x) = 200 - 0.4\left(e^{0.005x}\right)$, where D is in dollars, which of
the following is the demand x for a price D of $150?

(A) 966   (B) 1024   (C) 1368   (D) 1450   (E) 2048

37. What is the graph of the parametrically defined equations
$x = 4 + 2\cos\theta$ and $y = \sin\theta - 1$?

(A) Parabola
(B) Circle
(C) Ellipse
(D) Hyperbola
(E) Two perpendicular lines

38. If $g(x) = \sqrt[3]{\dfrac{x+1}{2}}$, then $g^{-1}(1.5) =$

(A) 4.25
(B) 5.75
(C) 6.52
(D) 7.12
(E) 8.45

39. On a math exam, the scores of ten students were 66, 81,
85, 97, 86, 58, 76, 73, 88, and 80. What is the standard
deviation of the scores?

(A) 10.72
(B) 12.29
(C) 12.88
(D) 13.16
(E) 13.58

GO ON TO THE NEXT PAGE

USE THIS SPACE FOR SCRATCHWORK.

40. Which of the following is the function of the graph in
     Figure 5?

    I. $f(x) = -x^3 + ax^2 + bx + c$

    II. $f(x) = x^5 + ax^4 + bx^3 + cx^2 + dx + e$

    III. $f(x) = x^7 + ax^6 + bx^5 + cx^4 + dx^3 + ex^2 + fx + g$

(A) I only
(B) II only
(C) II and III only
(D) I, II, and III
(E) None of those

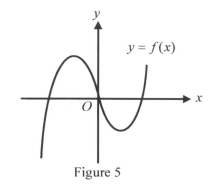

Figure 5

41. What is the smallest positive value of θ , in radians, which
     satisfies the equation $2\sin^2 \theta + 2\cos \theta - 1 = 0$?

(A) 0.56
(B) 0.86
(C) 1.24
(D) 1.56
(E) 1.95

42. Which of the following is the solution set of the equation
     $\log_3 (x - 5) = \log_9 (2x + 5)$?

(A) $\{2\}$
(B) $\{5\}$
(C) $\{10\}$
(D) $\{2, 10\}$
(E) $\{2, 5, 10\}$

GO ON TO THE NEXT PAGE

USE THIS SPACE FOR SCRATCHWORK.

43. What is the distance between two points of $(1, 2, 3)$ and $(0, -4, -2)$?

(A) 7.87
(B) 8.24
(C) 8.48
(D) 10.25
(E) 11.24

44. Which of the following could be the solution to
$[n]^2 - 2[n] = 3$, where $[n]$ is the greatest integer function?

(A) $2 \le n < 3$
(B) $0 \le n < 1$
(C) $-1 < n < 0$
(D) $-1 \le n < 0$
(E) $-1 < n \le 0$

45. In Figure 6, $ABCDE$ is a regular pentagon with side of length 6. What is the x-coordinate of D?

(A) 10.3
(B) 10.5
(C) 10.7
(D) 10.9
(E) 11.9

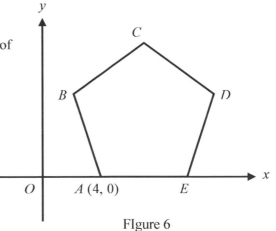

Figure 6

46. If the line $y = 3x + k$ is tangent to the hyperbola whose equation is $4x^2 - y^2 = 16$, which of the following could be the value of k?

(A) -2
(B) -1
(C) $\sqrt{5}$
(D) $2\sqrt{5}$
(E) $3\sqrt{5}$

GO ON TO THE NEXT PAGE

MATHEMATICS LEVEL 2 TEST - *Continued*

USE THIS SPACE FOR SCRATCHWORK.

47. What is the area of the polygon formed by the points (x, y) which satisfy the inequality $|x| + \dfrac{|y|}{2} \leq 1$?

(A) 2
(B) 3
(C) 4
(D) 8
(E) 10

48. If $\lim\limits_{x \to 1} \dfrac{x^2 + 2x + k}{x - 1} = 4$, then what is the value of k ?

(A) −4
(B) −3
(C) −2
(D) 3
(E) 4

49. What is the radius of the sphere whose equation is
$x^2 + y^2 + z^2 - 2x - 4y + 6z = 0$?

(A) 3
(B) 3.74
(C) 8.56
(D) 12.45
(E) 14

50. If $\vec{a} = (2, 1)$ and $\vec{b} = (1, -2)$, then $\left| 3\vec{a} - 2\vec{b} \right| =$

(A) 7.44
(B) 8.06
(C) 8.45
(D) 9.12
(E) 10.14

STOP

**IF YOU FINISH BEFORE TIME IS CALLED, YOU MAY CHECK YOUR WORK ON THIS TEST ONLY.
DO NOT TURN TO ANY OTHER TEST IN THIS BOOK.**

No Test Material on This Page

TEST 7			ANSWERS						

#	answer	#	answer	#	answer	#	answer	#	answer
1	B	11	E	21	A	31	D	41	E
2	B	12	C	22	B	32	D	42	C
3	C	13	E	23	A	33	B	43	A
4	A	14	E	24	B	34	C	44	D
5	A	15	D	25	E	35	B	45	E
6	D	16	D	26	B	36	A	46	D
7	E	17	B	27	B	37	C	47	C
8	A	18	B	28	E	38	B	48	B
9	B	19	E	29	B	39	A	49	B
10	E	20	D	30	D	40	C	50	B

Explanations: Test 7

1. **(B)** $\dfrac{x^{x+1} - x^x}{x^x} = \dfrac{x^x(x-1)}{x^x} = x - 1$

    Since $x = 10$, $x - 1 = 10 - 1 = 9$.

2. **(B)** $(x + y)(x - y) = 21$ (x and y are positive integers)

    $\begin{cases} x + y = 21 \\ x - y = 1 \end{cases}$ or $\begin{cases} x + y = 7 \\ x - y = 3 \end{cases}$

    $\quad 2x = 22 \qquad\qquad 2x = 10$

    $\quad\; x = 11 \qquad\qquad\; x = 5$

    Or, substitute choices and check.

3. **(C)** $y = 4x - 2 \;\;\rightarrow\;\; x = 4y - 2 \;\;\rightarrow\;\; f^{-1} : y = \dfrac{x + 2}{4}$

4. **(A)** The asymptotes of both graphs are $y = \pm x$.

    The graphs are as follows.

    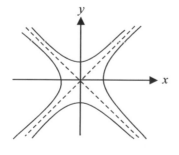

5. **(A)** $g(-5.4) = \left[-10.8\right] = -11 \;\;\rightarrow\;\; f(-11) = \left|-33\right| = 33$

6. (D) $\tan C = \dfrac{5}{5+5\sqrt{2}} \approx 0.414$

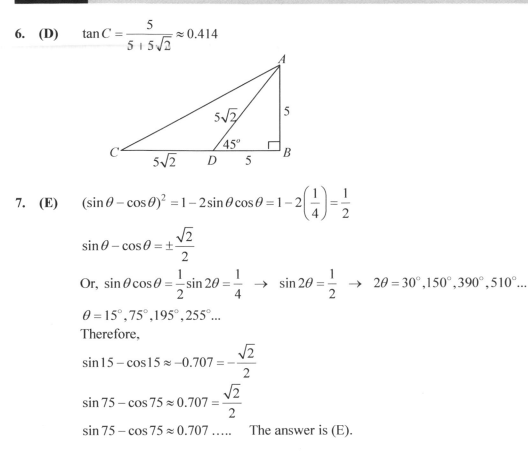

7. (E) $(\sin\theta - \cos\theta)^2 = 1 - 2\sin\theta\cos\theta = 1 - 2\left(\dfrac{1}{4}\right) = \dfrac{1}{2}$

$\sin\theta - \cos\theta = \pm\dfrac{\sqrt{2}}{2}$

Or, $\sin\theta\cos\theta = \dfrac{1}{2}\sin 2\theta = \dfrac{1}{4} \rightarrow \sin 2\theta = \dfrac{1}{2} \rightarrow 2\theta = 30°, 150°, 390°, 510°...$

$\theta = 15°, 75°, 195°, 255°...$
Therefore,

$\sin 15 - \cos 15 \approx -0.707 = -\dfrac{\sqrt{2}}{2}$

$\sin 75 - \cos 75 \approx 0.707 = \dfrac{\sqrt{2}}{2}$

$\sin 75 - \cos 75 \approx 0.707 .....$ The answer is (E).

8. (A) $\sec x = \dfrac{1}{\cos x}$

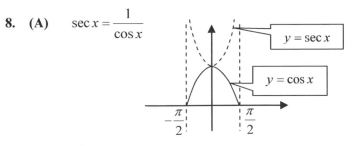

9. (B) Since $\dfrac{3x}{x-1} = 6 \rightarrow x = 2$, then $f(6) = 2^2 + 1 = 5$.

10. (E) $f(g) = \dfrac{g+1}{g-1} = \dfrac{1}{x} \rightarrow xg + x = g - 1 \rightarrow g(x) = \dfrac{1+x}{1-x}$

11. (E) The graph is as follows.

$\lim\limits_{x\to-\infty}\dfrac{1}{x} = 0$, $f(0) = 0$

Since $\lim\limits_{x\to 0}\dfrac{1}{x} = f(0)$, the range is all real numbers

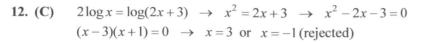

12. (C) $2\log x = \log(2x+3)$ $\rightarrow$ $x^2 = 2x+3$ $\rightarrow$ $x^2 - 2x - 3 = 0$

$(x-3)(x+1) = 0$ $\rightarrow$ $x = 3$ or $x = -1$ (rejected)

13. (E) Piecewise-defined function:

$$y = -\frac{|x|}{x} \begin{cases} x > 0, & -1 \\ x < 0, & 1 \end{cases}$$

14. (E) Reconstruct equation: conjugate roots

$$[x-(1-\sqrt{2})][x-(1+\sqrt{2})][x-i][x+i] = 0$$

$$[(x-1)^2 - (\sqrt{2})^2][x^2+1] = 0 \rightarrow (x^2 - 2x - 1)(x^2+1) = 0$$

$$\rightarrow x^4 - 2x^3 - 2x - 1 = 0$$

15. (D) Since $a = \log_5 9$ $\rightarrow$ $9 = 5^a$,

$$25^{2a} = 5^{4a} = (5^a)^4 = 9^4 = 6561.$$

16. (D) x: the length of an edge

Volume $= x^3 = 6^{3a}$ $\rightarrow$ $x = (6^{3a})^{\frac{1}{3}} = 6^a$

Surface area $= 6x^2 = 6(6^a)^2 = 6^{2a+1}$

17. (B) $\cos 2x = 1 - 2\sin^2 x = \dfrac{1}{2}$ $\rightarrow$ $\sin^2 x = \dfrac{1}{4}$ $\rightarrow$ $\sin x = \pm\dfrac{1}{2}$

Or, $2x = 60°, 300°$ $\rightarrow$ $x = 30°, 150°$

Therefore, $\sin 30° = \dfrac{1}{2}$ or $\sin 300° = -\dfrac{1}{2}$

18. (B) Use a calculator.

Or, $\text{Arcsin}\left(-\dfrac{\sqrt{3}}{2}\right) = k$ $\rightarrow$ $\sin k = -\dfrac{\sqrt{3}}{2}$, where $-90° \leq k \leq 90°$.

$\tan k = -\sqrt{3}$

19. (E) $N(x) = \sqrt{x-1}$ $\rightarrow$ $x \geq 1$

$D(x) = x - 2$ $\rightarrow$ $x \neq 2$

Domain: $\{x \mid x \geq 1 \text{ but } x \neq 2\}$

20. (D) $\quad _xC_{x-2} = \dfrac{x!}{2!(x-2)!} = \dfrac{x(x-1)}{2} \;\rightarrow\; \dfrac{x(x-1)}{2} = 21 \;\rightarrow\; (x-7)(x+6) = 0$

$x = 7$ (x must be a positive integer and greater than 2)

21. (A) $\quad P = {}_{20}C_{10}(0.2)^{10}(0.8)^{10} = 0.0020314137 \approx 0.002$

22. (B) $\quad$ Let $x = 1$ and $y = 1$.

$(x-2y)^4 = {}_4C_0(x)^4(-2y)^0 + {}_4C_1(x)^3(-2y)^1 + {}_4C_2(x)^2(-2y)^2 + {}_4C_3(x)^1(-2y)^3$
$+ {}_4C_4(x)^0(-2y)^4$

When you substitute $x = 1$ and $y = 1$, you can get the sum of the coefficients.

Both sides are equal for any x. Therefore, the sum of all coefficients is $(1 - 2\cdot 1)^4 = 1$.

23. (A) $\quad \displaystyle\sum_{n=1}^{100} i^n = i + i^2 + i^3 + i^4 + \dots + i^{100}$: Geometric sequence

$S_{100} = \dfrac{a(1-r^n)}{1-r} = \dfrac{i(1-i^{100})}{1\;i} = \dfrac{i(1-1)}{1-i} = 0$

Or, $i + i^2 + i^3 + i^4 = 0$: The sum of every four terms is 0. There are 25 of the terms.
$0 \times 25 = 0$.

24. (B) $\quad$ Since $3 - i\sqrt{2}$ is the root, the other root is $3 + i\sqrt{2}$.

Sum of the roots: $S = \dfrac{12}{a} = 6 \;\rightarrow\; a = 2$

Product of the roots: $P = \dfrac{c}{2} = (3 - i\sqrt{2})(3 + i\sqrt{2}) = 11 \;\rightarrow\; c = 22$

25. (E) $\quad$ From the graph: Period is 8 and frequency is $b = \dfrac{2\pi}{8} = \dfrac{\pi}{4}$.

Amplitude : 3 $\qquad y = 3\sin\dfrac{\pi}{4}\theta$

26. (B) $\quad x^2 + 4y^2 + 4x - 8y = 8 \;\rightarrow\; (x+2)^2 + 4(y-1)^2 = 16 \;\rightarrow\; \dfrac{(x+2)^2}{16} + \dfrac{(y-1)^2}{4} = 1$

$a = 4 \;\rightarrow\;$ Major axis $= 2a = 8$

27. (B)

The slope of line $m = \dfrac{5-1}{4-1} = \dfrac{4}{3}$

The slope of line $\ell = -\dfrac{3}{4}$

28. (E) $f(x)$ is periodic with period of $\dfrac{\pi}{2}$.

The period of $f(x) = 2\tan 2x$ is $\dfrac{\pi}{2}$.

29. (B) $\tan\angle CBE = \dfrac{CE}{BC} = \dfrac{a}{7a}$ and $\tan\angle EAD = \dfrac{ED}{AD} = \dfrac{b}{3b}$.

$\tan\angle BDA = \dfrac{AB}{AD} = \dfrac{a+b}{3b}$

Since $7a = 3b \;\rightarrow\; a = \dfrac{3b}{7}$,

$\dfrac{a+b}{3b} = \dfrac{\dfrac{3b}{7}+b}{3b} = \dfrac{10b}{21b} = \dfrac{10}{21} \approx 0.476$.

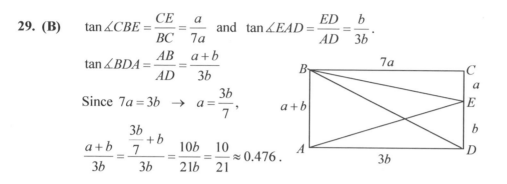

30. (D)   The graph of f : Transformation of $y = \dfrac{1}{x}$: shift to the right by 3 and up by 2

The range: $y \neq 2$

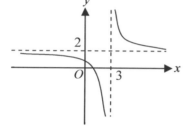

31. (D)   From the graph:

$$\begin{cases} \text{If } x \geq 1, & y = 2 \\ \text{If } -1 \leq x < 1, & y = 2x \\ \text{If } x < -1, & y = -2 \end{cases}$$

Choice (D): If $x \geq 1$, then $y = (x+1)-(x-1) = 2$

If $-1 \leq x < 1$, then $y = (x+1)+(x-1) = 2x$

If $x < -1$, then $y = -(x+1)+(x-1) = -2$

32. (D)   Since the ratio of the lengths is 1:2,

the ratio of their volumes is $1^3 : 2^3 = 1:8$.

Therefore, the ratio of the volumes is 1:7.

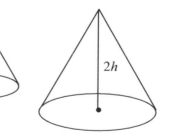

33. (B)   The rational zero test:

$\dfrac{\pm 1, \pm 2, \pm 4}{\pm 1, \pm 2} = \pm 1, \pm 2, \pm 4, \pm \dfrac{1}{2}$: 8 possible rational zeros

34. (C) Since $r^2 = x^2 + y^2$ and $r\cos\theta = x$,

$$x^2 + y^2 - 4x = 0 \quad \rightarrow \quad r^2 - 4r\cos\theta = 0 \quad \rightarrow \quad r = 4\cos\theta$$

35. (B) $\displaystyle\lim_{x\to 1}\frac{x-1}{x^3 - x^2 + x - 1} = \lim_{x\to 1}\frac{(x-1)}{x^2(x-1)+(x-1)} = \lim_{x\to 1}\frac{\cancel{(x-1)}}{\cancel{(x-1)}(x^2+1)} = \frac{1}{2}$

36. (A) $150 = 200 - 0.4\left(e^{0.005x}\right) \quad \rightarrow \quad 125 = e^{0.005x} \quad \rightarrow \quad x = (\ln 125) \div 0.005 \simeq 966$

37. (C) $\cos\theta = \dfrac{x-4}{2}$, $\sin\theta = y+1$

Since $\cos^2\theta + \sin^2\theta = 1$, $\dfrac{(x-4)^2}{4} + (y+1)^2 = 1$: Ellipse

38. (B) $g^{-1}(1.5) = k \quad \rightarrow \quad (1.5, k)$

Since $g^{-1}(x)$ is the inverse of $g(x)$, point $(k, 1.5)$ must be on $g(x)$.

Therefore, $\sqrt[3]{\dfrac{k+1}{2}} = 1.5 \quad \rightarrow \quad \dfrac{k+1}{2} = 1.5^3 \quad \rightarrow \quad k = 2\cdot 1.5^3 - 1 = 5.75$.

Or, you can find $g^{-1}(x)$.

39. (A) Use your calculator : Statistics. $\sigma_x = 10.72$

40. (C) Check the end of the graph. $f(x)$ have three real roots.

Therefore, II and III could be $f(x)$.

I. $\displaystyle\lim_{x\to\infty} f(x) = -\infty$ (False)

II. $\displaystyle\lim_{x\to\infty} f(x) = \infty$ and $\displaystyle\lim_{x\to-\infty} f(x) = -\infty$. Three real and two imaginary roots.

III. $\displaystyle\lim_{x\to\infty} f(x) = \infty$ and $\displaystyle\lim_{x\to-\infty} f(x) = -\infty$. Three real and four imaginary roots.

41. (E) Use a graphic utility:

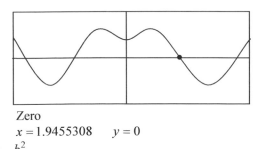

Zero
$x = 1.9455308 \qquad y = 0$

42. (C) Theorem: $\log_a b = \log_{a^2} b^2$

$\log_3(x-5) = \log_9(2x+5) \quad \rightarrow \quad \log_9(x-5)^2 = \log_9(2x+5) \quad \rightarrow \quad (x-5)^2 = 2x+5$
$(x-2)(x-10) = 0 \quad \rightarrow \quad x = 2 \text{ or } x = 10$
But $x - 5 > 0$, $x = 2$ rejected.

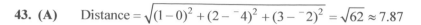

43. (A) Distance $= \sqrt{(1-0)^2 + (2 - {}^-4)^2 + (3 - {}^-2)^2} = \sqrt{62} \approx 7.87$

44. (D) Let $[n] = x$. $x^2 - 2x - 3 = 0 \rightarrow (x-3)(x+1) = 0 \rightarrow x = 3$ or $x = -1$

If $[n] = 3$, then $3 \leq n < 4$.

If $[n] = -1$, then $-1 \leq n < 0$.

45. (E)

$x = 10 + 6\cos 72° = 11.854\cdots \approx 11.9$

46. (D) Discriminant: Substitute $y = 3x + k$ into the equation of the hyperbola.

$4x^2 - (3x + k)^2 = 16 \rightarrow 5x^2 + 6kx + k^2 + 16 = 0$

$D = (6k)^2 - 4(5)(k^2 + 16) = 0 \rightarrow k^2 = 20$

Therefore, $k = \pm 2\sqrt{5}$.

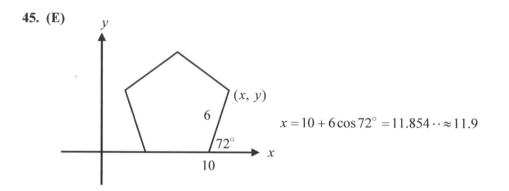

$4x^2 - y^2 = 16 \rightarrow \dfrac{x^2}{4} - \dfrac{y^2}{16} = 1$

Since $a = 2$ and $b = 4$,

Asymptotes: $y = \pm 2x$.

$y = 3x + 2\sqrt{5}$

$y = 3x - 2\sqrt{5}$

47. (C)   Remember: The graph of $|x| + |y| = 1$ is as follows.

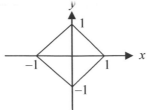

Therefore, the graph of $|x| + \dfrac{|y|}{2} \le 1$ is

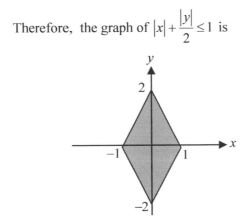

The area $= \dfrac{2 \times 1}{2} \times 4 = 4$

48. (B) $\displaystyle\lim_{x \to 1} \dfrac{x^2 + 2x + k}{x - 1} = 4$:   Numerator must have a factor of $(x - 1)$.

$N(1) = 1 + 2 + k = 0 \;\rightarrow\; k = -3$

$\displaystyle\lim_{x \to 1} \dfrac{x^2 + 2x + k}{x - 1} = 4 \;\rightarrow\; \lim_{x \to 1} \dfrac{x^2 + 2x - 3}{x - 1} = 4 \;\rightarrow\; \lim_{x \to 1} \dfrac{(x + 3)\,\cancel{(x - 1)}}{\cancel{(x - 1)}} = 4$

49. (B)   Since $(x - 1)^2 + (y - 2)^2 + (z + 3)^2 = 14$, $r = \sqrt{14} \approx 3.74$.

50. (B) $3\vec{a} - 2\vec{b} = 3(2,1) - 2(1,-2) = (4,7)$

$\left| 3\vec{a} - 2\vec{b} \right| = \sqrt{4^2 + 7^2} = \sqrt{65} \approx 8.06$

END

No Test Material on This Page

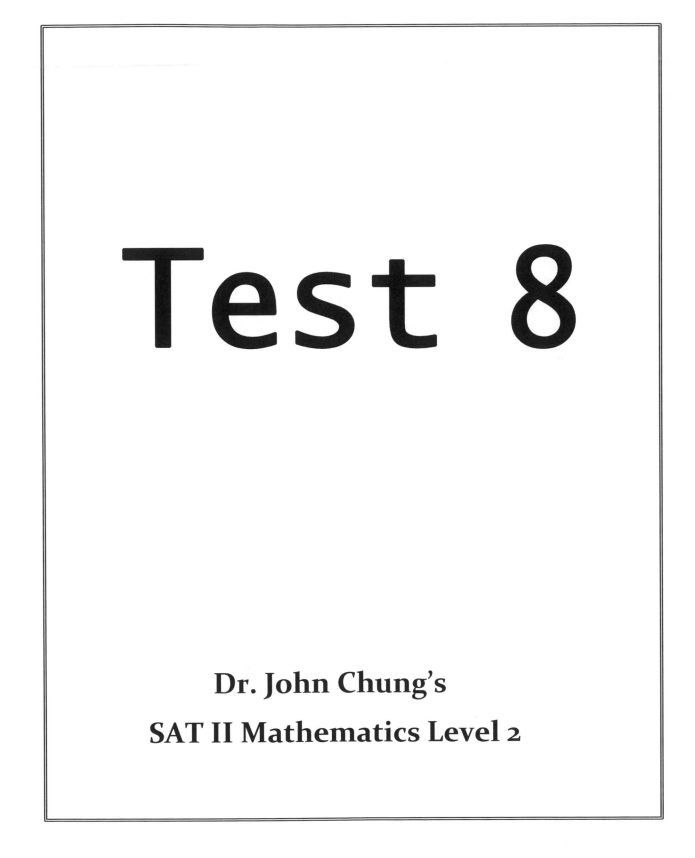

Test 8

Dr. John Chung's

SAT II Mathematics Level 2

MATHEMATICS LEVEL 2 TEST

REFERENCE INFORMATION

THE FOLLOWING INFORMATION IS FOR YOUR REFERENCE IN ANSWERING SOME OF THE QUESTIONS IN THIS TEST

Volume of a right circular cone with radius r and height h: $V = \dfrac{1}{3}\pi r^2 h$

Lateral Area of a right circular cone with circumference of the base c and slant height ℓ: $S = \dfrac{1}{2}c\ell$

Volume of a sphere with radius r: $V = \dfrac{4}{3}\pi r^3$

Surface Area of a sphere with radius r: $S = 4\pi r^2$

Volume of a pyramid with base area B and height h: $V = \dfrac{1}{3}Bh$

Dr. John Chung's SAT II Math Level 2

Answer Sheet

01 Ⓐ Ⓑ Ⓒ Ⓓ Ⓔ		26 Ⓐ Ⓑ Ⓒ Ⓓ Ⓔ
02 Ⓐ Ⓑ Ⓒ Ⓓ Ⓔ		27 Ⓐ Ⓑ Ⓒ Ⓓ Ⓔ
03 Ⓐ Ⓑ Ⓒ Ⓓ Ⓔ		28 Ⓐ Ⓑ Ⓒ Ⓓ Ⓔ
04 Ⓐ Ⓑ Ⓒ Ⓓ Ⓔ		29 Ⓐ Ⓑ Ⓒ Ⓓ Ⓔ
05 Ⓐ Ⓑ Ⓒ Ⓓ Ⓔ		30 Ⓐ Ⓑ Ⓒ Ⓓ Ⓔ
06 Ⓐ Ⓑ Ⓒ Ⓓ Ⓔ		31 Ⓐ Ⓑ Ⓒ Ⓓ Ⓔ
07 Ⓐ Ⓑ Ⓒ Ⓓ Ⓔ		32 Ⓐ Ⓑ Ⓒ Ⓓ Ⓔ
08 Ⓐ Ⓑ Ⓒ Ⓓ Ⓔ		33 Ⓐ Ⓑ Ⓒ Ⓓ Ⓔ
09 Ⓐ Ⓑ Ⓒ Ⓓ Ⓔ		34 Ⓐ Ⓑ Ⓒ Ⓓ Ⓔ
10 Ⓐ Ⓑ Ⓒ Ⓓ Ⓔ		35 Ⓐ Ⓑ Ⓒ Ⓓ Ⓔ
11 Ⓐ Ⓑ Ⓒ Ⓓ Ⓔ		36 Ⓐ Ⓑ Ⓒ Ⓓ Ⓔ
12 Ⓐ Ⓑ Ⓒ Ⓓ Ⓔ		37 Ⓐ Ⓑ Ⓒ Ⓓ Ⓔ
13 Ⓐ Ⓑ Ⓒ Ⓓ Ⓕ		38 Ⓐ Ⓑ Ⓒ Ⓓ Ⓔ
14 Ⓐ Ⓑ Ⓒ Ⓓ Ⓔ		39 Ⓐ Ⓑ Ⓒ Ⓓ Ⓔ
15 Ⓐ Ⓑ Ⓒ Ⓓ Ⓔ		40 Ⓐ Ⓑ Ⓒ Ⓓ Ⓔ
16 Ⓐ Ⓑ Ⓒ Ⓓ Ⓔ		41 Ⓐ Ⓑ Ⓒ Ⓓ Ⓔ
17 Ⓐ Ⓑ Ⓒ Ⓓ Ⓔ		42 Ⓐ Ⓑ Ⓒ Ⓓ Ⓔ
18 Ⓐ Ⓑ Ⓒ Ⓓ Ⓔ		43 Ⓐ Ⓑ Ⓒ Ⓓ Ⓔ
19 Ⓐ Ⓑ Ⓒ Ⓓ Ⓔ		44 Ⓐ Ⓑ Ⓒ Ⓓ Ⓔ
20 Ⓐ Ⓑ Ⓒ Ⓓ Ⓔ		45 Ⓐ Ⓑ Ⓒ Ⓓ Ⓔ
21 Ⓐ Ⓑ Ⓒ Ⓓ Ⓔ		46 Ⓐ Ⓑ Ⓒ Ⓓ Ⓔ
22 Ⓐ Ⓑ Ⓒ Ⓓ Ⓔ		47 Ⓐ Ⓑ Ⓒ Ⓓ Ⓔ
23 Ⓐ Ⓑ Ⓒ Ⓓ Ⓔ		48 Ⓐ Ⓑ Ⓒ Ⓓ Ⓔ
24 Ⓐ Ⓑ Ⓒ Ⓓ Ⓔ		49 Ⓐ Ⓑ Ⓒ Ⓓ Ⓔ
25 Ⓐ Ⓑ Ⓒ Ⓓ Ⓔ		50 Ⓐ Ⓑ Ⓒ Ⓓ Ⓔ

The number of right answers: ☐

The number of wrong answers: ☐

$$\underbrace{\boxed{}}_{\text{\# of correct}} - \frac{1}{4} \times \underbrace{\boxed{}}_{\text{\# of wrong}} = \underbrace{\boxed{}}_{\text{Raw score}}$$

Score Conversion Table

Raw Score	Scaled Score	Raw Score	Scaled Score	Raw Score	Scaled Score
50	800	28	640	6	480
49	800	27	630	5	470
48	800	26	620	4	470
47	800	25	620	3	460
46	800	24	610	2	460
45	800	23	610	1	450
44	800	22	600	0	450
43	800	21	600		
42	800	20	590		
41	800	19	590		
40	780	18	580		
39	760	17	570		
38	750	16	560		
37	740	15	550		
36	720	14	540		
35	710	13	530		
34	700	12	520		
33	690	11	510		
32	680	10	500		
31	670	9	490		
30	660	8	490		
29	650	7	480		

MATHEMATICS LEVEL 2 TEST

For each of the following problems, decide which is the BEST of the choices given. If the exact numerical value is not one of the choices, select the choice that best approximates this value. Then fill in the corresponding circle on the answer sheet

Note: (1) A scientific or graphing calculator will be necessary for answering some (but not all) of the questions in this test. For each question you will have to decide whether or not you should use a calculator.

(2) For some questions in this test you may have to decide whether your calculator should be in the radian mode or the degree mode.

(3) Figures that accompany problems in this test are intended to provide information useful in solving the problems. They are drawn as accurately as possible EXCEPT when it is stated in a specific problem that its figure is not drawn to scale. All figures lie in a plane unless otherwise indicated.

(4) Unless otherwise specified, the domain of any function f is assumed to be the set of all real numbers x for which $f(x)$ is a real number. The range of f is assumed to be the set of all real numbers $f(x)$, where x is in the domain of f.

(5) Reference information that may be useful in answering the questions in this test can be found on the page preceding Question 1.

USE THIS SPACE FOR SCRATCHWORK

1. If $e^x = 3^2$, then $x =$

    (A) 1.4
    (B) 1.7
    (C) 1.9
    (D) 2.2
    (E) 2.4

2. If $f\left(\sqrt{x}\right) = x^2 + 4x$, then $f(3) =$

    (A) 21
    (B) 46
    (C) 84
    (D) 117
    (E) 256

GO ON TO THE NEXT PAGE

USE THIS SPACE FOR SCRATCHWORK.

3.   If $3 - \dfrac{1}{x} = 9 - \dfrac{3}{x}$, then $3 - \dfrac{1}{x} =$

(A) −3   (B) −1   (C) 0   (D) 3   (E) 9

4. $\dfrac{\dfrac{3}{ax}}{\dfrac{6}{bx}} =$

(A) $\dfrac{ab}{18}$ (B) $\dfrac{2a}{b}$ (C) $\dfrac{2b}{a}$ (D) $\dfrac{b}{2a}$ (E) $\dfrac{a}{2b}$

5.   If $3^{2y+1} = 5$, then $y =$

(A) 0.23   (B) 0.32   (C) 2.75   (D) 3.12   (E) 3.44

6.   Which of the following could be the graph of the polar equation $r = 2\cos\theta$?

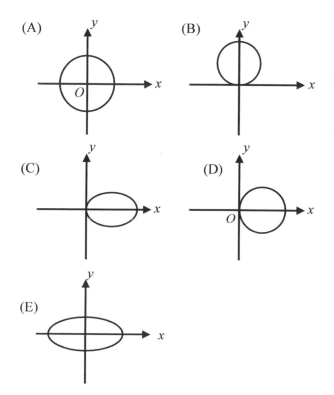

MATHEMATICS LEVEL 2 TEST - *Continued*

USE THIS SPACE FOR SCRATCHWORK.

7. Which of the following ordered pairs is not an element of

the greatest- integer function $y = \left[\dfrac{x}{2}\right]$?

    (A) $(8, 4)$

    (B) $(2.78, 1)$

    (C) $(-4.8, -3)$

    (D) $(-5.64, -2)$

    (E) $(\sqrt{10}, 1)$

8. What is the range of the function $f(x) = |x+2|$ for the
domain $-3 \le x \le 3$?

    (A) $3 \le y \le 5$

    (B) $1 \le y \le 5$

    (C) $0 \le y \le 5$

    (D) $-1 \le y \le 5$

    (E) $-3 \le y \le 5$

9. If $\left(2+\sqrt{5}\right)\left(3-\sqrt{5}\right) = a + b\sqrt{5}$, where a and b are rational
numbers, then $a + b =$

    (A) 1   (B) 2   (C) 3   (D) 4   (E) 5

10. $\sqrt{a\sqrt{a}} \times \sqrt[4]{a} =$

    (A) $a^{\frac{3}{16}}$

    (B) $a^{\frac{1}{8}}$

    (C) $a^{\frac{3}{4}}$

    (D) a

    (E) a^2

GO ON TO THE NEXT PAGE

MATHEMATICS LEVEL 2 TEST - *Continued*

USE THIS SPACE FOR SCRATCHWORK.

11. Figure 1 shows the prism with dimensions 3, 5, and 7. What is the perimeter of the triangle ABC?

(A) 15
(B) 17.45
(C) 20.71
(D) 22.38
(E) 23.12

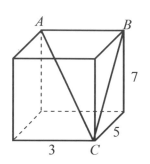

Figure 1

12. $\cos^4 \theta - \sin^4 \theta =$

(A) 1
(B) $\sin(2\theta)$
(C) $2\cos\theta$
(D) $\cos(2\theta)$
(E) $\sin\theta + \cos\theta$

13. If $2 + \sqrt{3}$ is a root of the polynomial $P(x)$, then a factor of $P(x)$ is

(A) $x^2 - 3$
(B) $x^2 - 4$
(C) $x^2 + 4x + 1$
(D) $x^2 - 4x - 1$
(E) $x^2 - 4x + 1$

14. The angle of elevation from point A to point B is $40°$ and the angle of elevation from D to B is $60°$. If the length of $\overline{AD}$ is 100, then what is the length of $\overline{BC}$?

(A) 80.50
(B) 93.97
(C) 98.56
(D) 120.45
(E) 162.76

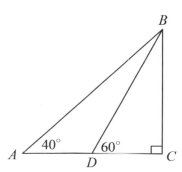

Note: Figure not drawn to scale.

Figure 2

GO ON TO THE NEXT PAGE

USE THIS SPACE FOR SCRATCHWORK.

15. If $f(x) = \dfrac{1}{x-1}$ and $f(g(x)) = x$, then which of the following is $g(x)$?

(A) $x-1$

(B) $\dfrac{x}{x+1}$

(C) $\dfrac{x+1}{x}$

(D) $\dfrac{x-1}{x}$

(E) $\dfrac{x}{1-x}$

16. In $\triangle ABC$, if $\angle A = 30°$, $b = 1$, and $c = \sqrt{3}$, then $\angle B =$

(A) $30°$
(B) $45°$
(C) $52°$
(D) $60°$
(E) $75°$

17. If $\sin\theta = 0.4$, then which of the following could be $\cos(90 - \theta)$?

(A) 0.2
(B) 0.4
(C) 0.5
(D) 0.6
(E) 0.8

USE THIS SPACE FOR SCRATCHWORK.

18. The set of points (x, y, z) such that

$(x-1)^2 + (y-1)^2 + z^2 = 0$ is

(A) A point
(B) A circle
(C) A plane
(D) A sphere
(E) Empty

19. If the graph of the rational function $R(x) = \dfrac{x^2 - ax + b}{x(x-1)}$

does not have vertical asymptotes, then what is the value of a?

(A) 0
(B) 1
(C) 2
(D) 3
(E) 4

20. If the four numbers $\log 3$, x, $\log 81$, and y form a geometric sequence in that order, which of the following could be the value of y?

(A) $\log 126$
(B) $\log 162$
(C) $\log 324$
(D) $\log 1296$
(E) $\log 6561$

21. If $5^{2x+3} = 7^{x+1}$, then $x =$

(A) 4.35
(B) 2.26
(C) 1.32
(D) −2.26
(E) −4.35

GO ON TO THE NEXT PAGE

USE THIS SPACE FOR SCRATCHWORK.

22. If $\lim\limits_{x\to\infty} \dfrac{ax^2 + bx + 1}{2x + 5} = 4$, then what is the value of $a + b$?

(A) 4
(B) 6
(C) 8
(D) 10
(E) 14

23. $\lim\limits_{n\to\infty} \sum\limits_{i=2}^{n} \dfrac{1}{3^i} =$

(A) $\dfrac{1}{6}$

(B) $\dfrac{1}{3}$

(C) $\dfrac{2}{3}$

(D) $\dfrac{3}{2}$

(E) $\dfrac{4}{3}$

24. If a and b are values in the domain of $f(x)$ and
$f(a) > f(b)$, where $b > a$, then which of the following
must be true?

(A) $f(x)$ is an odd function.
(B) $f(x)$ is an even function.
(C) $f(x)$ increases as x increases.
(D) $f(x)$ decreases as x increases.
(E) $f(x)$ is a linear function.

GO ON TO THE NEXT PAGE

USE THIS SPACE FOR SCRATCHWORK.

25. What is the measure of the largest angle in a triangle with sides of lengths 3, 4, and 6?

(A) $62°$

(B) $84°$

(C) $98°$

(D) $117°$

(E) $128°$

26. If $f(x) = \left(\dfrac{1}{2}\right)^{x-3} + 2$ and $g(x)$ is the inverse of f, then what is the value of a which satisfies $g(a) = 5$?

(A) 2

(B) 2.25

(C) 2.5

(D) 4.45

(E) 5.25

27. If $f(x) = 3^{-|x|}$, then what is the range of the function?

(A) $y > 0$

(B) $y < 0$

(C) $y \le 1$

(D) $y \ge 1$

(E) $0 < y \le 1$

28. Figure 3 shows the graph of $y = 3^{-x}$ and three inscribed rectangles. What is the sum of the areas of the rectangles?

(A) 0.25

(B) 0.50

(C) 2.45

(D) 6.26

(E) 12.68

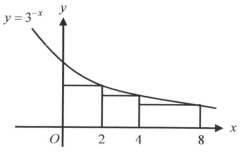

Note: Figure not drawn to scale.

Figure 3

GO ON TO THE NEXT PAGE

USE THIS SPACE FOR SCRATCHWORK.

29. What is the domain of $f(x) = (x^2 - 4)^{\frac{2}{3}}$?

(A) $x \geq 0$
(B) $x \leq -2$ or $x \geq 2$
(C) $-2 \leq x \leq 2$
(D) $-2 < x < 2$
(E) All real numbers

30. If $\sin A = \dfrac{3}{5}$, A is acute, $\sec B = -\dfrac{5}{3}$, and B is obtuse,

then what is the value of $\tan(A + B)$?

(A) 0.58
(B) 0.29
(C) −0.29
(D) −0.58
(E) −0.86

31. If $f(3x - 4) = 6x + 5$ for all real numbers x, then $f(x) =$

(A) $3x + 4$
(B) $2x - 15$
(C) $2x + 13$
(D) $2x - 10$
(E) $3x - 13$

32. Which of the following is true for the graph of the equation $x^2 + y^2 = kx$, where k is a positive constant?

(A) A circle with center on the y-axis is tangent to the x-axis.
(B) A circle with center on the x-axis is not tangent to the y-axis.
(C) A circle with center on the x-axis is tangent to the y-axis.
(D) An ellipse with center on the x-axis is tangent to the y-axis.
(E) None of these

GO ON TO THE NEXT PAGE

USE THIS SPACE FOR SCRATCHWORK.

33. What is the area of an equilateral triangle that is inscribed in a circle of radius 2?

   (A) $3\sqrt{3}$
   (B) $2\sqrt{3}$
   (C) $3\sqrt{2}$
   (D) $2\sqrt{2}$
   (E) $4\sqrt{2}$

34. What is the remainder when the polynomial $x^4 - 3x^2 + 10$ is divided by $x^2 + 1$?

   (A) 10
   (B) 14
   (C) $x + 10$
   (D) $x + 14$
   (E) $2x + 5$

35. In Figure 4, if the radius of the base is 6 and the height of the cone is 8, what is the surface area of the cone?

   (A) 36π
   (B) 64π
   (C) 96π
   (D) 136π
   (E) 148π

FIgure 4

36. A cylinder with height 10 is inscribed in a sphere with radius 8. What is the volume of the cylinder?

   (A) 201
   (B) 652
   (C) 844
   (D) 1225
   (E) 1412

GO ON TO THE NEXT PAGE

USE THIS SPACE FOR SCRATCHWORK.

37. If one zero of $f(x) = x^2 - kx + k + 7$ is 3, where k is a constant, then what is the other zero of f ?

(A) 1
(B) 2
(C) 3
(D) 4
(E) 5

38. If \$5,000 is invested in a bank at a rate of 5% annual interest compounded monthly for 3 years, what is the amount of the balance after 3 years?

(A) \$5300.45
(B) \$5800.12
(C) \$5807.36
(D) \$6000.50
(E) \$6900.56

39. If $f\left(\dfrac{2x-3}{3}\right) = 4x - 8$, then $f(2) =$

(A) 8
(B) 10
(C) 12
(D) 14
(E) 16

40. In Figure 5, if the volume of the inscribed circular cone is 100, then what is the volume of the square pyramid?

(A) 112.43
(B) 127.32
(C) 135.25
(D) 151.38
(E) 167.12

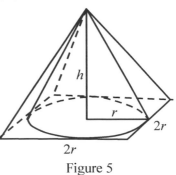

Figure 5

GO ON TO THE NEXT PAGE

USE THIS SPACE FOR SCRATCHWORK.

41. Which of the following is the point(s) of intersection of
$x^2 + y^2 = 16$ and $-y^2 + x = 4$?

(A) $(4, 0)$

(B) $(5, 0)$

(C) $(4, 0)$ and $(-5, -3)$

(D) $(4, 0)$ and $(-4, 0)$

(E) $(5, 0)$ and $(-5, 0)$

42. What is the coefficient of x^3 in the expansion of $(5x - 1)^9$?

(A) 5

(B) 25

(C) 125

(D) 9500

(E) 10500

43. The standard deviation of a data set is 8.5. If a new data set
is created by subtracting 5.5 from each data value, what is
the standard deviation of the new data set?

(A) 3.0

(B) 5.5

(C) 7.0

(D) 8.5

(E) 8.7

44. Which of the following is the unit vector of $\vec{a} = (3, 4, 12)$?

(A) $(1, 0, 0)$

(B) $(1, 1, 1)$

(C) $(0.31, 0.23, 0.92)$

(D) $(0.23, 0.31, 0.92)$

(E) $(-0.23, 0.92, -0.31)$

GO ON TO THE NEXT PAGE

MATHEMATICS LEVEL 2 TEST - *Continued*

45. The polynomial equation $xy - x + 2 = 0$ can be expressed by a set of parametric equations as a function of t. If $y(t) = 2t - 3$, then $x(t) =$

(A) $1 - 3t$

(B) $\dfrac{1}{2 - t}$

(C) $\dfrac{1}{t - 2}$

(D) $\dfrac{1 - 3t}{2}$

(E) $3t - 1$

46. If $i = \sqrt{-1}$, what is the third term in the binomial expansion of $(2 - 3i)^6$?

(A)   1120

(B)   1120i

(C)   2160

(D)   −2160

(E)   −2160i

47. If there are 10 points on a circle, how many line segments can be made by connecting any two given points?

(A) 100

(B) 90

(C) 80

(D) 72

(E) 45

48. In $\triangle ABC$, if $\angle A = 45°$, $a = 7$, and $b = 10$, how many distinct triangles can be formed?

(A) 0

(B) 1

(C) 2

(D) 3

(E) 4

GO ON TO THE NEXT PAGE

MATHEMATICS LEVEL 2 TEST - *Continued*

USE THIS SPACE FOR SCRATCHWORK.

49. Which of the following could be the curve represented by

the parametric equations $x = \dfrac{1}{\sqrt{t}}$ and $y = \dfrac{2t-1}{t}$?

(A)
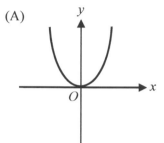

(B)
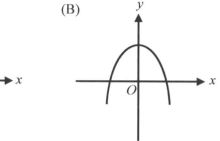

(C)
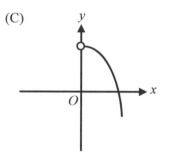

(D)
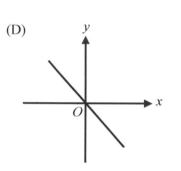

(E)
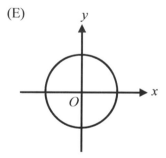

GO ON TO THE NEXT PAGE

USE THIS SPACE FOR SCRATCHWORK.

50.   Figure 6 shows the rectangular solid with dimensions 3, 4, and 5.
      If $\overline{PQ}$ is the diagonal of the solid, what is the value of θ formed
      by the diagonals and the side QR ?

(A) $30°$

(B) $32.07°$

(C) $34.45°$

(D) $46.28°$

(E) $55.55°$

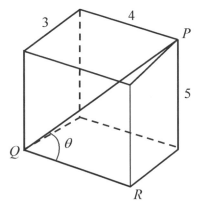

Note: Figure not drawn to scale.

Figure 6

STOP

IF YOU FINISH BEFORE TIME IS CALLED, YOU MAY CHECK YOUR WORK ON THIS TEST ONLY.

DO NOT TURN TO ANY OTHER TEST IN THIS BOOK.

#	answer	#	answer	#	answer	#	answer	#	answer
1	D	11	C	21	D	31	C	41	A
2	D	12	D	22	C	32	C	42	E
3	C	13	E	23	A	33	A	43	D
4	D	14	E	24	D	34	B	44	D
5	A	15	C	25	D	35	C	45	B
6	D	16	A	26	B	36	D	46	D
7	D	17	B	27	E	37	E	47	E
8	C	18	A	28	A	38	C	48	A
9	B	19	B	29	E	39	B	49	C
10	D	20	E	30	C	40	B	50	E

TEST 8 — **ANSWERS**

Explanations: Test 8

1. **(D)** $x = \ln 9 = 2.2$

2. **(D)**   Since $\sqrt{x} = 3 \;\rightarrow\; x = 9.$ $f(\sqrt{9}) = 9^2 + 4(9) = 117$

3. **(C)** $3x - 1 = 9x - 3 \;\rightarrow\; 6x = 2 \;\rightarrow\; x = \dfrac{1}{3} \;\rightarrow\; 3 - 3 = 0$

4. **(D)** $\dfrac{\left(\dfrac{3}{ax}\right)(abx)}{\left(\dfrac{6}{bx}\right)(abx)} = \dfrac{3b}{6a} = \dfrac{b}{2a}$

5. **(A)** $2y + 1 = \log_3 5 = \dfrac{\log 5}{\log 3} \;\rightarrow\; y = \dfrac{1}{2}\left(\dfrac{\log 5}{\log 3} - 1\right) = 0.23$

6. **(D)**   Since $r = \sqrt{x^2 + y^2}$ and $x = r\cos\theta,$

   $r = 2\cos\theta \;\rightarrow\; \sqrt{x^2 + y^2} = 2\dfrac{x}{\sqrt{x^2 + y^2}} \;\rightarrow\; x^2 + y^2 - 2x = 0 \;\rightarrow\; (x-1)^2 + y^2 = 1.$

7. **(D)** $\left[\dfrac{-5.64}{2}\right] = [-2.82] = -3$

8. **(C)**   From the graph of $f(x) = |x + 2|$, the range is
   $0 \le y \le 5$

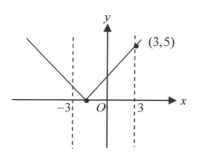

9. (B)   The equation can be simplified as follows. $1 + \sqrt{5} = a + b\sqrt{5}$
Since a and b are rational numbers, $a = 1$ and $b = 1$. $a + b = 2$.

10. (D) $\sqrt{a \cdot a^{\frac{1}{2}}} = \sqrt{a^{\frac{3}{2}}} = \left(a^{\frac{3}{2}}\right)^{\frac{1}{2}} = a^{\frac{3}{4}}$.   Therefore, $a^{\frac{3}{4}} \cdot a^{\frac{1}{4}} = a^{\frac{4}{4}} = a$.

11. (C) $AC = \sqrt{3^2 + 5^2 + 7^2} = \sqrt{83}$ $BC = \sqrt{5 + 7} = \sqrt{74}$ $AB = 3$
Perimeter $= \sqrt{83} + \sqrt{74} + 3 \approx 20.71$

12. (D) $\cos^4 \theta - \sin^2 \theta = \left(\cos^2 \theta + \sin^2 \theta\right)\left(\cos^2 \theta - \sin^2 \theta\right) = \cos^2 \theta - \sin^2 \theta = \cos 2\theta$

13. (E) $\left(x - \left(2 + \sqrt{3}\right)\right)\left(x - \left(2 - \sqrt{3}\right)\right) = 0$, $\left(x - 2 - \sqrt{3}\right)\left(x - 2 + \sqrt{3}\right) = \left(x - 2\right)^2 - 3 = x^2 - 4x + 1 = 0$

14. (E)   Law of sines: $\dfrac{\sin 20}{100} = \dfrac{\sin 40}{y}$ → $y = \dfrac{100 \sin 40}{\sin 20}$

$\rightarrow \quad z = y \sin 60 = \dfrac{100 \sin 40 \cdot \sin 60}{\sin 20} \simeq 162.76$

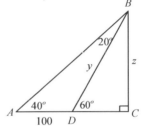

15. (C)   If $f\left(g(x)\right) = x$, then $g(x) = f^{-1}$.

For f^{-1}, $x = \dfrac{1}{y - 1}$ → $y - 1 = \dfrac{1}{x}$ → $y = \dfrac{1}{x} + 1$

Or, $f(g) = \dfrac{1}{g - 1} = x$ → $g - 1 = \dfrac{1}{x}$ → $g = \dfrac{1}{x} + 1 = \dfrac{x + 1}{x}$

16. (A)   Law of cosines:
$a^2 = \left(\sqrt{3}\right)^2 + 1^2 - 2\left(\sqrt{3}\right)(1)\cos 30° = 4 - 3 = 1$
$a = 1$.
Since $AC = BC$, $\angle A = \angle B$. $\angle B = 30°$

17. (B) $\cos(90 - \theta) = \cos 90 \cos \theta + \sin 90 \sin \theta = \sin \theta = 0.4$

18. (A)   It is not a sphere because the radius is 0. It indicates the point (1, 1, 0).

19. (B)   In order not to have any vertical asymptotes, $x^2 - ax + b$ must have factors of $x(x - 1)$.
Therefore, $N(0) = b = 0$ and $N(1) = 1 - a = 0$. $a = 1$.

20. (E) $r = \dfrac{x}{\log 3} = \dfrac{\log 81}{x}$ → $x = \pm 2\log 3$.   Therefore, $r = 2$ or -2.
$y = \log(81) \times 2 = \log 6561$

21. (D) $5^{2x+3} = 7^{x+1}$ → $(2x+3)\log 5 = (x+1)\log 7$ → $x(2\log 5 - \log 7) = \log 7 - 3\log 5$

$x = \dfrac{\log 7 - 3\log 5}{2\log 5 - \log 7} \approx -2.26$

22. (C) To have a finite limit value, degree of numerator and degree of denominator should be same. Therefore, a must be 0. To have limit value of 4, b must be 8. Therefore, $a+b=8$.

23. (A) Sum of geometric infinite series: $S = \dfrac{a}{1-r}$, where a is the first term and $|r| < 1$.

$$\lim_{n\to\infty} \sum_{t=2}^{n} \frac{1}{3^t} = \frac{1}{9} + \frac{1}{27} + \frac{1}{81} + \cdots = \frac{\frac{1}{9}}{1 - \frac{1}{3}} = \frac{1}{6}$$

24. (D) Since $f(b) < f(a)$ where $b > a$, $f(x)$ is decreasing for all real number x.

25. (D) The longest side is opposite the greatest angle.

$\cos C = \dfrac{a^2 + b^2 - c^2}{2ab} = \dfrac{3^2 + 4^2 - 6^2}{2(3)(4)} = -\dfrac{11}{24}$

$C = \cos^{-1}\left(-\dfrac{11}{24}\right) \approx 117°$

26. (B) If $g(a) = 5$, then $f(5) = a$. Therefore, $\left(\dfrac{1}{2}\right)^{5-3} + 2 = a$ → $a = \dfrac{9}{4}$.

27. (E) $f(x)$ has a maximum at $x = 0$ and $\lim\limits_{x\to\pm\infty} 3^{-|x|} = 0$.

Therefore, $0 < y \leq 1$. Or use graphic utility.

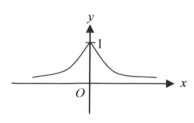

28. (A) The areas $= 2f(2) + 2f(4) + 4f(8) = 2\left(\dfrac{1}{9}\right) + 2\left(\dfrac{1}{81}\right) + 4\left(\dfrac{1}{6561}\right) \approx 0.25$

29. (E) Using a graphic utility:
Domain: All real numbers.

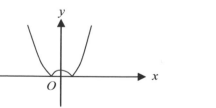

30. (C) Since $\tan A = \dfrac{3}{4}$ and $\tan B = -\dfrac{4}{3}$,

$$\tan(A+B) = \frac{\tan A + \tan B}{1 - \tan A \tan B} = \frac{\dfrac{3}{4} + \left(-\dfrac{4}{3}\right)}{1 - \left(\dfrac{3}{4}\right)\left(-\dfrac{4}{3}\right)} \approx -0.29 \,.$$

31. (C) Let $f(3k-4) = 6k+5$. Then $x = 3k-4$ or $k = \dfrac{x+4}{3}$.

Therefore, $f(x) = 6\left(\dfrac{x+4}{3}\right) + 5 = 2x + 13$.

32. (C) $x^2 + y^2 = kx \;\rightarrow\; \left(x - \dfrac{k}{2}\right)^2 + y^2 = \left(\dfrac{k}{2}\right)^2$

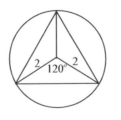

33. (A) The area of triangle is $A = \dfrac{(2)(2)\sin 120}{2} \times 3 = 3\sqrt{3}$.

34. (B) Use long division.

$$
\begin{array}{r}
x^2 - 4 \\
x^2 + 1 \overline{\smash{)}\, x^4 - 3x^2 + 10} \\
\underline{x^4 + x^2} \\
-4x^2 + 10 \\
\underline{-4x^2 - 4} \\
14
\end{array}
$$

35. (C) Lateral area $= \pi r \ell$ where ℓ is a slant height. $\ell = 10$. Therefore, the lateral area is $\pi(6)(10) = 60\pi$ and the base area is 36π. The surface area is 96π.

36. (D) The radius of the base is $\dfrac{\sqrt{156}}{2} = \sqrt{39}$. Therefore, the volume of the cylinder is

$$V = \pi r^2 h = \pi \left(\sqrt{39}\right)^2 10 = 390\pi \approx 1225.$$

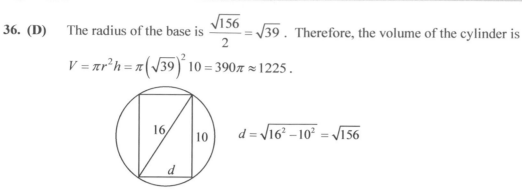

$$d = \sqrt{16^2 - 10^2} = \sqrt{156}$$

37. (E) Because 3 is a zero of $f(x)$, $f(3) = 0$. $f(3) = 9 - 3k + k + 7 = 0 \;\rightarrow\; k = 8$.

$$f(x) = x^2 - 8x + 15 = (x-3)(x-5) = 0$$

Therefore, the other root is 5.

38. (C) $A = 5{,}000\left(1 + \dfrac{0.05}{12}\right)^{12(3)} \approx 5807.36$

39. (B) $\dfrac{2x-3}{3} = 2 \;\rightarrow\; x = \dfrac{9}{2}$ Therefore, $f(2) = 4\left(\dfrac{9}{2}\right) - 8 = 10$.

40. (B) Since $\pi r^2 h = 100$, $r^2 h = \dfrac{100}{\pi}$.   The volume of a pyramid $V = 4r^2 h = 4\left(\dfrac{100}{\pi}\right) \approx 127.32$.

41. (A) Substitute $y^2 = x - 4$ in the other equation. That is,

$$x^2 + x - 4 = 16 \;\rightarrow\; x^2 + x - 20 = 0 \;\rightarrow\; (x+5)(x-4) = 0, \quad x = 4, -5$$

But when $x = -5$, $y^2 = -5 - 4 = -9$ (rejected).

When $x = 4$, $y^2 = 4 - 4 = 0 \;\rightarrow\; y = 0$. Therefore, the intersection is $(4,0)$.

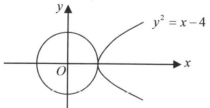

42. (E) For the coefficient of each term $\dbinom{9}{r}(5x)^{9-r}(-1)^r$, $r = 6$ to have x^3.

Therefore, the coefficient is $\dbinom{9}{6}(5)^3(-1)^6 - 10500$.

43. (D) Because all data values have been decreased by 5, the standard deviation has not been changed.

44. (D) $\vec{u} = \dfrac{\vec{a}}{|\vec{a}|}$, $|\vec{a}| = \sqrt{3^2 + 4^2 + 12^2} = 13$. Therefore $\vec{u} = \dfrac{1}{13}(3,4,12) = (0.23,\ 0.31,\ 0.92)$

45. (B)   Since $y = 2t - 3$, the polynomial equation will be as follows.

$$x(2t-3) - x + 2 = 0 \ \rightarrow \ x(2t-4) = -2 \ \rightarrow \ x = \dfrac{-2}{2t-4} \ \rightarrow \ x = \dfrac{1}{2-t}$$

46. (D)   The third term is $\dbinom{6}{2}(2)^4(-3i)^2 = -2160$.

47. (E) $\dbinom{10}{2} = 45$

48. (A)   Law of sines:
$$\dfrac{7}{\sin 45} = \dfrac{10}{\sin B} \ \rightarrow \ \sin B = \dfrac{10 \sin 45}{7} \approx 1.01 \ , \ \sin B \neq 1.01 \ (\text{No solution})$$

49. (C) $x = \dfrac{1}{\sqrt{t}} \geq 0$ and $t = \dfrac{1}{x^2}$. $y = \dfrac{2t-1}{t} = 2 - \dfrac{1}{t} \ \rightarrow \ y = 2 - x^2 \ (\text{Domain} : x > 0)$.

50. (E) $PQ = \sqrt{3^2 + 4^2 + 5^2} = \sqrt{50}$ and $QR = 4$.

$$\cos\theta = \dfrac{4}{\sqrt{50}} \ \rightarrow \ \theta = \cos^{-1}\!\left(\dfrac{4}{\sqrt{50}}\right) \approx 55.55^o$$

END

No Test Material on This Page

Test 9

Dr. John Chung's

SAT II Mathematics Level 2

MATHEMATICS LEVEL 2 TEST

REFERENCE INFORMATION

THE FOLLOWING INFORMATION IS FOR YOUR REFERENCE IN ANSWERING SOME OF THE QUESTIONS IN THIS TEST

Volume of a right circular cone with radius r and height h: $V = \dfrac{1}{3}\pi r^2 h$

Lateral Area of a right circular cone with circumference of the base c and slant height ℓ: $S = \dfrac{1}{2}c\ell$

Volume of a sphere with radius r: $V = \dfrac{4}{3}\pi r^3$

Surface Area of a sphere with radius r: $S = 4\pi r^2$

Volume of a pyramid with base area B and height h: $V = \dfrac{1}{3}Bh$

Dr. John Chung's SAT II Math Level 2

Answer Sheet

01 Ⓐ Ⓑ Ⓒ Ⓓ Ⓔ   26 Ⓐ Ⓑ Ⓒ Ⓓ Ⓔ
02 Ⓐ Ⓑ Ⓒ Ⓓ Ⓔ   27 Ⓐ Ⓑ Ⓒ Ⓓ Ⓔ
03 Ⓐ Ⓑ Ⓒ Ⓓ Ⓔ   28 Ⓐ Ⓑ Ⓒ Ⓓ Ⓔ
04 Ⓐ Ⓑ Ⓒ Ⓓ Ⓔ   29 Ⓐ Ⓑ Ⓒ Ⓓ Ⓔ
05 Ⓐ Ⓑ Ⓒ Ⓓ Ⓔ   30 Ⓐ Ⓑ Ⓒ Ⓓ Ⓔ
06 Ⓐ Ⓑ Ⓒ Ⓓ Ⓔ   31 Ⓐ Ⓑ Ⓒ Ⓓ Ⓔ
07 Ⓐ Ⓑ Ⓒ Ⓓ Ⓔ   32 Ⓐ Ⓑ Ⓒ Ⓓ Ⓔ
08 Ⓐ Ⓑ Ⓒ Ⓓ Ⓔ   33 Ⓐ Ⓑ Ⓒ Ⓓ Ⓔ
09 Ⓐ Ⓑ Ⓒ Ⓓ Ⓔ   34 Ⓐ Ⓑ Ⓒ Ⓓ Ⓔ
10 Ⓐ Ⓑ Ⓒ Ⓓ Ⓔ   35 Ⓐ Ⓑ Ⓒ Ⓓ Ⓔ
11 Ⓐ Ⓑ Ⓒ Ⓓ Ⓔ   36 Ⓐ Ⓑ Ⓒ Ⓓ Ⓔ
12 Ⓐ Ⓑ Ⓒ Ⓓ Ⓔ   37 Ⓐ Ⓑ Ⓒ Ⓓ Ⓔ
13 Ⓐ Ⓑ Ⓒ Ⓓ Ⓔ   38 Ⓐ Ⓑ Ⓒ Ⓓ Ⓔ
14 Ⓐ Ⓑ Ⓒ Ⓓ Ⓔ   39 Ⓐ Ⓑ Ⓒ Ⓓ Ⓔ
15 Ⓐ Ⓑ Ⓒ Ⓓ Ⓔ   40 Ⓐ Ⓑ Ⓒ Ⓓ Ⓔ
16 Ⓐ Ⓑ Ⓒ Ⓓ Ⓔ   41 Ⓐ Ⓑ Ⓒ Ⓓ Ⓔ
17 Ⓐ Ⓑ Ⓒ Ⓓ Ⓔ   42 Ⓐ Ⓑ Ⓒ Ⓓ Ⓔ
18 Ⓐ Ⓑ Ⓒ Ⓓ Ⓔ   43 Ⓐ Ⓑ Ⓒ Ⓓ Ⓔ
19 Ⓐ Ⓑ Ⓒ Ⓓ Ⓔ   44 Ⓐ Ⓑ Ⓒ Ⓓ Ⓔ
20 Ⓐ Ⓑ Ⓒ Ⓓ Ⓔ   45 Ⓐ Ⓑ Ⓒ Ⓓ Ⓔ
21 Ⓐ Ⓑ Ⓒ Ⓓ Ⓔ   46 Ⓐ Ⓑ Ⓒ Ⓓ Ⓔ
22 Ⓐ Ⓑ Ⓒ Ⓓ Ⓔ   47 Ⓐ Ⓑ Ⓒ Ⓓ Ⓔ
23 Ⓐ Ⓑ Ⓒ Ⓓ Ⓔ   48 Ⓐ Ⓑ Ⓒ Ⓓ Ⓔ
24 Ⓐ Ⓑ Ⓒ Ⓓ Ⓔ   49 Ⓐ Ⓑ Ⓒ Ⓓ Ⓔ
25 Ⓐ Ⓑ Ⓒ Ⓓ Ⓔ   50 Ⓐ Ⓑ Ⓒ Ⓓ Ⓔ

The number of right answers: ☐

The number of wrong answers: ☐

$$\underline{\quad\quad} - \frac{1}{4} \times \underline{\quad\quad} = \underline{\quad\quad}$$
# of correct   # of wrong   Raw score

Score Conversion Table

Raw Score	Scaled Score	Raw Score	Scaled Score	Raw Score	Scaled Score
50	800	28	640	6	480
49	800	27	630	5	470
48	800	26	620	4	470
47	800	25	620	3	460
46	800	24	610	2	460
45	800	23	610	1	450
44	800	22	600	0	450
43	800	21	600		
42	800	20	590		
41	800	19	590		
40	780	18	580		
39	760	17	570		
38	750	16	560		
37	740	15	550		
36	720	14	540		
35	710	13	530		
34	700	12	520		
33	690	11	510		
32	680	10	500		
31	670	9	490		
30	660	8	490		
29	650	7	480		

MATHEMATICS LEVEL 2 TEST

For each of the following problems, decide which is the BEST of the choices given. If the exact numerical value is not one of the choices, select the choice that best approximates this value. Then fill in the corresponding circle on the answer sheet

Note: (1) A scientific or graphing calculator will be necessary for answering some (but not all) of the questions in this test. For each question you will have to decide whether or not you should use a calculator.

(2) For some questions in this test you may have to decide whether your calculator should be in the radian mode or the degree mode.

(3) Figures that accompany problems in this test are intended to provide information useful in solving the problems. They are drawn as accurately as possible EXCEPT when it is stated in a specific problem that its figure is not drawn to scale. All figures lie in a plane unless otherwise indicated.

(4) Unless otherwise specified, the domain of any function f is assumed to be the set of all real numbers x for which $f(x)$ is a real number. The range of f is assumed to be the set of all real numbers $f(x)$, where x is in the domain of f.

(5) Reference information that may be useful in answering the questions in this test can be found on the page preceding Question 1.

USE THIS SPACE FOR SCRATCHWORK

1. If $2(a-b) = 5(a-b)$, then which of the following must be true?

    (A) $a = 0$
    (B) $b = 0$
    (C) $a = b$
    (D) $a = -b$
    (E) $a + b > 0$

2. If $f(x) = -f(-x)$ for all real x and a point $(3, 5)$ is on the line, then which of the following points is also on the line?

    (A) $(-3, 5)$
    (B) $(3, -5)$
    (C) $(-5, -3)$
    (D) $(-3, -5)$
    (E) $(5, 3)$

GO ON TO THE NEXT PAGE

USE THIS SPACE FOR SCRATCHWORK.

3. If $\dfrac{10!}{90 \cdot 56} = n!$, then $n =$

(A) 3   (B) 4   (C) 5   (D) 6   (E) 7

4. Figure 1 shows the graph of the linear function whose equation is defined by $f(x) = -\dfrac{3}{4}x + 3$. What is the value of θ formed by the line and x-axis ?

(A) 36.9
(B) −36.9
(C) 45.5
(D) −45.5
(E) 55.8

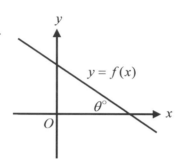

$y = f(x)$

$\theta°$

Note: Figure not drawn to scale.

Figure 1

5. If $f(x) = \sqrt[3]{x-1}$ and $g(x) = 5$, then $g\big(f(-7.82)\big) =$

(A) −10.3
(B) −5
(C)   5
(D) 10.3
(E) 15.6

6. Two circles are symmetric with respect to $y = x$. If the equation of a circle is $x^2 + y^2 - 2x - 4y + 1 = 0$, then which of the following is the equation of the other circle ?

(A) $(x-2)^2 + (y-1)^2 = 4$

(B) $(x-1)^2 + (y-2)^2 = 2$

(C) $(x-1)^2 + (y-2)^2 = 4$

(D) $(x-2)^2 + (y-2)^2 = 4$

(E) $(x+1)^2 + (y+2)^2 = 4$

GO ON TO THE NEXT PAGE

USE THIS SPACE FOR SCRATCHWORK.

7. If $\left|6 - \dfrac{n}{2}\right| - 3 < 4$, which of the following is the solution set?

  (A) $-1 < n < 13$
  (B) $-2 < n < 13$
  (C) $-2 < n < 26$
  (D) $n < -1$ or $n > 26$
  (E) $n < -2$ or $n > 13$

8. If $\tan\theta = 4.5$, what is the value of $\sqrt{\cos\theta}$?

  (A) 0.116
  (B) 0.201
  (C) 0.217
  (D) 0.328
  (E) 0.466

9. If $x < 3$, then $\sqrt{(x-10)^2} =$

  (A) $10 - x$
  (B) $10 + x$
  (C) $x - 10$
  (D) $-x - 10$
  (E) $\pm(x-10)$

10. Which of the following is true?

  (A) $\sin(-\theta) = \sin\theta$
  (B) $\cos(-\theta) = -\cos\theta$
  (C) $\tan(-\theta) = \tan\theta$
  (D) $\sec(-\theta) = \sec\theta$
  (E) $\csc(-\theta) = \csc\theta$

GO ON TO THE NEXT PAGE

USE THIS SPACE FOR SCRATCHWORK.

11.　When a polynomial $P(x) = x^2 + ax + b$ is divided by $(x-1)$, the remainder is 3, and when the polynomial is divided by $(x-2)$, the remainder is -3. What are the values of a and b?

　　(A) $a = 9, b = -11$
　　(B) $a = -9, b = 11$
　　(C) $a = -5, b = 3$
　　(D) $a = -5, b = -3$
　　(E) $a = -3, b = -5$

12.　If $\sin a° = \cos(2a + 30)°$, then what is the value of $\tan a°$?

　　(A) 0.21
　　(B) 0.36
　　(C) 0.42
　　(D) 0.60
　　(E) 0.75

13.　What is the range of the function $f(x) = -\sqrt{3x - 9} + 4$?

　　(A) $y \geq 3$
　　(B) $y \leq 3$
　　(C) $y \geq 4$
　　(D) $y \leq 4$
　　(E) $y \leq -4$

14.　If line ℓ is perpendicular to the line $y = 3x$, then what is the area of $\triangle ABO$?

　　(A) 1
　　(B) 1.5
　　(C) 2
　　(D) 2.5
　　(E) 3

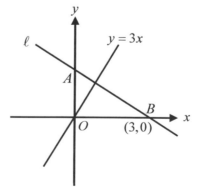

Note: Figure not drawn to scale.

GO ON TO THE NEXT PAGE ⇨

USE THIS SPACE FOR SCRATCHWORK.

15. If $xy = 1$, then $\dfrac{x}{x+1} + \dfrac{y}{y+1} =$

(A) 1   (B) 2   (C) 3   (D) 4   (E) 5

16. If one of the roots of $2x^2 + ax + b = 0$ is $-1 + 2i$, what is the value of b?

(A) -2
(B)   2
(C) -5
(D)   5
(E)   10

17. If $\log_{\sqrt{3}} x = 10$, then $\log_3 x^3 =$

(A) 10   (B) 15   (C) 30   (D) 45   (E) 60

18. If $\tan \theta = 3$ and $\pi < \theta < \dfrac{3\pi}{2}$, what is the value of $\cos(2\theta)$?

(A)   0.2
(B)   0.4
(C)   0.8
(D) -0.8
(E) -0.4

19. If the surface area of a cylinder, whose height is twice the radius, is 50, then what is the value of the radius?

(A) 1.63
(B) 1.84
(C) 2.45
(D) 3.87
(E) 4.56

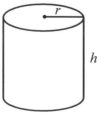

FIgure 3

GO ON TO THE NEXT PAGE

USE THIS SPACE FOR SCRATCHWORK.

20. If $f(x) = \log(x+1) + \log(x-1)$, then $f^{-1}(x) =$

   (A) 10^{x^2-1}

   (B) $x^2 - 10$

   (C) $\sqrt{10^x + 1}$

   (D) $-\sqrt{10^x + 1}$

   (E) $\pm\sqrt{10^x + 1}$

21. In Figure 2, $f(x) = x + b$ is tangent to the graph of a circle whose equation is $x^2 + y^2 = 4$. What is the value of b?

   (A) −5.45

   (B) −3.48

   (C) −2.14

   (D) −2.21

   (E) −2.83

Figure 4

22. What is the distance between the two points of intersection of the circles whose equations are $x^2 + y^2 = 16$ and $(x-4)^2 + (y-4)^2 = 16$?

   (A) 1.12

   (B) 2.73

   (C) 3.35

   (D) 4.87

   (E) 5.66

23. If $\vec{a} = (3, 2, 3)$ and $\vec{b} = (1, 5, 2)$, which of the following is the value of $\left|\vec{a} - \vec{b}\right|$?

   (A) 2.52

   (B) 3.74

   (C) 4.25

   (D) 7.58

   (E) 8.02

GO ON TO THE NEXT PAGE

USE THIS SPACE FOR SCRATCHWORK.

24. A pencil holder contains only five black pencils and three white pencils. If three pencils are drawn at random, what is the probability to have two black pencils and one white pencil?

(A) $\dfrac{3}{5}$ (B) $\dfrac{3}{8}$ (C) $\dfrac{15}{28}$ (D) $\dfrac{5}{7}$ (E) $\dfrac{2}{3}$

25. If $\dfrac{(x-1)^2}{x} \geq 0$, then which of the following is the complete solution set of the inequality?

(A) $\{x \leq 0\}$

(B) $\{0 \leq x < 1\}$

(C) $\{x > 0\}$

(D) $\{x < 0 \text{ or } x > 1\}$

(E) $\{x \leq 0 \text{ or } x > 1\}$

26. Which of the following includes all asymptotes of the rational function $f(x) = \dfrac{x^3}{x^2 - 1}$?

(A) $x = 1,\ x = -1$

(B) $x = 1,\ y = 0$

(C) $x = 1,\ x = -1,$ and $y = 0$

(D) $x = 1,\ x = -1,$ and $y = x$

(E) $x = 1,\ x = -1,$ and $y = -1$

27. Which of the following is the distance from the origin to the plane $x - y - z - 3 = 0$?

(A) $\sqrt{2}$

(B) $\sqrt{3}$

(C) 2

(D) $\sqrt{5}$

(E) $\sqrt{6}$

GO ON TO THE NEXT PAGE

MATHEMATICS LEVEL 2 TEST - *Continued*

USE THIS SPACE FOR SCRATCHWORK.

28. If $\cos^2 \theta - 3\cos \theta - 1 = 0$, then what is the smallest positive value of θ ?

(A) 8.16
(B) 4.40
(C) 1.88
(D) 0.92
(E) 0.46

29. What is the interquartile range of the following set of data
10, 13, 15, 18, 25, 30, 40, 60, 75, 80, 80 ?

(A) 20
(B) 40
(C) 50
(D) 60
(E) 70

30. If angle A is obtuse and $\tan A = -\dfrac{3}{2}$, which of the following is the value of $\cos 2A$?

(A) −0.38
(B) −0.30
(C) −0.15
(D) 1.5
(E) 3.6

31. What is the value of $\arccos\left(\dfrac{\sqrt{3}}{2}\right) + \arcsin\left(-\dfrac{\sqrt{3}}{2}\right)$?

(A) 0°
(B) −30°
(C) −45°
(D) 30°
(E) 45°

GO ON TO THE NEXT PAGE

MATHEMATICS LEVEL 2 TEST - *Continued*

USE THIS SPACE FOR SCRATCHWORK.

32. If $f(x) = \sqrt[3]{2x+3}$, then $f^{-1}(3) =$

    (A) 3.6
    (B) 5
    (C) 8
    (D) 10
    (E) 12

33. The function $f(x) = x^2 - 4x + 9$ is a shift of $f(x) = x^2$

    (A) 4 units to the right and 9 units up
    (B) 2 units to the right and 5 units down
    (C) 2 unit to the left and 5 units up
    (D) 4 units to the left and 9 units up
    (E) 2 units to the right and 5 units up

34. If $(\cos\theta + i\sin\theta)(\cos\theta - i\sin\theta) = a - 1 + bi$, where a and b are real numbers, which of the following is true?

    (A) $a = 1, b = 1$
    (B) $a = 1, b = 0$
    (C) $a = 2, b = 0$
    (D) $a = 2, b = -2$
    (E) $a = -2, b = -2$

35. If the difference of the roots of $x^2 + 2mx = 7$ is 8, then what is the positive integer value of m?

    (A) 0   (B) 1   (C) 2   (D) 3   (E) 4

GO ON TO THE NEXT PAGE

MATHEMATICS LEVEL 2 TEST - *Continued*

USE THIS SPACE FOR SCRATCHWORK.

36. What is the measure of one of the larger angles of a parallelogram in the xy-plane that has vertices with coordinates $(3, 2), (6, 2), (4, 6)$ and $(7, 6)$?

    (A) $76.0°$

    (B) $98.2°$

    (C) $104.0°$

    (D) $103.5°$

    (E) $108.6°$

37. A used car was purchased for \$20,000 and the car loses $k\%$ of its value each year. If the car is worth \$10,000 after 5 years, what is the value of k ?

    (A) 10.5
    (B) 11.6
    (C) 12.9
    (D) 13.6
    (E) 14.8

38. Which of the following is the polar form of the rectangular equation $y = 4$?

    (A) $r = 3$
    (B) $r = 4$
    (C) $r = 4\sin\theta$
    (D) $r = 4\cos\theta$
    (E) $r = 4\csc\theta$

39. If function $f(x) = \dfrac{1}{4}x - 3$, and $f^{-1}(x)$ is the inverse function of $f(x)$, then $f^{-1}\left(f^{-1}(-3)\right) =$

    (A) 0
    (B) 3
    (C) 6
    (D) 12
    (E) 18

 **GO ON TO THE NEXT PAGE**

MATHEMATICS LEVEL 2 TEST - *Continued*

USE THIS SPACE FOR SCRATCHWORK.

40. If $2\left(3^{2x-5}\right)-5=10$, what is the value of x?

(A) 1.28
(B) 2.46
(C) 3.42
(D) 3.68
(E) 4.12

41. What is the domain of $f(x)=\dfrac{\sqrt{x-1}}{\sqrt{x^2-x-6}}$?

(A) $x<-3$
(B) $x>1$
(C) $1\le x<3$
(D) $x>3$
(E) $1<x<5$

42. $\displaystyle\lim_{x\to 1}\dfrac{x^2-x}{x^2+x-2}=$

(A) $\dfrac{1}{3}$

(B) $\dfrac{1}{2}$

(C) 1

(D) 2

(E) Undefined

43. How many integer values of x satisfy the inequality
$x(x-6)(x+8)(x-2)<0$?

(A) 4   (B) 6   (C) 8   (D) 10   (E) 11

USE THIS SPACE FOR SCRATCHWORK.

44. What is the range of the following function?

$$f(x) = \begin{cases} 1 - x, & \text{if } x < 1 \\ \sqrt{x-1} + 1, & \text{if } x \geq 1 \end{cases}$$

(A) $(-\infty, 0]$

(B) $[0, 1]$

(C) $(0, 1)$

(D) $[0, +\infty)$

(E) $(0, +\infty)$

45. In how many ways can a 10 question true-false math exam be answered? (Assume that no questions are omitted.)

(A) 10
(B) 100
(C) 1024
(D) 2048
(E) 4096

46. What is the coefficient of x in the binomial expansion of $\left(\sqrt{x} + 5\right)^4$?

(A) 20
(B) 150
(C) 500
(D) 625
(E) 875

47. If $14 \cdot {}_nP_3 = {}_{n+2}P_4$, then which of the following could be the value of n?

(A) 6
(B) 7
(C) 8
(D) 9
(E) 15

GO ON TO THE NEXT PAGE

USE THIS SPACE FOR SCRATCHWORK.

48. Assume that the probability of having a boy is 40%. In a family with three children, what is the probability that there is at least one boy?

(A) 0.40
(B) 0.486
(C) 0.562
(D) 0.765
(E) 0.784

49. Figure 5 shows the graph of an ellipse whose equation is
$$\frac{(x-h)^2}{a^2} + \frac{(y-k)^2}{b^2} = 1.$$ If the area A of an ellipse is given
by $A = \pi ab$, then what is the area of the ellipse in Figure 5?

(A) 9.42

(B) 15.71

(C) 28.42

(D) 47.12

(E) 52.25

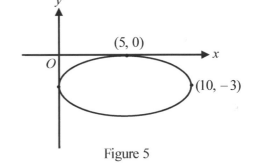

Figure 5

GO ON TO THE NEXT PAGE

USE THIS SPACE FOR SCRATCHWORK.

50. Which of the following could be the graph of the parametric
equations $x = \sqrt{t-1}$ and $y = t - 2$?

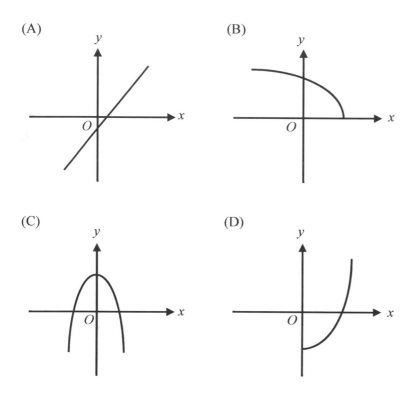

(A)

(B)

(C)

(D)

(E)

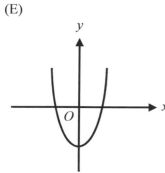

STOP

IF YOU FINISH BEFORE TIME IS CALLED, YOU MAY CHECK YOUR WORK ON THIS TEST ONLY.

DO NOT TURN TO ANY OTHER TEST IN THIS BOOK.

No Test Material on This Page

TEST 9				ANSWERS					

#	answer	#	answer	#	answer	#	answer	#	answer
1	C	11	B	21	E	31	B	41	D
2	D	12	B	22	E	32	E	42	A
3	D	13	D	23	B	33	E	43	D
4	A	14	B	24	C	34	C	44	E
5	C	15	A	25	C	35	D	45	C
6	A	16	E	26	D	36	C	46	B
7	C	17	B	27	B	37	C	47	A
8	E	18	D	28	C	38	E	48	E
9	A	19	A	29	D	39	D	49	D
10	D	20	C	30	A	40	C	50	D

Explanations: Test 9

1. **(C)** $a - b = 0 \;\to\; a = b$

2. **(D)** Since $f(x)$ is an odd function, $(-3, -5)$ must be on the line.

3. **(D)** $\dfrac{10!}{90 \cdot 56} = \dfrac{10!}{10 \cdot 9 \cdot 8 \cdot 7} = 6!$, $n = 6$

4. **(A)** Since $\tan\theta = \dfrac{3}{4}$, $\theta = \tan^{-1}\left(\dfrac{3}{4}\right) \approx 36.9°$.

5. **(C)** $g(x) = 5$ is a constant function for any value of x.

6. **(A)** Switch x and y. $y^2 + x^2 - 2y - 4x + 1 = 0 \quad\to\quad (x-2)^2 + (y-1)^2 = 4$

7. **(C)** $\left|6 - \dfrac{n}{2}\right| = \left|\dfrac{n}{2} - 6\right| < 7 \;\to\; -7 < \dfrac{n}{2} - 6 < 7 \;\to\; -1 < \dfrac{n}{2} < 13 \;\to\; -2 < n < 26$

8. **(E)** Since $\tan\theta = 4.5$ and $\cos\theta \geq 0$, θ lies in Quadrant I.

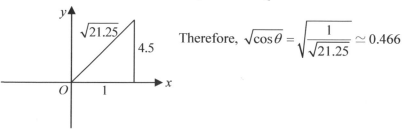

Therefore, $\sqrt{\cos\theta} = \sqrt{\dfrac{1}{\sqrt{21.25}}} \simeq 0.466$

9. **(A)** $\sqrt{(x-10)^2} = |x-10|$
    If $x < 3$, then $|x-10| = -x + 10$.

10. (D) $\sec\theta$ is an even function.

11. (B) $P(1) = 1 + a + b = 3$ and $P(2) = 4 + 2a + b = -3$.

$$\begin{array}{r} a + b = 2 \\ -\underline{\left| 2a + b = -7 \right.} \\ -a \quad = 9 \end{array} \qquad a = -9 \text{ and } b = 11$$

12. (B) Cofunction:
$$a + 2a + 30 = 90 \rightarrow a = 20 \rightarrow \tan 20° \approx 0.36$$

13. (D) Check with a graphing calculator. $f(x) = -\sqrt{3x-9} + 4 = -\sqrt{3(x-3)} + 4$

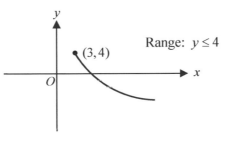

Range: $y \le 4$

14. (B) The equation of line ℓ is $y = -\dfrac{1}{3}x + b$. The line passes through a point $(3,0)$. Therefore, the equation of line ℓ is $y = -\dfrac{1}{3}x + 1$. $AO = 1$ and $OB = 3$. The area is $\dfrac{3 \times 1}{2} = 1.5$.

15. (A) Since $xy = 1$, $\dfrac{x}{x+1} + \dfrac{y}{y+1} = \dfrac{x(y+1) + y(x+1)}{xy + x + y + 1} = \dfrac{2xy + x + y}{xy + x + y + 1} = \dfrac{x+y+2}{x+y+2} = 1$.

Or, since $y = \dfrac{1}{x}$, $\dfrac{y}{y+1} = \dfrac{\frac{1}{x}}{\frac{1}{x}+1} = \dfrac{1}{x+1}$. Therefore, $\dfrac{x}{x+1} + \dfrac{1}{x+1} = \dfrac{x+1}{x+1} = 1$.

16. (E) Product of the roots: $(-1 + 2i)(-1 - 2i) = \dfrac{b}{2} \rightarrow 5 = \dfrac{b}{2} \rightarrow b = 10$

17. (B) $\log_{\sqrt{3}} x = \log_3 x^2 = 10 \rightarrow 2\log_3 x = 10 \rightarrow \log_3 x = 5$

$\log_3 x^3 = 3\log_3 x = 3(5) = 15$

18. (D) Since θ lies in Quadrant III, $\cos\theta = -\dfrac{1}{\sqrt{10}}$. $\cos 2\theta = 2\cos^2\theta - 1 = 2\left(\dfrac{-1}{\sqrt{10}}\right)^2 - 1 = -\dfrac{4}{5}$

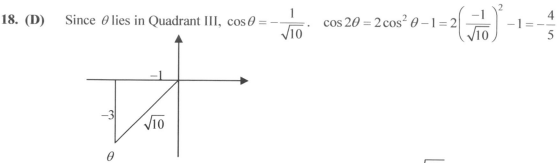

19. (A) Surface area $= 2\pi r^2 + 2\pi r(2r) = 50 \;\rightarrow\; 6\pi r^2 = 50 \;\rightarrow\; r = \sqrt{\dfrac{50}{6\pi}} \approx 1.63$

20. (C) $f(x) = \log(x+1) + \log(x-1) = \log(x^2-1)$ (Domain: $x > 1$)

For the inverse f^{-1}:

$$x = \log\left(y^2 - 1\right) \;\rightarrow\; y^2 - 1 = 10^x \;\rightarrow\; y = \sqrt{10^x + 1} \quad (\text{Range: } y > 1)$$

21. (E) $y = x + b$ and $x^2 + y^2 = 4$ intersect at one point. Substitute $y = x + b$ into a circle equation.

$$x^2 + (x+b)^2 = 4 \;\rightarrow\; 2x^2 + 2bx + b^2 - 4 = 0$$

To have two equal roots, its discriminant should be zero.

$$D = \left(2b\right)^2 - 4(2)(b^2 - 4) = -4b^2 + 32 = 0 \;\rightarrow\; b^2 = 8 \;\rightarrow\; b = 2\sqrt{2} \text{ or } -2\sqrt{2}$$

In Figure 2, the y-intercept b is negative. Therefore, $b = -2\sqrt{2}$.

Or, the distance from the origin to $x - y + b = 0$ is

$$d = \frac{\left|0 - 0 + b\right|}{\sqrt{1^2 + (-1)^2}} = 2 \;\rightarrow\; |b| = 2\sqrt{2} \;\rightarrow\; b = -2\sqrt{2} : \text{the } y\text{-intercept is negative.}$$

22. (E)

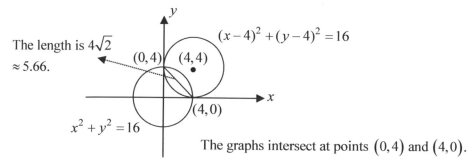

The length is $4\sqrt{2}$ ≈ 5.66.

$(x-4)^2 + (y-4)^2 = 16$

$x^2 + y^2 = 16$

The graphs intersect at points $(0,4)$ and $(4,0)$.

23. (B) $\vec{a} - \vec{b} = (3,\, 2,\, 3) - (1,\, 5,\, 2) = (2,\, -3,\, 1)$

$\left|\vec{a} - \vec{b}\right| = \left|(2, -3, 1)\right| = \sqrt{2^2 + (-3)^2 + 1^2} = \sqrt{14} \approx 3.74$

24. (C) $P = \dfrac{_5C_2 \times {_3}C_1}{_8C_3} = \dfrac{15}{28}$

Or, find the probability to have BBW, BWB, and WRR.

$P(BBW) = \dfrac{5}{8} \times \dfrac{4}{7} \times \dfrac{3}{6} = \dfrac{5}{28}$. $P(BBW) = P(BWB) = P(WBB)$.

Therefore, $\dfrac{5}{28} \times 3 = \dfrac{15}{28}$.

25. (C) $\dfrac{(x-1)^2}{x} \geq 0 \;\rightarrow\; \text{multiply by } x^2 \;\rightarrow\; \left(x^2\right)\dfrac{(x-1)^2}{x} \geq 0\left(x^2\right) \;\rightarrow\; x(x-1)^2 \geq 0 \;\left(x \neq 0\right)$

Using graphic solution: The complete solution set is $\{x > 0\}$.

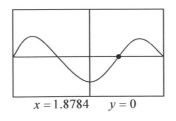

Or, use test value.

26. (D) $f(x) = \dfrac{x^3}{x^2 - 1} = x + \dfrac{x}{x^2 - 1}$

Vertical asymptotes : $D(x) = (x+1)(x-1) = 0 \;\rightarrow\; x = -1,\ x = 1$

Slant asymptote: $y = x$ as $x \to \infty$.

27. (B) $D = \dfrac{|0 - 0 - 0 - 3|}{\sqrt{1^2 + 1^2 + 1^2}} = \dfrac{3}{\sqrt{3}} = \sqrt{3}$

28. (C) Use a graphing calculator: Radian mode.

$x = 1.8784 \qquad y = 0$

Algebraic Solution: Quadratic formula.

$\cos\theta = \dfrac{3 \pm \sqrt{13}}{2} \;\rightarrow\; \cos\theta = 3.30277\,(\text{rejected}) \text{ or } -0.3027756377$

$\cos^{-1}(-0.3027756377) = 1.8783999 \approx 1.88$

29. (D) Interquartile range $=$ upper quartile $-$ lower quartile $= 75 - 15 = 60$

10, 13, (15), 18, 25, (30), 40, 60, (75), 80, 80

Box and Whisker Plot

10 15 30 75 80

30. (A)   Method 1: Find the angle using a calculator.

$$\tan A = -\frac{3}{2} \quad \rightarrow \quad A = \tan^{-1}\left(-\frac{3}{2}\right) = -56.30993247 + 180 = 123.6900675 \ \left(A \text{ is obtuse}\right)$$

$$\cos 2A = \cos(2 \times 123.6900675) = -0.3846153846 \approx -0.38$$

Method 2: Using diagram

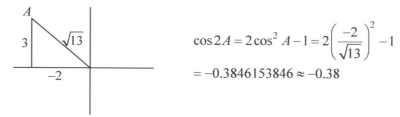

$$\cos 2A = 2\cos^2 A - 1 = 2\left(\frac{-2}{\sqrt{13}}\right)^2 - 1$$

$$= -0.3846153846 \approx -0.38$$

31. (B)   Method 1: Using a calculator (Degree mode)

$$\arccos\left(\frac{\sqrt{3}}{2}\right) + \arcsin\left(-\frac{\sqrt{3}}{2}\right) = -30°$$

Method 2: Algebraic solution

Let $\theta = \arccos\dfrac{\sqrt{3}}{2}$, where $0° \leq \theta \leq 180°$. $\cos\theta = \dfrac{\sqrt{3}}{2} \quad \rightarrow \quad \theta = 30°$

Let $\theta = \arcsin\left(-\dfrac{\sqrt{3}}{2}\right)$, where $-90° \leq \theta \leq 90°$. $\sin\theta = -\dfrac{\sqrt{3}}{2} \quad \rightarrow \quad \theta = -60°$

Therefore, $30° - 60° = -30°$

32. (E)   Method 1: $x = \sqrt[3]{2y+3} \quad \rightarrow \quad f^{-1}: y = \dfrac{x^3 - 3}{2} \quad \rightarrow \quad f^{-1}(3) = 12$

Method 2: $3 = \sqrt[3]{2y+3} \quad \rightarrow \quad 27 = 2y+3 \quad \rightarrow \quad y = 12$

33. (E) $f(x) = (x-2)^2 + 5$:   Two units to the right and 5 units up

34. (C) $\cos^2\theta + \sin^2\theta = a - 1 + bi \quad \rightarrow \quad 1 = a - 1 + bi \quad \rightarrow \quad a - 1 = 1 \text{ and } b = 0$
Therefore, $a = 2$ and $b = 0$.

35. (D)   If $r_1 > r_2$, then $r_1 - r_2 = 8$, $r_1 + r_2 = -2m$, and $r_1 \cdot r_2 = -7$.

$$\left(r_1 + r_2\right)^2 = \left(r_1 - r_2\right)^2 + 4r_1 r_2 \quad \rightarrow \quad 4m^2 = 64 - 28 \quad \rightarrow \quad m^2 = 9 \quad \rightarrow \quad m = 3$$

Or, substitute the choices into the equation. For $m = 3$,

$$x^2 + 6x - 7 = (x-1)(x+7) = 0 \quad \rightarrow \quad x = 1, -7 \quad \text{(Difference is 8.)}$$

36. (C)

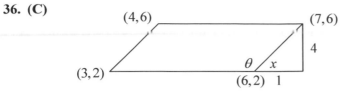

$$\tan x = 4 \quad \rightarrow \quad x = \tan^{-1} 4 \approx 75.96 \qquad \text{Therefore,} \ \theta = 180 - 75.96 \approx 104.0.$$

37. (C)   Compound decay yearly: $A = P(1-r)^t$

$$10,000 = 20,000(1 - 0.01k)^5 \quad \rightarrow \quad \frac{1}{2} = (1 - 0.01k)^5 \quad \rightarrow \quad \left(\frac{1}{2}\right)^{\frac{1}{5}} = 1 - 0.01k$$

$$k = \frac{1 - (0.5)^{\frac{1}{5}}}{0.01} = 12.94404367 \approx 12.9$$

38. (E) $y = 4 \quad \rightarrow \quad r\sin\theta = 4 \quad \rightarrow \quad r = \dfrac{4}{\sin\theta} = 4\csc\theta$

39. (D) $f^{-1}(x) = 4x + 12 \quad \rightarrow \quad f^{-1}(-3) = 0 \quad \rightarrow \quad f^{-1}(0) = 12$

40. (C) $2(3^{2x-5}) = 15 \quad \rightarrow \quad 3^{2x-5} = \dfrac{15}{2} = 7.5 \quad \rightarrow \quad 2x - 5 = \log_3 7.5$

Therefore, $x = \dfrac{1}{2}\left(\dfrac{\log 7.5}{\log 3} + 5\right) = 3.417021884 \approx 3.42$

41. (D) $N(x) = \sqrt{x-1} \quad \rightarrow \quad x \geq 1$

$D(x) = \sqrt{x^2 - x - 6} \quad \rightarrow \quad x^2 - x - 6 > 0 \quad \rightarrow \quad (x-3)(x+2) > 0 \quad \rightarrow \quad x > 3 \text{ or } x < -2$

$\{x \geq 1\} \cap \{x > 3\} = \{x > 3\}$ or $\{x \geq 1\} \cap \{x < -2\} = \phi$

Therefore, the solution set is $\{x > 3\}$.

42. (A) $\lim\limits_{x \to 1} \dfrac{x(x-1)}{(x+2)(x-1)} = \lim\limits_{x \to 1} \dfrac{x}{x+2} = \dfrac{1}{3}$

43. (D)   The graph of $y = x(x-6)(x+8)(x-2) < 0$ is as follows.

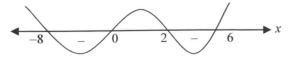

Therefore, the intervals for $y < 0$ is $-8 < x < 0$ or $2 < x < 6$.

The integers x are $-7, -6, -5, -4, -3, -2, -1$ and $3, 4, 5 \rightarrow 10$ integers

44. (E) The graph of the piecewise function is as follows.

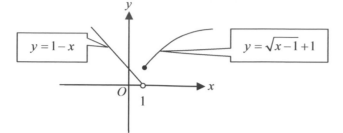

Therefore, the range is $(0, \infty)$.

45. (C) $2^{10} = 1024$

46. (B) $\binom{4}{r}\left(\sqrt{x}\right)^{4-r}(5)^r \;\rightarrow\; \binom{4}{r}(x)^{\frac{4-r}{2}}(5)^r \;\rightarrow\; r$ must be 2

Therefore, $\binom{4}{2}\left(\sqrt{x}\right)^2(5)^2 = 150x$

47. (A) $14 \cdot {}_nP_3 = {}_{n+2}P_4 \;\rightarrow\; 14 \cdot n\cancel{(n-1)}(n-2) = (n+2)(n+1)\,n\cancel{(n-1)}$

$14n - 28 = n^2 + 3n + 2 \;\rightarrow\; n^2 - 11n + 30 = 0 \;\rightarrow\; (n-6)(n-5) = 0$

Therefore, $n = 5$ or 6.

48. (E) Since $P(B) = \dfrac{2}{5}$ and $P(G) = \dfrac{3}{5}$,

The probability is $\binom{3}{1}\left(\dfrac{2}{5}\right)^1\left(\dfrac{3}{5}\right)^2 + \binom{3}{2}\left(\dfrac{2}{5}\right)^2\left(\dfrac{3}{5}\right)^1 + \binom{3}{3}\left(\dfrac{2}{5}\right)^3\left(\dfrac{3}{5}\right)^0 = \dfrac{98}{125} = 0.784$

Or, $1 - P(\text{all three girs}) = 1 - \binom{3}{3}(0.6)^2(0.4)^0 = 0.784$.

49. (D) Since $a = 5$ and $b = 3$, $A = \pi ab = 15\pi \approx 47.12$.

50. (D) Since $x = \sqrt{t-1} \geq 0$ and $x^2 = t - 1 \;\rightarrow\; t = x^2 + 1$, $y = t - 2 = x^2 + 1 - 2 \;\rightarrow\; y = x^2 - 1$.

Therefore, $y = x^2 - 1$ and $x \geq 0$.

END

Test 10

Dr. John Chung's

SAT II Mathematics Level 2

MATHEMATICS LEVEL 2 TEST

REFERENCE INFORMATION

THE FOLLOWING INFORMATION IS FOR YOUR REFERENCE IN ANSWERING SOME OF THE QUESTIONS IN THIS TEST

Volume of a right circular cone with radius r and height h: $V = \dfrac{1}{3}\pi r^2 h$

Lateral Area of a right circular cone with circumference of the base c and slant height ℓ: $S = \dfrac{1}{2}c\ell$

Volume of a sphere with radius r: $V = \dfrac{4}{3}\pi r^3$

Surface Area of a sphere with radius r: $S = 4\pi r^2$

Volume of a pyramid with base area B and height h: $V = \dfrac{1}{3}Bh$

Dr. John Chung's SAT II Math Level 2

Answer Sheet

01 ⒶⒷⒸⒹⒺ   26 ⒶⒷⒸⒹⒺ
02 ⒶⒷⒸⒹⒺ   27 ⒶⒷⒸⒹⒺ
03 ⒶⒷⒸⒹⒺ   28 ⒶⒷⒸⒹⒺ
04 ⒶⒷⒸⒹⒺ   29 ⒶⒷⒸⒹⒺ
05 ⒶⒷⒸⒹⒺ   30 ⒶⒷⒸⒹⒺ
06 ⒶⒷⒸⒹⒺ   31 ⒶⒷⒸⒹⒺ
07 ⒶⒷⒸⒹⒺ   32 ⒶⒷⒸⒹⒺ
08 ⒶⒷⒸⒹⒺ   33 ⒶⒷⒸⒹⒺ
09 ⒶⒷⒸⒹⒺ   34 ⒶⒷⒸⒹⒺ
10 ⒶⒷⒸⒹⒺ   35 ⒶⒷⒸⒹⒺ
11 ⒶⒷⒸⒹⒺ   36 ⒶⒷⒸⒹⒺ
12 ⒶⒷⒸⒹⒺ   37 ⒶⒷⒸⒹⒺ
13 ⒶⒷⒸⒹⒺ   38 ⒶⒷⒸⒹⒺ
14 ⒶⒷⒸⒹⒺ   39 ⒶⒷⒸⒹⒺ
15 ⒶⒷⒸⒹⒺ   40 ⒶⒷⒸⒹⒺ
16 ⒶⒷⒸⒹⒺ   41 ⒶⒷⒸⒹⒺ
17 ⒶⒷⒸⒹⒺ   42 ⒶⒷⒸⒹⒺ
18 ⒶⒷⒸⒹⒺ   43 ⒶⒷⒸⒹⒺ
19 ⒶⒷⒸⒹⒺ   44 ⒶⒷⒸⒹⒺ
20 ⒶⒷⒸⒹⒺ   45 ⒶⒷⒸⒹⒺ
21 ⒶⒷⒸⒹⒺ   46 ⒶⒷⒸⒹⒺ
22 ⒶⒷⒸⒹⒺ   47 ⒶⒷⒸⒹⒺ
23 ⒶⒷⒸⒹⒺ   48 ⒶⒷⒸⒹⒺ
24 ⒶⒷⒸⒹⒺ   49 ⒶⒷⒸⒹⒺ
25 ⒶⒷⒸⒹⒺ   50 ⒶⒷⒸⒹⒺ

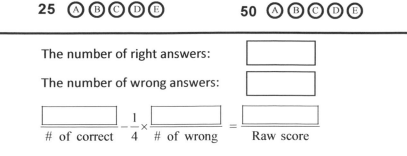

The number of right answers: ▢

The number of wrong answers: ▢

$$\boxed{} - \frac{1}{4} \times \boxed{} = \boxed{}$$

\# of correct   \# of wrong   Raw score

Score Conversion Table

Raw Score	Scaled Score	Raw Score	Scaled Score	Raw Score	Scaled Score
50	800	28	640	6	480
49	800	27	630	5	470
48	800	26	620	4	470
47	800	25	620	3	460
46	800	24	610	2	460
45	800	23	610	1	450
44	800	22	600	0	450
43	800	21	600		
42	800	20	590		
41	800	19	590		
40	780	18	580		
39	760	17	570		
38	750	16	560		
37	740	15	550		
36	720	14	540		
35	710	13	530		
34	700	12	520		
33	690	11	510		
32	680	10	500		
31	670	9	490		
30	660	8	490		
29	650	7	480		

MATHEMATICS LEVEL 2 TEST

For each of the following problems, decide which is the BEST of the choices given. If the exact numerical value is not one of the choices, select the choice that best approximates this value. Then fill in the corresponding circle on the answer sheet

Note: (1) A scientific or graphing calculator will be necessary for answering some (but not all) of the questions in this test. For each question you will have to decide whether or not you should use a calculator.

(2) For some questions in this test you may have to decide whether your calculator should be in the radian mode or the degree mode.

(3) Figures that accompany problems in this test are intended to provide information useful in solving the problems. They are drawn as accurately as possible EXCEPT when it is stated in a specific problem that its figure is not drawn to scale. All figures lie in a plane unless otherwise indicated.

(4) Unless otherwise specified, the domain of any function f is assumed to be the set of all real numbers x for which $f(x)$ is a real number. The range of f is assumed to be the set of all real numbers $f(x)$, where x is in the domain of f.

(5) Reference information that may be useful in answering the questions in this test can be found on the page preceding Question 1.

USE THIS SPACE FOR SCRATCHWORK

1.　　If $a < 0$, then $\sqrt{(-2a)^2} - \sqrt{9a^2} =$

(A)　a

(B)　$2a$

(C)　$5a$

(D) $-2a$

(E) $-5a$

2.　　If $\sqrt{28k}$ is an integer, which of the following is the smallest integer value of k ?

(A)　2

(B)　4

(C)　6

(D)　7

(E)　28

GO ON TO THE NEXT PAGE

USE THIS SPACE FOR SCRATCHWORK.

3. If $a^3 = -64$ and $\sqrt{a^2} = b$, then $b =$

(A) 4
(B) −4
(C) 8
(D) −8
(E) 16

4. How many positive values of a are there to satisfy that $\sqrt{40 - a}$ is an integer?

(A) 3   (B) 4   (C) 5   (D) 6   (E) 7

5. Which of the following sets of data has a standard deviation of 0 ?

(A) $\{-3, -2, -1, 0, 1, 2, 3\}$
(B) $\{-3, -3, -3, 1, 3, 3, 3\}$
(C) $\{-2, -2, -2, 0, 2, 2, 2\}$
(D) $\{0, 0, 0, 3, 5, 5, 5\}$
(E) $\{5, 5, 5, 5, 5, 5, 5\}$

6. How many integers satisfy with the inequality $5 < \sqrt{x^2} < 10$?

(A) 4
(B) 6
(C) 8
(D) 10
(E) Infinitely many

7. If $a = -3$, then $\sqrt{a^2} + \sqrt{(a-2)^2} =$

(A) −8
(B) −5
(C) −3
(D) 5
(E) 8

GO ON TO THE NEXT PAGE

USE THIS SPACE FOR SCRATCHWORK.

8.   Which of the following is true?

(A) $\left(\sqrt{5}\right)^2 = \pm 5$

(B) $\sqrt{25} = \pm 5$

(C) $\sqrt{(-11)^2} = 11$

(D) $\sqrt{(-6)^2} = -6$

(E) $\left(\sqrt{16}\right)^{\frac{1}{2}} = 4$

9.   If $x^2 = 5$, then $(x+3)(x+2) + (x+1)(x-6) =$

(A) -4 (B) -2 (C) 0   (D) 5   (E) 10

10.   If the polynomial $x^2 + kx - 1$ has a factor of $(x-2)$,
then $k =$

(A) $\dfrac{2}{3}$ (B) $\dfrac{3}{2}$ (C) $-\dfrac{2}{3}$ (D) $-\dfrac{3}{2}$ (E) $-\dfrac{5}{2}$

11.   If $x^2 + 10x - a = (x+b)^2$ for all real x, where a and b are
constants, what is the value of a?

(A) 30   (B) 20   (C) 0   (D) -25 (E) -30

12.   If one root of the equation $x^2 - 10x + a + 2 = 0$ is $5 + \sqrt{10}$,
what is the value of the constant a?

(A) 7
(B) 13
(C) 15
(D) 18
(E) 23

GO ON TO THE NEXT PAGE

USE THIS SPACE FOR SCRATCHWORK.

13. Which of the following equations has no solution?

(A) $x^3 = -8$

(B) $\sqrt{x^2} = -4$

(C) $x^2 - 2x - 1 = 0$

(D) $e^x = 0.5$

(E) $|x - 5| = 2$

14. If $f(x) = 8\sin x + 2$, which of the following includes all values of x in the interval $0 \le x \le \pi$, where $f(x) = 6$?

(A) $\dfrac{\pi}{3}$

(B) $\dfrac{\pi}{6}$ and $\dfrac{\pi}{3}$

(C) $\dfrac{5\pi}{6}$

(D) $\dfrac{\pi}{6}$ and $\dfrac{5\pi}{6}$

(E) $\dfrac{\pi}{3}$ and $\dfrac{2\pi}{3}$

15. If the coordinates of the vertex of $f(x) = x^2 - 4x + k$ are $(2, 5)$, what is the value of k?

(A) 5   (B) 7   (C) 9   (D) 11   (E) 14

16. What is the range of the quadratic function $f(x) = -x^2 + 7x - 12$?

(A) $\{y \mid y \le 4.25\}$

(B) $\{y \mid y \le 3.50\}$

(C) $\{y \mid y \le 2.36\}$

(D) $\{y \mid y \le 1.25\}$

(E) $\{y \mid y \le 0.25\}$

GO ON TO THE NEXT PAGE

USE THIS SPACE FOR SCRATCHWORK.

17. If the minimum value of $y = x^2 - 2kx + k$ is -12, then what is all value of k?

(A) $\{3\}$

(B) $\{-3\}$

(C) $\{-3, -4\}$

(D) $\{-3, 4\}$

(E) $\{4, 5\}$

18. In Figure 1, a circular cone is inscribed in the sphere at center O with radius 10. If $AH = 16$, what is the volume of the cone?

(A) 4188.8

(B) 3217.0

(C) 2495.2

(D) 1072.3

(E) 1010.6

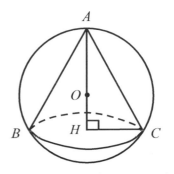

Note: Figure not drawn to scale.

Figure 1

19. If $f(x) = 2x^3 - 1$, then the inverse of $f(x)$ is

(A) $-2x^2 + 1$

(B) $\sqrt[3]{x+1}$

(C) $\dfrac{\sqrt[3]{x+1}}{2}$

(D) $\sqrt[3]{\dfrac{x+1}{2}}$

(E) $\sqrt[3]{\dfrac{x-1}{2}}$

GO ON TO THE NEXT PAGE

USE THIS SPACE FOR SCRATCHWORK.

20. If the period of the function $y = 2\sec(2kx + 0.3) + 5$ is 2, then what is the value of k?

   (A) 6.28
   (B) 4.77
   (C) 3.14
   (D) 1.57
   (E) 0.79

21. If a sphere has a volume of 64π, then what is its surface area?

   (A) 166
   (B) 175
   (C) 184
   (D) 225
   (E) 289

22. Which of the following functions has an inverse function?

   (A) $f(x) = x^2$
   (B) $f(x) = |x - 5|$
   (C) $f(x) = x^3 - x + 1$
   (D) $f(x) = x^3$
   (E) $f(x) = -x^2 + 10$

23. In Figure 2, the surface area of the cylinder is 24π and the volume of the cylinder is 12π. Which of the following is the value of the radius?

   (A) 0.52
   (B) 1.33
   (C) 1.59
   (D) 2.77
   (E) 3.78

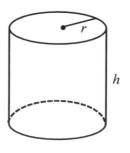

Figure 2

USE THIS SPACE FOR SCRATCHWORK.

24. If two six-sided dice are tossed, what is the probability that a total of 7 is rolled?

(A) $\dfrac{1}{18}$

(B) $\dfrac{1}{12}$

(C) $\dfrac{3}{6}$

(D) $\dfrac{2}{6}$

(E) $\dfrac{1}{6}$

25. If a vector $\vec{P}$ has the magnitude of 10 and the same direction as the vector $\vec{Q} = (3, -4)$, which of the following is the vector $\vec{P}$?

(A) $(6, 8)$

(B) $(10, 1)$

(C) $(-3, 4)$

(D) $(6, -8)$

(E) $(9, -12)$

26. If $\sin t = \dfrac{4}{5}$, then $\sin(\pi - t) =$

(A) $\dfrac{3}{5}$

(B) $-\dfrac{3}{5}$

(C) $\dfrac{4}{5}$

(D) $-\dfrac{4}{5}$

(E) $\dfrac{3}{4}$

GO ON TO THE NEXT PAGE

USE THIS SPACE FOR SCRATCHWORK.

27. If $f(t) = \sin t$, $g(t) = \cos t$, and $h(t) = f(t)g(t)$, which of the following is not true?

(A) $f(t)$ is an odd function.

(B) $g(t)$ is an even function

(C) $h(t)$ is an odd function

(D) $h(t)$ is an even function

(E) $\dfrac{f(t)}{g(t)}$ is an odd function

28. Which of the following is the equation of the graph in Figure 3 ?

(A) $y = 2\sin\dfrac{1}{2}x + 2$

(B) $y = -2\cos 2x + 2$

(C) $y = 2\cos\dfrac{1}{2}x + 2$

(D) $y = -2\cos\dfrac{1}{2}x + 2$

(E) $y = -2\cos\dfrac{1}{4}x + 2$

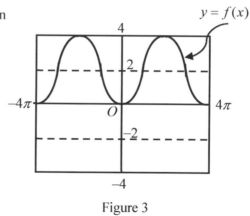

Figure 3

29. In the *xy*-coordinate plane, which of the following is the set of points whose distance from the origin is two times the distance from the point $(6, 0)$?

(A) a line
(B) a parabola
(C) a hyperbola
(D) an ellipse
(E) a circle

GO ON TO THE NEXT PAGE

340

USE THIS SPACE FOR SCRATCHWORK.

30. If $f(x) = \sqrt{2x+1}$ and $g(x) = x^2 - 2x + 1$, then $(f \cdot g)(4) =$

(A) $\sqrt{19}$
(B) $\sqrt{10}$
(C) 3
(D) 9
(E) 27

31. If $g(x)$ is the inverse function of $f(x)$, which of the
following is not true?

   I. The graphs of $g(x)$ and $f(x)$ are reflections of
      each other in the line $y = x$.

  II. $f\big(g(x)\big) = x$

 III. $g\big(f(x)\big) = -x$

(A) I only
(B) II only
(C) III only
(D) I and II only
(E) I and III only

32. If a soft-drink manufacturer has daily production costs of
$C(n) = 80,000 - 120n + 0.05n^2$, where C is the total cost in
dollars and n is the number of units produced, what is the
minimum cost each day?

(A) 8,000
(B) 7,500
(C) 7,000
(D) 6,700
(E) 6,000

GO ON TO THE NEXT PAGE

MATHEMATICS LEVEL 2 TEST - *Continued*

USE THIS SPACE FOR SCRATCHWORK.

33. In Figure 4, if a line is drawn around the box from vertex P to Q, what is the length of the shortest distance of the line?

(A) 12.6
(B) 13.9
(C) 14.6
(D) 15.1
(E) 15.8

Note: Figure not drawn to scale.

Figure 4

34. If a polynomial function $y = -x^7 - 100x^2 - 5x + 4$, what is the right-end and left-end behavior of the graph of the function?

(A) The graph falls to the left and rises to the right.
(B) The graph falls to the left and falls to the right.
(C) The graph rises to the left and rises to the right.
(D) The graph rises to the left and falls to the right.
(E) The graph approaches to the x – axis.

35. If $\dfrac{(x-2)(x-5)^2}{(x+3)} \leq 0$, which of the following is the solution set of the inequality?

(A) $\{x \mid x < -3\}$

(B) $\{x \mid -3 \leq x < 2\}$

(C) $\{x \mid -3 < x \leq 2\}$

(D) $\{x \mid 2 \leq x \leq 5\}$

(E) $\{x \mid -3 < x \leq 2\} \vee \{x \mid x = 5\}$

36. If $\log_3(ab) = 10$, $\log_3\left(\dfrac{a}{b}\right) = 2$, and $b > 0$, what is the value of a?

(A) 9
(B) 81
(C) 243
(D) 729
(E) 2187

GO ON TO THE NEXT PAGE

MATHEMATICS LEVEL 2 TEST - *Continued*

USE THIS SPACE FOR SCRATCHWORK.

37. If the ellipse $x^2 + 2y^2 - 2x + 4y = k$ has a major axis of 10, where k is a constant, then what is the value of k?

(A) 5
(B) 10
(C) 15
(D) 22
(E) 25

38. If $x^{\frac{2}{3}} = 4$, which of the following is the complete solution set?

(A) $\{x \mid x = 8\}$
(B) $\{x \mid x = -8\}$
(C) $\{x \mid x = 4\}$
(D) $\{x \mid x = 8 \text{ or } -8\}$
(E) $\{x \mid x = 4 \text{ or } -4\}$

39. What is the amplitude of $y = 3\sin\theta + 4\cos\theta$?

(A) 3.5
(B) 4
(C) 5
(D) 5.8
(E) 7

40. $\displaystyle\lim_{n \to \infty} \sum_{k=1}^{n} 5(0.2)^k =$

(A) 1
(B) 1.25
(C) 5
(D) 6.26
(E) Infinite

USE THIS SPACE FOR SCRATCHWORK.

41. What is the coefficient of the term $x^6 y^5$ in the expansion of

$(2x - 5y)^{11}$?

(A) $-3,125$
(B) $29,568$
(C) $-324,567$
(D) $90,400,000$
(E) $-92,400,000$

42. Matrices A, B, C, and D are of orders 2×3, 2×3, 3×2, and 2×2, respectively. Which of the following matrices are of proper order to perform the operation?

(A) $A + 3C$
(B) $B - 2C$
(C) AB
(D) $BC - 3D$
(E) $CB - 2D$

43. If the sum of the first n terms of a series is $S_n = n^2 + 4n$, then what is the 10th term?

(A) 23
(B) 40
(C) 85
(D) 125
(E) 140

44. In how many ways can 5 different prizes be given to any 5 of 12 people, if no person receives more than one prize?

(A) 124020
(B) 95040
(C) 7650
(D) 792
(E) 60

GO ON TO THE NEXT PAGE

MATHEMATICS LEVEL 2 TEST - *Continued*

USE THIS SPACE FOR SCRATCHWORK.

45. If $_nC_2 = {}_{n-1}P_2$ and $n \geq 3$, then $n =$

(A) 7
(B) 6
(C) 5
(D) 4
(E) 3

46. If three people are randomly chosen, what is the probability that all were born on different days of the week?

(A) 0.084
(B) 0.096
(C) 0.125
(D) 0.358
(E) 0.612

47. If three marbles are chosen at random from a bag containing 4 red marbles and 5 white marbles, what is the probability that exactly two marbles are red?

(A) 0.36
(B) 0.42
(C) 0.52
(D) 0.63
(E) 0.81

48. $\lim\limits_{x \to 0} \dfrac{1 - \sqrt{1+x}}{x} =$

(A) −1.5
(B) −0.5
(C) 1.5
(D) 2.0
(E) Undefined

GO ON TO THE NEXT PAGE

MATHEMATICS LEVEL 2 TEST - *Continued*

USE THIS SPACE FOR SCRATCHWORK.

49. The frequency table in Figure 5 shows the test score for students sampled in a statistics class. What is the standard deviation of the data?

(A) 5.9

(B) 6.1

(C) 6.6

(D) 7.2

(E) 7.5

Test score	70	78	82	92
Frequency	3	8	5	2

Figure 5

50. What is the surface area of the cast iron solid in Figure 6?

(A) 100π

(B) 120π

(C) 132π

(D) 165π

(E) 190π

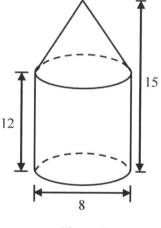

Figure 6

STOP

IF YOU FINISH BEFORE TIME IS CALLED, YOU MAY CHECK YOUR WORK ON THIS TEST ONLY.

DO NOT TURN TO ANY OTHER TEST IN THIS BOOK.

No Test Material on This Page

TEST 10			ANSWERS						
#	answer	#	answer	#	answer	#	answer	#	answer
1	A	11	D	21	A	31	C	41	E
2	D	12	B	22	D	32	A	42	D
3	A	13	B	23	D	33	B	43	A
4	E	14	D	24	E	34	D	44	B
5	E	15	C	25	D	35	E	45	D
6	C	16	E	26	C	36	D	46	E
7	E	17	D	27	D	37	D	47	A
8	C	18	D	28	D	38	D	48	B
9	E	19	D	29	E	39	C	49	B
10	D	20	D	30	E	40	B	50	C

Explanations: Test 10

1. (A) Since $\sqrt{x^2} = |x|$, $\sqrt{(-2a)^2} - \sqrt{9a^2} = \sqrt{4a^2} - \sqrt{9a^2} = |2a| - |3a| = -2a - (-3a) = a$.

2. (D) Since $\sqrt{28k} = \sqrt{2 \cdot 2 \cdot 7 \cdot k}$, k should be 7. (Prime factorization)

3. (A) $a^3 = -64 \rightarrow a = -4$ and $b = \sqrt{a^2} = \sqrt{(-4)^2} = \sqrt{16} = 4$.

4. (E) $\sqrt{40 - a} = 0, 1, 2, 3, 4, 5, 6 \rightarrow 40 - a = 0, 1, 4, 9, 16, 25, 36 \rightarrow a = 40, 39, 36, 31, 24, 15, 4$

5. (E) If all data are equal, the standard deviation is 0.

6. (C) Since $\sqrt{x^2} = |x|$, $5 < |x| < 10$. Therefore,
$|x| = 6, 7, 8, 9 \rightarrow x = \pm 6, \pm 7, \pm 8, \pm 9$ (8 integers).

7. (E) $|a| + |a - 2| = |-3| + |-3 - 2| = 8$

8. (C) (A) $\left(\sqrt{5}\right)^2 = 5$ (B) $\sqrt{25} = 5$ (C) $\sqrt{(-11)^2} = 11$ (D) $\sqrt{(-6)^2} = 6$ (E) $\left(\sqrt{16}\right)^{\frac{1}{2}} = 2$

9. (E) $(x + 3)(x + 2) + (x + 1)(x - 6) = \left(x^2 + 5x + 6\right) + \left(x^2 - 5x - 6\right) = 2x^2$
Since $x^2 = 5, \rightarrow 2x^2 = 10$.

10. (D) Factor Theorem:
Let $x^2 + kx - 1 = (x - 2)Q(x)$. When $x = 2$, $4 + 2k - 1 = 0 \rightarrow k = -\dfrac{3}{2}$.

11. (D) $x^2 + 10x - a = (x+b)^2 \rightarrow x^2 + 10x - a = x^2 + 2bx + b^2$

Therefore, $b = 5$ and $-a = b^2$. $a = -25$.

12. (B) Substitution: $(5+\sqrt{10})^2 - 10(5+\sqrt{10}) + a + 2 = 0 \rightarrow 35 + 10\sqrt{10} - 50 - 10\sqrt{10} + a + 2 = 0$

$\rightarrow -15 + a + 2 = 0 \rightarrow a = 13$

Or,

Product of the roots: $(5+\sqrt{10})(5-\sqrt{10}) = a+2 \rightarrow 15 = a+2 \rightarrow a = 13$

13. (B) (A) $x^3 = -8 \rightarrow x = -2$ (B) $\sqrt{x^2} = -4 \rightarrow |x| \neq -4$

(C) $x^2 - 2x - 1 = 0 \rightarrow$ Discriminant $= 8 > 0$: two real roots

(D) $e^x = 0.5 \rightarrow x = \ln 0.5$ (E) $|x-5| = 2 \rightarrow x = 7$ or 3

14. (D) $8\sin x + 2 = 6 \rightarrow \sin x = \dfrac{1}{2} \rightarrow x = \dfrac{\pi}{6}$ or $\dfrac{5\pi}{6}$

15. (C) $f(2) = 4 - 8 + k = 5 \rightarrow k = 9$

16. (E) Axis of symmetry: $x = \dfrac{-7}{-2} = 3.5$, $f(3.5) = -(3.5)^2 + 7(3.5) - 12 = 0.25$

The range: $y \leq 0.25$

Graphing utility:

Maximum	
$x = 3.4999$	$y = 0.25$

17. (D) Axis of symmetry: $x = \dfrac{2k}{2} = k$ $f(k) = k^2 - 2k^2 + k = -12 \rightarrow k^2 - k - 12 = 0$

$(k-4)(k+3) = 0 \rightarrow k = 4$ or -3

18. (D) The radius of the circular base is 8 and the height of the cone is 16.

$V = \dfrac{\pi r^2 h}{3} = \dfrac{64\pi \cdot 16}{3} = 1072.330292 \approx 1072.3$

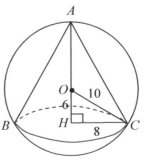

19. (D) $f(x) = 2x^3 - 1 \rightarrow f^{-1}(x): x = 2y^3 - 1 \rightarrow y = \sqrt[3]{\dfrac{x+1}{2}}$

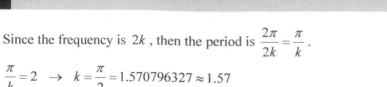

20. (D) Since the frequency is $2k$, then the period is $\dfrac{2\pi}{2k} = \dfrac{\pi}{k}$.

$$\dfrac{\pi}{k} = 2 \quad \rightarrow \quad k = \dfrac{\pi}{2} = 1.570796327 \approx 1.57$$

21. (A) $V = \dfrac{4}{3}\pi r^3 = 64\pi \quad \rightarrow \quad r = 48^{\frac{1}{3}}$

The surface area: $4\pi r^2 = 4\pi \left(48^{\frac{1}{3}}\right)^2 = 4\pi \cdot 48^{\frac{2}{3}} = 165.9729662 \approx 166$

22. (D) Since $f(x) = x^3$ is a one-to-one function, its inverse is also a function.

(C) $y = x^3 - x + 1$ is not one-to-one. Use a graphing utility to show the graph.

23. (D) Since $2\pi r^2 + 2\pi rh = 24\pi$ and $\pi r^2 h = 12\pi$, then $r^2 + rh = 12$ and $r^2 h = 12$.

$$h = \dfrac{12}{r^2} \quad \rightarrow \quad r^2 + r\left(\dfrac{12}{r^2}\right) = 12 \quad \rightarrow \quad r^2 + \dfrac{12}{r} = 12 \quad \rightarrow \quad r^3 - 12r + 12 = 0$$

$$\begin{cases} x = 1.1157494 \quad y = 0 \\ x = 2.7687343 \quad y = 0 \end{cases}$$

Zero
$x = 2.7687343 \quad y = 0$

Therefore, $r = 1.12$ or 2.77.

24. (E) The total of 7: $\rightarrow (1,6)(2,5)(3,4)(4,3)(5,2)(6,1)$

$$P = \dfrac{6}{36}$$

25. (D) Choice (D): Magnitude $\sqrt{6^2 + (-8)^2} = 10 \qquad (6,-8) = 2(3,-4)$: Same direction

Because $\left|\vec{P}\right| = 10$ and $\left|\vec{Q}\right| = \sqrt{3^2 + (-4)^2} = 5$, $\vec{P} = 2\vec{Q}$.

26. (C) $\sin(\pi - t) = \sin\pi\cos t - \cos\pi\sin t = \sin t \qquad \rightarrow \quad \sin t = \dfrac{4}{5}$

27. (D) $h(t) = \sin t\cos t = \dfrac{1}{2}\sin 2t$: odd function

28. (D) period $= 4\pi$, middle line $= 2$, frequency $= \dfrac{2\pi}{4\pi} = \dfrac{1}{2}$

Therefore, $y = -2\cos\left(\dfrac{1}{2}x\right) + 2$

29. (E)

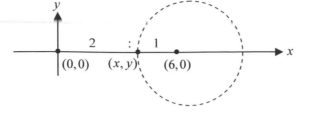

$$\frac{\sqrt{x^2+y^2}}{\sqrt{(6-x)^2+(0-y)^2}}=\frac{2}{1} \rightarrow x^2+y^2=4(36-12x+x^2+y^2) \rightarrow 3x^2+3y^2-48x+144=0$$

$$x^2+y^2-16x+48=0 \rightarrow (x-8)^2+y^2=4^2 : \text{a circle}$$

30. (E) Multiplication : $(f\cdot g)(x)=\left(\sqrt{2x+1}\right)\cdot\left(x^2-2x+1\right) \rightarrow (f\cdot g)(4)=3\cdot 9=27$

cf. $(f\circ g)(x)$; composition

31. (C) $f\left(f^{-1}(x)\right)=x$, $y=f(x)$ and $y=f^{-1}(x)$ is symmetric with respect to $y=x$.

32. (A) Axis of symmetry: $x=\dfrac{120}{2\cdot(0.05)}=1200$

$$f(1,200)=80,000-120(1,200)+0.05(1,200)^2=8,000$$

33. (B) Since $\overline{PQ}$ is the shortest distance, $PQ=\sqrt{5^2+13^2}=13.92838828\approx 13.9$

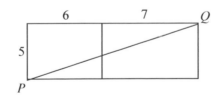

34. (D) $\lim\limits_{x\to-\infty} f(x)=+\infty$: rises to the left

$\lim\limits_{x\to\infty} f(x)=-\infty$: falls to the right

35. (E) By multiplying $(x+3)^2$ to both sides:

$$\frac{(x-2)(x-5)^2}{(x+3)} \le 0 \quad \rightarrow \quad (x+3)(x-2)(x-5)^2 \le 0, \text{ where } x \ne -3.$$

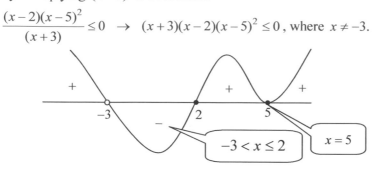

The solution set: $-3 < x \le 2$ or $x = 5$. At $x = 5$, the inequality is also true.
Or, you can use test value method.

36. (D) Since $ab = 3^{10}$ and $\dfrac{a}{b} = 3^2 = 9$, then $b = \dfrac{a}{9}$ and $a\left(\dfrac{a}{9}\right) = 3^{10}$.

$$a^2 = 3^{12} \quad \rightarrow \quad a = 3^6 = 729$$

37. (D) $x^2 + 2y^2 - 2x + 4y = k \quad \rightarrow \quad (x-1)^2 + 2(y+1)^2 = k+3 \quad \rightarrow \quad \dfrac{(x-1)^2}{k+3} + \dfrac{(y+1)^2}{\dfrac{(k+3)}{2}} = 1$

$a^2 = k+3 \quad \rightarrow \quad a = \sqrt{k+3}$

Major axis : $2a = 2\sqrt{k+3} = 10 \quad \rightarrow \quad k+3 = 25 \quad \rightarrow \quad k = 22$

38. (D) Algebraic solution: $x^{\frac{2}{3}} = 2 \quad \rightarrow \quad \left(x^{\frac{1}{3}}\right)^2 = 4 \quad \rightarrow \quad \left(x^{\frac{2}{3}}\right)^3 = 4^3 = 64 \quad \rightarrow \quad x^2 = 64 \quad \rightarrow \quad x = \pm 8$

Graphing calculator:

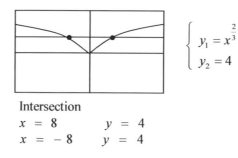

$$\begin{cases} y_1 = x^{\frac{2}{3}} \\ y_2 = 4 \end{cases}$$

Intersection
$x = 8 \qquad y = 4$
$x = -8 \qquad y = 4$

39. (C) If $y = a\sin\theta$ and $y = b\cos\theta$, then the amplitude of $y = a\sin\theta + b\cos\theta$ is $\sqrt{a^2 + b^2}$.

The amplitude is $\sqrt{3^2 + 4^2} = 5$.

Because $y = 5\left(\dfrac{3}{5}\sin\theta + \dfrac{4}{5}\cos\theta\right) = 5\sin(\theta + \theta_1)$, where $\sin\theta_1 = \dfrac{4}{5}$ and $\cos\theta_1 = \dfrac{3}{5}$.

40. (B)   Infinite series:

$$\lim_{n\to\infty}\sum_{k=1}^{n}5(0.2)^{k}=5\lim_{n\to\infty}\sum_{k=1}^{n}0.2^{k}=5\left(\frac{0.2}{1-0.2}\right)=1.25$$

41. (E) $_{11}C_{r}(2x)^{11-r}(-5y)^{r}\ \to\ {}_{11}C_{r}(2)^{11-r}(-5)^{r}(x)^{11-r}(y)^{r}$

r must be 5. Therefore, $_{11}C_{5}(2)^{6}(-5)^{5}x^{6}y^{5}=-92,400,000$

42. (D)   Dimension operation:

(A) $A+3C\ \to\ (2\times3)+(3\times2)$: wrong

(B) $B-2C\ \to\ (2\times3)-(3\times2)$: wrong

(C) $AB\ \to\ (2\times3)(2\times2)$:wrong

(D) $BC-3D\ \to\ (2\times3)(3\times2)-(2\times2)=(2\times2)-(2\times2)=(2\times2)$: true

(E) $CB-2D\ \to\ (3\times2)(2\times3)-(2\times2)=(3\times3)-(2\times2)$: wrong

43. (A) $a_{10}=S_{10}-S_{9}=\left(10^{2}+4(10)\right)-\left(9^{2}+4(9)\right)=140-117=23$

44. (B)   Choose 5 people and assign them to the 5 prizes: $_{12}C_{5}\times5!=95040$

45. (D) $_{n}C_{2}={}_{n-1}P_{2}\ \to\ \dfrac{n(n-1)}{2!}=(n-1)(n-2)\ \to\ \dfrac{n}{2}=(n-2)\quad\because n\neq1$

Therefore, $n=4$.

46. (E) $P=\dfrac{7\times6\times5}{7^{3}}=\dfrac{210}{343}=0.612244898\approx0.612$

people #1	people #2	people #3
M	M	M
T	T	T
W	W	W
TH	TH	TH
F	F	F
SA	SA	SA
S	S	S

All possible outcomes: $7\times7\times7=343$

47. (A)   Probability: $P=\dfrac{_{4}C_{2}\times{}_{5}C_{1}}{_{9}C_{3}}=\dfrac{30}{84}=0.3571428571\approx0.36$

48. (B) $\lim\limits_{x \to 0} \dfrac{\left(1-\sqrt{1+x}\right)\left(1+\sqrt{1+x}\right)}{x\left(1+\sqrt{1+x}\right)} = \lim\limits_{x \to 0} \dfrac{-x}{x\left(1+\sqrt{1+x}\right)} = \lim\limits_{x \to 0} \dfrac{-1}{\left(1+\sqrt{1+x}\right)} = -\dfrac{1}{2}$

49. (B) Calculator: statistics
$S_x = 6.097251068 \approx 6.1$

50. (C) Lateral area of the cone $= \pi rs = \pi \cdot 4 \cdot 5 = 20\pi$
Lateral area of the cylinder $= 2\pi rh = 96\pi$
The area of the base $= 16\pi$
Therefore, $20\pi + 96\pi + 16\pi = 132\pi$

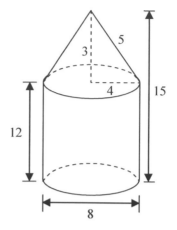

END

Test 11

Dr. John Chung's

SAT II Mathematics Level 2

MATHEMATICS LEVEL 2 TEST

REFERENCE INFORMATION

THE FOLLOWING INFORMATION IS FOR YOUR REFERENCE IN ANSWERING SOME OF THE QUESTIONS IN THIS TEST

Volume of a right circular cone with radius r and height h: $V = \dfrac{1}{3}\pi r^2 h$

Lateral Area of a right circular cone with circumference of the base c and slant height ℓ: $S = \dfrac{1}{2}c\ell$

Volume of a sphere with radius r: $V = \dfrac{4}{3}\pi r^3$

Surface Area of a sphere with radius r: $S = 4\pi r^2$

Volume of a pyramid with base area B and height h: $V = \dfrac{1}{3}Bh$

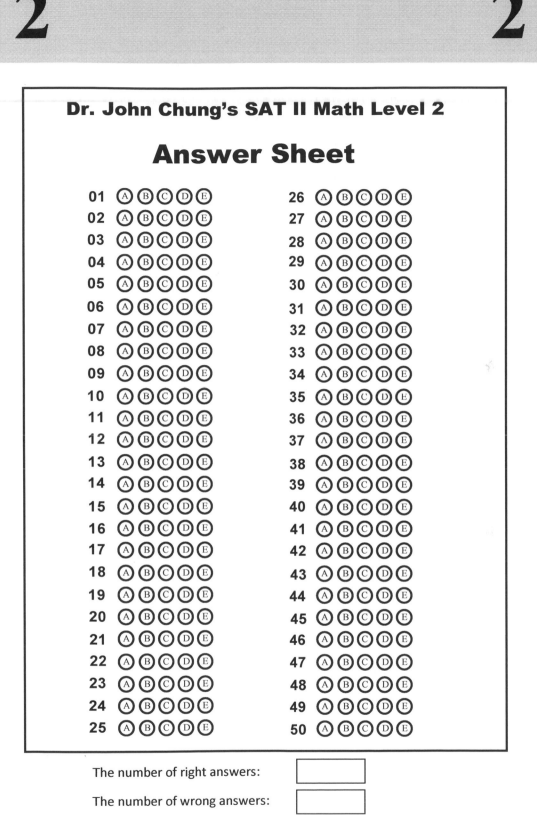

Dr. John Chung's SAT II Math Level 2

Answer Sheet

01 Ⓐ Ⓑ Ⓒ Ⓓ Ⓔ   26 Ⓐ Ⓑ Ⓒ Ⓓ Ⓔ
02 Ⓐ Ⓑ Ⓒ Ⓓ Ⓔ   27 Ⓐ Ⓑ Ⓒ Ⓓ Ⓔ
03 Ⓐ Ⓑ Ⓒ Ⓓ Ⓔ   28 Ⓐ Ⓑ Ⓒ Ⓓ Ⓔ
04 Ⓐ Ⓑ Ⓒ Ⓓ Ⓔ   29 Ⓐ Ⓑ Ⓒ Ⓓ Ⓔ
05 Ⓐ Ⓑ Ⓒ Ⓓ Ⓔ   30 Ⓐ Ⓑ Ⓒ Ⓓ Ⓔ
06 Ⓐ Ⓑ Ⓒ Ⓓ Ⓔ   31 Ⓐ Ⓑ Ⓒ Ⓓ Ⓔ
07 Ⓐ Ⓑ Ⓒ Ⓓ Ⓔ   32 Ⓐ Ⓑ Ⓒ Ⓓ Ⓔ
08 Ⓐ Ⓑ Ⓒ Ⓓ Ⓔ   33 Ⓐ Ⓑ Ⓒ Ⓓ Ⓔ
09 Ⓐ Ⓑ Ⓒ Ⓓ Ⓔ   34 Ⓐ Ⓑ Ⓒ Ⓓ Ⓔ
10 Ⓐ Ⓑ Ⓒ Ⓓ Ⓔ   35 Ⓐ Ⓑ Ⓒ Ⓓ Ⓔ
11 Ⓐ Ⓑ Ⓒ Ⓓ Ⓔ   36 Ⓐ Ⓑ Ⓒ Ⓓ Ⓔ
12 Ⓐ Ⓑ Ⓒ Ⓓ Ⓔ   37 Ⓐ Ⓑ Ⓒ Ⓓ Ⓔ
13 Ⓐ Ⓑ Ⓒ Ⓓ Ⓔ   38 Ⓐ Ⓑ Ⓒ Ⓓ Ⓔ
14 Ⓐ Ⓑ Ⓒ Ⓓ Ⓔ   39 Ⓐ Ⓑ Ⓒ Ⓓ Ⓔ
15 Ⓐ Ⓑ Ⓒ Ⓓ Ⓔ   40 Ⓐ Ⓑ Ⓒ Ⓓ Ⓔ
16 Ⓐ Ⓑ Ⓒ Ⓓ Ⓔ   41 Ⓐ Ⓑ Ⓒ Ⓓ Ⓔ
17 Ⓐ Ⓑ Ⓒ Ⓓ Ⓔ   42 Ⓐ Ⓑ Ⓒ Ⓓ Ⓔ
18 Ⓐ Ⓑ Ⓒ Ⓓ Ⓔ   43 Ⓐ Ⓑ Ⓒ Ⓓ Ⓔ
19 Ⓐ Ⓑ Ⓒ Ⓓ Ⓔ   44 Ⓐ Ⓑ Ⓒ Ⓓ Ⓔ
20 Ⓐ Ⓑ Ⓒ Ⓓ Ⓔ   45 Ⓐ Ⓑ Ⓒ Ⓓ Ⓔ
21 Ⓐ Ⓑ Ⓒ Ⓓ Ⓔ   46 Ⓐ Ⓑ Ⓒ Ⓓ Ⓔ
22 Ⓐ Ⓑ Ⓒ Ⓓ Ⓔ   47 Ⓐ Ⓑ Ⓒ Ⓓ Ⓔ
23 Ⓐ Ⓑ Ⓒ Ⓓ Ⓔ   48 Ⓐ Ⓑ Ⓒ Ⓓ Ⓔ
24 Ⓐ Ⓑ Ⓒ Ⓓ Ⓔ   49 Ⓐ Ⓑ Ⓒ Ⓓ Ⓔ
25 Ⓐ Ⓑ Ⓒ Ⓓ Ⓔ   50 Ⓐ Ⓑ Ⓒ Ⓓ Ⓔ

The number of right answers: ☐

The number of wrong answers: ☐

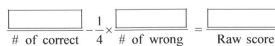

$$\boxed{} - \frac{1}{4} \times \boxed{} = \boxed{}$$
# of correct　　　# of wrong　　Raw score

Score Conversion Table

Raw Score	Scaled Score	Raw Score	Scaled Score	Raw Score	Scaled Score
50	800	28	640	6	480
49	800	27	630	5	470
48	800	26	620	4	470
47	800	25	620	3	460
46	800	24	610	2	460
45	800	23	610	1	450
44	800	22	600	0	450
43	800	21	600		
42	800	20	590		
41	800	19	590		
40	780	18	580		
39	760	17	570		
38	750	16	560		
37	740	15	550		
36	720	14	540		
35	710	13	530		
34	700	12	520		
33	690	11	510		
32	680	10	500		
31	670	9	490		
30	660	8	490		
29	650	7	480		

MATHEMATICS LEVEL 2 TEST

For each of the following problems, decide which is the BEST of the choices given. If the exact numerical value is not one of the choices, select the choice that best approximates this value. Then fill in the corresponding circle on the answer sheet

Note: (1) A scientific or graphing calculator will be necessary for answering some (but not all) of the questions in this test. For each question you will have to decide whether or not you should use a calculator.

   (2) For some questions in this test you may have to decide whether your calculator should be in the radian mode or the degree mode.

   (3) Figures that accompany problems in this test are intended to provide information useful in solving the problems. They are drawn as accurately as possible EXCEPT when it is stated in a specific problem that its figure is not drawn to scale. All figures lie in a plane unless otherwise indicated.

   (4) Unless otherwise specified, the domain of any function f is assumed to be the set of all real numbers x for which $f(x)$ is a real number. The range of f is assumed to be the set of all real numbers $f(x)$, where x is in the domain of f.

   (5) Reference information that may be useful in answering the questions in this test can be found on the page preceding Question 1.

USE THIS SPACE FOR SCRATCHWORK

1. $\left(\dfrac{3x^{-3}}{5y^{-2}}\right)^{-2} =$

   (A) $\dfrac{3x^4}{5y^5}$ (B) $\dfrac{9x^6}{25y^4}$ (C) $\dfrac{25y^4}{9x^6}$ (D) $\dfrac{25x^6}{9y^4}$ (E) $\dfrac{9x^4}{25y^6}$

2. What is the value of k for which $x^2 + 2kx + k^2$ is a perfect square?

   (A) 1
   (B) 4
   (C) 9
   (D) 16
   (E) Any real number

GO ON TO THE NEXT PAGE

USE THIS SPACE FOR SCRATCHWORK.

3. If $x^2 + x + 3$ is a factor of $2x^3 + px + q$, what are the values of p and q?

(A) $p = 4$ and $q = -6$
(B) $p = -8$ and $q = 4$
(C) $p = -8$ and $q = -6$
(D) $p = 8$ and $q = 6$
(E) $p = 8$ and $q = -6$

4. What is the sum of the roots of the equation $x^3 - 3x + 52 = 0$?

(A) -3
(B) 0
(C) 2
(D) 3
(E) 52

5. If a polynomial $P(x)$ has a remainder of three when divided by $(x - 1)$ and remainder of one when divided by $(x + 1)$, then the remainder when divided by $(x^2 - 1)$ is

(A) 4
(B) $x + 2$
(C) $x + 4$
(D) $x - 2$
(E) $x - 4$

6. If $x < -3$, then $\left| 1 - \left| x + 2 \right| \right| =$

(A) $x + 3$
(B) $x - 3$
(C) $-x + 3$
(D) $-x - 3$
(E) $-x + 1$

GO ON TO THE NEXT PAGE

7. Which of the following values of x is true for the inequality $\sin x < \cos x$?

   (A) $\dfrac{\pi}{4}$ (B) $\dfrac{\pi}{2}$ (C) $\dfrac{3\pi}{4}$ (D) $\dfrac{5\pi}{4}$ (E) $\dfrac{3\pi}{2}$

8. In Figure 1, a right cylinder is inscribed in a cube. If the cube has an edge of 10, what is the ratio of the volume of the cylinder to the volume of the cube?

   (A) $\dfrac{\pi}{4}$ (B) $\dfrac{\pi}{2}$ (C) $\dfrac{4}{\pi}$ (D) $\dfrac{2}{\pi}$ (E) $\dfrac{3}{4}$

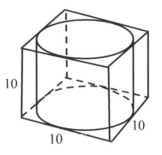

Figure 1

9. What is the product of $3 - 4i$ and its conjugate?

   (A) -7
   (B) 7
   (C) -25
   (D) 25
   (E) 6

10. If $\dfrac{a}{a-2} = 4 + \dfrac{2}{a-2}$, then $a =$

    (A) -2
    (B) 2
    (C) 4
    (D) 6
    (E) No solution

11. If $\sqrt[3]{27 - x^3} = -3$, then $x =$

    (A) ± 3
    (B) $3\sqrt[3]{2}$
    (C) $\pm 3\sqrt[3]{2}$
    (D) 9
    (E) ± 9

GO ON TO THE NEXT PAGE

USE THIS SPACE FOR SCRATCHWORK.

12. What is the domain of $f(x) = \sqrt{\dfrac{x}{10-x}}$?

(A) $x \geq 0$
(B) $0 < x < 10$
(C) $0 < x \leq 10$
(D) $0 \leq x \leq 10$
(E) $0 \leq x < 10$

13. Which of the following is the slant asymptote(s) of

$$f(x) = \frac{2x^2 - 3x + 1}{x+1} \ ?$$

(A) $x = -1$
(B) $y = 2$
(C) $y = 2x$
(D) $y = 2x - 5$
(E) $y = 2x - 10$

14. If $f\left(\dfrac{2}{x}\right) = 3x + 5$, then $f(x) =$

(A) $\dfrac{3x}{2} + \dfrac{5}{2}$

(B) $\dfrac{3x}{2} - \dfrac{5}{2}$

(C) $\dfrac{3}{x} + \dfrac{1}{5}$

(D) $\dfrac{6}{x} + 5$

(E) $\dfrac{6}{x} + \dfrac{1}{5}$

15. If $f(x) = \sqrt{x} - 1$, what value does the inverse function
$f^{-1}(x)$ have at the point $x = 9$?

(A) 8   (B) 10   (C) 100   (D) 120   (E) 125

GO ON TO THE NEXT PAGE

MATHEMATICS LEVEL 2 TEST - *Continued*

USE THIS SPACE FOR SCRATCHWORK.

16. The symbol $[x]$ is the greatest integer which is less than or equal to x. If $[x]^2 - 6[x] = -9$, which of the following could be the value of x?

(A) -3.3
(B) 1.3
(C) 2.5
(D) 3.9
(E) 4.01

17. How many real numbers are equal to their multiplicative inverses?

(A) 4   (B) 3   (C) 2   (D) 1   (E) 0

18. How many ways can 8 books be arranged on a shelf if 5 of them are math books and must be kept together?

(A) 24
(B) 120
(C) 360
(D) 2880
(E) 40320

19. Find all values of k which satisfy the determinant $\begin{vmatrix} k & 3 \\ 2k & k \end{vmatrix} = 27$?

(A) 9
(B) -3
(C) 6
(D) 6 or -3
(E) 9 or -3

20. If y varies directly as x and inversely as the square of z, and $y = 15$ when $x = 3$ and $z = 5$, what is the value of y when $x = 5$ and $z = 2.5$?

(A) 1   (B) 25   (C) 50   (D) 100   (E) 125

USE THIS SPACE FOR SCRATCHWORK.

21. What is the number of points of intersection of the graphs of
$x^2 + y^2 = 1$ and $x^2 + 4y^2 = 4$?

(A) 0   (B) 1   (C) 2   (D) 3   (E) 4

22. If the equation of the graph in Figure 2 is $y = -|x - 10| + k$,
where k is a constant, what is the area of $\triangle ABO$?

(A) 100
(B) 75
(C) 50
(D) 25
(E) 12.5

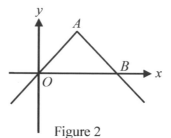

Figure 2

23. If the length of a diagonal of a cube is 10, then what is the
volume of the cube?

(A) 100
(B) 192.5
(C) 225
(D) 475.8
(E) 1000

24. If $\cos x = x$, then how many real solutions are there?

(A) 0
(B) 1
(C) 2
(D) 3
(E) 4

25. Which of the following is the graph of the polar equation
$r = \dfrac{1}{\cos\theta + \sin\theta}$?

(A) A line
(B) A circle
(C) An ellipse
(D) A parabola
(E) An hyperbola

GO ON TO THE NEXT PAGE

USE THIS SPACE FOR SCRATCHWORK.

26. What is the distance between the line $y = 2x + 5$ and the point (1, 4)?

 (A) 3.25
 (B) 1.75
 (C) 1.34
 (D) 1.19
 (E) 0.75

27. If the area of the triangle bounded by the lines $y = 2x$, $x = k$, and $y = 6$ is 16, what is the positive value of k?

 (A) 4
 (B) 5
 (C) 6
 (D) 7
 (E) 8

28. What is the sum of all factors of 210?

 (A) 556
 (B) 576
 (C) 584
 (D) 616
 (E) 625

29. If $\log_2(x^2 - 3x + 2) - \log_2(x - 1) = 5$, what is the value of x?

 (A) 10
 (B) 30
 (C) 34
 (D) 40
 (E) 48

30. If $10^{3x} = 27$, then $10^{-2x} =$

 (A) $\dfrac{1}{3}$ (B) $\dfrac{1}{6}$ (C) $\dfrac{1}{9}$ (D) $\dfrac{1}{18}$ (E) $\dfrac{1}{27}$

GO ON TO THE NEXT PAGE

USE THIS SPACE FOR SCRATCHWORK.

31.　If $\log 2 = 0.3010$, what is the number of digits in 2^{100}?

(A) 50
(B) 46
(C) 34
(D) 31
(E) 30

32.　If $2i$ is a root of $x^3 - 2x^2 + 4x - 8 = 0$, which of the following are the other roots?

(A) $-2i$
(B) $-2i$ and 3
(C) $-2i$ and 2
(D) $-2i$ and -1
(E) $-2i$ and -2

33.　$\lim\limits_{n\to\infty}\left(\dfrac{1}{n^2} + \dfrac{2}{n^2} + \dfrac{3}{n^2} + \dfrac{4}{n^2} + \cdots + \dfrac{n}{n^2}\right) =$

(A) 0　　(B) $\dfrac{1}{2}$　　(C) 1　　(D) $\dfrac{3}{2}$　　(E) 2

34.　Three numbers have a sum of 30 and a product of 640. If these three numbers form an arithmetic sequence, what is the smallest number?

(A) 1
(B) 2
(C) 4
(D) 10
(E) 16

35.　If $f(x) = 2^{2x}$ and $g(x) = \log_4 x$, then $(f \circ g)(x) =$

(A) $0.5x$
(B) x
(C) $1.5x$
(D) $2x$
(E) $2.5x$

GO ON TO THE NEXT PAGE

MATHEMATICS LEVEL 2 TEST - *Continued*

USE THIS SPACE FOR SCRATCHWORK.

36. Which of the following is not a function?

(A) $y = \left(\dfrac{1}{2}\right)^x$

(B) $y = x^5$

(C) $xy = -9$

(D) $y = \sqrt{10 - x^2}$

(E) $y^2 = 4x$

37. In Figure 3, what is the value of the angle θ between
the lines $y = x - 1$ and $y = -3x + 5$?

(A) 63.4
(B) 65.8
(C) 69.2
(D) 72.5
(E) 75.6

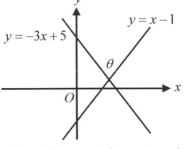

Note: Figure not drawn to scale.

Figure 3

38. $\dfrac{\sin 2\theta}{1 - \cos 2\theta} -$

(A) $\sin \theta$
(B) $\cos \theta$
(C) $\tan \theta$
(D) $\cot \theta$
(E) $\sec \theta$

39. If $\cos \theta = 0.61$, then $\cos(\pi - \theta) =$

(A) -0.61
(B) -0.39
(C) 0.39
(D) 0.61
(E) 0.93

GO ON TO THE NEXT PAGE

USE THIS SPACE FOR SCRATCHWORK.

40. If $\dfrac{x^2}{9} - \dfrac{y^2}{16} = 1$, then which of the following is the foci of the hyperbola?

(A) $(0, \pm 3)$

(B) $(0, \pm 4)$

(C) $(\pm 3, 0)$

(D) $(\pm 4, 0)$

(E) $(\pm 5, 0)$

41. Which of the following is the graph of the curve represented by the parametric equations $x = \sqrt{t-2}$ and $y = t + 5$?

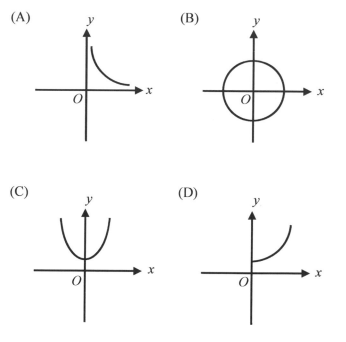

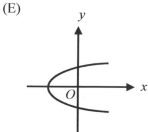

GO ON TO THE NEXT PAGE

USE THIS SPACE FOR SCRATCHWORK.

42. In Figure 4, if $AB = 3$, $BC = 5$, and $CD = 7$, what is the degree measure of angle ADF ?

(A) 50.2
(B) 48.4
(C) 46.8
(D) 45.6
(E) 43.1

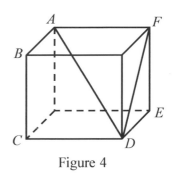

Figure 4

43. If the rectangular equation is $x^2 + y^2 - 4x = 0$, which of the following is an equivalent equation in polar form?

(A) $r^2 + r = 0$
(B) $r - 2\cos\theta = 0$
(C) $r - 4\cos\theta = 0$
(D) $r - 2\sin\theta = 0$
(E) $r + 4\cos\theta = 0$

44. If the matrices $A = \begin{bmatrix} -2 & 0 \\ 1 & 4 \end{bmatrix}$ and $B = \begin{bmatrix} -1 & 2 \\ 3 & 1 \end{bmatrix}$, what is the determinant of $A+B$?

(A) 12
(B) −12
(C) 23
(D) −23
(E) 28

45. If the equation of a sphere is given by $x^2 + y^2 + z^2 - 4x - 6z = 0$, what is the surface area of the sphere?

(A) 13π
(B) 52π
(C) 84π
(D) 128π
(E) 169π

GO ON TO THE NEXT PAGE

USE THIS SPACE FOR SCRATCHWORK.

46. If the plane passes through the point $(3, 2, 5)$ and is parallel to the xy-plane, then what is the equation of the plane?

(A) $x = 3$
(B) $y = 5$
(C) $x = 5$
(D) $z = 5$
(E) $y = z$

47. If $\lim\limits_{x \to 1} \dfrac{x^2 + px + q}{x - 1} = 5$, where p and q are constants, what is the value of p?

(A) -2
(B) -1
(C) 1
(D) 3
(E) 4

48. What is the minimum value of the function defined as
$$f(x) = \begin{cases} |x|, & |x| \le 2 \\ 2, & |x| > 2 \end{cases} ?$$

(A) 4
(B) 2
(C) 0
(D) -1
(E) -2

49. How many positive integers are there in the solution set of $\dfrac{(x - 5)(x + 2)}{x - 1} \le 0$?

(A) 2
(B) 3
(C) 4
(D) 5
(E) 6

GO ON TO THE NEXT PAGE

USE THIS SPACE FOR SCRATCHWORK.

50. What is the constant term in the binomial expansion of

$$\left(x^2 + \frac{1}{x} \right)^{12} ?$$

(A) 924
(B) 792
(C) 495
(D) 220
(E) 66

STOP

IF YOU FINISH BEFORE TIME IS CALLED, YOU MAY CHECK YOUR WORK ON THIS TEST ONLY.

DO NOT TURN TO ANY OTHER TEST IN THIS BOOK.

No Test Material on This Page

TEST 11   ANSWERS

#	answer	#	answer	#	answer	#	answer	#	answer
1	D	11	B	21	C	31	D	41	D
2	E	12	E	22	A	32	C	42	A
3	A	13	D	23	B	33	B	43	C
4	B	14	D	24	B	34	C	44	D
5	B	15	C	25	A	35	B	45	B
6	D	16	D	26	C	36	E	46	D
7	E	17	C	27	D	37	A	47	D
8	A	18	D	28	B	38	D	48	C
9	D	19	E	29	C	39	A	49	C
10	E	20	D	30	C	40	E	50	C

Explanations: Test 11

1. (D) $\left(\dfrac{3x^{-3}}{5y^{-2}}\right)^{-2} = \dfrac{3^{-2}x^{6}}{5^{-2}y^{4}} = \dfrac{25x^{6}}{9y^{4}}$

2. (E) Since $\left(\dfrac{2k}{2}\right)^{2} = k^{2}$, then $k^{2} = k^{2}$. It is always true for all real number k.

3. (A) Long division:

$$
\begin{array}{r}
2x - 2 \\
x^{2}+x+3\overline{)\,2x^{3}+px+q} \\
\underline{2x^{3}+2x^{2}+6x} \\
-2x^{2}+(p-6)x+q \\
\underline{-2x^{2}-2x-6} \\
(p-4)x+q+6
\end{array}
$$

remainder

Therefore, $p=4$ and $q=-6$.

4. (B) Sum of the roots of polynomial equation $a_{n}x^{n}+a_{n-1}x^{n-1}+a_{n-2}x^{n-2}+\cdots+a_{1}x+a_{0}$

is $-\dfrac{a_{n-1}}{a_{n}}$. Therefore, $S=-\dfrac{0}{1}=0.$

5. (B) $P(x)$ can be expressed in three different ways as follows.

$$
P(x) = \begin{cases} (x-1)Q_{1}(x)+3 & (1) \\ (x+1)Q_{2}(x)+1 & (2) \\ (x-1)(x+1)Q(x)+ax+b & (3) \end{cases}
$$

When $x = 1$

$$P(1) = \begin{cases} 3 & (1) \\ a+b & (3) \end{cases} \quad \rightarrow \quad a+b = 3$$

When $x = -1$

$$P(-1) = \begin{cases} 1 & (2) \\ -a+b & (3) \end{cases} \quad \rightarrow \quad -a+b = 1$$

Therefore, $a = 1$ and $b = 2 \quad \rightarrow \quad$ remainder $= x + 2$

6. (D) Since $x < -3$, $\left|1 - |x+2|\right| = \left|1 + (x+2)\right| = |x+3| = -(x+3) = -x - 3$.

7. (E) Graphing calculator:
Check each choice:

$$\sin x < \cos x \quad \rightarrow \quad \begin{cases} \text{If } x = \dfrac{\pi}{4}, \text{ then } \sin\dfrac{\pi}{4} = \cos\dfrac{\pi}{4}. \\[2mm] \text{If } x = \dfrac{\pi}{2}, \text{ then } \sin\dfrac{\pi}{2} > \cos\dfrac{\pi}{2} \\[2mm] \text{If } x = \dfrac{3\pi}{4}, \text{ then } \sin\dfrac{3\pi}{4} > \cos\dfrac{3\pi}{4} \\[2mm] \text{If } x = \dfrac{5\pi}{4}, \text{ then } \sin\dfrac{5\pi}{4} = \cos\dfrac{5\pi}{4} \\[2mm] \text{If } x = \dfrac{3\pi}{2}, \text{ then } \sin\dfrac{3\pi}{2} < \cos\dfrac{3\pi}{2} \text{(True)} \end{cases}$$

8. (A) Volume of the cylinder: $\pi r^2 h = 250\pi$
Volume of the cube: $10^3 = 1000$
Therefore, the ratio: $\dfrac{250\pi}{1000} = \dfrac{\pi}{4}$.

9. (D) $(3 - 4i)(3 + 4i) = (3)^2 - (4i)^2 = 25$

10. (E) Multiply by the common denominator $(a - 2)$:
$a = 4(a - 2) + 2 \quad \rightarrow \quad a = 2.$ (Extraneous root)

11. (B) $\sqrt[3]{27 - x^3} = -3 \quad \rightarrow \quad 27 - x^3 = -27 \quad \rightarrow \quad x^3 = 54 \quad \rightarrow \quad x = 3\sqrt[3]{2}$

12. (E) Domain of $f(x) = \sqrt{\dfrac{x}{10-x}}$ is $\dfrac{x}{10-x} \geq 0$, where $x \neq 10$.

$(10 - x) \cdot x \geq 0 \quad \rightarrow \quad x(x - 10) \leq 0 \quad \rightarrow \quad 0 \leq x < 10$

Or, find the critical points; From $\dfrac{x}{10-x} = 0$, critical points are $x = 0$ and $x = 10$.

Therefore, for $0 \le x < 10$, $\dfrac{x}{10-x}$ is positive.

13. (D)   Since $f(x) = \dfrac{2x^2 - 3x + 1}{x+1} = 2x - 5 + \dfrac{6}{x+1}$, $y = \lim\limits_{x \to \infty}\left(2x - 5 + \dfrac{6}{x+1}\right) = 2x - 5$.

14. (D)   Method 1:

If x is replaced with $\dfrac{2}{x}$, $f\left(\dfrac{2}{x}\right)$ is changed to $f\left(\dfrac{2}{\frac{2}{x}}\right) = f(x)$

Therefore, $f(x) = 3\left(\dfrac{2}{x}\right) + 5 = \dfrac{6}{x} + 5$

Method 2:

Let $f\left(\dfrac{2}{k}\right) = 3k + 5$ and $x = \dfrac{2}{k}$.

$k = \dfrac{2}{x}$. Replace k with $\dfrac{2}{x}$.

$f\left(\dfrac{2}{k}\right) = 3k + 5$ $\to$ $f(x) = 3\left(\dfrac{2}{x}\right) + 5$ $\to$ $f(x) = \dfrac{6}{x} + 5$

15. (C)   Method 1:

The inverse function: $f^{-1}(x) = (x+1)^2$ $\to$ $f^{-1}(9) = 100$

Method 2:

From $f(x)$: $f^{-1}(9) = y$ is equivalent to $9 = \sqrt{y} - 1$. $y = 100$

16. (D) $[x]^2 - 6[x] = -9$ $\to$ $[x]^2 - 6[x] + 9 = 0$ $\to$ $([x] - 3)^2 = 0$

$[x] = 3$ $\to$ $3 \le x < 4$

17. (C) $k = \dfrac{1}{k}$ $\to$ $k^2 = 1$ $\to$ $k = \pm 1$

18. (D)

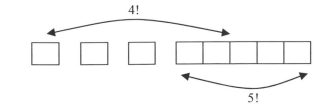

$4! \cdot 5! = 2880$

19. (E)   Determinant:

$\begin{vmatrix} k & 3 \\ 2k & k \end{vmatrix} = k^2 - 6k$ $\to$ $k^2 - 6k = 27$ $\to$ $k^2 - 6k - 27 = 0$

$(k-9)(k+3)=0 \rightarrow k=9$ or $k=-3$

20. (D)   Compound proportion: $y=k\dfrac{x}{z^2}$

$15=k\dfrac{3}{25} \rightarrow k=125 \quad , \quad y=125\times\dfrac{5}{2.5^2}=100$

21. (C) $x^2+y^2=1$ and $x^2+4y^2=4 \rightarrow \dfrac{x^2}{4}+\dfrac{y^2}{1}=1$

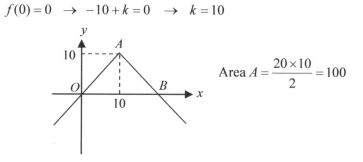

22. (A) $f(0)=0 \rightarrow -10+k=0 \rightarrow k=10$

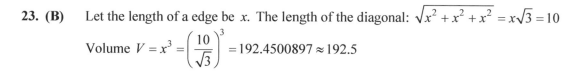

Area $A=\dfrac{20\times10}{2}=100$

23. (B)   Let the length of a edge be x. The length of the diagonal: $\sqrt{x^2+x^2+x^2}=x\sqrt{3}=10$

Volume $V=x^3=\left(\dfrac{10}{\sqrt{3}}\right)^3=192.4500897\approx192.5$

24. (B)   Graphic utility:
One point of intersection.

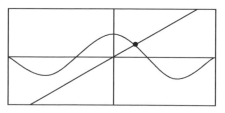

25. (A) $r=\dfrac{1}{\cos\theta+\sin\theta} \quad \rightarrow \quad r\cos\theta+r\sin\theta=1 \quad \rightarrow \quad r\dfrac{x}{r}+r\dfrac{y}{r}=1$

$\rightarrow \quad x+y=1$

26. (C) Distance between $(1,4)$ and $2x - y + 5 = 0$.

$$D = \frac{|2(1) - 4 + 5|}{\sqrt{2^2 + (-1)^2}} = \frac{3}{\sqrt{5}} = 1.341640786 \approx 1.34$$

27. (D)

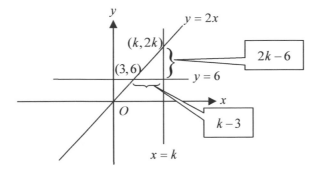

The area of $\triangle = \dfrac{(k-3)(2k-6)}{2} = 16$. $(k-3)^2 = 16 \;\rightarrow\; k - 3 = 4, -4 \;\rightarrow\; k = 7, \cancel{-1}$

because $k > 0$.

28. (B) Prime factorization: $210 = 2^1 \times 3^1 \times 5^1 \times 7^1$
Therefore, the sum of all factors $= (1+2)(1+3)(1+5)(1+7) = 576$

29. (C) $\log_2(x^2 - 3x + 2) - \log_2(x-1) = 5 \;\rightarrow\; \log_2 \dfrac{(x-2)(x-1)}{(x-1)} = \log_2(x-2) = 5$

$x - 2 = 2^5 \;\rightarrow\; x = 34$

30. (C) $10^{3x} = 27 \;\rightarrow\; \left(10^{3x}\right)^{-\frac{2}{3}} = 27^{-\frac{2}{3}} \;\rightarrow\; 10^x = \left(3^3\right)^{-\frac{2}{3}} = 3^{-2}$

$3^{-2} = \dfrac{1}{9}$

31. (D) Using a calculator: $2^{100} = 1.2676506 \times 10^{30} \;\rightarrow\;$ The number of digits $= 30 + 1 = 31$
Algebraically: Let $X = 2^{100} \;\rightarrow\; \log X = \log 2^{100} = 100\log 2 = 30.10$
$$X = 10^{30.10} \;\rightarrow\; 10^{30} \le X < 10^{31}$$
Therefore, the number of digits is 31.
Ex. $2^{10} = 1024$ (4 digits number)
$\log 2^{10} = 10\log 2 = 10 \times 0.3010 = 3.010$. $3 < \log 2^{10} < 4$. Therefore, it is 4 digits number.

32. (C) Sum of the roots of $x^3 - 2x^2 + 4x - 8 = 0$ is $-\dfrac{b}{a} = -\dfrac{-2}{1} = 2$.

Since $2i$ is a root, then $-2i$ is also a root. Let the third root be w.
Sum of the roots: $2i + (-2i) + w = 2 \;\rightarrow\; w = 2$
Therefore, the roots are $2i, -2i$, and 2.

33. (B) $\displaystyle\lim_{n\to\infty}\left(\frac{1}{n^2}+\frac{2}{n^2}+\frac{3}{n^2}+\frac{4}{n^2}+\cdots+\frac{n}{n^2}\right)=\lim_{n\to\infty}\frac{1+2+3+\cdots+n}{n^2}=\lim_{n\to\infty}\frac{\dfrac{n(1+n)}{2}}{n^2}$

$\displaystyle\lim_{n\to\infty}\frac{n(1+n)}{2n^2}=\lim_{n\to\infty}\frac{n+n^2}{2n^2}=\frac{1}{2}$

34. (C) Let three number be $a-d$, a, and $a+d$, where $d>0$.

$(a-d)+a+(a+d)=30 \;\rightarrow\; a=10$

$(a-d)a(a+d)=(10-d)(10)(10+d)=640 \;\rightarrow\; 100-d^2=64 \;\rightarrow\; d^2=36$

Since $d=6$, the smallest number is $10-6=4$.

35. (B) $(f\circ g)(x)=2^{2\log_4 x}=2^{\log_4 x^2}=2^{\log_{\sqrt 4}\sqrt{x^2}}=2^{\log_2 x}=x \;\; (x>0)$

36. (E) Choice (E): If $x=2$, then $y=\pm 2$. (Vertical line test fails.)

37. (A) $\tan\theta=\left|\dfrac{m_2-m_1}{1+m_1 m_2}\right|$

If $m_1=1$ and $m_2=-3$, then $\tan\theta=\left|\dfrac{-3-1}{1+(-3)(1)}\right|=2 \;\rightarrow\; \theta=\tan^{-1}(2)=63.43494882\approx 63.4$

Or,

$\tan\theta_1=1 \;\rightarrow\; \theta_1=45°$

$\tan\theta_2=3 \;\rightarrow\; \theta_2=\tan^{-1}3=71.56505118°\approx 71.565°$

$\theta=180-(45+71.565)=63.435\approx 63.4°$

38. (D) Because $\cos 2\theta=1-2\sin^2\theta$ and $\sin 2\theta=2\sin\theta\cos\theta$,

$\dfrac{\sin 2\theta}{1-\cos 2\theta}=\dfrac{2\sin\theta\cos\theta}{1-(1-2\sin^2\theta)}=\dfrac{2\sin\theta\cos\theta}{2\sin^2\theta}=\dfrac{\cos\theta}{\sin\theta}=\cot\theta$

39. (E) $\cos(\pi-\theta)=\cos\pi\cos\theta+\sin\pi\sin\theta=-\cos\theta=-0.61$

40. (E) $\dfrac{x^2}{a^2}-\dfrac{y^2}{b^2}=1 \;\rightarrow\; \dfrac{x^2}{9}-\dfrac{y^2}{16}=1 \;\rightarrow\; a=3$ and $b=4$

Since $c=\pm\sqrt{3^2+4^2}=\pm 5$, the foci are at $(-5,0)$ and $(5,0)$.

41. (D) $x=\sqrt{t-2} \;\rightarrow\; x\ge 0$

$x=\sqrt{t-2} \;\rightarrow\; t=x^2+2 \;\rightarrow\; y=(x^2+2)+5 \;\rightarrow\; y=x^2+7$

42. (A) Diagonal $AD=\sqrt{3^2+5^2+7^2}=\sqrt{83}$ and $DE=\sqrt{3^2+5^2}=\sqrt{34}$.

$\cos\angle ADF=\dfrac{\sqrt{34}}{\sqrt{83}} \;\rightarrow\; \angle ADF=\cos^{-1}\left(\dfrac{\sqrt{34}}{\sqrt{83}}\right)\approx 50.2°$

43. (C) Since $x = r\cos\theta$ and $y = r\sin\theta$, $x^2 + y^2 - 4x = 0 \rightarrow r^2 - 4(r\cos\theta) = 0$.

Therefore, $r - 4\cos\theta = 0$.

44. (D) $\begin{bmatrix} -2 & 0 \\ 1 & 4 \end{bmatrix} + \begin{bmatrix} -1 & 2 \\ 3 & 1 \end{bmatrix} = \begin{bmatrix} -3 & 2 \\ 4 & 5 \end{bmatrix}$

Determinant : $\begin{vmatrix} -3 & 2 \\ 4 & 5 \end{vmatrix} = (-3)(5) - (2)(4) = -23$

45. (B) $x^2 + y^2 + z^2 - 4x - 6z = 0 \rightarrow (x-2)^2 + y^2 + (z-3)^2 = 13$

Since $r = \sqrt{13}$, the surface area is $4\pi r^2 = 4\pi(13) = 52\pi$.

46. (D) The plane is parallel to xy-plane: $z = 5$

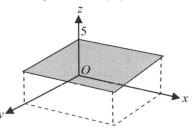

47. (D) Since $\lim_{x \to 1} \dfrac{x^2 + px + q}{x - 1} = 5$, $x^2 + px + q$ must have a factor of $(x - 1)$ to have a finite limit value.

$f(1) = 1 + p + q = 0 \rightarrow q = -1 - p$

$x^2 + px + q = x^2 + px - 1 - p \rightarrow x^2 + px - 1 - p = x^2 - 1 + p(x - 1)$

$= (x + 1)(x - 1) + p(x - 1) = (x - 1)(x + 1 + p)$

Therefore, $\lim_{x \to 1} \dfrac{x^2 + px + q}{x - 1} = \lim_{x \to 1} \dfrac{(x - 1)(x + 1 + p)}{(x - 1)} = \lim_{x \to 1} \dfrac{x + 1 + p}{1} = 2 + p$.

$2 + p = 5 \rightarrow p = 3$.

48. (C) The graph of f is as follows.

$f(x) = \begin{cases} |x|, & |x| \le 2 \\ 2, & |x| > 2 \end{cases}$

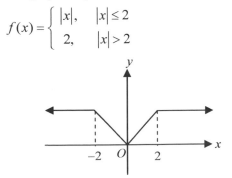

The minimum of $y = 0$.

49. (C) $\dfrac{(x-5)(x+2)}{x-1} \leq 0 \;\rightarrow\; (x-1)(x-5)(x+2) \leq 0$ and $x \neq 1$

Method 1: Graphic solution

The positive integers are 2, 3, 4, and 5.

Method 2: Test sign : Test at $x = 2$ in $(1, 5]$ $\;\rightarrow\; \dfrac{(x-5)(x+2)}{x-1} \leq 0 \;\rightarrow\; \dfrac{(-3)(4)}{1} \leq 0$ (ok)

Therefore, there are 4 positive integers, 1, 2, 3, 4 in $(1, 5]$.

50. (C) General term: $_{12}C_r \left(x^2\right)^{12-r} \left(\dfrac{1}{x}\right)^r = {}_{12}C_r x^{24-2r} x^{-r} = {}_{12}C_r x^{24-3r}$

For $r = 8$, it is constant. Therefore, $_{12}C_8 x^0 = 495$.

END

Test 12

Dr. John Chung's

SAT II Mathematics Level 2

MATHEMATICS LEVEL 2 TEST

REFERENCE INFORMATION

THE FOLLOWING INFORMATION IS FOR YOUR REFERENCE IN ANSWERING SOME OF THE QUESTIONS IN THIS TEST

Volume of a right circular cone with radius r and height h: $V = \dfrac{1}{3}\pi r^2 h$

Lateral Area of a right circular cone with circumference of the base c and slant height ℓ: $S = \dfrac{1}{2}c\ell$

Volume of a sphere with radius r: $V = \dfrac{4}{3}\pi r^3$

Surface Area of a sphere with radius r: $S = 4\pi r^2$

Volume of a pyramid with base area B and height h: $V = \dfrac{1}{3}Bh$

Dr. John Chung's SAT II Math Level 2

Answer Sheet

01 Ⓐ Ⓑ Ⓒ Ⓓ Ⓔ   26 Ⓐ Ⓑ Ⓒ Ⓓ Ⓔ
02 Ⓐ Ⓑ Ⓒ Ⓓ Ⓔ   27 Ⓐ Ⓑ Ⓒ Ⓓ Ⓔ
03 Ⓐ Ⓑ Ⓒ Ⓓ Ⓔ   28 Ⓐ Ⓑ Ⓒ Ⓓ Ⓔ
04 Ⓐ Ⓑ Ⓒ Ⓓ Ⓔ   29 Ⓐ Ⓑ Ⓒ Ⓓ Ⓔ
05 Ⓐ Ⓑ Ⓒ Ⓓ Ⓔ   30 Ⓐ Ⓑ Ⓒ Ⓓ Ⓔ
06 Ⓐ Ⓑ Ⓒ Ⓓ Ⓔ   31 Ⓐ Ⓑ Ⓒ Ⓓ Ⓔ
07 Ⓐ Ⓑ Ⓒ Ⓓ Ⓔ   32 Ⓐ Ⓑ Ⓒ Ⓓ Ⓔ
08 Ⓐ Ⓑ Ⓒ Ⓓ Ⓔ   33 Ⓐ Ⓑ Ⓒ Ⓓ Ⓔ
09 Ⓐ Ⓑ Ⓒ Ⓓ Ⓔ   34 Ⓐ Ⓑ Ⓒ Ⓓ Ⓔ
10 Ⓐ Ⓑ Ⓒ Ⓓ Ⓔ   35 Ⓐ Ⓑ Ⓒ Ⓓ Ⓔ
11 Ⓐ Ⓑ Ⓒ Ⓓ Ⓔ   36 Ⓐ Ⓑ Ⓒ Ⓓ Ⓔ
12 Ⓐ Ⓑ Ⓒ Ⓓ Ⓔ   37 Ⓐ Ⓑ Ⓒ Ⓓ Ⓔ
13 Ⓐ Ⓑ Ⓒ Ⓓ Ⓔ   38 Ⓐ Ⓑ Ⓒ Ⓓ Ⓔ
14 Ⓐ Ⓑ Ⓒ Ⓓ Ⓔ   39 Ⓐ Ⓑ Ⓒ Ⓓ Ⓔ
15 Ⓐ Ⓑ Ⓒ Ⓓ Ⓔ   40 Ⓐ Ⓑ Ⓒ Ⓓ Ⓔ
16 Ⓐ Ⓑ Ⓒ Ⓓ Ⓔ   41 Ⓐ Ⓑ Ⓒ Ⓓ Ⓔ
17 Ⓐ Ⓑ Ⓒ Ⓓ Ⓔ   42 Ⓐ Ⓑ Ⓒ Ⓓ Ⓔ
18 Ⓐ Ⓑ Ⓒ Ⓓ Ⓔ   43 Ⓐ Ⓑ Ⓒ Ⓓ Ⓔ
19 Ⓐ Ⓑ Ⓒ Ⓓ Ⓔ   44 Ⓐ Ⓑ Ⓒ Ⓓ Ⓔ
20 Ⓐ Ⓑ Ⓒ Ⓓ Ⓔ   45 Ⓐ Ⓑ Ⓒ Ⓓ Ⓔ
21 Ⓐ Ⓑ Ⓒ Ⓓ Ⓔ   46 Ⓐ Ⓑ Ⓒ Ⓓ Ⓔ
22 Ⓐ Ⓑ Ⓒ Ⓓ Ⓔ   47 Ⓐ Ⓑ Ⓒ Ⓓ Ⓔ
23 Ⓐ Ⓑ Ⓒ Ⓓ Ⓔ   48 Ⓐ Ⓑ Ⓒ Ⓓ Ⓔ
24 Ⓐ Ⓑ Ⓒ Ⓓ Ⓔ   49 Ⓐ Ⓑ Ⓒ Ⓓ Ⓔ
25 Ⓐ Ⓑ Ⓒ Ⓓ Ⓔ   50 Ⓐ Ⓑ Ⓒ Ⓓ Ⓔ

The number of right answers: ☐

The number of wrong answers: ☐

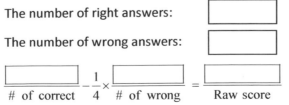

$$\underbrace{\boxed{}}_{\text{\# of correct}} - \frac{1}{4} \times \underbrace{\boxed{}}_{\text{\# of wrong}} = \underbrace{\boxed{}}_{\text{Raw score}}$$

Score Conversion Table

Raw Score	Scaled Score	Raw Score	Scaled Score	Raw Score	Scaled Score
50	800	28	640	6	480
49	800	27	630	5	470
48	800	26	620	4	470
47	800	25	620	3	460
46	800	24	610	2	460
45	800	23	610	1	450
44	800	22	600	0	450
43	800	21	600		
42	800	20	590		
41	800	19	590		
40	780	18	580		
39	760	17	570		
38	750	16	560		
37	740	15	550		
36	720	14	540		
35	710	13	530		
34	700	12	520		
33	690	11	510		
32	680	10	500		
31	670	9	490		
30	660	8	490		
29	650	7	480		

MATHEMATICS LEVEL 2 TEST

For each of the following problems, decide which is the BEST of the choices given. If the exact numerical value is not one of the choices, select the choice that best approximates this value. Then fill in the corresponding circle on the answer sheet

Note: (1) A scientific or graphing calculator will be necessary for answering some (but not all) of the questions in this test. For each question you will have to decide whether or not you should use a calculator.

(2) For some questions in this test you may have to decide whether your calculator should be in the radian mode or the degree mode.

(3) Figures that accompany problems in this test are intended to provide information useful in solving the problems. They are drawn as accurately as possible EXCEPT when it is stated in a specific problem that its figure is not drawn to scale. All figures lie in a plane unless otherwise indicated.

(4) Unless otherwise specified, the domain of any function f is assumed to be the set of all real numbers x for which $f(x)$ is a real number. The range of f is assumed to be the set of all real numbers $f(x)$, where x is in the domain of f.

(5) Reference information that may be useful in answering the questions in this test can be found on the page preceding Question 1.

USE THIS SPACE FOR SCRATCHWORK

1. If $\left(3x^a\right)^b = 81x^{12}$, then $a + b =$

   (A) 4   (B) 5   (C) 6   (D) 7   (E) 8

2. If $3a + b = 2a - b$, then $\dfrac{a-b}{a+b} =$

   (A) –3   (B) –2   (C) –1   (D) 2   (E) 3

3. If $2^{x+1} = 8$, then $\dfrac{2^{3x} + 2^{2x}}{2} =$

   (A) 20
   (B) 40
   (C) 48
   (D) 64
   (E) 80

GO ON TO THE NEXT PAGE

USE THIS SPACE FOR SCRATCHWORK.

4. What is the smallest integer value of x to satisfy the

inequality $\dfrac{x}{4} - \dfrac{2x-1}{2} < 1$?

(A) –1   (B) 0   (C) 1   (D) 2   (E) 3

5. In Figure 1, when the rectangle with dimensions 4 and 10 is rotated about line m, what is the volume of the resulting solid?

(A) 100π
(B) 120π
(C) 160π
(D) 320π
(E) 640π

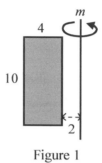

Figure 1

6. $\left(\log_3 16\right)\left(\log_2 9\right) =$

(A) 8
(B) $\log_6 144$
(C) 24
(D) $\log_5 25$
(E) 36

7. If $\sin\theta = \dfrac{1}{2}$ and θ is acute angle, what is the value of

$\sin 2\theta$?

(A) 0.20
(B) 0.42
(C) 0.50
(D) 0.87
(E) 0.95

8. Which of the following is an asymptote of $f(x) = \tan 2\theta$?

(A) $\theta = \dfrac{\pi}{8}$ (B) $\theta = \dfrac{\pi}{4}$ (C) $\theta = \dfrac{\pi}{2}$ (D) $\theta = \dfrac{2\pi}{3}$ (E) $\theta = \dfrac{5\pi}{3}$

GO ON TO THE NEXT PAGE

USE THIS SPACE FOR SCRATCHWORK.

9. In Figure 2, if triangle ABC has $BC = 10$, $\angle A = 30°$, and $\angle C = 70°$, then what is the area of the triangle?

    (A) 92.5
    (B) 97.3
    (C) 112.5
    (D) 125.8
    (E) 135.1

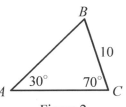

Figure 2

10. Which of the following is true for the graph of $f(x) = \sin 2x + 3$?

    (A) symmetric with respect to the y-axis
    (B) symmetric with respect to the x-axis
    (C) symmetric with respect to the origin
    (D) symmetric with respect to the point $(3, 0)$
    (E) symmetric with respect to the point $(0, 3)$

11. The graph of $x^2 + y^2 - 2x - 4y + 5 = 0$ is which of the following?

    (A) A point
    (B) A circle
    (C) An ellipse
    (D) A hyperbola
    (E) A parabola

12. If θ is a positive acute angle and $\sin 2\theta = \dfrac{1}{2}$, then

    $(\sin\theta + \cos\theta)^2 =$

    (A) 1
    (B) 1.5
    (C) 2.2
    (D) 2.5
    (E) 2.8

GO ON TO THE NEXT PAGE

USE THIS SPACE FOR SCRATCHWORK.

13. In which quadrant is the graph of an ellipse represented by
the equation $x^2 - 6x + 4y^2 + 16y + 17 = 0$ located?

(A) I
(B) II
(C) III
(D) IV
(E) III and IV

14. A cannonball is launched from a height of 80 feet. If the
height of the cannonball in feet, h, is defined by the
equation $h(t) = -18t^2 + 72t + 80$, where t is time in seconds
, how long does the rocket remain at or above 134 feet from
the ground , in seconds?

(A) 1   (B) 1.2   (C) 1.5   (D) 2   (E) 2.3

15. What is the fourth term in the expansion of $\left(x^2 - \dfrac{1}{x^2} \right)^5$?

(A) $-5x^{-4}$
(B) $-10x^{-2}$
(C) $-15x^{-3}$
(D) $10x^{-2}$
(E) $15x^{-3}$

16. What is the solution of the equation $2\log_9(5x) = 3$?

(A) 3
(B) 5
(C) 5.4
(D) 6
(E) 7.2

17. Find the sum of the first 30 terms of the recursive sequence
defined as $a_1 = 3$ and $a_n = a_{n-1} + 5$.

(A) 148
(B) 1680
(C) 2265
(D) 2340
(E) 3120

18. If two forces of 30 newton and 40 newton acting on a body form an angle of $50°$, what is the magnitude of the resultant force?

(A) 50.25 newton
(B) 54.78 newton
(C) 63.58 newton
(D) 76.45 ncwton
(E) 81.68 newton

19. If $a^2 - b^2 + (a-b)i = 10 + 5i$, where a and b are real numbers, what is the value of a?

(A) 2
(B) 2.5
(C) 3
(D) 3.5
(E) 4

20. $\lim\limits_{n \to \infty} \left(1 + \dfrac{1}{n}\right)^{2n} =$

(A) 1
(B) e
(C) e^2
(D) e^{-2}
(E) 0

21. What is the period of the function defined by

$$f(x) = 5 - 2\cos^2\left(\frac{\pi x}{3}\right)?$$

(A) 1
(B) 2
(C) 3
(D) 6
(E) 8

GO ON TO THE NEXT PAGE

USE THIS SPACE FOR SCRATCHWORK.

22. Which of the following is not an odd function?

   (A) $y = \sin 2x$

   (B) $y = x^5 + 3x^3$

   (C) $y = -x^3 + 2x$

   (D) $y = x^{\frac{1}{3}}$

   (E) $y = \dfrac{1}{x} + 1$

23. What is the value of $\sin\left(\operatorname{Arc\,tan} a\right)$, where $a < 0$?

   (A) $\dfrac{\sqrt{1+a^2}}{a}$

   (B) $\dfrac{\sqrt{a^2-1}}{a}$

   (C) $\dfrac{a}{\sqrt{1+a^2}}$

   (D) $\dfrac{a}{\sqrt{1-a^2}}$

   (E) $\dfrac{a}{1+a^2}$

24. If $f(x) = e^{x+1}$, what is $f^{-1}(x)$?

   (A) $\ln(x-1)$

   (B) $\ln(x+1)$

   (C) $\ln\left(\dfrac{x}{2}\right)$

   (D) $\ln\left(\dfrac{x}{e}\right)$

   (E) $\ln(ex)$

GO ON TO THE NEXT PAGE

MATHEMATICS LEVEL 2 TEST - *Continued*

USE THIS SPACE FOR SCRATCHWORK.

25. If $f(x) = 2x + 1$ and $g(x) = x - 3$, then $\left(\dfrac{f}{g}\right)(5) =$

   (A) 5.5
   (B) 10
   (C) 17
   (D) 22
   (E) 25

26. What is the domain of the function $f(x) = \sqrt{8 - 2x - x^2}$?

   (A) $\left[-\infty, -4\right]$
   (B) $\left[-\infty, 5\right]$
   (C) $\left[-4, 2\right]$
   (D) $\left[-1, 4\right]$
   (E) All real

27. What is the sum of the infinite geometric series
   $0.5 + 0.25 + 0.125 + \cdots$?

   (A) 0
   (B) 1
   (C) 2
   (D) 3
   (E) 4

28. Six students are to be seated in a row of 6 chairs. If three of these students must be seated together, how many ways could this be accomplished?

   (A) 24
   (B) 48
   (C) 120
   (D) 144
   (E) 210

GO ON TO THE NEXT PAGE

USE THIS SPACE FOR SCRATCHWORK.

29. Suppose the graph of $f(x) = -(x-1)^2 - 2$ is translated 2 units left and 3 units up. if the resulting graph represents $g(x)$, what is the value of $g(-2.5)$?

   (A) −29.25
   (B) −14.62
   (C) −1.25
   (D) 14.65
   (E) 18.75

30. If $\sin^2 x - \sin x = \cos^2 x$, then what is the smallest positive value of x?

   (A) $\dfrac{\pi}{3}$

   (B) $\dfrac{\pi}{2}$

   (C) $\dfrac{7\pi}{6}$

   (D) $\dfrac{4\pi}{3}$

   (E) $\dfrac{11\pi}{6}$

31. If $f(x) = \sqrt{2x - x^2}$ and $g(x) = x^2 - 2$, then what is the domain of $(g \circ f)(x)$?

   (A) $x \geq 0$
   (B) $x \leq 0$
   (C) $0 \leq x \leq 2$
   (D) $x \geq 2$ and $x \leq 0$
   (E) All real x

GO ON TO THE NEXT PAGE

32. If the function $f(x)$ is continuous, what is the value of k?

$$f(x) = \begin{cases} \dfrac{x^2 - 4}{x - 2} & \text{if } x \neq 2 \\ k & \text{if } x = 2 \end{cases}$$

(A) 1
(B) 2
(C) 3
(D) 4
(E) Undefined

33. A radioactive nuclide has a half-life of 10 days. At what rate does the substance decay each day?

(A) 5%
(B) 6.7%
(C) 8.5%
(D) 10%
(E) 12.5%

34. The graph of $f(x) = |x - 5| + 2$ is translated 6 units left and 3 units down. If the resulting graph is $g(x)$, then $g(-2)$ is

(A) 0
(B) 1
(C) 2
(D) 3
(E) 4

35. $\dfrac{1}{\sin^2 \theta} - \cot^2 \theta =$

(A) 1
(B) $\sin \theta$
(C) $\cos \theta$
(D) $\tan \theta$
(E) $\cot \theta$

USE THIS SPACE FOR SCRATCHWORK.

36. If $\dfrac{x+10}{x^2-4} = \dfrac{a}{x+2} + \dfrac{b}{x-2}$, then $a =$

(A) 3
(B) 2
(C) 1
(D) −1
(E) −2

37. If a die is rolled three times, what is the probability that all three numbers are different?

(A) $\dfrac{1}{3}$

(B) $\dfrac{1}{2}$

(C) $\dfrac{4}{9}$

(D) $\dfrac{5}{9}$

(E) $\dfrac{2}{3}$

38. In Figure 3, if line m is tangent to the circle at point P, which of the following is the equation of line m?

(A) $x + 2y = 26$
(B) $2x + 2y = 34$
(C) $3x + 4y = 60$
(D) $4x + 3y = 59$
(E) $5x + 2y = 58$

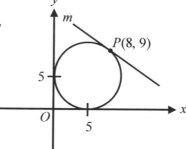

Note: Figure not drawn to scale.

Figure 3

GO ON TO THE NEXT PAGE

MATHEMATICS LEVEL 2 TEST - *Continued*

39. The graph in Figure 4 shows a portion of a function. Which of the following could be the function of f ?

    I. $f(x) = -x^3 + ax^2 - bx - 3$

    II. $f(x) = -x^5 + ax^4 + bx^3 + cx^2 + dx + 5$

    III. $f(x) = -x^7 + ax^6 + cx^5 + dx^4 + cx^3 + dx^2 + ex + 5$

    (A) I only
    (B) II only
    (C) I and II only
    (D) II and III only
    (E) I, II, and III

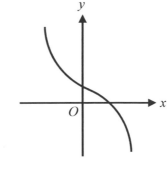

Figure 4

40. If $f(x) = 2^{5\log_2 x}$, then what is the smallest integral value of x such that $f(x) \geq 100$?

    (A) 2
    (B) 3
    (C) 50
    (D) 100
    (E) 1000

41. If $\log_{\sqrt{3}} k = \log_3 2 + \log_3 (k+4)$, then what is the value of k ?

    (A) −2 or 4
    (B) 2 or 5
    (C) 4 only
    (D) 4 or 8
    (E) Undefined

42. If triangle ABC with dimensions 10 and 16 is rotated about $\overline{AB}$, what is the surface area of the resulting solid?

    (A) 314.2
    (B) 592.8
    (C) 634.7
    (D) 906.9
    (E) 5026.6

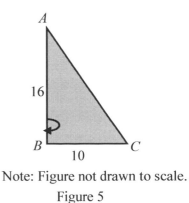

Note: Figure not drawn to scale.

Figure 5

MATHEMATICS LEVEL 2 TEST - *Continued*

USE THIS SPACE FOR SCRATCHWORK.

43. What is the measure of the angle between $\vec{a} = (1, 3)$ and $\vec{b} = (2, 1)$?

    (A) $22.5°$

    (B) $30°$

    (C) $45°$

    (D) $60°$

    (E) $75°$

44. Which of the following is the graph of the polar equation $r = 2\csc\theta$?

    (A) A point

    (B) A line

    (C) A circle

    (D) A parabola

    (E) An ellipse

45. If $\sin\theta = -\dfrac{5}{13}$ and $\pi < \theta < \dfrac{3\pi}{2}$, then what is the value of $\sin(2\theta)$?

    (A)   0.71

    (B)   0.50

    (C)   0.31

    (D) −0.31

    (E) −0.71

46. Figure 6 shows an isosceles trapezoid. What is the length of its diagonal?

    (A) 6.5

    (B) 7.4

    (C) 8.1

    (D) 8.7

    (E) 9.3

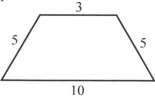

Figure 6

47. If $|5 - 6i| = |a + 2i|$, then a could be

    (A) 7.9   (B) 8.6   (C) 11.3   (D) −8.1   (E) −7.5

GO ON TO THE NEXT PAGE

MATHEMATICS LEVEL 2 TEST - *Continued*

USE THIS SPACE FOR SCRATCHWORK.

48. If the probability of rain on any given day is $\frac{1}{3}$, then what is

the probability of at most 2 days of rain during the next 4

days?

(A) 0.5
(B) 0.54
(C) 0.71
(D) 0.89
(E) 0.95

49. If the equation of a parabola is given by $y - 1 = \frac{1}{4}(x - 2)^2$,

then what is its focus?

(A) (0, 2)
(B) (1, 2)
(C) (2, 2)
(D) (2, 3)
(E) (2, −2)

50. If a hyperbola has the equation $y^2 - 25x^2 = 25$, what are the
equations of its asymptotes?

(A) $y = \pm \frac{1}{5}x$

(B) $y = \pm \frac{2}{5}x$

(C) $y = \pm 5x$

(D) $y = \pm 10x$

(E) $y = \pm 25x$

STOP

IF YOU FINISH BEFORE TIME IS CALLED, YOU MAY CHECK YOUR WORK ON THIS TEST ONLY.

DO NOT TURN TO ANY OTHER TEST IN THIS BOOK.

No Test Material on This Page

#	answer	#	answer	#	answer	#	answer	#	answer
1	D	11	A	21	C	31	C	41	C
2	E	12	B	22	E	32	D	42	D
3	B	13	D	23	C	33	B	43	C
4	B	14	D	24	D	34	A	44	B
5	D	15	B	25	A	35	A	45	A
6	A	16	C	26	C	36	E	46	B
7	D	17	C	27	B	37	D	47	E
8	B	18	C	28	D	38	C	48	D
9	A	19	D	29	C	39	D	49	C
10	E	20	C	30	B	40	B	50	C

TEST 12   **ANSWERS**

Explanations: Test 12

1. (D) $\left(3x^a\right)^b = 81x^{12} \rightarrow 3^b x^{ab} = 3^4 x^{12}$

Therefore, $b=4$, $ab=12$, and $a=3$. The answer is $a+b=7$.

2. (E) $3a+b = 2a-b \rightarrow a = -2b$

$\dfrac{a-b}{a+b} = \dfrac{-2b-b}{-2b+b} = \dfrac{-3b}{-b} = 3$

3. (B) $2^{x+1} = 8 \rightarrow 2^{x+1} = 2^3 \rightarrow x = 2$

$\dfrac{2^{3x} + 2^{2x}}{2} = \dfrac{2^6 + 2^4}{2} = 2^5 + 2^3 = 32 + 8 = 40$

4. (B) $4\left(\dfrac{x}{4} - \dfrac{2x-1}{2}\right) < 1(4) \rightarrow x - 2(2x-1) < 4 \rightarrow -3x < 2 \rightarrow x > -\dfrac{2}{3}$

The smallest integer is 0.

5. (D) $V = \pi(6)^2 10 - \pi(2)^2 10 = 320\pi$

6. (A) $\log_a b = \dfrac{\log b}{\log a}$

$$\left(\log_3 16\right)\left(\log_2 9\right) = \left(\dfrac{\log 16}{\log 3}\right)\left(\dfrac{\log 9}{\log 2}\right) = \left(\dfrac{4\log 2}{\log 3}\right)\left(\dfrac{2\log 3}{\log 2}\right) = 8$$

7. (D) Method 1:

$\sin\theta = \dfrac{1}{2} \;\to\; \theta = 30° \;\to\; \sin 2\theta = \sin 60° = \dfrac{\sqrt{3}}{2} = 0.8660254038 \approx 0.87$

Method 2:

In Quadrant I : $\cos\theta = \dfrac{\sqrt{3}}{2}$

$\sin 2\theta = 2\sin\theta\cos\theta = 2\left(\dfrac{1}{2}\right)\left(\dfrac{\sqrt{3}}{2}\right) = \dfrac{\sqrt{3}}{2}$

8. (B) Period of $\tan 2\theta$ is $\dfrac{\pi}{2}$.

Therefore, the asymptotes are at $x = \pm\dfrac{\pi}{4},\ \pm\dfrac{3\pi}{4},\ \pm\dfrac{5\pi}{4}, \cdots$

9. (A) Area of a triangle $= \dfrac{ab\sin C}{2}$:

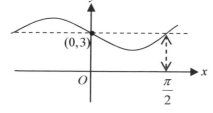

The law of sines:

$\dfrac{\sin 80}{b} = \dfrac{\sin 30}{10} \;\to\; b = \dfrac{10\sin 80}{\sin 30}$

$\text{Area} = \dfrac{1}{2}\left(10\cdot\dfrac{10\sin 80}{\sin 30}\right)\sin 70 = 92.54165784 \approx 92.5$

10. (E) Point of symmetry:

11. (A) $x^2 + y^2 - 2x - 4y + 5 = 0 \;\to\; (x-1)^2 + (y-2)^2 = 0 \;\to\; x = 1$ and $y = 2$.
Since the length of the radius is zero, it represents a point $(1, 2)$.

12. (B) $\left(\sin\theta + \cos\theta\right)^2 = 1 + 2\sin\theta\cos\theta = 1 + \sin 2\theta$

$1 + \sin 2\theta = 1 + \dfrac{1}{2} = \dfrac{3}{2}$

13. (D) $x^2 - 6x + 4y^2 + 16y + 17 = 0 \rightarrow x^2 - 6x + 4(y^2 + 4y) = -17$

$\rightarrow (x-3)^2 + 4(y+2)^2 = 8 \rightarrow \dfrac{(x-3)^2}{8} + \dfrac{(y+2)^2}{2} = 1$

$a^2 = 8 \rightarrow a = 2\sqrt{2}$, $b^2 = 2 \rightarrow b = \sqrt{2}$, and center at $(3, -2)$.

The graph is as follows.

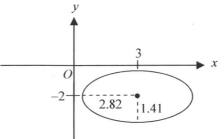

14. (D) $h(t) = -18t^2 + 72t + 80 = 134 \rightarrow 18t^2 - 72t + 54 = 0 \rightarrow t^2 - 4t + 3 = 0$

$(t-3)(t-1) = 0 \rightarrow t = 3, 1$

Therefore, $3 - 1 = 2$ seconds.

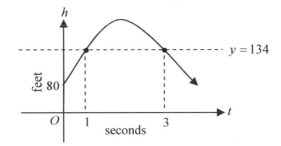

15. (B) $\left(x^2 - \dfrac{1}{x^2}\right)^5 \rightarrow$ The fourth term $= {}_5C_3\left(x^2\right)^2\left(-x^{-2}\right)^3 = 10x^4\left(-x^{-6}\right) \rightarrow -10x^{-2}$

16. (C) $2\log_9(5x) = 3 \rightarrow \log_9(5x) = \dfrac{3}{2} \rightarrow 5x = 9^{\frac{3}{2}} \rightarrow 5x = \left(3^2\right)^{\frac{3}{2}} = 27$

$x = \dfrac{27}{5}$ (Or, use a calculator: $9 \wedge (1.5) \div 2$)

17. (C) $a_n = a_{n-1} + 5 \rightarrow a_n - a_{n-1} = 5$: Common difference is 5 and the first term is 3.

$a_{30} = a_1 + (n-1)d = 3 + 29 \cdot 5 = 148$

Sum of the arithmetic sequence: $S_{30} = \dfrac{30(3 + 148)}{2} = 2265$

18. (C) The law of cosines:

The magnitude of the resultant $= \sqrt{30^2 + 40^2 - 2(30)(40)\cos 130} = 63.58215365 \approx 63.58$

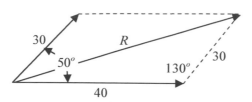

19. (D) $a^2 - b^2 + (a-b)i = 10 + 5i \;\rightarrow\; a^2 - b^2 = 10,\; a - b = 5$

$(a+b)(a-b) = 10$ and $a - b = 5 \;\rightarrow\; a + b = 2$.

Therefore, $a = 3.5$.

20. (C) Since $\lim\limits_{n\to\infty}\left(1 + \dfrac{1}{n}\right)^n = e$,

$$\lim_{n\to\infty}\left(1 + \frac{1}{n}\right)^{2n} = \lim_{n\to\infty}\left(1 + \frac{1}{n}\right)^{2n} = e^2$$

21. (C) Since the period of $\cos\left(\dfrac{\pi}{3}x\right)$ is $\dfrac{2\pi}{\dfrac{\pi}{3}} = 6$, the period of $\cos^2\left(\dfrac{\pi}{3}x\right)$ is $\dfrac{6}{2} = 3$.

22. (E) $f(x) = \dfrac{1}{x} + 1$ and $-f(-x) = -\left(\dfrac{1}{-x}\right) - 1 = \dfrac{1}{x} - 1$.

Since $f(x) \neq -f(-x)$, $f(x)$ is not an odd function.

23. (C) $y = \sin(\operatorname{Arctan} a)$: Let $X = \operatorname{Arctan} a. \;\rightarrow\; a = \tan X$ and $y = \sin X$

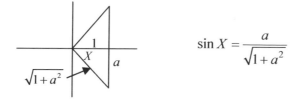

$$\sin X = \frac{a}{\sqrt{1+a^2}}$$

24. (D) $y = e^{x+1} \;\rightarrow\; f^{-1}(x):\; x = e^{y+1} \;\rightarrow\; y = \ln(x) - 1 \;\rightarrow\; y = \ln\dfrac{x}{e}$

25. (A) Quotient of functions: $\left(\dfrac{f}{g}\right)(5) = \dfrac{f(5)}{g(5)} = \dfrac{11}{2} = 5.5$

26. (C)   Domain: $8 - 2x - x^2 \geq 0 \;\rightarrow\; x^2 + 2x - 8 \leq 0 \;\rightarrow\; (x+4)(x-2) \leq 0$

Therefore, the domain is $-4 \leq r \leq 2$

27. (B)   The first term is 0.5 and the common ratio is 0.5.

$$S = \frac{a}{1-r} = \frac{0.5}{1-0.5} = 1$$

28. (D)   Permutation:

$$\rightarrow \quad {}_4P_4 = 4!$$

$${}_3P_3 = 3!$$

Therefore, $3! \times 4! = 144$.

29. (C) $g(x) = -\big((x+2)-1\big)^2 - 2 + 3 = -(x+1)^2 + 1 \;\rightarrow\; g(-2.5) = -(-2.5+1)^2 + 1 = -1.25$

30. (B) $\sin^2 x - \sin x = \cos^2 x \;\rightarrow\; \sin^2 x - \sin x = 1 - \sin^2 x \;\rightarrow\; 2\sin^2 x - \sin x - 1 = 0$

$(2\sin x + 1)(\sin x - 1) = 0$

Therefore, $\sin x = -\dfrac{1}{2}$ or $\sin x = 1$. The smallest positive value of x is $\dfrac{\pi}{2}$.

31. (C) $(g \circ f)(x) = -x^2 + 2x - 2$

The domain of $(g \circ f)(x)$ is $0 \leq x \leq 2$.

From above, it might appear that the domain of the composition is all real numbers. However, this is not true because the domain of f is $0 \leq x \leq 2$, the domain of $(g \circ f)$ is $0 \leq x \leq 2$.

32. (D) $\displaystyle \lim_{x \to 2} \frac{x^2 - 4}{x - 2} = \lim_{x \to 2} \frac{(x+2)(x-2)}{(x-2)} = \lim_{x \to 2} \frac{(x+2)}{1} = 4$

In order to be continuous, k should be equal to 4.

33. (B)   Radioactive decay: $P' = P\left(\dfrac{1}{2}\right)^{\frac{t}{10}}$

The rate each day: $P' = P\left(\dfrac{1}{2}\right)^{\frac{1}{10}} = 0.9330329915P$

Therefore, $1 - 0.9330329915 = 0.0669670085 \approx 6.7\%$ decay.

34. (A) $f(x) = |x - 5| + 2 \xrightarrow{\text{Shift 6 left and down 3}} g(x) = |x + 6 - 5| + 2 - 3 \;\rightarrow\; g(x) = |x + 1| - 1$

$g(-2) = |-2 + 1| - 1 = 0$

35. (A) $\dfrac{1}{\sin^2 \theta} - \cot^2 \theta = \dfrac{1}{\sin^2 \theta} - \dfrac{\cos^2 \theta}{\sin^2 \theta} = \dfrac{1 - \cos^2 \theta}{\sin^2 \theta} = \dfrac{\sin^2 \theta}{\sin^2 \theta} = 1$

36. (E) $\dfrac{x+10}{x^2-4}=\dfrac{a}{x+2}+\dfrac{b}{x-2}$ $\rightarrow$ $\dfrac{x+10}{x^2-4}=\dfrac{a(x-2)+b(x+2)}{(x+2)(x-2)}$

$\dfrac{x+10}{x^2-4}=\dfrac{(a+b)x-2a+2b}{(x+2)(x-2)}$

Therefore, $a+b=1$ and $-2a+2b=10$. $a=-2$

37. (D) The number of all possible outcomes (sample space) is $6\cdot6\cdot6=216$.
If the first roll is a 1, the second and third time cannot rolls cannot be 1.
If the second roll is a 2, the third cannot be a 2.
Therefore, $6\times5\times4=120$.

Probability $P=\dfrac{120}{216}=\dfrac{5}{9}$.

38. (C) The tangent is perpendicular to the diameter of the circle.

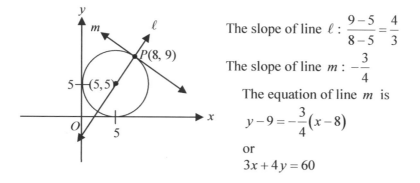

The slope of line ℓ : $\dfrac{9-5}{8-5}=\dfrac{4}{3}$

The slope of line m : $-\dfrac{3}{4}$

The equation of line m is

$y-9=-\dfrac{3}{4}(x-8)$

or

$3x+4y=60$

39. (D) The function has one positive real root, a positive y-intercept, rises to the left, and falls to the right.

   I. $f(x)=-x^3+ax^2-bx-3$ $\rightarrow$ Negative y-intercept

  II. $f(x)=-x^5+ax^4+bx^3+cx^2+dx+5$ $\rightarrow$ Four imaginary roots and one real root

 III. $f(x)=-x^7+ax^6+cx^5+dx^4+cx^3+dx^2+ex+5$ $\rightarrow$ Six imaginary roots and one real root

40. (B) $f(x)=2^{5\log_2 x}\geq100$ $\rightarrow$ $2^{\log_2 x^5}=x^5$

$x^5\geq100$ $\rightarrow$ $x\geq100^{\frac{1}{5}}=2.5118864$

The smallest integer value of x is 3.

41. (C) $\log_a b=\log_{a^n} b^n$:

$\log_{\sqrt{3}} k=\log_3 2+\log_3(k+4)$ $\rightarrow$ $\log_3 k^2=\log_3 2+\log_3(k+4)$

$\log_3 k^2=\log_3(2k+8)$ $\rightarrow$ $k^2=2k+8$ $\rightarrow$ $k^2-2k-8=0$

Therefore, $(k-4)(k+2)=0$. $k=4$ or $k=-2$.

From $\log_{\sqrt{3}} k$, k cannot be less than or equal to 0. The value of k is only 4.

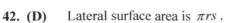
42. (D) Lateral surface area is $\pi r s$.

The Surface area: $\pi r s + \pi r^2$

$\pi(10)(\sqrt{356}) + \pi(10)^2 = 906.9137817 \approx 906.9$

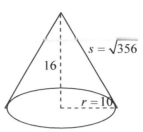

43. (C) $\tan\theta_1 = \dfrac{3}{1} \rightarrow \theta_1 = \tan^{-1}3$

$\tan\theta_2 = \dfrac{1}{2} \rightarrow \theta_2 = \tan^{-1}\left(\dfrac{1}{2}\right)$

$\theta = \theta_1 - \theta_2 = \tan^{-1}3 - \tan^{-1}\dfrac{1}{2} = 45°$

44. (B) $r = 2\csc\theta = \dfrac{2}{\sin\theta} \rightarrow r = \dfrac{2}{\dfrac{y}{r}} \rightarrow y = 2$

45. (A) θ is in Quadrant III.

$\sin\theta = -\dfrac{5}{13}$

$\cos\theta = -\dfrac{12}{13}$

$\sin(2\theta) = 2\sin\theta\cos\theta = 2\left(-\dfrac{5}{13}\right)\left(-\dfrac{12}{13}\right) = \dfrac{120}{169} = 0.7100591716 \approx 0.71$

46. (B) From the figure below:

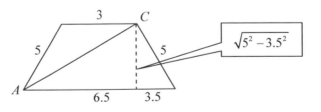

The length of the diagonal $\overline{AC} = \sqrt{6.5^2 + \left(5^2 - 3.5^2\right)} = 7.416198487 \approx 7.4$

47. (E) $|5-6i| = \sqrt{5^2 + (-6)^2} = \sqrt{61}$

$|a+2i| = \sqrt{a^2 + 4}$

$\sqrt{a^2 + 4} = \sqrt{61} \rightarrow a^2 + 4 = 61 \rightarrow a^2 = 57 \rightarrow a = \pm 7.549834435 \approx \pm 7.5$

48. (D) At most two rainy days: 0 days, I day, and 2 days

$$P = {}_4C_0 \left(\frac{1}{3}\right)^0 \left(\frac{2}{3}\right)^4 + {}_4C_1 \left(\frac{1}{3}\right)^1 \left(\frac{2}{3}\right)^3 + {}_4C_2 \left(\frac{1}{3}\right)^2 \left(\frac{2}{3}\right)^2 = 0.88888$$

Or

$$\text{binomcdf}\left(4, \frac{1}{3}, 2\right) = 0.888888 \approx 0.89$$

49. (C) $y - 1 = \frac{1}{4}(x-2)^2 \rightarrow (x-2)^2 = 4(1)(y-1)$

$p = 1$ and directrix $y = 0$.

The coordinates of the focus is $(2, 2)$.

50. (C) $y^2 - 25x^2 = 25 \rightarrow \dfrac{y^2}{5^2} - \dfrac{x^2}{1} = 1$

$a = 1$ and $b = 5$.

Asymptotes: $y = \pm \dfrac{b}{a}x = \pm \dfrac{5}{1}x = \pm 5x$

END